BYZANTINE SLAVERY AND THE MEDITERRANEAN WORLD

Youval Rotman

Translated by Jane Marie Todd

Byzantine Slavery and the Mediterranean World

HARVARD UNIVERSITY PRESS
Cambridge, Massachusetts, and London, England   2009

Publication of this book has been aided by a grant from the French Ministry of Culture.
Ouvrage publié avec le concours du Ministère français chargé de la Culture—Centre national du livre.

Originally published as *Les esclaves et l'esclavage: De la Méditerranée antique à la Méditerranée médiévale, VIe–XIe siècles,* copyright © 2004 by La Société d'Édition Les Belles Lettres, Paris

Library of Congress Cataloging-in-Publication Data

Rotman, Youval.
  [Esclaves et l'esclavage. English]
  Byzantine slavery and the Mediterranean world / by Youval Rotman ; translated by Jane Marie Todd.
    p.   cm.
  Originally published in French: Paris : Belles Lettres, 2004, under title Les esclaves et l'esclavage : De la Méditerranée antique à la Méditerranée médiévale, VIe–XIe siècles.
  Includes bibliographical references and index.
  ISBN 978-0-674-03611-6 (alk. paper)
    1. Slavery—Byzantine Empire—History.   2. Slaves—Byzantine Empire—History.
  3. Byzantine Empire—Social conditions.   4. Byzantine Empire—History—527–1081.
  5. Mediterranean Region—History—476–1517.   I. Todd, Jane Marie, 1957–   II. Title.
    HT865.R6713 2009
    306.3′6209495—dc22   2009009042

. . . this work is dedicated to Rivka Rotman,
daughter of Esther and David Bass, my grandmother,
whose mind and spirit have never left me . . .

Contents

Acknowledgments

This book came into being on boulevard Raspail in Paris in the spring of 1995, during my first meeting with Évelyne Patlagean. Subsequently, she directed my research at the Université de Paris X-Nanterre, oversaw my training as a Byzantinist, and followed the composition of this book, which was published thanks to her backing and support. Évelyne Patlagean passed away before this book was published in English. I was extremely fortunate to have had her as both a mentor and a friend and will forever feel her absence.

I thank Benjamin Isaac, my mentor at the University of Tel Aviv, who trained me as a Roman historian, encouraged me on this path, supervised my work, and always provided me with the help I needed.

I thank Jean Andreau, Henri Bresc, Jean-Michel Carrié, David Jacoby, and Baber Johansen for their remarks and help; Philippe Hoffmann, for the paleographical training he gave me and for his continuous encouragement; Glen Bowersock, David Brion Davis, Susan Reynolds, and Guy Stroumsa for their help and encouragement; Ioanna Rapti for her constant aid during the entire composition stage; Avshalom Laniado for his valuable references; Danielle Storper-Perez for her remarks and help; Jane Marie Todd for her attentive and thoughtful translation; and Sharmila Sen at Harvard University Press for the great care she has taken with this book.

This book could not have been undertaken and brought to completion without financial aid from the following institutions: the French embassy in Israel; AVI Fellowships Geneva; the Fondation du Judaïsme Français; the Yad Hanadiv Foundation; the University of Paris X-Nanterre; the University of Tel Aviv; the Program in Hellenic Studies, Princeton University; and the MacMillan Center for International and Area Studies, Yale University. My gratitude also extends to Orit Bashkin, Chava Boyarin, Sylvain Destephen,

Milette Gaifman, Francesca Trivellato, and Uri Yiftach, as well as to my colleagues and friends at Yale University.

And of course this book could not have seen the light of day without the constant support of my family. I therefore warmly thank Drora, David, Vered, and especially Kobi.

For abbreviations used in the tables, notes, appendixes, and bibliography, see pages 201–204.

BYZANTINE SLAVERY AND THE MEDITERRANEAN WORLD

Introduction

"If you do not venture outside antiquity to see what happens next, you cannot write the history of antiquity."[1] It seems to me that this statement by Fernand Braudel could not be more fitting than when applied to the history of slavery. Despite a large number of studies devoted to ancient slavery, the subject still remains an open question. To respond to it, I shall adopt a viewpoint that places the slavery of the Middle Ages rather than that of antiquity at the center of this book.

The evolution of the eastern Mediterranean—that is, of the Byzantine world—from antiquity to the Middle Ages offers an ideal framework for pursuing that approach, both because of the continuity between the Roman Empire and Byzantium and because of the major changes that shook the world during the medieval period. From this vantage point, the evolution of slavery can be seen as part of the evolution of medieval societies, one extending far beyond the economic context to which there has been a tendency to confine slavery. In this study I shall treat the institution of slavery in its relation to economic development, of course, but also in terms of developments in politics, social structures, religion, culture, and mentalities. It is only by situating slavery within that complex framework that I shall be able to reveal the modalities of its development.

The initial point of reference for my chronological axis is late antiquity, and specifically the reign of Justinian I (527–565), which marks a very important epoch in the history of the Roman Empire. Thanks to Emperor Justinian's military policy, the empire recaptured the lost territories of Italy, Africa, Armenia, and the Balkans. That policy went hand in hand with the growing centralization of power in Constantinople, manifested both in the revision and codification of the law and in Chalcedonian religious policy.

The eleventh century stands as the endpoint of the chronological axis.

1

Traditionally, that century has marked a break at the international level. With the arrival of the crusaders, the Mediterranean began a new phase in its history. My chronological framework thus embraces the six centuries during which the Mediterranean evolved from an ancient into a medieval world.

Between the sixth and eleventh centuries, the geopolitical world also underwent a great transformation. In the sixth century, the empire was still fighting against the Barbarian kingdoms in Africa and Italy, whereas, despite confrontations with the Persians, it still controlled the eastern provinces. In the early seventh century, imperial control weakened, the conquests of Justinian were threatened, and the Sassanid Empire seized the opportunity to conquer the rich Roman provinces in the East: Syria, Palestine, Arabia, and Egypt. It is not an overstatement to say that Heraclius (610–641) saved the empire. He recaptured all these provinces and annihilated the Sassanid Empire, Rome's age-old enemy. But the victory was short-lived: the empire lost all the reconquered territories and (with the Arab conquest) Africa as well, this time definitively. It now had a new rival on the geopolitical scene, and wars between the two states raged without respite in the seventh and eighth centuries.

In the East, what is now called the Byzantine Empire, though it still designated itself as Roman, maintained its grasp on Asia Minor despite the Arab expeditions into Anatolia and Caucasus. In the eighth century, the maritime threat from the Arabs was also brought to bear on Italy and Sicily. On the empire's other front, the Balkans and the Black Sea, the arrival of the Slavs, the Bulgars, and the "Russians" also brought geopolitical changes. But the map that was transformed in the seventh and eighth centuries was not only political but religious. In Byzantine eyes, what was at issue was no longer the world of the empire against that of the Barbarians, but of the Christian state versus the Muslim state. The Balkan regions, by contrast, served as the hinterland and were notable for their belated paganism.

From the early period of imperial Rome onward, public power was incarnated in the person of the emperor. After a period of internal instability in the late sixth century, imperial power began a new phase of its history, characterized by, among other things, the dynastic model. Nevertheless, as in the late Roman period, shifts from one dynasty to the next introduced new figures on the political scene. Sometimes of obscure origin, they achieved power by means of their military careers.

The sovereignty of imperial power continued to be made manifest in the law. The codification and compilation of imperial law continued throughout the period, in accordance with the models established by Justinian. The law was still in flux, however, as illustrated by the large number of imperial *Novellae* promulgated between the eighth and eleventh centuries.

To a certain extent, the organization of the empire into themata—military but also administrative units—replaced the old system of Roman provinces, and the partial decentralization of the imperial army allowed it to adapt to the empire's new geopolitical needs.

In the area of religion, the loss of all the provinces opposing the Chalcedonian Creed paradoxically led to a unification of church and state. That unity, particularly strong at the time because the empire was surrounded by non-Christian enemies, was shaken by the iconoclastic crisis in the eighth century. The church, or more precisely the ecclesiastical elite, emerged from the crisis stronger than ever.

In the economic realm, the power of the monasteries and of the dignitaries close to the public authorities grew in the ninth and tenth centuries, at the expense of public resources. The small landowners had a tendency to circumvent their tax obligations by becoming *paroikoi*, dependents of the large landowners. The public authorities became aware in the tenth century that they were losing out to those they defined as "the powerful," *oi dunatoi*. That century witnessed the failure of a legislative struggle against the economic expansion of this powerful elite. It may also be said that when the Doukai and Comneni came to power in the eleventh century, traditional tenth-century public authority was eclipsed by these two mighty aristocratic families, which would henceforth share power.

The entire era of concern here was characterized by its development of medieval civilizations, that is, of civilizations under the exclusive control of divine law. In the empire, that process, which had begun with Constantine I in the fourth century, continued until the eleventh century. The iconoclastic crisis did not prevent eighth-century emperors from introducing legislation that continued to adapt Roman law to the structures of a medieval empire.

The end of that crisis coincided with the monastic reform of Theodore Studites, which in the early ninth century led to the founding of new monasteries. There is a great wealth of extant documents in the monastic archives for the period extending from the ninth to the twelfth century. To a certain degree, they provide a counterpoint to the papyrological and epigraphic documents of late antiquity. The evolution of the empire into a Christian state can also be observed in the realm of private life—marriage and family—which preoccupied the public authorities, as indicated in the continuity of legislation from Justinian I to Alexius I Comnenus.

Apart from the documents left by the church, historians have available two types of literary sources for studying the empire's cultural life: hagiography and historiography. The hagiographical literature, though dating back to late antiquity, now treated its subjects in a new way and reflected the changes in society and in ways of thinking. It circulated more widely than Byzantine historiography, which in the eighth to tenth centuries no longer had the scope it had had in the sixth century. But that deficiency is offset by a very rich Arab historiography.

The phenomenon of slavery is directly related to all aspects of Byzantine history, which itself reflects the development of the medieval world in the eastern Mediterranean. I cannot begin, therefore, without referring to the historiography on the subject or, rather, to the problems it raises and has raised, and without defining the theoretical vantage point or points from which to examine slavery.

CHAPTER 1

Theoretical Approaches

The chronological parameters of my study of Byzantine slavery extend from the reign of Justinian I (527–565) in late antiquity through the central Middle Ages—that is, up to the beginning of the twelfth century, when the empire began a new phase in its history and the entire Mediterranean scene was transformed. The political and geographical space to be studied is the part of the world that was under the authority of the emperor of Constantinople at any given moment. The major changes occurring throughout the seventh century ultimately limited that space to the northeastern regions of the Mediterranean basin. The context is thus well defined. Defining slavery, by contrast, turns out to be more complex.

Previous definitions advanced by historians have excluded Byzantium from the history of slavery. I would like first to consider the reason for this exclusion and identify the notion or notions underlying what is termed "slavery."

Civil Status and Economic Status

No monograph has been devoted to Byzantine slavery since the work of Anna Hadjinicolaou-Marava,[1] though several Byzantinists have taken an interest in the subject.[2] Two different approaches can be distinguished in their work: one considers the question from an intrinsic point of view, emphasizing the major importance of slavery in Byzantine life—Helga Köpstein's writings are the standard reference[3]—whereas the other looks at its place within a chronology, particularly in relation to Roman slavery and its decline. It is clear that one cannot situate Byzantine slavery within its historical context without raising the question of the fate of late Roman institutions, including slavery.

Slavery in antiquity, and especially the way it has been perceived by historians, is of key importance to my thesis because I shall be concerned with the civilization that immediately followed the Classical Age. It is widely recognized that slavery was inherent to the Greco-Roman world. In studies on the subject, in fact, alongside modern slavery in the Americas, it is the institution as it existed in Greek and Roman societies that has attracted the greatest attention.[4] Since these societies are defined as slave-owning in contradistinction to those that followed, this immediately raises a question: what accounts for the decline of slavery?

Ramsay MacMullen dismisses that question, saying it is incongruous to explain the transition from the Roman era to the Middle Ages in terms of slavery because slaves were no longer a decisive force of economic production even in the late Roman Empire.[5] On the basis of his regional survey, MacMullen demonstrates that, outside Italy, the role slaves played in agriculture was marginal at the time.[6] And since "it is agreed on all hands that what counted in the economy was agriculture," he concludes that, despite the other functions that slaves performed, the Roman world cannot be said to have been a "slave-owning society."[7] In other words, the slaves' nonproductivity excluded them from economic and then from social discourse. Hence he evaluates the importance of slavery in economic terms, and the nonproductivity of slaves is said to have coincided with their inconsequential presence in society. That is, MacMullen associates the economic role of slaves with their number.[8]

Like many others, Panayotis Yannopoulos analyzes slavery in economic terms, focusing on Byzantium in the seventh to ninth centuries. According to him, as soon as slaves ceased to be a productive force and were confined to functions characterized as "decorative" or even "parasitical" (both terms appear in his bibliography), they no longer had any social importance: "The sectors that owned slaves were exactly those that did not produce. Hence the slave was not productive, contrary to the case in the classical period and the Roman era." Yannopoulos concludes, "Byzantine slaves lived in a society to which they did not belong as active members—they had a place in it but not a situation."[9]

Even historians who do not accept the thesis of the decline of slavery in the late Roman Empire speak of the institution from an economic standpoint. They argue that the productive labor of slaves continued to be significant throughout the period[10] and, in the West, even into the early Middle Ages.[11] I have grouped together specialists on different periods to underscore the importance given to that economic definition of slavery. Pierre Bonnassie, seeking plausible explanations for the extinction of slavery in western Europe during the early medieval period, rules out religious factors and the difficulties in acquiring slaves, then goes on to argue: "In the present day, one increasingly appeals to economics to explain the end of slavery."[12] But is this truly a perspective of the "present day"?

According to such theories, slavery persists only so long as it has economic importance. When that is no longer the case, other economic agents must come to replace slaves, or economic life will be organized in a different manner. That point of view appears to be inseparable from a historical analysis of slavery.

Slavery was first defined as a means of production in the nineteenth century by Karl Marx.[13] It is therefore indispensable to consider slavery as it appears in his writings. Marx addresses the question only to demonstrate that in every society, social debate or conflict is materialist in nature, centered on the distribution of the means of production. The division of labor determines class divisions. For Marx, Roman slavery constituted an exemplary case. "In Italy, on the other hand,[14] the concentration of landed property . . . and its conversion into grazing land . . . brought about the almost total disappearance of the free population; the slaves died out again and again, and had constantly to be replaced by new ones. Slavery remained the basis of the entire production process. The plebeians, midway between freemen and slaves, never succeeded in becoming more than a proletarian rabble [*lumpenproletariat*]."[15] I shall not concern myself here with what the Marxists, in developing historical determinism, made of these ideas;[16] let me merely note that Marx's economic analysis established an equivalence between economic status, social status, and civil status.

By "civil status" I mean a legal definition that constitutes a group of people into a distinct entity before the law: for example, the group has certain obligations or is granted special privileges. Other considerations may also come into play. This definition determines the criteria for placing persons in the same civil category, and its objective is to give the group a particular status. I make a distinction between legal and civil status, in that civil status can be applied only to human beings. Hence Roman and Byzantine law dictated how the slave could be distinguished from the free person, just as, for example, the criterion of age for minors or gender for women defines the civil status of those groups.

The Marxist view developed within a framework that defined slaves as res mobiles. It is beyond the scope of this argument to critique Marx's theory; in exploring the dynamic of his definition, I simply wish to note the elements it introduced into the scholarly work on slavery. For example, the Marxist analysis excludes domestic slavery, believing it lies outside any economic discourse. In Roman society, however, there was no difference in the eyes of the law between rural and domestic slaves: they had the same civil status. Marxists may reply that domestic slaves were socially marginal. Although that may have been true in ancient Greece, it was not so in Byzantium or in the late Roman Empire.

Although the Marxist analysis does not tally with the definition of slavery in antiquity, it perfectly characterizes slavery in the Americas. In the nineteenth century, American slavery was the "living" model for European historians, and in fact it received a great deal more attention in Marxist economic theory than did ancient slavery. For Marx, the schema was clear: "productive" is the equivalent of "not free," "unproductive" of "free." Marx's political aim was to achieve a society in which the productive forces would also be free. Freedom, from his point of view, is the state of being in possession of one's own productivity. According to that argument, artisans were free, the only exception to Marx's schema.[17] And it was this schema that gave rise to the idea that slavery, with the unfreedom it implies, is a means of production.

The second example Marx proposes for his economic and social analysis is feudalism, under which serfs replaced slaves as the productive economic class. The analysis of medieval Europe is important for his theory because the society of the Middle Ages developed into a capitalist society. Moreover, Marx's definition of medieval economic life in terms of the relation between feudal lords and serfs in Western feudalism tallies with his model of nonproductive owners and productive nonowners (who are unfree by his definition). I shall set aside the conflict that in his view gave birth to medieval society and consider what became of ancient slavery according to medievalists.

In an etymological study of the Latin terms *servus, servitium,* and *servitus,* Marc Bloch argues that the new meanings acquired by these words—namely "serf," "serfdom," and "servitude"—marked an evolution from slavery to serfdom (a *servus* was originally a "slave"; *servitium* and *servitus* both meant "slavery").[18] Bloch grants a central place to the parceling up of large demesnes in the Carolingian era and, more precisely, in the second half of the ninth century. That process went hand in hand with the installation of free peasants and enfeoffed emancipated slaves, the *casati,* as tenant farmers on the "new parcels of land."[19] These tenant farmers would give rise to serfs in the second stage of the feudal system, between the tenth and twelfth centuries. Serfs replaced slaves not only as a productive economic force but also, as etymology demonstrates, as unfree persons whose form of servitude was different from that of the ancient slaves. Slaves remained marginal in feudal society, serving primarily as domestics.[20]

Pierre Toubert's regional study of Sabina posits the same process during the same period. Hence, from the mid-eighth to the early eleventh century, the dissolution of the demesnial economy, which preceded *incastellamento* (the construction of castles throughout the countryside, from which local lords could dominate the population), changed the form of agricultural operations by turning slaves into emancipated tenant farmers.[21] But in that case there was no chronological continuity between slavery and serfdom. Similarly, according to Jean-Pierre Poly and Éric Bournazel, "The few descendants of the ninth-century *servi* gradually became indistinguishable from the formerly free small peasantry, who were now bound to a tenancy."[22]

In these studies, which attempt to explain the birth of feudalism, both slavery and serfdom are analyzed from an economic standpoint. Pierre Dockès views them the same way, though he posits the collapse of the state as the cause of ancient slavery's decline.[23] And Pierre Bonnassie, opposing the idea of a continuity between slavery and serfdom, proffers the solution that technological development was the catalyst that brought slavery to an end.[24] Not surprisingly, those historians who do not analyze serfdom in economic terms say very little about slavery.[25]

In referring to slavery in Byzantium, historians try to explain the transformation of that society during its transition to the medieval era. Hence they situate the extinction of slavery in the late Roman age or have it extend into the tenth century; in either case, they consider slavery to have been on the decline.[26] But although it is presented in the scholarly literature as an institution in the process of disappearing, slavery was omnipresent throughout the medieval period. That contradiction requires an explanation.

The response can be found in the economic field. Documents preserved in the Mount Athos archives often note the existence of *paroikoi*, dependent peasants.[27] Their dependency made them very different from the serfs of medieval western Europe.[28] Those who have analyzed the local documents agree on the central institutional role of *paroikoi* in the Byzantine countryside. Having adopted the traditional view that rural slavery existed in the Roman Empire, they then attempt to identify a transformation or a shift. In Byzantium as in the West, free land-owning peasants lived in rural communities.[29] In the tenth to twelfth centuries, the changes in the Byzantine countryside were part of the redistribution of economic forces: the small peasantry that had formerly owned land often became leaseholders under the large landowners. At the time, the *dunatoi,* the powerful elite, were pitted against the small landowners, who are designated as "the poor" in the sources of the time.[30]

As for slavery in the rural areas, historians of Byzantium see it as an instrument for producing the small peasantry. Thus some advance the hypothesis that in the major conflict of the age, the imperial authority, in its battle against the large landowners, tended to turn slaves into peasants dependent on itself.[31] According to these theories, emancipation contributed toward the creation of a social stratum, the dependent peasants, that stood opposed to the power elite. The common ground between historians of Byzantium and Western medievalists is the argument that the emancipated slaves became dependent peasants: Browning and Oikonomides invoke the *servi casati* in the same manner as Marc Bloch and Toubert.

The equivalence among economic, civil, and social statuses is thus maintained in the view that emancipated slaves became *paroikoi,* giving rise to a new institution, and that medieval slaves were only "unproductive" domestics and "parasites" lacking any economic raison d'être. In one way or another, these theories seek to answer the question: what became of Roman slavery? I wonder, however, whether the positing of the decline of Roman slavery might not have preceded the theories. In other words, the axiom that Roman slavery disappeared may have called forth a search for explanations. But historians of both Byzantium and western Europe seem to be forgetting a part of the Roman Empire. By this I mean the African, Asian, and Iberian territories that, along with their populations, were inherited by the medieval Arab world. It is not by chance that Arab slavery has been left out of the discussion of Roman slavery's fate.

Of course, Arab civilization was a world apart. Its significance for my inquiry lies in the importance that slavery assumed there during the period under study. I shall not deal at length with Arab slavery: for the most part, it will provide points of comparison, as it often directly affected the Byzantine population.[32] In the theories that deal with medieval slavery, however, Arab slavery lies well within my area of concern. It differs in several ways from that of the Roman world. What was noteworthy about the Arab world, especially when compared with that of classical antiquity, was its use of slaves not only for domestic and agricultural labor but also in the army,[33] which was almost unthinkable in Roman civilization.[34]

In modern scholarship, it is clear that slavery of that kind does not correspond to a means of production model. Despite the presence of rural slaves in the Arab world, civil status was not the equivalent of economic status. That was also the case in Byzantium. Rural slaves did not disappear there but were present throughout the period under discussion. In addition, though slaves did not serve in the Byzantine army,[35] they performed functions that were not productive in the strict sense as, for example, domestics, administrators, shop foremen, private soldiers, and palace servants. Yet they all continued to have a common civil status distinguishable from that of people the law called "free." To speak of slaves as "parasites" is still to see them in terms of production while leaving them outside economic and subsequently social discourse. This point of view does not tally with medieval slavery as it existed. That is why I will not consider slaves solely in terms of their economic role. I shall begin by establishing a separation between civil status and economic function or functions. Some might object that Byzantium, unlike ancient Greece and Rome, was not a slave-owning society. It is necessary, however, to revise the definition of "slave-owning society," which tends to encompass not only ancient Greece and the Roman Empire but also Brazil, the American South, and the Caribbean.[36]

The decline of Byzantine slavery has been disputed by Köpstein, who relies on Byzantine sources and shows the omnipresence of slaves in the empire.[37] In her article "Die byzantinische Sklaverei in der Historiographie der letzten 125 Jahre" (Byzantine slavery in historiography over the last 125 years), she critiques discussions of the subject and expounds the different approaches of Kazhdan, Sjuzjumov, and Browning, who were writing in the 1950s. Sjuzjumov points to the presence of slaves in artisanal production in the cities, whereas Browning indicates the existence of slave labor on farms; hence they too analyze Byzantine slavery in economic terms. By contrast, Kazhdan, who was attuned to the changes in Byzantine society, emphasizes the use of slaves in the ninth to eleventh centuries by the emperor and the aristocracy. The fact that Köpstein and Kazhdan, who avoid the "formulas" of medievalists of western Europe, support this view demonstrates how closely connected the theory of slavery is to the historiographical space of the discussion. All the same, in approaching Byzantine slavery from a standpoint intrinsic to Byzantium, these two historians disassociate it from ancient slavery and from the medieval Mediterranean world.

It is not by chance that only Charles Verlinden has managed to integrate Byzantine slavery with its Mediterranean environment.[38] His work, which was not only pioneering but also established the methodology for everything having to do with medieval slavery in Europe, confines itself, in the case of Byzantium, solely to slaves' legal status. Without attempting to demonstrate the role of slaves in Byzantine society and in its economy, Verlinden places the emphasis on the Mediterranean scene—that is, on international relations and trade. He thus situates Byzantine slavery within its geographical context. But, inattentive to the transition from the late Roman Empire to the Byzantine state, he does not deal with its historical context. He pays little attention to the period prior to the eleventh and twelfth centuries, except in his discussion of Ostrogothic and Lombard Italy and in a brief passage on the role of slavery in the evolution of serfdom in Carolingian Italy.[39] Verlinden focuses on the late Middle Ages (thirteen to fifteen centuries) and on European societies. The reason for his success may be that he does not explain the existence of medieval slavery by using an economic argument. And that is also why Bonnassie finds him disappointing.[40] In Verlinden's book, which is some two thousand pages long, the example of the Byzantine world takes up only about twenty, and of those, only three are devoted to Byzantine slavery before the twelfth century.[41]

Jacques Heers also rejects economic definitions of slavery.[42] He disassociates medieval slavery not only from serfdom but also from ancient slavery, focusing, like the others, on the western Mediterranean. Unlike Verlinden, Heers examines the social positions of slaves. But his rejection of the economic dimension leads him to speak almost exclusively of domestic slavery, Byzantium still being absent from the discussion.

Since not all Byzantine slaves had the same economic roles and since they performed functions also carried out by nonslaves, they did not have an economic role specific to them. In other words, in Byzantium as in the medieval Arab world, the civil status of slaves did not correspond to a productive role and as a result was not equivalent to an economic status.[43] But if civil status does not necessarily tally with economic status, what is distinctive about slaves? Is it possible to refer to slaves as a social category?

Civil Status and Social Status: Free versus Slave, Free Labor versus Forced Labor

In historical terms, medieval slavery is as far from that of ancient Greece as from slavery in modern societies. But the scholarship dealing with slavery has often had a tendency to attenuate the distance between ancient slavery and that of the modern era without taking medieval slavery into account.

It is impossible to speak of ancient slavery without reference to the thesis of Moses Finley, who believes that the Marxist analysis of classical society in terms of the means of production is irrelevant. According to Finley, the slaves of antiquity cannot be assimilated to the "proletariat." But did they in fact constitute a social class?

Pierre Vidal-Naquet defines social class on the basis of three criteria.[44] It entails, first, a well-defined place on the social ladder (as "grande bourgeoisie" or "lower classes," for example); second, a defined place in relations of production (Marx); and third, a consciousness of common interests, a common language, and collective action at the political and social levels (also Marx).

Vidal-Naquet establishes that definition by using an approach that recognizes a specific economic role for each class. Therein lies the origin of the equation between social and economic status. I have shown that in scholarship on Rome and Byzantium, modern slavery and its definitions shaped the analysis of slavery as a social class. Vidal-Naquet and Vernant too point out that the economic role of slaves in classical Greece was not uniform,[45] which was also true in Byzantium. It is therefore clear that, according to Vidal-Naquet's definition, slaves in these societies did not constitute a social class. So how should they be situated?

Any analysis of the institution of slavery based on the means of production entails introducing a cleavage between slaves and owners. Finley proposes a different interpretation of the structure of ancient Greek society, founded on an opposition between slaves and free persons, one not defined by economic status. He maintains, however, that this opposition is based on the notion of forced labor.[46] In fact, Finley distinguishes between what English-speaking historians call "chattel slavery" and other forms of "servitude," such as that of the helots in Sparta. Chattel slavery and its raison d'être, forced labor, are therefore at the heart of his theory on the origin of ancient slavery and its "replacement" (in his view) in the late period of the Roman Empire. According to Finley, slavery as an institution came about in Greece because free persons were not ready to submit to the large landowners.[47] In other words, the free labor force—by Finley's definition, it was "free" in the sense that labor was done for the benefit of the laborers themselves or for their families—could not become a labor force for someone else. In the absence of an internal labor force, chattel slavery, which could be imported, provided a solution. As for slavery in antiquity, it was simply replaced by other forms of unfree labor that developed within the late Roman Empire among the group that had once been free.[48]

At the center of his theory Finley places the peculiarity that distinguishes classical Greece from all other ancient civilizations: "the advance, hand in hand, of freedom *and* slavery."[49] For Finley as for Vidal-Naquet, freedom needs chattel slavery to define itself, because in Greece forced labor and chattel slavery were established in contradistinction to the freedom of the citizen. Here, then, is the explanation for the cleavage that the law instates in society: those who are "inside" can define themselves socially. In other words, the legal cleavage is equivalent to a social cleavage. The insiders define themselves in relation to the outsiders. Behind that viewpoint I discern the desire to explain what constitutes "citizenship" and what to modern eyes ought to characterize classical Greece (and more exactly, Athens) and Rome, what marks them off from all other ancient societies, where freedom as we moderns understand it—that is, as citizenship—did not exist. The definition of freedom, like that of slavery, is here a civil definition. Hence Vidal-Naquet's distinction between chattel slavery and other forms of servitude that were part of ancient Greece.

But if it is conceded that freedom or citizenship defines itself by means of slavery, does it necessarily follow that slavery existed on a large scale only where there was freedom? I believe that such a perspective conflates the notion of freeman with that of freedom, or more precisely confuses the cleavage between slave and freeman with the dichotomy between slavery and freedom. On this question, it is essential to examine Henri Wallon's writings, which are the foundation for all modern historical scholarship on ancient slavery.

Wallon deserves particular mention because he too places the cleavage between slaves and freemen at the center. Let us not forget that he was writing in the nineteenth century, before the abolition of slavery in the Caribbean possessions of France, his native country.[50] He explains that behind his work lay his desire to show the effects of slavery in the labor relations of freemen. According to Wallon, slavery deforms and destroys society from a moral but also an economic standpoint. He presents his conclusion in the introduction to his book: one must abolish slavery to preserve or save the society of freemen. Here again, the driving force of social change is said to be the two key elements of slavery and freedom, expressed as the opposition between forced labor and free labor.[51]

It is interesting to note that Wallon constructs his schema on the same dichotomy as Finley: slave versus free. Although Finley focuses exclusively on chattel slavery, like Wallon he speaks in the first place of the implications of such a dichotomy. Yet the two historians advance opposing theories: for Finley, slavery is necessary for freedom to be able to define itself, whereas for Wallon slavery destroys freedom. I shall not undertake here to compare Finley's and Wallon's theses, which belong to two different eras. But having identified the cleavage between slavery and freedom, I shall attempt to grasp more precisely what it entails.[52]

Why, or rather how, might slavery play a role in defining freedom? Vernant and Vidal-Naquet clarify this point by focusing on exclusion: the slave is the absolute Other who finds himself completely excluded from society because of his position as chattel and, even more, his lack of civil status.[53]

In an article devoted to the institution of slavery, Alain Testart shows that stripping slaves of civil status made their economic exploitation possible.[54] The approach of Vernant and Vidal-Naquet is different: civil status does not correspond to an economic position but to a place (or nonplace) in society. The absolute Other, imported and without rights, defines by his very exclusion those who constitute society. In other words, the lack of civil status coincides with or gives rise to a lack of social status. For these historians, the institution of slavery makes it possible to define, *a contrario,* the civil and social status of free persons while leaving slaves outside any social discourse and, as a result, without recourse to any possible social struggle.[55]

According to Finley, chattel slavery provides the resolution to a conflict arising from the opposition between citizens (hence free) who refuse to become subordinate to others they judge to be their equals. Unlike other societies where slavery exists, the character of a slave-owning society consists in the fact that the exclusion of slaves, further reinforced by their status as imported chattel, serves to define the majority who are not slaves. Orlando Patterson, who casts into relief the social relation between master and slave by examining it within a broad historical context extending from antiquity to the modern age, similarly identifies slavery as the antithesis of freedom.[56] Freedom exists by virtue of the form of social domination that slavery entails. In this respect, there is no difference between slaves working in the fields and those working in a palace. That relation of domination, therefore, by its very definition, places slaves on the margins of society.

But the assertion of a causal relationship between exclusion and the absence of civil status remains problematic. I shall later show that the slave condition is in fact a civil status. And as possessors of a civil status, slaves are part of the same society as free people. I call into question the standard definition of slaves as res: that definition is not the only one possible. And I believe that it constitutes an obstacle or even a trap for the historian.

To concede that slaves are outsiders to society is to consider them inferior (not economically but socially) to all others who are "members" of society. That inferiority, characterized by the exclusive right of members of society to appropriate slaves, makes patent the importance of the definition of chattel slavery. But in my view, the social inferiority of slaves is relative; it exists solely in relation to their masters. To perceive it as an inferiority to every free person is already to infer a form (the most simple) of social stratification. Even if historians do not make the argument, it is obvious that the idea of exclusion implies that the outsider is inferior to the insider. As outsiders, slaves are inferior to free persons. That simple form of social stratification between two groups is based on the dichotomy between slave and free; social stratification is posited on the basis of a definition of civil stratification. Herein lies the misunderstanding: the delimitation of groups in society has been assimilated to a social stratification model. But it is possible to define groups in terms of different civil statuses without placing these groups in a hierarchy. I believe the misunderstanding stems from the fact that historians have imposed freedom as a criterion for a stratifying model.

In addition, modern historians do not perceive this civil delimitation, corresponding to a civil and then a social stratification, as limited to two groups, superior and inferior. Between total freedom (that of citizens) and total unfreedom (that of chattel slaves), they posit a broad spectrum of intermediate statuses of unfreedom. In opposing that understanding of slavery as part of a stratifying model, I find myself called upon to examine more closely where such a perspective and its problematic originated and to consider its consequences for the definition of slavery.

The Social Stratification Model

The analysis of social organization in terms of a hierarchy is inspired primarily by Marx, who provides several examples of it in *Das Kapital*. For Marx, however, it is the distribution of the means of production that establishes the stratification. The world (or society) is divided into the labor force (means of production) on the one hand and the owners of the means of production on the other. I have already noted that a socioeconomic stratification proceeds from that division. Marx's objective is to explain how capitalist society operates. The advent of capital transformed the entire historical topography of the economy by introducing an element that ceaselessly swallows or appropriates all other means of production. The accumulation and mobilization of capital represented major innovations in the economy.

For Marx, the other societies that exist or have existed—that is, noncap-italist societies—are only examples destined to explain the birth of the cap-italist system (in this Marx is a historian) and to illustrate the perpetual struggle to control the means of production (in this he is both a historian and an economist).

As a man of the nineteenth century, Marx understood ancient slavery through the prism of the reality of his age: slavery in the New World, where economic, social, and civil stratifications were perfectly coextensive. The slave-owning societies of the New World came about through the importa-tion of chattel slaves who were outsiders to society. Slave systems in the Americas did have a purely economic rationale, but since they were created ex nihilo, their civil and social aspects coincided with their economic objec-tive. Although it is correct that the law confers legitimacy on the structures of the society that produced it, it does not follow that social or economic need always precedes the civil code. In other words, the effort to know which comes first, the law of a society or societal structures, leads to a vicious circle, though the case of the New World may be an exception. In the medieval world, the institution of slavery was not simply tacked on. Once slavery has been placed within the context of the development of a society and its laws, it will be possible to grasp its specificity in the Middle Ages.

The cleavage brought about by exclusion in the stratification model en-tails more than a division into two groups. In Finley's and Vidal-Naquet's writings, chattel slavery stands as the absolute opposite of freedom. Vidal-Naquet explains that in a society that defines its freedom in contradistinction to chattel slavery (in Finley's sense), other groups also lack freedom. Yet these groups, included in society because they are composed of nonslaves, can aspire to freedom. It is within this framework that what historians call "forms of servitude" can be situated. For example, the helots cannot be classi-fied as chattel slaves. It would be interesting in this regard to consider the coloni as well, who were defined in historiography, first, as "quasi-slaves who do not have freedom of movement," then as an intermediate group between slaves and free persons.[57]

Clearly, I do not support the view that helots were the archetype for coloni or that they had the same kind of unfreedom. I think, however, that both oc-cupy the same place within historical scholarship, which tends to construct a civil stratification based on the "distance from freedom" it posits for each group. But that perspective is based on an anachronistic definition of the concept of freedom. In addition, not all these forms of unfreedom can be placed on the same continuum, not only because their point of reference, "freedom," is fictive but also because these forms differ in nature. Thus, for example, a female Athenian citizen was not more free than a slave, because her unfreedom belonged to a different register.

The Definition of Freedom and Its Problematic

To establish a hierarchy of freedom with slavery at the bottom is to take the definition of freedom as a given. According to Finley, for instance, in Athens the free were citizens; imported foreigners were unfree slaves; and nonslave foreigners, not being citizens, were not completely free. I shall show, however, that this scale of freedom is remote from Roman and Byzantine reality. In constructing a model that ranks degrees of freedom or unfreedom along a hierarchy, modern historians find a way to categorize freedmen, coloni, and every other social group that they cannot designate as "completely free." Yet that stratification raises major problems as one approaches medieval societies and, more generally, societies under an autocratic regime.

Freedom as a point of reference becomes problematic when it is used to define a society on the basis of the dichotomy between free and slave. Such a dichotomy, which might function perfectly well in the case of democratic Athens, republican Rome, or even republican France, is not applicable to an autocratic society. When compared to the king, emperor, caliph, or any other figure embodying public authority under such a system, other members of society can be designated only as "less free." In the same way, in autocratic regimes there is no clear dichotomy between slaves and free persons. It is for that reason that Finley calls all ancient societies, with the exception of Greece and Rome, "nonslave" societies, whereas Vernant and Vidal-Naquet are obliged to admit that, outside the Greco-Roman world, no societies were free. Hence the claim that in the late Roman Empire slavery failed, declined, or was replaced tallies well with the shift away from the republican political system. According to the same logic, medieval societies cannot be designated as "slave-owning" quite simply because they are not considered free. That is, there is no freedom that would stand in opposition to slavery. The fact that slavery was in full flower under the Roman Empire and in Byzantium and the Arab world proves that this perspective is problematic.

As a civil status, freedom, unlike slavery, is not defined in the law—in this case Roman and Byzantine law—in terms of its existence proper.[58] In fact, the only definition of freedom dating from that time is found in the legal definition of slavery:

Of the Law of Persons:

The principal division in the law of persons is that all men are either free or slaves.

1. Freedom [*libertas*], from which we get the description of men as free [*liberi*], is a man's natural capacity of doing what he pleases unless he is prevented by force or law. 2. Slavery [*servitus*] is an institution of the jus gentium [or *ius gentium*, law of peoples] by which one man is made the property of another contrary to nature [*nature*, i.e., natural law]. 3. Slaves (servi) are so-called because military commanders order their captives to be sold, and so are used to preserve them alive (servare) instead of killing them. They are also called mancipia because they are taken from the enemy by the strong hand (manu capiuntur). 4. Slaves are either born slaves or made slaves. They are born of our female slaves [*ancillae*]. They are made slaves either by the jus gentium, that is by being taken captive, or by civil law [*ius civile*], as when a free man upwards of twenty years of age suffers himself to be sold in order to share the price. 5. There is no difference in the condition of slaves. In the condition of free men there are many differences; for they are either born free (ingenui) or made free (libertini).[59]

Hence there is no legal definition either for freedom or for the status of being free, except as "a man's natural capacity of doing what he pleases unless he is prevented by force or law," which is merely a rhetorical argument. Conversely, the definition of a slave is well formulated:[60]

a person who is the property of another and who can be alienated by sale, purchase, or gift;

a person whose slave condition comes either from the mother, and who is therefore a slave by birth, or from captivity, hence by "the law of peoples," or from sale, hence by imperial law.

These criteria define two distinct groups within a society. A person cannot belong both to the group of slaves and to the group of nonslaves because, according to the Roman legislative system, in being the property of another, he or she cannot also be the owner of property.[61] In addition, the definition determines how one moves from the group of nonslaves to the group of slaves, as well as the reverse process of emancipation, how a slave becomes free.[62] That definition is what I mean by "civil status," and it determines a cleavage between slaves and nonslaves in human societies generally. The definition of the group of persons having free status is thus established by default or by negation, in other words, in opposition to the definition of the slave's status.

Finley's and Wallon's approaches make it possible to grasp the criterion that defines a slave-owning society in historiography: the coexistence of slavery and what is called "freedom" but is in fact citizenship. Hence the French Caribbean in the nineteenth century and the American South would correspond to democratic Athens and republican Rome in the ancient world.

Modern scholarship, therefore, projects onto its object the current concept of freedom: republican citizenship.[63] As I see it, in each society the definitions of freedom and slavery must be sought separately and not reciprocally. By that I mean that one term does not necessarily define the other.

But though slavery and freedom are not necessarily opposites, it is true that the slave's personal freedom is limited. That is, the institution of slavery implies a notion that could be called "unfreedom." The unfreedom of slaves may be specific, and it does stem from the definition of the institution of slavery, but it does not depend on the existence of an absolute freedom.

The Different Dimensions of Unfreedom

Within the context of a social stratification based on the exclusion of the Other, designated as the barbarian, the alien, the black, or as something else and projected onto a civil stratification, mobility is no easy thing. Let me cite as a counterexample the Arab world, where the son born of a master and his slave is free. As Murray Gordon explains, that law establishes a high degree of mobility among the children of an (unmarried) slave woman in the direction of the free status of their father.[64] That might also have been so in Rome or Byzantium for the descendants of a mistress and her male slave, since, according to Roman law, the status of slave comes from the mother; but that case, which was not well accepted socially, is rarely attested.[65] In any event, it is clear that the Arab institution of slavery did not have, or was not based on, a social stratification, because there was no social stability for the progeny of slaves.

For Greco-Roman and Romano-Byzantine societies, the case of the freedman illustrates the existence of a certain social mobility. Finley concedes that the problem with his model lies in the place that freedmen occupy within it. How to explain the possibility of their becoming free persons and citizens in Rome and the frequency with which that possibility was realized?[66] In fact, the civil status of the freedman in Roman law falls within that of the free person and as a result is not located "between" the status of a free person and that of a slave. This shows that the cleavage between free and slave does not necessarily entail the idea of exclusion, something that was especially true in Byzantium. Another case of civil mobility in Byzantium and the Roman Empire, but in the opposite direction, was that of persons who sold themselves; in Byzantium, there was also the case of parents selling their children. These examples also do not fit Finley's model.

In the slave-owning societies of the New World, the number of freedmen existing before the abolition of slavery was insignificant. Freedmen rarely became integrated into these societies as slave owners. What was at issue was a social and civil stratification, to which the factor of racial discrimination was added. Hence, in these same societies, a free (white) person could not become a (black) slave.

In fact, the better delineated the economic stratification and the better defined the roles economically, the more difficult social mobility becomes. In India, for example, castes persist even after the complete legal abolition of the caste system because they perform traditional economic functions. In the same way, in western Africa, descendants of former freedmen are even today identified as such because they have the same economic role once attributed to their ancestors.[67] Marx would have proposed class struggle as their political solution.

For Vidal-Naquet, social struggle can be engaged in only by members of society, not by those who are "totally excluded": slaves. But what about the other means of mobility whereby "outsiders" become integrated—through emancipation, for example? Clearly, it is difficult to apply to ancient societies or, for my purposes, to medieval ones the characterization of slaves as socially excluded.

Moreover, the argument that slavery is a complete loss of freedom is always weakened by the fact that it isolates the definition of slavery from that of any other form of servitude. It considers slaves solely in terms of chattel without proposing any definition for other kinds of servants apart from "less free but not slave."

The term *douleia* and its Latin equivalent, *servitium,* designate both the institution of slavery and the social relation of submission. That is, *douleia* expresses different notions in different contexts, concerning, on the one hand, the slave's civil status and, on the other, the slave's relation to the owner. Whereas the first sense of the term clearly refers to slaves as a group, the second may designate other relations of social submission. The Greek language therefore reveals two different dimensions, civil and social. The definition of slavery divides society into slaves and free persons. But the submission of slaves, as Keith Bradley shows, does not come about in relation to free persons in general, but exclusively in relation to the slaves' masters, their owners.[68] Thus Bradley declares that the institution of Roman slavery is a social institution. All the same, within the civil dimension, society is clearly divided into slaves and free persons, whereas in the social dimension the relation between slave and master is one social relation among many. It is therefore clear that, even after the economic dimension is set aside, the civil place of slaves does not coincide with their social place.

As a result, it is important to make explicit how I am defining unfreedom. The civil status of slaves, in making them the property of another, is an expression of their civil unfreedom. But how does their social unfreedom manifest itself? Here caution is required. There is sometimes a tendency, under the influence of Marx and the example of American slavery, to propose a stratifying social schema: upper classes, lower classes, and so on. This model is also an invitation to invoke degrees of freedom; that is why some historians insist on positing a whole gamut of statuses between free and slave. But anthropological studies show that a society's social relations cannot be analyzed solely in terms of a hierarchical model.[69]

Without a doubt, a semantic difference exists between the current meanings of the terms "freedom" and "slavery" and those of the ancient terms. As it happens, anthropological studies on slavery show that the institution of slavery can be identified even without any knowledge of the terms corresponding to it. But by what criteria?

To grasp the notion of slavery, anthropology proposes criteria regarding the acquisition of another (such as purchase, war captivity, or debt) or the ways of subjecting a person to forced labor.[70] These criteria also define the transition from the civil status of freeman to that of slave and vice versa, as I noted with respect to Roman and Byzantine law. That is exactly what I understand by the civil definition, which establishes a delimitation within society: the groups concerned and, if need be, the transition from one group to the other must be well defined. It is in this way that the civil status of slaves manifests itself. Such a definition presumes that a person is not at the same time property and the owner of property.

This analysis leads me to consider slavery an institution fixed by its civil definitions. At the same time, in referring to slavery as a social relation, I shall need to examine its implications within each society. That is what anthropologists attempt to do.[71] To understand the institution of slavery, they try to constitute its legal definition and to discern what makes one person "subject" to another, even without taking the economic factor into consideration. Anthropological models do not define the status of slave in terms of how slaves are acquired or how another's labor is put to use. They base themselves on a civil status for slaves, indicating that it is only one civil status among many. The same is true for social relations. I shall therefore analyze slavery as an extreme form of dependency without placing it within a social stratification model.

Slave status, then, is to be considered one social relation among many. By definition, dependency implies an element of unfreedom, which is embodied in a relation between two people. In regard to the slave's relation of dependency, it is essential to clarify that the discussion is confined strictly to social relations. I have shown that social status and civil status operate on two different registers. In the case of slavery, civil status assigns a place or grants legitimacy to social status. In other words, civil status offers the possibility of establishing a relation of private possession between owner and slave. That relation expresses the social unfreedom of the slave, who is completely dependent on the master. It is the public authorities—in the era in question, the imperial authorities—who confer legitimacy on a relation of private submission; it is also these authorities that, through the power of law, can change that relation.

In examining separately the nature of dependency in any social relation, I have found that other forms of unfreedom cannot be hierarchized along a continuum of freedom. Hence the dependency of coloni is to be explained in a manner completely different from that of slaves.[72] I have shown that in Rome and Byzantium, economic, social, and civil situations did not necessarily coincide. The status of freedmen, who occupied no position on the freedom continuum, can be understood both in terms of a civil dimension, since under Roman law emancipated slaves explicitly had the status of free persons, and in terms of a social dimension, since they were dependent on their former owners.

Those who define slavery as the ultimate form of unfreedom not only take as a given the scale ranking degrees of freedom. They also invert the hierarchy by defining slavery and all other degrees of unfreedom in relation to freedom, which is defined in Roman and Byzantine law only *a contrario* or by omission. In addition, those who adopt that model for a study of slavery run the risk of having the word *doulos* refer solely to the slave and thus cover only civil unfreedom. When the unfree in a society—in this case Byzantium—are defined as slaves of a sort, the word *douleia* becomes a synonym for "servitude," and all other meanings of the word are eliminated. The example of the coloni is in this respect the most instructive: since they were called, among other things, *douloi*, they have been perceived by historiography as "almost slaves." In Byzantium, the social context of the word *doulos* extended beyond the semantic field of the concept of slavery and entailed a whole range of social relations.

In addition, those who do not recognize that different dimensions are at issue may be led to conclude that nonslave *douloi* replaced slaves. That is why some historians decided to translate the word *doulos* automatically as "servant," believing that slaves were replaced by other unfree types. To evaluate the extent to which Byzantine slavery expresses a dependency, I shall therefore examine in each case the relation of slaves to their masters, to the public authorities, and to the other institutions concerned—for example, the church. That will allow me to grasp the social dimension of the phenomenon.

Byzantine slaves can be perceived from several angles: civil, social, and economic. Unfreedom and dependency constitute two criteria in this study. I shall not confine myself to examining slaves in their relations with their masters, since that would be to neglect other aspects of the institution of slavery. I shall also take into account social dependency of a private nature, which entails a certain unfreedom. Within a historiographical perspective that defines social status in terms of personal relations, Muslim and Byzantine slavery and the other forms of social dependency can coexist within a common framework. Nevertheless, were I to judge them solely from the angle of individual relations, I would be limiting myself to a single aspect of institutional slavery.

As a result, the question of which definitions of slave and free person are correct cannot be resolved through the adoption of the traditional definitions of historiographical scholarship. It will first be necessary to examine how the delimitation between the free person and the slave occurs. In the medieval Mediterranean world, that delimitation and the way it came into being took a particularly dynamic form.

CHAPTER 2

Medieval Slavery in a New Geopolitical Space

The Provenance of Slaves

According to the legal definition of slavery in Byzantium, there were three ways to become a slave: first, by being born of a slave mother (slavery by birth); second, by selling oneself (which, by law, only persons older than twenty could do); or third, by being taken into captivity.

The first two cases applied to the population within the empire, the third to slaves of foreign provenance. In addition to these three legal means for procuring slaves, there were the slave trade and the forced enslavement of a free person, which could be legal or illegal depending on the circumstances. Note that these five ways of acquiring slaves, which date from the late period of the Roman Empire, were still valid and applicable to the medieval Mediterranean world throughout the entire period under study. To grasp how this system operated, I take as my starting point the law, and in particular the institutions of the Roman Empire.

Roman law determined that the free status of a child came from the mother.[1] If she had the status of *eleuthera* during her pregnancy (even if she was later reduced to slavery), the child received the status of *eugenēs*.[2] In the same way, the children of a slave mother and her master were slaves until they and their mother were freed,[3] whereas the children of a *doulos* and his mistress were *eleutheroi*.[4]

The situation of free persons who sold themselves to acquire money or who were obliged to become slaves because of a debt had been known since antiquity. An important moment in the evolution of that matter was the *Novella* of Leo VI that declared the act of selling oneself no longer valid.[5] The same law, however, permitted the voluntary enslavement of a person who wanted to marry a slave.[6] The act of selling one's own children can also be included here, since it too entailed reducing a *eugenēs* (in Latin, *ingenuus*) to slavery. Although children did not have a legal personality, third-century Roman law recognized their freeborn status.[7] All the same, cases of parents selling, abandoning, or prostituting their children were not uncommon.

Trade, though not included in the legal definition, remained the privileged method for circulating slaves, whether they originated in the empire or were imported. Of course, the alienation of a formerly free person who had been illegitimately enslaved was still illegal. Normally, however, in the case of an imported slave (as opposed to one born in the empire), it was less important to know whether he or she had been enslaved legitimately because, from the standpoint of Roman law, the imported slave's original status was defined by the *ius civile* of another state.

Within the category of forced reduction to slavery, Roman and Byzantine legislation distinguished between the forced enslavement of a freeborn person and the enslavement of a freedman (under certain conditions, it was the legal right of a master to reclaim a freedman as a slave). Byzantine legislation, which followed the prohibitions of Roman law, banned the capture of a free person to be sold as a slave.[8] But that act was legally permitted if the state itself reduced the person to slavery. In Roman civilization, the reduction to slavery was traditionally a legal punishment. But the only authority that could impose it was the emperor, by virtue of his judicial power.

Among the illegitimate means were the abduction of children and the sale of one's own freeborn children. These two scenarios preoccupied lawmakers from the sixth to the eleventh century.[9]

During the entire era concerned, the Byzantine Empire was in a constant state of war and not only in the border regions. Wars affected the civilian populations in several regions of the empire, bringing about significant geopolitical shifts. The situation was particularly critical in the sixth and seventh centuries, but it continued to exist later on. The *Prochiros Nomos* cites ancient legislation stipulating that "according to the law of war, the conquered belong to the conquerors."[10] As a result, the empire had an unlimited supply of slaves. The obverse of that phenomenon was that many Byzantines were conquered by the enemy, becoming its captives and then its slaves.

For the Byzantine population living within the empire, the delimitation between slaves and free persons was clearly marked by law.[11] Things were less clear, however, for Byzantines taken into captivity or for populations outside the empire. It would be helpful to examine how the delimitation between the free person and the slave came about in the most complex situation, namely, slavery by captivity.

Civilian Captives, Prisoners of War, and Christian Marriage

Between Slave and Captive

In a world where the conquered belonged to the conquerors, the winners literally held the losers' lives in their hands. It was altogether legitimate to kill the conquered, and if the conquerors decided to let their captives live they could dispose of them as they wished. For that reason, captives had since antiquity become the conquerors' slaves. That rule also made war a legitimate means for procuring slaves. There is no dearth of examples from the Roman era.

The practice continued on a large scale in the Middle Ages, but it was no longer suited to the new geopolitical map of the Mediterranean world. Two problems arose as a result. On the one hand, enslaving prisoners of war was the general rule among both the Arabs and the Byzantines. When the Byzantines could not defeat their enemy, they became victims of that custom. On the other hand, the evolution of Christian marriage introduced a new definition of that institution and of the captive's marital status. Within the context of the Roman legal system, these two factors were in contradiction. Christian marriage, indissoluble by its very nature (except in special cases), made maintaining the free status of both spouses obligatory, even if one was enslaved following a war. The emperors of the Syrian dynasty in the eighth century undertook to resolve that contradiction by changing the law; they introduced new definitions regarding the status of the freeman and of the slave.

The expression "war captives" groups together warriors—particularly soldiers—and the conquered civilian population. In fact, throughout the era concerned, it is possible to distinguish four types of war captives in the sources: first, soldiers taken prisoner during a military operation; second, the residents of a city or region taken by the enemy after a military defeat; third, the population captured by the enemy during a raid; and fourth, persons kidnapped by pirates. Although there was a difference between a raid by the enemy and one conducted by pirates, both were criminal acts and therefore had to be distinguished from the others. The aim of these raids was neither military nor political; they were directed exclusively at taking captives and at making a profit from their sale. But is a raid not itself a military operation? The distinctions between these categories of captives are necessarily conventional. This is made clear by the Greek terminology used to refer to them. All sorts of captives were designated by a single term: *aikhmalōtos* (parallel to *aikhmalōtizō*, "to take into captivity"). The matter at hand was to determine whom the captives belonged to and, more precisely, who had the right to draw a profit from their market value. In other words, were "the conquerors" victorious soldiers, pirates, or the state?

Closely linked to the subject of prisoners of war was the phenomenon of exchanging them (in Greek, *allagia*). Such an exchange by adversaries could occur during a truce or upon the signing of a peace treaty. This was an innovation in the Mediterranean world and developed especially during the Arab-Byzantine wars. Exchanges of prisoners, whether soldiers or civilians, played a key role at that time. Simultaneously, however, sources continued to cite cases of prisoners of war who were not held for exchange but were sold as slaves.[12]

The practice of exchanging captives is linked to my primary concern: the evolution of their slave status. The development of the practice in the case of prisoners of war has been studied for the most part from the Arab perspective,[13] which corresponds to a difference between Arab and Greek historiography. Despite the absence of references on the Byzantine side, however, Byzantium not only played an important role in developing the practice but in fact initiated it.

Thus far I have spoken of the dichotomy between the conquerors and the conquered. That is, I have adopted an international vantage point from which to view the captives. From the Byzantine perspective, however, there were two types of captured slaves: Byzantines captured by the enemy and enemies captured by the Byzantines. (I shall not call the inhabitants of the Byzantine Empire "Greeks" because Greeks also lived in territories beyond the reach of Byzantine imperial power and because the Byzantine population was not exclusively Greek.) This is an important distinction, because it conditioned the practice of exchanging captives. Those taken by the Byzantines were legally defined as slaves. But free Byzantines who became slaves in enemy territory raised a real problem for the Byzantine legal system, one not raised in Roman law.

During the classical and the late Roman era, a free person captured by the enemy and made a slave was recognized as such in Roman territories as well.[14] As a captive, hence a slave in another state, that person no longer had the right to own property and thus lost his *usucapio*.[15] Although his property did not revert to the fisc, it could not be claimed by an heir: a slave, not having a legal personality, could have no heirs. The property therefore remained in abeyance (those of slave status also could not draw up wills).[16] Because the captive was assigned the status of a slave, his familial status and his ownership rights were affected: he lost his potestas over his own children, and his marriage was dissolved.[17] In short, all his rights that in the empire had been granted him as a person of free status were rendered void. Here Roman law, which—though no longer in force—continued to be cited throughout the Byzantine era, had the character of "universal law" in that it stipulated the same fate for Roman captives and for captives of the Romans. For this reason, Roman law attributed that norm not to *ius civile*—Roman civil law— but to *ius gentium*, a Roman definition of "the law of peoples."

The exchange of prisoners of war was very rarely mentioned in the Roman world.[18] In fact, the definition that reduced the Roman captive to slave status in his native state posed a difficulty for the argument that his citizenship should be restored to him by public means. A good example is the story told by the historian Malchus regarding the strategos Heraclius, who was captured by the Goths. Emperor Zeno offered to ransom him from the Goths but asked Heraclius's family to supply the ransom money; had someone other than a family member ransomed Heraclius, he could still have been considered a slave.[19]

As for captives who had returned to the Roman Empire, their status was complicated.[20] According to classical and imperial Roman law, a captive who succeeded in escaping the enemy or who was liberated did not automatically recover his original status upon returning to his native country. All the same, through the institution of postliminium, he received a transitional status that allowed him to recover the ownership rights he had had before his captivity.[21] Things were even more complex if the captive was ransomed by a third party (in Latin, *redemptus ab hostibus*). Historians have attempted to reconstruct a coherent theory of the different imperial regulations (*CJ* 8.50) and of Roman jurisprudence (*Dig.* 49.15). That is impossible, since, as Marco Melluso correctly argues, a complete theory of the subject never existed.[22] The debate has to do with the status of the captive ransomed by a third party. That captive did not benefit de jure from the *ius postliminii* so long as he did not ransom himself from his purchaser—in other words, so long as he did not reimburse his purchase price. At the time, there was an *ius pignoris* that bound him to his buyer.[23] But since he could not use his former ownership rights, he did not have the means to purchase himself.[24] The only solution was for him to be ransomed by his family or friends, as is indicated in the case reported by Malchus. So long as the captive had not reimbursed his purchase, his status and his former property remained in abeyance.

Third-century jurists spoke much more often of the status of the slave captured and ransomed by a third party.[25] By *ius postliminii,* such a slave would be returned to his or her former master. But for that institution to enter into force, the purchaser had to be reimbursed. Jurists were much less concerned by the subject of Romans of free status who were captured and ransomed by a third party because there was no dispute over property, as there was in the case of the ransomed slave. It is true that the case of the ransomed slave aptly demonstrates that the ransoming of a person from the enemy was also recognized within the empire. As for captives of free status who returned to the empire as slaves, I believe there is another explanation for why Roman law did not automatically restore their free status. From the Roman point of view, defeat was shameful. Roman jurists say so explicitly, explaining why weapons, unlike horses, were not restored by *ius postliminii.*[26] Traditionally, therefore, the Roman soldier was supposed to fight until victory or his death. Those who became captives of the enemy were believed to have preferred slavery to death.[27]

Hence a Roman captured by the enemy who returned to the empire as chattel did not attract a great deal of attention from lawmakers because his case did not raise any legal problems. Roman law allowed him to be restored to his former status provided that his purchaser was reimbursed. It was understood, of course, that such a course of action by the captive or his family was possible only if they had the financial means. For that reason, jurists allowed a captive in that situation to draw on an inheritance, which was considered a potential ransom provided by a member of his family.[28] If the ransomed captive or his family did not have sufficient money, he became de facto the slave of his purchaser, who could legally alienate him.[29]

Redemption by individuals thus existed, but not the possibility of ransom by public or imperial authorities. The fact that Roman law of the classical and late Roman era never envisioned the ransoming of captives by the state clearly indicates that exchanges of prisoners of war were not customary.

The traditional Roman point of view still had currency in the fifth and sixth centuries. But an evolution was occurring in the status of the captive. A constitution of Honorius (395–423) dating from 409 allowed the captive purchased by a third party to ransom himself from the latter.[30] If he could not pay the ransom, the constitution fixed a period of five years of labor, after which he regained his free status.[31] The sack of Rome by Alaric probably created the political circumstances surrounding the law.[32] To apply that law, Honorius named not only the curials but also the Christians "nearby" *(Christiani proximorum locorum);* these may have been devout people in general or the local clergy.

In addition, the redemption of captives as an act of Christian charity or even as a duty is mentioned during the same period by Ambrose of Milan, who establishes an opposition between Christians and Barbarian enemies.[33] Ambrose speaks of private individuals ransoming Christians and also argues that the church should melt down its sacred gold vessels to ransom captives.[34] The landed property that the church owned was not at issue because it was inalienable.

In fact, the state had also sometimes returned Roman prisoners in the fourth century, even prior to the rule of Ambrose. Julian the Apostate made a special request to the Alamans to return the Roman soldiers they had captured.[35]

The act of ransoming Christians taken into captivity was twice officially recognized by Justinian: *Novella* 120 authorizes the church to alienate otherwise inalienable lands to redeem captives,[36] and *Novella* 131 names the bishop responsible for an act of ransom mentioned in the will of a person from his diocese.[37] The practice is also attested in the will of Flavios Theodoros, an employee in the offices of the dux of Thebais.[38] In that document of 567, the author stipulates that upon his death his parents' house will be sold to ransom captives *(eis anarrēsin aikhmalōtōn).* Sixth-century historiography also contains an echo of that new provision. According to Procopius, in 540 the bishop of Sergiopolis ransomed the twelve thousand inhabitants of Sura captured by Khosrow.[39]

The Talmud of Babylonia reflects a parallel development in Jewish law, demonstrating that in the eastern provinces of the empire, especially Palestine, Syria, and Mesopotamia, the problem of captives was very real in the sixth century.[40] To redeem captives, interpreters of the Talmud say, even a synagogue can be sold, provided it has not yet been used. The similarity in this regard to Ambrose and especially to the *Novellae* of Justinian is noteworthy.[41] Let me point out that the Talmud of Babylonia originated in Pumbeditha and Sura, where the ransoming of Christians is attested by Procopius.

The parallel development, in Christianity and Judaism, of the custom of ransoming coreligionists also points to the emergence of a new sense of community, which would later be found in Islam as well. All these examples attest to the individual's identification with a religious community that preserved the free status of its members. As for Byzantium, it came to identify itself as a Christian empire, defined as a community of Christians.

This process also had consequences for marital status: in 536, a new *Novella* abolished as grounds for dissolving a marriage the difference in status that arises when one of the spouses is taken captive and enslaved.[42] That legislation was part of *Novella* 22, whose subject was Christian marriage. The notion of the status of captive and that of marital status thus influenced each other.[43]

Once again, this was a case of a Byzantine taken into captivity by the enemy. The origin of the distinction between a captive taken by the Byzantines and a Byzantine taken by the enemy can be seen here. The former was defined as a slave, whereas the latter preserved his status as a free person because his religion coincided with that of his state. Christian residents had to be saved from the infidels. No longer was the world of the empire pitted against that of the Barbarians, but rather the world of the Christian empire was pitted against the infidels. As Ambrose said, the new "Barbarians" were the non-Christians. And it was the development of that distinction that changed the civil status of the Christian captive and brought into being prisoner-of-war exchanges.

Justinian's marriage legislation created a contradiction between the Roman captive's marital and civil status. In decreeing that a marriage remained in force after a person was taken into captivity, the Roman legal system of the sixth century recognized the marriage of a person who had the civil status of a slave, as the *Novella* explicitly indicates. It is true that it applied only to persons remaining outside the empire, but that contradiction necessarily had repercussions within the empire as well.

The following example illustrates the paradox that Justinian's legislative innovation introduced. A Byzantine captive was sold as a slave in enemy territories and reintroduced as chattel within the empire. According to the traditional system, at the time of his captivity he would have been deprived of his status as husband and as free person. But according to the new law of Justinian, there was a contradiction between his marital rights, preserved as those of a free person, and that of the law of purchase, according to which, having been purchased legally by another Byzantine, he was considered property and not a free person so long as he had not reimbursed his purchaser. In other words, though the change in marital status did not raise a problem while the captive remained abroad, once he returned to the empire as a slave, if he was not ransomed by his family or by the church, he found himself with two contradictory statuses: married, which belonged to the status of a free person, but de facto also a slave.

That paradox was resolved by legislation in the eighth century that stipulated that a formerly free Byzantine taken into captivity and reintroduced into the empire as a slave regained his status as a free person; that legislation did not take the *ius postliminii* into account. But if that paradox truly existed until the eighth century, why had the legislation of Justinian not addressed the problem stemming from the innovation?

War Captives and the Political Situation

For a proper understanding of the origins of that evolution, it is important to examine the relationship between captivity and slavery before the Arab-Byzantine wars. Consider the late Roman Empire and its relations with the Persians, who had posed a major difficulty for Rome since the second century. The sources are very rich, especially the historiography, but they come solely from the Romano-Byzantine side.

During the long period of war in the sixth to seventh centuries, a large portion of the empire's population found itself in a region invaded by the enemy. The military expeditions pursued by the Persians greatly affected people's lives. Inhabitants abandoned cities, and people of the Roman Empire were forced to live under foreign occupation much more often than before, especially in the eastern regions. The abduction of civilians as a military objective is rarely mentioned by the Roman sources, however.[44]

Samuel Lieu, who studied the fate of the Romans captured by the Persians, shows that the Persians used the conquered population to fulfill their demographic needs.[45] Hence they established captives (soldiers or civilians) in colonies in the interior of the Sassanid Empire, far from the borders. Take as an example the case of Antioch, whose residents, captured by the Persian army, were driven to the middle of the Sassanid Empire to create a "new Antioch."[46] Similarly, the inhabitants of Theodosiopolis in Armenia were transferred to the Persian capital,[47] and Khosrow threatened to empty Edessa of its inhabitants by taking them to his empire.[48] Lieu studies only the fourth century, but the Sassanid authorities' policy remained the same throughout late antiquity, as shown in Procopius, Agathias, Menander Protector, and the fifth-century historians Eunapius, Olympiodorus, Priscus, and Malchus.

Exchanges of prisoners of war were never at issue. The question was not even raised in the peace treaties or in the diplomatic relations between the Romans and the Persians for which we have documentation.[49] The texts refer either to massacres of prisoners, to their transfer within the Sassanid Empire for purposes of colonization, or to their imprisonment.[50] In no case were the captives who had been taken by the Persians sold as slaves, unlike the captives of the Romans. In fact, the Persians considered their captives not enemies but residents of the recovered Persian provinces. Hence in 503, when the Persians conquered Amida, they allowed some of the residents to live and ultimately liberated them.[51]

By "Roman prisoners" I mean Romans who were captured by the enemy. But that is not the case for the empire's historiographers: in Priscus, for example, the *aikhmalōtoi romaioi* were the prisoners taken *by* the Romans.[52] Priscus mentions cases in which the return of prisoners was stipulated by peace treaties of the fifth century. But only the Romans had to return their prisoners, whom they had captured at the Balkan border.[53]

As for Persians captured by the Romans, they belonged to the Roman authorities. The emperor could make use of them, sell them, or return them to the Sassanid Empire in support of his diplomacy. Hence Tiberius II decided to free the Persian captives who were prisoners in Constantinople and send them to Khosrow.[54] Sebeos and Theophanes attribute that act to Heraclius.[55]

Although the captives taken by the Persians were not reduced to slavery, they were considered slaves by the *law of peoples* as it was understood in Rome. It is clear that the supposedly universal character of that law turned out to be unilateral on the international scene of the late Roman era.

Nevertheless, the norms of Roman law existing in the first to third centuries corresponded to the situation of the late Roman period as well. The case of a person of free status who was captured, sold, and returned to the empire as a slave was not common in sixth-century political reality. The act of redemption motivated by charity returned the captive to the empire; if he had had free status before his capture, he probably regained it at that time. The reduction to slavery of free persons, or rather the transition from the status of a free person to that of a slave, was unilaterally fixed by Roman law. That action thus remained in the hands of the Romano-Byzantine authorities, and that is why *Novella* 22 of Justinian raised no problems at the time it was promulgated. The paradox was introduced into the legal system at a later time, when the person who was a captive of the enemy retained the rights of a free person within the empire, even though he actually became a slave and returned to the empire as such.

From a global viewpoint, however, the paradox emerged for two more general reasons. On the one hand, the legal system persisted in believing in a universal law according to which "the conquered belong to the conquerors"; on the other, changes took place within the empire in sociocultural structures, such as Christian marriage, which remained in force even for the captive. That aspect of Christian marriage no longer tallied with any so-called universalism. But can it really be said that, from the Roman point of view, Roman law of the early imperial period was universal? And why did Roman law claim to recognize a "law of peoples" if such a law was disadvantageous to Roman captives or to the empire's population?

The situation that would have allowed the reduction to slavery of Roman citizens[56] was not common during the Roman era as a whole. To understand why, consider Rome's strategy toward its own enemies in the early imperial era but also in the republican period. Roman policy did not want to acknowledge permanent enemies; it gave them the choice between concluding a peace treaty or being definitively subjugated.[57] Such subjugation, especially if it was the result of a war or the repression of a revolt, sometimes led to the enslavement of the conquered population. That strategy explains the "universal" Roman law on prisoners of war, which always gave the advantage to the victor. Clearly, Rome never imagined losing, and the Romans also did not tolerate rivals on the political scene. Within its universal perspective, the Roman law of peoples could serve only Roman interests because Rome never had the intention of sharing its world with a rival.

The only real threat of slavery for the Roman population was piracy. That phenomenon, omnipresent in antiquity throughout the Mediterranean, greatly preoccupied the Romans from the first century B.C. to the first century A.D. Roman law considered both enslavement by pirates and any act of abduction, whether of a free person or of a slave, illegal within the empire.[58] And among the empire's first military actions in this regard were Marcus Antonius's failed attempt to eliminate sea pirates in 74–72 B.C. and Pompeius's successful efforts in 70–67 B.C.[59]

It was vis-à-vis the Persians that Roman ideology encountered difficulties, not only because the adversary remained unconquered but also because the wars with the Persians affected the civilian population of the empire. That situation, however, did not raise a problem in terms of the slave status of Roman captives because, once settled in the Sassanid Empire, they did not return.

Although the preservation of captives' marriages did not pose a difficulty in the sixth century, that was no longer the case in the seventh and eighth centuries, when the Arabs replaced the Sassanid Empire on the Byzantine geopolitical scene. Unlike what had happened among the Persians, the enslavement of captives was the general rule among the Arabs, as it was in Byzantium.[60] These captives were not inhabitants of the vast regions that the Arabs had conquered in the seventh century but rather were Byzantine soldiers. In the eighth century, the Arabs' strategy changed, and from that time on the civilian Byzantine population itself became a target of the Arab forces.

The paradox introduced by the *Novella* of Justinian found expression in another universal law, that of commercial exchange. Some of the Byzantine captives reduced to slavery by the Arabs were reintroduced into Byzantium as chattel or as part of the tribute. Since they retained their marital status, they found themselves slaves married to free persons. That was the contradiction the *Ekloga* attempted to resolve in the eighth century, stipulating that such persons would be free by law but would have to pay their masters their own value—that is, their price as slaves—to ransom themselves. If the captives did not have the means to do so, the new masters would pay their wages until the captives could accumulate that sum.[61] The constitution of Honorius was probably the source for that provision, though it is unknown whether it was ever applied to Byzantium.[62] In any case, from the eighth century on, the forced reduction to slavery of a Byzantine, both in and outside the empire, was not recognized de jure, even though the laws of commerce were respected. Under no pretext did the law prohibit purchasing such slaves or render their acquisition null and void.

The new law of the *Ekloga* had other consequences. It put an end to the trade in such slaves within the empire, because their sale was now prohibited. In other words, no trader would purchase a slave of Byzantine origin in Arab countries to be sold in Byzantium. Hence the legislative innovation introduced by the *Ekloga* indirectly modified the slave traffic itself.

For Byzantines captured by the Arabs, that legislation paved the way for the practice of exchanging prisoners of war in Byzantium.

The Captives of the Arab-Byzantine Wars

Maria Campagnolo-Pothitou has studied thirteen exchanges of Arab-Byzantine prisoners of war reported by al-Maqrīzī between 804–805 and 946.[63] In addition, Arnold Toynbee provides a list of the exchanges between the two empires between 769 and 969, a list that Athina Kolia-Dermitzaki completes.[64] The first exchange for which we possess evidence is that of 769 attested by Theophanes.[65] This exchange took place under the reign of Constantine V, the emperor who promulgated the *Ekloga* with Leo III,[66] which confirms the hypothesis that the development of that custom on the Byzantine side was linked to the change in the definition of a free person and of a slave.

Further evidence is provided in the *Leges militares* (Military law), a collection of rules of military discipline that probably dates back to the era of the *Ekloga*.[67] The second version of this collection, edited by E. Korzenszky, contains a paragraph dealing with booty: captives are not considered booty, and the strategos must keep them with him or take them to the emperor for a possible exchange of prisoners of war.[68] This collection must therefore date to an era when the exchange of prisoners of war was beginning to be an established practice.[69] The origin of that change lies both in the process by which Byzantine law initially became a Christian law and in the transformation of the geopolitical map of the Mediterranean in the eighth century.

In general, the exchanges between Byzantium and the Arabs are reported much more regularly by Arab historiographers than by the Byzantines. But even among the Arabs no mention of exchanges can be found before the eighth century. That is even more surprising in historiographers such as al-Balādhurī, who gives a great deal of information on the seventh and eighth centuries. Note, in this regard, the story in al-Mas'ūdī of a proposal for exchange coming from Mu'āwiya in the seventh century.[70] The Arabic term used is *fidā*, which refers to the ransoming of captives and not specifically to exchange. The story ends with the return of the captive to Arab territory, but there is no mention of a corresponding return of Byzantine captives. Another case of redemption of Muslim prisoners captured by the Byzantines is that of 710–720 mentioned by al-Balādhurī.[71] It is worth pondering whether these stories do not attest to a custom of public ransoming (that is, one organized by the public authorities) among the Arabs, which might have preceded a need for such a practice among the Byzantines.

The ransoming of captives, or *fidā*, was carried out either through the payment of money or through the exchange of captives. The Koran makes provisions for the liberation and redemption of war captives. These were prisoners of the enemy who found themselves in captivity among the Arabs. The Koran counsels a moderate attitude, recommending that the captive's life be spared.[72] It does not consider Muslim prisoners.[73] Did the Koran not anticipate that Arabs might fall into the enemy's hands? This is not known. In any case, it is clear that for the ransoming of prisoners of war, the starting point of Islamic law was the same as that of Byzantine law. In both cases, the practice was in a state of flux.[74]

Although the Koran made provisions for the ransoming of its prisoners by the enemy, such an act is not attested for the seventh century. As a result, it is clear that Byzantine prisoners were sold as slaves. As al-Mas'ūdī says: "In the time of the Umayyads, there was no major, well-known ransoming of which we may make mention."[75] All the same, al-Mas'ūdī states that private acts of ransoming did take place in the time of the Umayyads. Parallel to the situation in the Roman Empire, the private ransoming of Arab prisoners preceded public redemptions. It remains an open question whether public redemptions of Arab prisoners were necessary.[76] Campagnolo-Pothitou has attempted a response, arguing that the military, especially the new Arab navy formed by Mu'āwiya in the late seventh century, needed to supply itself with soldiers. The term *fidā*, in the sense of "redemption of Arab captives," is used by the same eighth- to tenth-century historians who describe acts of public redemption in exchange for money or prisoners: once again, the eighth century was the starting point. Nevertheless, truces and peace treaties between the two camps did exist before 769, despite the long duration of the war between the Arabs and the Byzantines.

In the seventh century, the Arabs conducted a holy war aimed at the total defeat of the Byzantines; the sieges of Constantinople in the seventh and eighth centuries are proof of that. But throughout the period, peace treaties were signed between the two states, and it was not always Byzantium that initiated them. I have already noted that prisoners of war had no place in these treaties. But all of them do mention slaves as part of the tribute offered by the state in the more disadvantageous situation, the side asking for the treaty.[77] The number of slaves to be provided, like the number of horses and the amount of money, was usually fixed as an annual base figure.[78] These treaties attest to the significant number of slaves who found themselves in the hands of the Byzantine emperor and of the caliph.

By contrast, in all the peace treaties signed after 769, no mention is found of slaves as part of the tribute. This absence argues in favor of the hypothesis that the strategy toward captives and the definition of their civil status had changed. Were the slaves who had been provided as tribute in the previous treaties war captives? That is likely, but information on slaves as part of a tribute comes solely from Byzantine documentation, which does not mention the fate of these slaves (or captives). Hence, to introduce the custom of prisoner-of-war exchanges, or even of public redemptions of war captives, Byzantine law had to change. The acknowledgment that captives retained their civil status as free persons was the first step necessary toward making that status correspond to their marital status.[79]

The political map of the Arab world changed in the eighth century when the Abbasids replaced the Umayyads. In particular, that change translated into the transfer of the capital to the new city of Baghdad. Although the wars on the Byzantine border did not end, they took a different form.

After the lifting of the Arab siege of Constantinople in the winter of 717–718 under the reign of Leo III, the Arabs seem to have given up the prospect of a complete conquest of Byzantium. In the eighth century, they no longer conducted wars but simply made occasional incursions to the interior of Asia Minor to weaken the geographical defenses of the Byzantines. To do so, they besieged cities of strategic importance. In addition, for the Arabs victory entailed sacking the city and capturing its population, which was then sold into slavery, as, for example, during the siege and capture of Heraclea.[80] That strategy was common to both adversaries. This was no longer the same war as in the seventh and early eighth centuries. The failure of the Arab sieges of Constantinople in 677–678 and then in 717–718 marked a decisive turning point in favor of the Byzantines and consolidated their state.

With the advent of the Abassids in the Arab world, the total defeat of the enemy and the holy war were no longer political objectives. The Abassids gave priority to gaining a foothold in the interior against the opposing forces there, to establishing themselves, and to strengthening their empire. That new situation influenced Arab-Byzantine relations as well. The form of war changed, and with it the way the infidel enemy was perceived. Relations were not merely adversarial but also material and intellectual.[81]

The Byzantine Perspective on Captives

The case of deserters was an important consideration in defining the free person and the slave on the geopolitical scene. If deserters returned to the empire, their punishment was enslavement, a practice that the central authorities had legitimated since the eighth century.[82]

Within the context of Byzantium's international relations between the fifth and seventh centuries, the question of refugees was elaborated even more fully than that of captives, which shows just how widespread the phenomenon was.

Menander Protector provides detailed documentation on the peace treaty of 561–562 between the Roman Empire and the Sassanid Empire.[83] Not only did no clause deal with the exchange of prisoners of war; such prisoners were not even mentioned.[84] By contrast, the sixth clause concerned refugees. These were actually deserters (*automoleō* in Greek). The difference between a refugee and a deserter depends on the point of view of the two parties: here I shall use the more neutral term "refugee." The provision in question gave permission to those who, during the war, had sought refuge with the enemy to return to their homeland. As for those who took refuge in peacetime, they would be returned to those "from whom they had escaped."

Roger Blockley explains that this clause expresses the concern of both sides to control the civilian population at a time when there was a dearth of residents in the rural areas. He argues that those who escaped in peacetime were slaves.[85] The text is not explicit, however, and these may also have been civilians who found better living conditions in the enemy empire: those "from whom they escaped" could simply designate the empire from which they fled and not specifically "their masters."[86] In any case, the problem of refugees was a burning issue in the border regions. It arose repeatedly in many peace treaties not only between Byzantium and the Sassanid Empire but also in the Balkans, between Byzantium and the Avars, the Huns, and then the Slavs and Bulgars.[87] The aim of the treaties governing the problem of refugees was to ensure their freedom when they returned to their homes even if they had done harm to their state.[88]

Within the context of Byzantine-Arab relations, this was also a religious battle, which influenced the fate of the deserters-refugees. The best-known example is the epic of Digenis Akritas, which dates from the ninth or tenth century. It concerns an emir (the father of Digenis Akritas), a dignitary in the Arab army who directed attacks against the civilian population of Asia Minor. Having deserted to the Byzantines, he embraced the Christian faith and married a young woman from an illustrious Byzantine family.[89] This story attests to the role the Christian faith played in establishing "national" identity, especially in Byzantine-Arab relations: consider the moving letter from the emir's mother, who implores him to return to his country and his religion.[90] In this story, Christian faith goes hand in hand with Christian marriage, which is the motive for the emir's desertion.

The story is not unique but reveals Byzantine policy in the tenth century. In *De cerimoniis aulae byzantinae*, Constantine VII Porphyrogenitus attested to the demographic use, for military ends, of captive Arab prisoners belonging to the state.[91] According to this account, captives could be emancipated if they converted, married, and remained in Byzantine territories, especially in the border regions. Nevertheless, they were not delivered from their *douleia* to the Byzantine emperor, which now took the form of either fiscal or military obligations (which were also of a fiscal nature). The two acts, conversion to Christianity and marriage, not only transformed captives into free Byzantines (they may have already been married in their native country, but that changed nothing) but also made them trustworthy.[92] According to the imperial edict mentioned in the *Life of Athanasia of Aegina,* also dating from the early tenth century, unmarried (widowed or single) Greek women were to marry foreigners who had settled in Byzantium.[93] Arab prisoners may have been included among these foreigners.[94] Al-Mas'ūdī also attests to the presence, in 923, of twelve thousand Christianized Arab horsemen among the Byzantine forces.[95]

As Marius Canard has noted, parallels existed on the Arab side as well.[96] While there is no mention of a conversion to Islam by Andronikos Doukas (906),[97] other renegades, such as Leo of Tripoli and Damian, governor of Tarsus, attained high positions in Arab society, often thanks to military careers.[98] It is interesting to note that the Arabs told stories of Byzantine and Arab renegades, whereas the Byzantines refrained from speaking of their own renegades.[99] Hence, for example, Theophanes tells how Elpidios, the strategos of Sicily, took refuge in Africa, without mentioning his conversion to Islam.[100]

By contrast, the theme treated in *Digenis Akritas* is also found in Arabic literature, for example, in the story told by Abū al-Faraj, *Kitāb al-Aghānī* (The Book of Songs)—a collection of songs from the time of Caliph Harun al-Rashid. It is the story of a reciter of the Koran who, after his voluntary exile, arrives in Constantinople, converts to Christianity, and marries a Christian. "The envoy of Caliph 'Umar b. 'Abd al-'Aziz, coming to Constantinople to negotiate an exchange of prisoners and passing through the streets of the capital on a mule, hears a sad voice singing an Arabic verse. Moved by the beauty of the voice and intrigued by the strangeness of such a song in such a place, he enters the house from which the voice is coming. He sees the reciter, who is tirelessly singing the same verse, all the while weeping. He entreats him to return to Islam to be redeemed with the prisoners. 'But I have a Christian wife and two children,' he replies. 'How can I return to Islam?' and he rejects the proposal."[101]

I mentioned three interrelated factors that determined the delimitation between slave and free in Byzantium: first, captivity; second, the shift from the status of free person to that of slave; and third, the institution of marriage (i.e., Christian marriage).

These three criteria applied only to slavery by captivity. But they indicate that there is a difference between having the status of slave and being a slave or, in other words, between a slave de jure and a slave de facto. That difference, which later existed between a free person de jure and a free person de facto, can be observed in the first place in the case of captivity, because two different societies and two different legal systems met at that point.

But the real catalyst in that case was the change in status of Byzantine marriage, which was related to a person's Christian faith or Christian identity. Here as well the difference between the Byzantine society of that era and the surrounding world becomes apparent. Nevertheless, the empire was also evolving toward a Christian civilization, and that evolution was accompanied by an internal adaptation.[102]

I have emphasized the relation between the status of a free person and a Christian identity. Khosrow's discourse cited by Menander Protector shows how the international and even political perspective of Byzantium had changed as a result of the Christian factor. The Sassanid king explained that the Romans could not conduct a war within the Sassanid Empire because they would find there a Christian population that they could not defeat.[103] It is clear that Menander was reflecting the point of view of the Byzantines. And in fact when Belisarius captured the Persian city of Sisauranon in 541, he released all residents who had once been Christians and "Romans" *(Khristianoi te kai Rōmaioi to anekathen)* but sent the "Persians" to Constantinople.[104] In this case, the Romans were perceived as Christians, whereas the Persians were non-Christians; in the sixth century, that was a uniquely Roman point of view.

Despite the correlation established between the state and religion, the population in the territories under Arab domination was not entirely Muslim (on the contrary, Muslims were a minority in the seventh to ninth centuries), just as not all those subject to the Byzantine emperor were Christian. Hence the Byzantines also took Christian captives from Islam countries, as attested by the exchange of captives in 855 or 856.[105]

Thus far, I have been interested in the Byzantine-Arab border, where the religious dichotomy coincided with the political dichotomy. But that equivalence did not correspond to the dichotomy between slave and free. In other words, though Byzantium made efforts to recover its soldiers and its residents captured and enslaved by the Arabs by defining them as free, and though the same thing happened on the Arab side,[106] in Byzantium not all free persons were Christian, and not all Christians were free. The same was true of Muslims in the Arab world. In Byzantium, the Christianization of non-Christian slaves was the general rule, the master preferring to convert his slaves to his own religion.

The laws dealing with the difference in religion between master and slave shed light on another case of correlation between the state and religion. Byzantine law forbade a non-Christian, whether Jewish, Samaritan, or pagan, to have Christian slaves.[107] The ownership of Christians by non-Christians continued to concern lawmakers, indicating that the situation was not rare.[108] The legislation tried to foresee all possible situations: for example, a slave who wanted to convert to the Christian faith even though his master was opposed to it, or a master who forced his slaves to become Jewish or Samaritan. The objective of that legislation was to stand in the way of a Christian's being subjected to a non-Christian. It was self-evident that Christians could have Christian slaves.

The legislation was almost identical on the Arab side: laws forbade non-Muslims from having Muslim slaves.[109] It is clear, however, that the Muslims themselves had Muslim slaves, but these were of foreign origin. Hence they were not Muslims by birth but were Islamized after being imported to the Arab world.[110] The capture of prisoners of war was thus crucial since, apart from commercial importation, it was the only means for acquiring such slaves. But did not the practice of exchanging prisoners of war cause a problem by limiting that source of slaves?

On the Byzantine-Arab border, which extended from Caucasus to southern Italy, the religious opposition was therefore clearly defined. It is time to see what was happening on the other active front of Byzantium, that is, in the Balkans. In Byzantine documentation, no case is found of an exchange of prisoners of war between the Byzantines and the Slavs, Bulgars, or Russians. It is true that diplomatic relations between Byzantium and the Balkans in the seventh to ninth centuries are much less well documented than those involving the Arabs, particularly since the Slavonic sources are much less rich than Arab historiography. That is not sufficient for concluding that no exchange took place between Byzantium and the Slavs or Bulgars. In fact, the inscription published by Veselin Beševliev, which concerns the Bulgar-Byzantine peace treaty of 816, mentions an exchange of prisoners (*psukhin anti psukhis*—"soul for soul").[111] The exchange took place between the Byzantines and the Arabs at a time when the Bulgars were still pagans.

I have emphasized that one of the conditions for the exchange of prisoners was that both parties treat the prisoners they captured in the same manner. Within the context of Arab-Byzantine relations, that meant that both parties, unlike the Persians, reduced their prisoners to slavery. As for the treatment of prisoners by the Slavs and Bulgars, the little extant documentation comes especially from the Byzantine side. These are saints' Lives from the tenth century. *The Life of Luke the Younger* mentions the Bulgar attacks by Simeon.[112] Blaise of Amorion is captured when he goes to Rome and is then sold to a "Scythian."[113] His *Life* also mentions pirates on the Danube.[114] Finally, the *Life of Fantinos the Younger* tells the story of a slave abducted by the Bulgars and imprisoned.[115] And it was not only enemies who abducted Byzantine residents. Hence, in the *Life of Nikon Metanoeite,* the peasants are threatened by bandits who pillage the countryside and kidnap free persons to sell as slaves.[116] The saint rescues a kidnapped girl and returns her to her parents, and he makes the bandits swear to never again engage in pillaging.[117] Similarly, Gregory the Decapolite runs into Slav bandits on the waterway while traveling to Thessalonica.[118] The Byzantines sometimes asked for these captives to be returned through diplomatic means, but no exchange of captives is mentioned after that of 816.[119]

Each of the three fronts of Byzantium imposed a different policy. Since the Roman era, the Caucasian front had been the scene of several battles against the Eastern adversary (the Persians, then the Arabs). The Caucasian peoples did not themselves conduct an offensive policy against Byzantium. Recall that the alliances between the Khazars and Byzantium were strengthened by imperial marriage connections: in 733, Constantine V married the daughter of the Khazar khan.[120] In addition, Armenia, though not Chalcedonian, had been Christian since the fourth century. The Balkans were thus notable for their belated paganism.

The difference in the religion and laws of the non-Christian Balkan peoples, when compared to the Arabs and Byzantines, lay in the fact that Arabs and Byzantines developed a new practice requiring them to rescue and redeem those of "their own" who had fallen into captivity. The religious criterion determined who these were.

Judaism developed a parallel doctrine during the same era.[121] The mitzvah (precept) of redeeming captives took on greater scope in the tenth and eleventh centuries as a result of the piracy in the eastern Mediterranean.[122] The practice is attested by the documents of the Cairo Genizah.[123] It is interesting to see that the development of the practice of redeeming captives as a religious duty among the Jews varied by region. Hence in the eleventh century, the Jewish population of Jerusalem accused the gaon Solomon ben Yehuda of having refused to help in redeeming captives. That gaon was then obliged to leave Jerusalem less than two weeks later to return to Ramla.[124]

The difference between the two fronts of Byzantium, the northern and the southern, thus lay in religion. That situation continued until the Christianization of the Slavs and Bulgars, that is, until the ninth century. But what happened subsequently?

I have shown that the dichotomy between Christianity and Islam corresponded to the situation of Byzantium in its relations with the Arabs. On the Balkan front, until the ninth century the enemies of Byzantium were pagans. There as well the Byzantines conducted a war against the infidels. But they also took advantage of the fact that their Balkan enemies were pagans, and they conducted a policy of Christianization. The Christianization of pagans was easier than that of a people with a monotheistic religion. In addition, the church was much better prepared to convert pagans, an area in which it had a great deal of experience.

Byzantine legislation attests to the persistence of the custom of enslaving Bulgars, particularly in the tenth and eleventh centuries. The *Novellae* in question, because of their legislative nature, have to do with slaves of any origin, but they give details about the Bulgar slaves especially. The *Novella* of John I Tzimisces, dating to between 972 and 975, fixed a tax that Byzantine soldiers had to pay when they sold the prisoners of war they had enslaved. That tax applied only to sales to a person outside the military.[125] That *Novella*, the only one attributed to John I Tzimisces that has come done to us, has been discussed by Helga Köpstein and by Taxiarchis Kolias.[126] The two authors adopt different points of view: Köpstein considers the *Novella* evidence of the imperial authorities' struggle against the powerful elite, whereas Kolias concentrates more on its fiscal aspect. It is of interest here for two reasons: first, because it deals with prisoners of war privately owned by the military men who had captured them, whether in the Byzantine infantry or navy, and specifies that these were Bulgar captives;[127] and second, because the taking of Bulgarian captives occurred at a time when the Bulgars were Christians.

The *Novella* attests to a well-known fact: the Bulgaro-Byzantine wars continued well after the Christianization of the Bulgars (864) and after the church of Bulgaria came under the religious hegemony of the patriarchate of Constantinople.[128] The correlation between the Eastern enemy's religion and its politics might lead to the conclusion that once those in the Balkans were no longer religious foes, they would also not be political adversaries. But that reasoning, which may have encouraged Byzantium in its politico-religious strategy, ultimately did not apply to the Balkans of the ninth to tenth centuries, especially where the Bulgars were concerned.

In fact, Byzantium did not seek to make its enemies in the Balkans its equals. The proof is that the Byzantine authorities insisted on obedience to the patriarchate of Constantinople. In that respect it found itself in competition with the Latin West. Religious dependency must also have translated into political submission, the cause of the battle conducted by the Bulgar king Simeon and later by Kings Boris II and Samuel.[129] On the Byzantine side, however, the view that stipulated the submission of these peoples to the imperial authority combined the political sense of the word *douloi*, expressed, for example, in the political treatises of Constantine VII Porphyrogenitus, and the sense of "slaves," the reality being that the Byzantines procured slaves for themselves among these same peoples.[130]

The military success of the Byzantines, which was greater on the Balkan front than against the Arabs, was thus expressed as the benefit to be drawn from taking captives. The difference between the two fronts of Byzantium was also reflected in the ethnic profile of Byzantine slaves of foreign origin— the war captives who remained in Byzantium without being exchanged were Slavs, Bulgars, and Russians. The term assigned to most of these prisoners was "Scythians."[131]

Byzantium continually enslaved Slavs and Bulgars even after they had converted to Christianity. In fact, the political enslavement of the Balkans went hand in hand with their conversion. The counterpart to that policy in the private domain was the practice of converting slaves while keeping them in the same legal and social positions.

This occurred among the Jews as well. Simha Assaf, who has studied the subject in the *Responsa* of the geonim in the ninth to eleventh centuries, shows that the conversion of slaves to Judaism was not only recommended but obligatory.[132] In the Hebrew sources, the process is called *Tevilah le-avdut,* "ritual immersion for slavery," that is, the obligation to immerse the person with the aim of making him or her a Jewish slave, parallel to the *Tevilah-le-geirut,* which, as the sources explain, is the immersion of a person not a slave who wishes to convert to Judaism.[133] All the same, in the era concerned, Jews who wanted to "immerse slaves to have them as Jewish slaves," had to contend with the state's legislation, which placed limits on the phenomenon. In addition, Jews were not always ready to convert their slaves because, once the slaves had become Jews, they had to be emancipated after seven years, following the rule for the *eved ivri* (Hebrew slave).[134] The evidence in the *Responsa* and in the documents of the Genizah shows that people preferred to convert their slaves to Judaism, but they sometimes did so in their wills, while also making provisions for the slaves' emancipation after the owners' death.[135]

The Byzantines' Loss of Freedom

Piracy was a particularly effective means for procuring slaves. It was an old phenomenon, but it took a new form in the Byzantine world, especially in the Mediterranean, and was increasingly present in the literary sources from the ninth century on, especially in historiography and hagiography. These raids disturbed the Byzantine population along the coast, especially after 826, when Arab forces succeeded in occupying Crete. The island served as a base for Arab piracy against the Byzantines until 963–969, when Nicephorus II Phocas recaptured it.[136] Nevertheless, the Arab forces that had been expelled from Spain and that occupied Crete appear to have been independent from the other Arab forces (Egyptian, Syrian, and African).[137] This can be discerned by their strategy: the aim was not to conquer all Byzantine lands, with Constantinople as the final objective, but to abduct the Byzantine population for its market value. It is obvious that this operation was dictated by a commercial demand for slaves in the Arab territories. Hence in the ninth century, slavery became one of the most important issues on the Arab-Byzantine Mediterranean scene and the major concern of the Byzantines. And not only because of the Arabs: the sacking of Thessalonica in 904 was committed by Egyptian forces, without the knowledge of the Arabs of Crete.[138] In fact, there were not only acts of sea piracy but also raids organized and carried out by infantries. In the ninth and tenth centuries, that became a strategy of the Arab forces, which launched raids on the Byzantine cities in Asia Minor and withdrew after capturing and enslaving the local population—in the attack on Heraclea, for example.

In the tenth century, raids against the Byzantine population were conducted in the Balkans as well.[139] The Bulgaro-Byzantine wars brought about instability in the regions of continental Greece, especially during the reign of Simeon the Bulgarian. All these military operations profoundly marked the Byzantine population and also had economic consequences. In the *Life of Luke the Younger*, for example, the family flees the Arab pirate attacks on the

isle of Aegina in Hellas, to Thebes and Peloponnesus. The father finally set-
tles in a village in Phocis, but there he faces the opposition of the villagers.
He therefore travels to Constantinople to ask for help from the emperor. An
imperial envoy arrives in the village to again divide up the lands.[140] The rav-
ages of the Bulgars are also predicted by Luke the Younger. Many are taken
captive, then killed or reduced to slavery; some residents take refuge in the
cities, while others, especially peasants, flee to the south, to Euboea, the
Peloponnesus, and the Gulf of Corinth.[141] The same people who fled the
Greek isles for the continent found themselves threatened from the north
as well.

In the Byzantine hagiographical sources, only Arab piracy is mentioned.
But raids organized by the Byzantines also occurred. The Byzantine navy
raided parts of Syria, Palestine, and even Egypt, as al-Balādhurī relates for
the year 710.[142] On the reign of Theophilus, Michael the Syrian wrote:
"During that time, the Romans came to Antioch by sea, as far as the port;
they pillaged merchants, took captives, and left again on their ships."[143] Similarly, in 988 Ibn Hawqal, in his description of the Mediterranean, related:
"In our time, the Byzantines were relentless in attempting raids on the coast
of Syria and the beaches of Egypt. They drove off the ships of the coastal residents along all the coasts and captured them everywhere. No help, no aid
was procured from the Muslims, and no one cared."[144]

The eleventh-century documents of the Cairo Genizah also refer to Byzantine piracy: its victims included the Jews of Palestine, who were sold as
slaves to Byzantium or redeemed by their Byzantine coreligionists. Consider,
for example, the letter from the leader of a Jewish community who collected
five thousand dinars to ransom two hundred people.[145] The author mentions
a large number of Jewish captives returning from Byzantium *(Edom)*, where
they were redeemed by the local communities. Upon their return to Palestine, they passed through the city of the author, whose name is not indicated,
and the community there provided for them. These two hundred ransomed
persons were only part of a much larger group of captives sold as slaves. The
letter is a response to a request from the Jewish community of Al-Fustāt.

The objective of the Byzantine assaults, exactly like that of the Arabs, was
to abduct civilians, who were then taken to Constantinople, where they were
sold or kept with an exchange in view: witness the *Sylloge Tacticorum*, attributed to Leo VI, and the first-person description by Hārūn ibn Yahyā, who
recounts how he arrived at the Byzantine court as a captive abducted in
Ashkelon.[146] Although this type of tale suggests that war captives went to the

court of the caliph or of the emperor, that was not always the case. Hence Emperor Leo VI asserted that if the enemy did not want an exchange of prisoners, they could be disposed of as desired, attesting that the custom of selling them still existed.[147] In the exchange of 845, the number of Arab prisoners in the hands of the Byzantines was far greater than the number of Byzantines who were captives of the Arabs. Thus, to make their numbers even, al-Wathiq ordered the Byzantine slaves who had been sold in Baghdad and Rakka to be ransomed, and he personally brought out the Byzantine women from his own harem.[148]

In Asia Minor, the Byzantines used the same strategy. According to the *Tactica* of Leo VI, the Arabs of Cilicia were to be attacked by sea when they attacked by land, and vice versa.[149] And in 855 the Byzantines seized the city of Anazarbus without warning and took into captivity the Zutt tribe—including the women, children, and livestock—which the Arabs had installed there in 835.[150]

Prisoners were also used as spies. The unavoidable reference is the story "Abū Qir wa Abū Sir," recounted in the *Thousand and One Nights*, in which Abū Qir wrongly accuses Abū Sir (both natives of Alexandria) of being a spy for the Byzantines. He explains to the Arab king that both were prisoners of the "sultan of Christians" and that Abū Sir, to liberate his wife and his child from the Roman sultan, promised the sultan to return to Arab territory and kill the king *(malik)*.[151]

For the duration of the Arab occupation of Crete, the Byzantines repeatedly tried to recapture that island, with short-lived successes.[152] At the same time, they—like the Arab forces—launched maritime attacks intended to abduct the civilian population, though the Byzantine attacks are less well attested. They conducted a similar strategy in Asia Minor. In 942–943, for example, Byzantine forces arrived in Diyarbakir and captured a large number of residents before devastating the entire region as far as Arzen.[153] Al-Muqaddasī (d. late tenth century) describes how the Byzantine ships took Arab prisoners to Palestine, where they were exchanged or ransomed (three for a hundred dinars). He names the following guard stations *(ribāt)* where such exchanges occurred: Gaza, Mimas, Ashkelon, Mahuz (port of) Ashdod, Mahuz Yubna, Jaffa, and Arsuf (the former Apollonia).[154]

In the episode of the miracle of the mother and of the dragon of Theodore Tyron, the hero, Theodore the Recruit, is the leader of a military expedition conducted with the objective of abducting Arabs and taking them to the emperor.[155] Theodore arrives in Syria, where he captures forty men, eighty women, and a hundred children. Upon their return, the men are thrown into prison and the women enslaved. That narrative, a Byzantine version of *King Kong*, is very unusual in that it mentions the Byzantine raids. But why are the Byzantine sources silent about their offensive side in such a war? It is quite possible that an ideological motive is concealed behind that silence.

Despite the raids by the Byzantine army, those launched by the Arabs, especially during the period of their domination in Crete, continued to disturb the population on the Byzantine coast of the Mediterranean. As a result, a considerable number of Byzantine inhabitants were kidnapped by Arab pirates and sold as slaves in the Arab world. That was the situation in the Greek isles, Sicily, southern Italy, Peloponnesus, the coasts of continental Greece, and the Aegean coast of Asia Minor. The Byzantine strategic response, especially in the Greek isles, Peloponnesus, and Sicily, was sometimes to evacuate the local population. All the hagiographical narratives of that time that are set in these Mediterranean regions attest to this. The raids were not limited to the coastal cities and villages but also threatened areas inland.[156]

The motivation for these acts was the market value of the persons abducted, who could be sold in the Arab territories. For the pirates, however, that price could also be obtained if the families redeemed the abducted. That custom was very widespread, as detailed, for example, in Methodius's *In Praise of Nicholas of Myra*. The author recounts the attack on Lesbos by the Arabs of Crete. These Arabs capture a priest from Mytilene and his three disciples. Nicholas then goes to Crete and liberates them.[157] Another source for the same saint's Life—*Three Miracles of Nicholas of Myra*—relates how the son of a peasant is captured by the Arabs of Crete; the saint returns him to his father.[158] Similarly, in the *Spiritually Beneficial Tales of Paul of Monembasia* and in the *Life of Nilus of Rossano,* a bishop, a metropolitan, and a monk leave for the Arab countries in search of captured persons—who are in all cases their spiritual responsibility—in order to redeem them.[159]

In another example, a widow sells a property to the monastery of Iviron for fifteen *nomismata* to redeem her son captured by the Arabs.[160] The act of redemption is portrayed as being carried out by an individual, which accorded with the pirates' objective and differed from the exchanges organized by the public authorities. Redemption was not always viewed favorably. Hence Nilus of Rossano opposes the journey of the Calabrian metropolitan to redeem members of his flock because that act requires negotiations with the infidels. But he himself sends a hundred *nomismata* to the emir of Palermo to ransom three monks from his monastery. The metropolitan, named Blattōn (Vlaton), manages to emancipate captives in Africa because he persuades the Arab governor of Africa that the woman the governor married, herself a captive abducted by the Arabs, is in fact Blattōn's sister.[161] In any case, individual redemptions and public exchanges did not always succeed in rescuing the abducted persons, who, as Ibn Butlān attests, were sold at Arab markets.[162]

Another result of the frequent abductions was a new type of sainthood. Theoctiste of Lesbos, for example, whose Life dates from the early tenth century, is captured by the Arabs of Crete but manages to escape during a stop in Paros.[163] Her sainthood is essentially attributable to her abduction, as is that of Joseph the Hymnographer, whose Life (late ninth century) describes his captivity and imprisonment in Crete, where he becomes the spiritual leader of the Christian captives.[164] In these cases, sainthood is linked either to escape or to capture by the Arabs. The two themes, in fact—suffering as destiny and the misfortunes caused by the Muslim infidels—merge. The story of Joseph the Hymnographer is a characteristic example, but the phenomenon reaches its apogee with the story of Elias the Younger, whose vocation manifests itself through his abductions by the infidels, his loss of freedom, and his sale as a slave, which lead him to serve as a missionary in the Muslim countries.[165] Sainthood adapted itself to the extremely difficult situation of that Byzantine population and developed a new model. It proved to be advantageous to set oneself up as a unique victim.

The Byzantine Jews were a special case: they could be redeemed by their coreligionists living in Arab territories, as attested by the documents of the Cairo Genizah. The community of Alexandria occupied a strategic position propitious for the purchase of Byzantine Jews abducted by the Arab pirates and sold in the ports of Damietta and Alexandria. But that community did not always have the financial means necessary, and they corresponded with the rich community of Al-Fustāt to obtain ransom money. A letter dated 1028 attests to the abduction of ten Jews from Attaleia (*Anatalia* in the text).[166] Another relates the case of an abducted Byzantine Jewish woman.[167] Still another speaks of Byzantine Jewish captives, including a woman, a child of ten, and a doctor and his wife, clearly attesting that the Jews abducted in Byzantium were not necessarily merchants.[168] This same letter states that the rich Ephraïm bn. Shemarya of Al-Fustāt did everything in his power to see that Jews not remain slaves of the Muslims. A document published by Jacob Mann attests to the abduction of five young Jews of *Assarbilo* (which David Jacoby has identified as Strobilos) who were taken to Alexandria.[169] Furthermore, a letter from the community of Alexandria dated 1026 and addressed to the Palestinian Jewish community of Al-Fustāt concerns the redemption of the Byzantine Jews.[170] The most lively description is found in a letter to Yehuda bn. Sa'adya, probably composed by the captives themselves.[171] Attacked at sea by Arab pirates, they were taken to Egypt and purchased by Muslims (*Ishma'elim*—"Ismaelites") and Christians (*'arelim*—"the uncircumcised"). But the leader of the local Jewish community intervened with the authorities, who ordered the purchasers to return their new slaves to the pirates within five days. And since the community did not have the means to redeem or to provide for them, they turned to Yehuda bn. Sa'adya le Naguid, the leader of the Jewish community of Al-Fustāt. As for the Arab pirates (*shodedim*—"plunderers"), who were anxious to dispose of their captives so that they could conduct another raid in Byzantium *(Iavan),* they planned to sell the captives to Muslims and Christians or to kill them if they were not redeemed by the deadline.

Another letter, written by two brothers in Jerusalem in 1053 and sent to their sister in Toledo, tells the story of two Spanish Jews abducted by the Byzantines on their way to Palestine. They were sold in Ramla and probably redeemed by the local community.[172] That practice was also followed in Spain. Hence three letters from Yehuda Halevi (1075–1141) speak of his attempt to pay the ransom price of a Jewish woman who had been abducted and sold in Toledo.[173]

Like Byzantine hagiography, the Hebrew literature of that time also depicted the captive. The story that comes to mind is that of the four Jewish captives in the seventh part of *Sefer Ha-Qabbalah* (The book of tradition) by Abraham Ibn Daud (mid-twelfth century). The four great scholars *(hahamim gedolim),* who leave by boat from Bari, are abducted by Arab forces. They are then sold to different countries (Egypt, Ifriqiya, and Spain). Three of them become the founders of major rabbinical schools: in Al-Fustāt, Qairawan, and Cordova.[174]

Despite the change in the status of Byzantine captives introduced by the *Ekloga* in the mid-eighth century, the Roman and Byzantine legal systems did not foresee the situation of the ninth and tenth centuries, where so many civilians found themselves slaves in enemy territory. One of the social consequences of that political reality can be found in the legislation of Leo VI in the late ninth and early tenth centuries, which included 113 *Novellae*, a number comparable only to that of the *Novellae* of Justinian.

Leo VI's legislation was very concerned with the problems of the time. For example, *Novella* 40 resolves the difficulty of the property belonging to a Byzantine in captivity.[175] Previously, such a captive had been prohibited from preparing a will.[176] Leo VI modified that law to allow captives to draw up a will valid in the empire provided that they not bequeath to the enemy. That case suggests that relations existed between captives and their families. In the same way, that legislation affirmed (in *Novella* 36) the son's right to inherit if his father died a captive. But though the captive now had the right to prepare a will, the question remains: what notaries could he have used to do so?[177]

The delimitation between slave and nonslave in the Roman Empire was defined and imposed by the Roman authorities on the basis of its legal categories. These categories aspired to be universal, but that universality turned out to favor the Roman conqueror. Hence the delimitation between slave and free was also in the empire's hands. That was no longer the case in the Byzantine world after the seventh century. From that time on, this delimitation did not depend solely on the Byzantines, because it was no longer their empire alone that set the rules of the game on the geopolitical scene.

Thus far, I have examined the delimitation between slave and nonslave from the point of view of the reduction to slavery. As for the reverse procedure, emancipation, prisoner-of-war exchanges became the means to restore freedom to persons who had become slaves at the hands of the enemy. Although at first glance redemption resembles the exchange of prisoners, it deserves special attention. In such cases, a ransom price had to be agreed upon, even though, from the eighth century on, the person was free de jure. Moreover, ransoming was an altogether private economic transaction. The public authorities, despite the exchanges of captives they conducted, proved to be unable to secure de facto the freedom of their subjects, and it was up to the subjects to take care of such matters. Nevertheless, using their judicial authority, the public powers modified the delimitation between slave and nonslave within the empire: when such captives entered Byzantine territories, they were de facto free.

That development in the definitions and delimitations of legal status went hand in hand with an evolution in Byzantine law: it became a Christian law. I mentioned the similarity between Byzantine law and Islamic law with respect to these definitions. But unlike Islamic law, which was a religious law from the start, Byzantine law had its roots in a nonreligious system and outlook and conserved its nonreligious structures and rationales. The evolution of Byzantine law concerning the delimitation between slave and free person, though it began in late antiquity, can also be understood within the context of the influences and adaptations of the emergent medieval world in which Byzantium found itself in the seventh century. For the first time, its primordial adversary came to be its religious foe as well.

Another innovation appears in Byzantine treaties of the tenth century, which include a paragraph dealing with slaves who flee to the adversary. The problem of fugitive slaves had always existed. For example, many slaves had taken advantage of Alaric's siege of Rome by fleeing; Olympiodorus points out that these slaves were "especially of Barbarian origin."[178] In the fourth century, Procopius spoke of fugitive Ethiopian slaves who deserted the Ethiopian army. They created an independent force and staged a coup d'état in the Himyarite kingdom (Yemen), having chosen as their leader a certain Abramos, the slave of a Roman. They constituted a political threat that the Ethiopian king could not rid himself of.[179] The first military expedition he sent to oppose Abramos defected and joined forces with the slave leader. The second returned without success. The episode ended with Abramos agreeing to a tribute to the Ethiopian king.

A special provision in certain peace treaties resolved the question of refugees by decreeing that they had the right to return to their native countries. It is clear that, in a politically and economically unsettled situation, residents would try to find a better life where they could.[180] For the state, that meant not only a loss of residents, especially in the border regions, but also a loss of the money these residents paid in taxes.

In the fifth and sixth centuries, some Byzantines sought to settle outside the ravaged region and thus escape their fiscal obligations. Later, however—when the neighboring state was Muslim—refuge was no longer such a simple solution. The Byzantines became *dhimmīs* in Muslim territory, and as such had to pay special taxes. Conversion to Islam, moreover, often proved to be too radical a change, though it could be useful to abducted Byzantines, to refugees no longer able to maintain their social position, or to conquered Byzantines. Hence Nikon Metanoeite traveled to Crete to bring Christians who had converted to Islam during the Arab occupation back to Christianity.[181] In other words, in the new medieval world, where the political adversary of Byzantium was also its religious adversary, the phenomenon of refugees was not widespread. On the contrary, the state now had a new role, that of protecting the religion of its residents. (During the iconoclastic era, however, that role was undermined: the Byzantine authorities persecuted those who venerated icons, and territories under Arab control were no longer considered an adequate refuge.)[182] Hence refugees are no longer mentioned in the Byzantine-Arab treaties but are still mentioned in those between Byzantium and the Bulgars so long as the Bulgars remained pagans—in the treaty of 813, for example.[183] I have emphasized this theme to show that refugees of free status had ceased to be an international issue. That was not true in the case of slaves.

The two Russo-Byzantine treaties of 911 and 944, reported in the *Laurentian Chronicle* (the so-called *Chronicle of Nestor*), contain an article that committed at least one party to return fugitive slaves to the other.[184] In the treaty of 911, it was the Byzantines who agreed to return fugitive slaves to Russian traders, whereas in the treaty of 944 that obligation applied to both sides. The Arab-Byzantine treaty of Aleppo in 969, described by Ibn al-'Adim, committed only the Arabs to return fugitive slaves, whether Christian or Muslim, to the Byzantines.[185] The importance that tenth-century treaties granted refugee slaves indicates that there must have been a significant number of them at the time. Theophanes, for example, relates the case of an Arab slave who stole money and then fled to the Byzantines.[186] There is also evidence of that phenomenon in the *Life of Luke the Younger*, dating from the tenth century: the imperial authority has the saint arrested by soldiers who are looking for fugitive slaves.[187] In a *Novella* dating from between 949 and 959, Constantine VII Porphyrogenitus again banned granting refuge to fugitive slaves within the empire and established the rate of compensation for anyone who returned a slave to his master.[188] That measure encouraged slaves to seek refuge in an enemy state where they could enjoy a different life and a new status. The twelfth article of the Arab-Byzantine treaty of 969 addresses that problem precisely: "If a Muslim or Christian slave, man or woman, flees to a country other than the territories designated, so long as the slave remains in those territories, the Muslims must not hide the slave but must denounce him or her. The slave's owner will pay a price of thirty Greek dinars for a man, twenty dinars for a woman, and fifteen for a young boy or young girl; if the owner does not have the means to purchase the slave, the emir will charge the owner a duty of three dinars and will remit the slave to the owner." The thirteenth article specifies that "if the fugitive slave is baptized, the Muslims will not have the right to keep the slave: the emir will charge the slave's owner a duty and will return the slave to the owner."[189]

The Russo-Byzantine treaty of 911 contains an important diplomatic innovation. There is a paragraph stipulating that a person who finds a captive from the other camp reduced to slavery in a third country must ransom him or her.[190] The redeemed captive would then be transferred to his or her native country and would repay the person. Through that clause, the two sides decided to form a common defensive front against the abduction of their subjects. This was not a religious front, however, because at the time the Russians were not officially Christianized, as this treaty attests.[191]

That clause proves that the redemption of persons abducted from their country and enslaved had already become the rule. Recall the case related in the *Life of Nahum:* Byzantine diplomats in Venice found disciples of Methodius who had been abducted in Moravia and sold as slaves. Having redeemed them, the diplomats took the disciples with them to Constantinople.[192]

I believe that this diplomatic innovation developed as a continuation of the Byzantine legislative evolution in the status of Byzantines captured by the enemy. For them to be recognized as free by another state, they first had to be considered so in their own state. Hence this article contains the same rule as the law that originally changed the status of Byzantine captives— *Ekloga* 8.2. It concerns the case in which the redeemed captive does not have the means to reimburse his purchaser. The treaty of 911, like the *Ekloga*, decreed that he had to pay his price to the person who had acquired him by working for him until he accumulated the sum paid.

The appearance of these new subjects in tenth-century peace treaties attests to the importance of mobility—from the status of slave to that of free person and vice versa. The articles also show that this was an international problem or even that the specific international context of Byzantium made that mobility possible, unlike what had occurred in the geopolitical space of the Roman Empire. It is also clear that the problem preoccupied the Byzantines, since it was they who were risking their freedom; in other words, they too were becoming victims of the political situation.

The response of Byzantium was not simply to change its internal definitions of the slave and the free person through legislation. It went further, attempting to establish through peace treaties a new international law that would allow slaves and free Byzantines to be recognized as such outside the empire. The custom of exchanging captives was the first stage in this course of action.[193] Byzantium was thus obliged to recognize the same statuses among its adversaries. It is also clear that, in the fifth and sixth centuries, the difference in religion was the source of the custom of redeeming captured Christian Byzantines, and that in the tenth century that practice became widespread.

That change on the political scene raised a problem for Byzantium: how to procure slaves? I mentioned the *Novella* of John I Tzimisces (dating from between 972 and 975) that points to the continuous wars and raids in the Balkans as a permanent source of slaves.[194] This supply source was combined with the no less important one provided by trade.

The Slave Trade: The New Commercial Map of the Medieval World

The Commercial and Political Context for the Traffic in Slaves

Since trade was an important means for procuring slaves, the place of the slave market must be situated within the general context of trade in the Mediterranean basin. My starting point is the sixth century, when the Roman Empire succeeded in extending its borders to the maximum degree. By the eighth century, this was no longer the same empire. The major changes in the geopolitical map had consequences both for slavery and for trade in Byzantium and the surrounding world.

In the fifth to seventh centuries, the empire possessed vast resources for providing all sorts of commodities. Importation was one means, especially in the case of luxury goods. That was also true for slaves. Take as an example the importation occurring via the Red Sea, as described by Cosmas Indicopleutes, who mentions slaves imported to Egypt from Ethiopia.[195] They are attested as well by sixth-century Egyptian papyri.[196] Although castration was prohibited in the empire, it was practiced illegally, and eunuchs were luxury slaves with a higher value from the start.[197] They were imported from Eastern regions such as Mesopotamia, Caucasus, and even India, which was a source of other precious commodities.[198]

This commercial outlook changed in the seventh century for both international and domestic trade. In the early seventh century, Heraclius, exarch of Carthage, made a wager with his vice general Gregoras: which was the quickest way to go from Carthage to Constantinople, by land (attempted by Niketas, son of Gregoras) or by sea (attempted by Heraclius the Younger)?[199] By the end of the century, such a venture was no longer possible. The new geopolitical map also imposed a new economic and commercial map.[200]

On this new medieval map, the Jews occupied an important position in international trade, especially the slave trade. Ibn Khordādhbih's description of the "al-Rādhāniyya" (*Kitāb al-Masālik wa'l-mamālik,* or Book of routes and kingdoms) is central to the entire debate by historians regarding the slave trade in the Middle Ages.[201] The *Radhaniyya,* Jewish merchants of slaves and other goods, have been much written about in modern scholarship. They were not the only Jewish merchants specializing in the slave trade,[202] but Ibn Khordādhbih's description has the most geographical details and is also the oldest (the first version of his book was completed in about 846).[203]

In modern scholarship, Évelyne Patlagean's "Byzance et les marchés du grand commerce vers 830–vers 1030. Entre Pirenne et Polanyi" (Byzantium and the large trade markets from ca. 830 to ca. 1030: From Pirenne to Polanyi) places Byzantium at the center for the first time, granting it the role of a commercial power active in the global trade of its time (ninth to eleventh century). I shall extend that chronological framework back to the seventh century, when the Mediterranean map underwent its great geopolitical shift.

Despite the number of works devoted to the *Radhaniyya* and to Jewish merchants generally, until now there has been no map of the global slave traffic for that time.[204] That explains why Byzantium has been excluded from the historical debate centering on the questions raised by medieval commerce. In other words, had a map existed, the occultation of Byzantium, an integral part of it, would not have been possible. In the belief that such a map may prove enlightening as to the particular position of Byzantium, I have constructed one, based on the most notable geographical accounts and the corresponding studies. But where to begin with such a geographical map?

The episode of the conquest of Constantinople by Heraclius is an invitation to examine the position of Byzantium in relation to the Mediterranean. There has been a tendency to consider that basin the navel of the world. Since the time Rome made the Mediterranean its own *mare domesticum,* that image has been perpetuated, even in modern scholarship. Whether in Henri Pirenne's thesis or in Fernand Braudel's conception, the Mediterranean has always remained at the center of any economic and commercial discussion.[205] According to this view, the Mediterranean world is a unit apart. But though that was true for the Roman Empire and for the Italian cities in the late Middle Ages and Renaissance, it was less true between these two eras. As for Byzantium, it has been placed outside the debate because Constantinople is considered to be geographically on the margins.

I cannot speak of the place of the Mediterranean on the commercial medieval map without referring to Michael McCormick's writings.[206] His *Origins of the European Economy: Communications and Commerce, A.D. 300–900* (2001) not only demonstrates a new commercial dynamic in the eighth to eleventh centuries but also situates it within the new geopolitical-economic medieval context. The Mediterranean functions as the commercial intermediary between the European side and the Arab side, as the arena in which and around which the movement of people and commodities occurred. The slave trade had a central role in that dynamic, which always depended on the wealth of the Arab world. As for Byzantium, though it participated in that economic activity and played its part in this new world of medieval communication, it does not appear to have had a very determining role there.

Yet Byzantium lived its political, economic, and commercial life between three seas. I shall therefore return the city of Constantinople to its place at the center of the international map; after all, Constantinople was founded to occupy that place. Along the edges of the map, the surrounding countries played an important role in the world market: to the west, the Spain of the Umayyads, a major consumer of imported slaves; to the north, the Baltic Sea, where Arab and Byzantine coins attest to the commercial link between eastern Europe and the Arab world and Byzantium; to the south, the Red Sea, which opened the maritime route to India and China; and to the east, the Caspian Sea and Khorāsān, important regions for international trade because of the Khazars and the Samanids. It immediately becomes clear that Byzantium's centrality is much more than a geographical position.

Nevertheless, a geographical map, however detailed it may be, is not sufficient for following the chronology. It also cannot situate the sources, which provide key information on trade in the space concerned but do not speak of commercial routes. That is why I have provided a table with significant information concerning the commercial map of Byzantium (table 1). This information is organized both chronologically and geographically. The regions are defined from west to east: western Europe, Spain, and the western Mediterranean, Italy-Sicily-the Adriatic Sea and the central Mediterranean (as far as Ifriqiya and Tripolitania), the eastern Mediterranean (as far as Syria, Palestine, and Egypt), Byzantium (its regions in Asia Minor and the Balkans), the Balkans (outside the Byzantine Empire), Caucasus-Russia-the Black Sea,[207] and Iran-Iraq.

Let me first mention a few general elements that played a role in shaping international trade in the Byzantine world. The Balkan region, and especially its Slavic and Bulgar populations, constituted the most important source of slaves for Byzantium. In the Balkans, war turned out to be an effective means for procuring slaves. The same was true of international trade: the Slavs and the Bulgars were the principal source of slaves throughout the regions mentioned. Africa was also an important source of slaves, even in late antiquity.[208] Nevertheless, African slaves were not imported to the Arab world in numbers sufficient to satisfy demand. The Arabs in fact made a

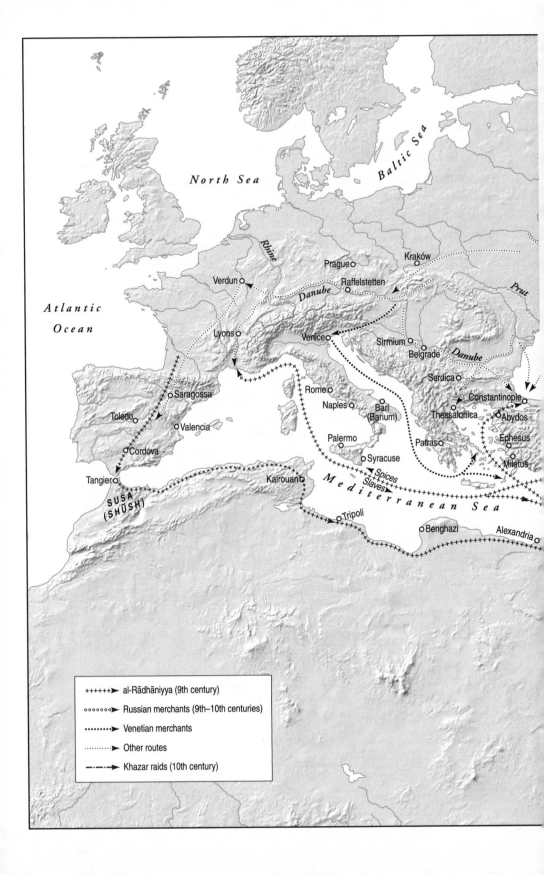

North Sea

Baltic Sea

Atlantic
Ocean

Rhine

Prague○

Kraków○

Verdun ○

Raffelstetten

Danube

Prut

Lyons ○

Venice○

Sirmium○

Danube

Belgrade○

Serdica○

Rome ○

Constantinople○

Naples ○

Bari
(Barium)

Thessalonica

Abydos○

Saragossa

Toledo○

Valencia○

Patras○

Ephesus○

Cordova○

Palermo○

Miletus○

Syracuse○

Tangier○

Kairouan○

Spices
Slaves

Mediterranean Sea

SUSA
(SHŪSH)

Tripoli○

Benghazi○

Alexandria○

+++++► al-Rādhāniyya (9th century)

○○○○○○► Russian merchants (9th–10th centuries)

●●●●●► Venetian merchants

........► Other routes

–·–·–► Khazar raids (10th century)

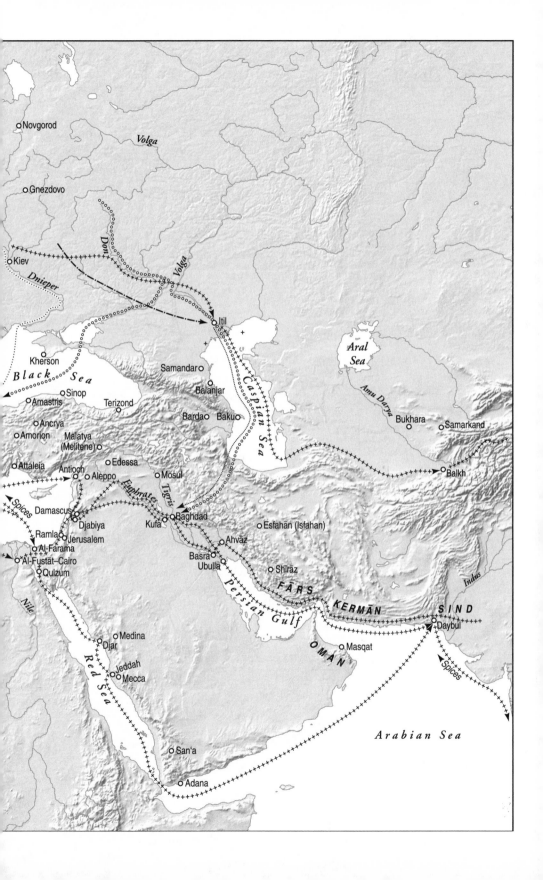

Novgorod

Volga

Gnezdovo

Don

Kiev

Dnieper

Itil

Kherson

Black   Sea

Aral Sea

Samandar

Sinop

Balanjar

Caspian Sea

Amastris

Terizond

Amu Darya

Ancrya

Bardao Bakuo

Amorion

Malatya
(Melitene)

Bukhara

Samarkand

Attaleia

Edessa

Antioch

Aleppo

Mosul

Euphrates

Tigris

Balkh

Spices

Damascus

Baghdad

Kufa

Esfahãn (Isfahan)

Djabiya

Ramla

Ahvaz

Jerusalem

Al-Farama

Basra

Shĩraz

Al-Fustãt–Cairo

Ubulla

FÃRS

Qulzum

Nile

Persian Gulf

KERMÃN

SIND

Indus

Daybul

Medina

Spices

Djar

OMAN

Masqat

Red Sea

Jeddah

Mecca

Spices

San'a

Arabian Sea

Adana

Table 1   Trade in the Eighth to Eleventh Centuries

Western Europe	Central Europe	Central Mediterranean: Italy-Adriatic Sea	Eastern Mediterranean: Syria-Palestine-Egypt
			688: presence of Arabs in Cyprus
		776: letter from Pope Adrian I to Charlemagne	
822–852: al-Ghzāl on the Spain-Baltic routes		812/814: the Franks leave the Adriatic Sea	824: Arab conquest of Crete
825: privileges granted by Louis the Pious to a Jewish merchant of Sargossa		814–820: Byzantine-Venetian edict against trade with the Arabs	
			833–844: Arab raids in Sicily and Peloponnesus; Byzantine raids in Syria
846: Agobard of Lyons writes against the Jewish slave traders		830–860: Arab raids in southern Italy	
		831: Arab conquest of Palermo	
		872/875: the Arabs in Dalmatia, a Byzantine-Venetian operation	
		876: Venetian edict against the slave trade	
		878: Arab conquest of Syracuse	

Byzantium	Balkans	Caucasus-Black Sea-Russia	Iraq-Iran
685–695: Justinian II (first reign): sales of Slavic slaves in Asia Minor (seals of the *kommerkiarioi)* Rhodian Sea Law (7th–8th centuries) 728: last known sigillographical mention of *apothēkai*	712: first *kommerkiarioi*, attested in Thessalonica	729: Itil the Khazar capital (first evidence) 740: documents attesting Jews among the Khazars	762: Abbassids settle in Baghdad
801: Irene lowers taxes 809: tax on slaves entering by the Dodecanese (Nicephorus I) 831–833: new *kommerkiarioi*	*Abydikoi* (officials in charge of import taxes) of Thessalonica attested 860: the Serbs pay their tribute to the Bulgars in slaves 864: Christianization of Boris of Bulgaria	841: the thema of Kherson mid-ninth century: —*Life of George* of *Amastris* (tax in Trebizond). —Russian merchants in Constantinople 860/1: Christian mission in Russia; a Jewish Khazar dynasty 867–886: coins of Basil I in Russia	846: first version of *Kitāb al-Masālik wa'l-mamālik*, by Ibn Khordādhbih 874: Samanids settle in Bukhara
Leo VI (886–912)	893: transfer of Bulgar commerce from Constantinople to Thessalonica; Vladimir the Bulgar returns to paganism	895: coins of Leo VI and Samanid coins in Kiev	

continued

Table 1   *(continued)*

Western Europe	Central Europe	Central Mediterranean: Italy-Adriatic Sea	Eastern Mediterranean: Syria-Palestine-Egypt
The *Responsa* of the geonim: Jewish merchants between France and Spain (tenth century)	903/906: Raffelstetten (Linz) Customs Regulations 906: Moravian and Russian slave trade in Byzantium	945: Venetian edict against the slave trade 960: prohibition on Venetian ships transporting Jewish slave merchants	904: sack of Thessalonica Muhammad Ibn 'Umar, *Faqīh* 911/912: Byzantine-Russian expedition in Crete
968: Liutprand of Cremona writes of castration in Verdun of slaves destined for Spain	960: Abraham Iakobi, Jewish slave merchant in Prague 961: Hungarian Jewish merchants in Russia	968: Liutprand of Cremona: Byzantine customs in Corfu	964/5: conquest of Crete and Cyprus (Nicephorus II) 969/970: treaty of Aleppo
		971: edict against Venetian weapons trade with the Arabs	
		992: Byzantine privileges in Venice at the customs of Abydos	
		1082: Chrysobull of Alexius Comnenus to the Venetians 1090: taxes on the Jewish merchants of Salerno	

Byzantium	Balkans	Caucasus-Black Sea-Russia	Iraq-Iran
911–912: *Book of the Prefect*	906: Moravian and Russian slave trade in Byzantium	907/911: Byzantine-Russian commercial treaties	922: Ibn Fadlān, envoy to the Bulgars of Volga: route from Baghdad to the Caspian Sea
Constantine VII (913–959) *(De administrando imperio)*		912: Russians participate in the Byzantine attack on Crete River slave traffic by the Russians	
			988: *Kitāb Sūrat al-ard,* by Ibn Hawqal
		944: Byzantine-Russian commercial and military treaty	999: the destruction of the kingdom of the Samanids
Nicephorus II Phocas (963–969)	961: Hungarian Jewish merchants in Russia	957: Olga's journey to Constantinople	
John I Tzimisces (969–976)		968: Byzantine-Russian victory over the Bulgars 969: the Russians destroy Itil 971: Byzantine victory over the Russians and Bulgars 988: Christianization of Vladimir 989: Kherson under Russian control	
			Ibn Butlān (mid-eleventh century: description of the slave markets in Cairo (Greek and Armenian slaves)

distinction between black and white slaves and granted a greater value to whites. In the Arabic language of Spain, black slaves continued to be called *'abīd* (slaves), whereas white slaves were designated by the term *saqaliba*.[209] This word, which attests to the Slavic origin of these slaves, corresponds to the word *sklavos*, which from the twelfth century on was the Greek synonym for the word "slave."[210] In Ibn Khordādhbih's description (from ninth-century Iraq), *saqaliba* designates simply "the Slavs," whereas for Ibn Fadlān this word refers to the Bulgars. The Slavs and Bulgars therefore appear as the principal source of slaves on the commercial map.

As for the importation of African slaves, it merely responded to the demand of the Arab market. Hence the slave trade seems to have moved north to south and, in the Arab world, also from south (Africa) to north (Arab territories). The Arab world therefore extended the Roman Empire to the east, importing African slaves. The Slavs and Balkans in the Ural Mountains did not mint coins before the tenth century: that explains the demand in these regions for Arab and Byzantine coins, which have been found as far north as the shore of the Baltic Sea and as far east as Oka Lake on the Volga. These finds provide a more complete portrait of commercial exchanges.[211]

The Radhaniyya

Modern specialists in the *Radhaniyya* have searched for their origin and have tried to discover whether Ibn Khordādhbih's description of them is authentic.[212] Historians who have examined them within the more general context of Jewish trade at the time have studied the specificity of these traders. The scholarship has illustrated that Jewish communities were found everywhere and were thus able to serve as a network for these merchants. In fact, their special merchandise, slaves, was not their only one. Eliyahou Ashtor speaks of precious fabrics and pearls—luxury goods.[213] Ibn Khordādhbih also mentions sabers. This is important because, as in the case of slaves, these goods traveled between the Muslim and Christian worlds.

Before studying the Jews' routes more closely, let me point out that the Jews were restricted in the slaves they could purchase. Unable to buy Christian slaves in the Byzantine Empire or Muslim slaves in the Arab world, they legally procured only imported slaves. Recall on this matter the conversion to Judaism of slaves purchased by the Jews, as attested by the documents of the Genizah. In fact, Jews were prohibited from converting slaves to Judaism in Byzantium and in Islamic regions. Legally, therefore, the Jews could "immerse to have as Jewish slaves" only foreign slaves before they arrived at their destination. In other words, slave merchants had to convert them before selling them.²¹⁴ It is therefore clear that demand from a Jewish market also played a role in the development of the specialization in slave trafficking.

To quote from Ibn Khordādhbih's description of the *Radhaniyya:*

Itinerary/itineraries of the Jewish merchants (known as) Rādhāniyya, who speak Arabic, Persian, Rūmī (= Greek), Frankish (= French), Andalusian (= Romance), and Slavonic, and travel from the East to the West and vice-versa, by land and by sea. From the West they import eunuchs *(khadam)*, young slaves of both sexes *(djawārī* and *ghilmān)*, silk brocade *(dībadj)*, beaver pelts *(djulud al-khazz)*, [pelts of] the sable *(sammūr)* and [other] furs, as well as swords.

[First itinerary] They embark in the land of the Franks *(Firandja)* on the Western Sea (= the Mediterranean) and disembark at al-Faramā (= ancient Pelusium), then they transport their merchandise by land *('ala 'l-zahr)* as far as al-Kulzum (ancient Clysma), a distance of 25 parasangs; they then traverse the Eastern Sea (= the Red Sea) from al-Kulzum to al-Djār (the port of Medina) and to Djudda. From here, they continue their journey to Sind, to India, and to China. From China, they bring back musk *(misk)*, wood of aloes *('ūd)*, camphor *(kāfūr)*, cinnamon *(dār sīnī)* and other [products] which are imported from these countries. Thus they return to al-Kulzum, then transport their [consignment] to al-Faramā and embark on the Mediterranean. Sometimes, they made a detour through Constantinople *(Al Kustantīnyya)* with their merchandise, which they sold to the Byzantines. Sometimes furthermore, they went to sell them [in the land of the] king of Firandja.

[Second itinerary] When they chose to do so, on leaving Firandja, they transported their merchandise by sea, on the Mediterranean, disembarking at Antioch *(Antākiya)*, whence they made their way, in three overland stages to al-Djābiya; they then sailed on the Euphrates *(al-Furāt)* to Baghdād, then on the Tigris *(Didjla)* to al-Ubulla, and from here they gained access to Oman *('Umān)*, Sind, India and China, all these countries being contiguous with one another.

[Third itinerary] Their overland route: those among them who set out from al-Andalus or from Firandja, cross over [the strait] to Lower Sūs *(al-Sūs al Aksā)* and arrived in Tangier, whence they make their way to Ifrīkiya (approximately equivalent to present-day Tunisia, but more specifically

Kayrawān), To Misr (Egypt, but more specifically al-Fustāt), they subsequently pass through al-Ramla (in Palestine), Damascus *(Dimashk)*, Kūfa, Baghdād, Basra (these last three in 'Irāk), al-Ahwāz (in Khūzistān), Fārs and Kirmān, arriving in Sind, India and China.

[Fourth itinerary] Sometimes they take a route to the rear of Rome *(Rūmiya)*, through the land of the Slavs *(al-Sakāliba)*, reaching Khamlīdj (or Khamlīkh), capital of the Khazars, then [they sail] on the sea of Djurdjān (= the Caspian), [arriving] at Balkh (in northern Afghanistan) and in Transoxiana *(Mā warā' al-Nahr)* before attaining the camp *(wurt)* of the Toghuzghuz and moving into China.[215]

There were therefore sea, river, but also land routes (see map). Several questions have been raised about these *Radhaniyya:* their origin, their name, their routes, their merchandise, their raison d'être, and even whether they really existed. I will not investigate whether these routes corresponded to the reality. But I shall take on the task of comparing these routes to other information. Ibn Khordādhbih's description is situated within an Arab geographical perspective, especially since he was writing in Iraq. Nevertheless, it reveals international commercial traffic, with the slaves originating in central and eastern Europe (the Balkans), whereas the markets were located in the southeast. Yet these traders did not travel directly from the northwest to the southeast but made long and arduous detours in conveying the slaves.[216]

The Position of the Byzantine Empire

The routes retraced by Ibn Khordādhbih indicate that Constantinople was among the destinations of the *Radhaniyya* traders, but only as a spice market. The other routes, by contrast, including those for slaves, did not pass through the Byzantine Empire, even though a slave market existed in Constantinople.[217] To the east (Balkans-Caucasus-Caspian Sea) and to the west (a maritime route from the Mediterranean coast of present-day France to Antioch, which in the ninth century was under Arab domination), they circumvented Byzantium. Yet a single glance at the map shows that Byzantium was exactly between the sources of slaves and the slave markets. Why did these routes not pass through that empire?

Unlike the other ninth-century states, the Byzantine Empire had enjoyed political continuity since the Roman era. And that included a central economic authority located in Constantinople from the fourth century on. The Byzantine market radically changed in the seventh century, after the loss of the wealthiest provinces. Any consideration of the question of Byzantine routes must take into account the new geopolitical reality to which Byzantium had to adapt. That adaptation took place between the late seventh and the mid-ninth centuries, an era prior to Ibn Khordādhbih's description.

The Byzantine authority's control over the circulation of goods in the seventh to eighth centuries was manifested above all in the *kommerkiarioi,* the officials responsible for the collection of taxes on goods, as attested by their seals, which date back to the reign of Justinian II. That control was also exerted through the imposition of taxes *(kommerkion)* and special bonds or fees *(apothēkai)* on the circulation of goods. This subject has been studied by Hélène Antoniadis-Bibicou, Michael F. Hendy, and Nicolas Oikonomides.[218] They all agree that through their system of bonds and customs duties, the Byzantine authorities controlled not only the circulation of goods within the empire, since the *kommerkion* was actually a tax on circulation and not on sale, but also, by virtue of the location of the Byzantine ports, international circulation between the Black Sea, the Aegean Sea, and the Adriatic Sea.

There was another aspect to that control: legal regulation of the private transfer of goods. That regulation of commercial maritime transport has come down to us in the *Rhodian Sea Law,* a collection of rules dating from the seventh to eighth century.[219] This source clearly attests to the circulation of slaves by sea. It regulates, among other things, the captain's responsibility for the value of the slaves entrusted to him to be transported from one trader to another. That responsibility applies even if the slaves escape, a risk that distinguishes slaves from any other merchandise.[220]

The seals discovered in seven provinces of Asia Minor, dating from between 694 and 695, attest to a major sale of Slavic slaves *(andrapoda; sklabōn* in the Bithynian seals) conducted by the *kommerkiarios* George, *apo khupaton* under the reign of Justinian II.[221] Oikonomides interprets this evidence within the political context: the slave sale was a punishment inflicted on the families of Slavic soldiers established in Asia Minor who deserted to join the Arab camp.[222] According to him, the seals attest that the *kommerkiarioi,* being close to power, also enjoyed privileges, such as a monopoly on that type of sale. Hendy's interpretation is entirely different: according to him, these seals attest to the role played by the *kommerkiarioi* in supplying soldiers, who were Slavic war captives established in Asia Minor.[223] In any case, these seals are not the only evidence of the empire's control over the slave trade. I would like to insist here on the importance of the role of Byzantine customs duties.

In 801 Empress Irene lowered taxes on imported goods to appease public opinion, which was unfavorable following her coup d'état of 797 against her son Constantine VI, whom she arranged to have blinded.[224] The tax cut led to lower prices in Constantinople.[225] Nicephorus I restored the taxes, adding a special tax on the circulation of slaves in 809.[226] In accordance with that special tax, slaves who did not pass through customs at Abydos would be taxed at the rate of two *nomismata* apiece (10 percent of the average price of a slave). Theophanes explains that this measure particularly targeted slaves who passed through the Dodecanese. Either these slaves, intended for the markets of Constantinople, arrived through the Dodecanese so that the traders could avoid paying the tax (that hypothesis does not explain why slaves are the only goods mentioned, however), or these slaves were not intended for these markets. I interpret this to mean that the *Radhaniyya* took the detour to avoid Byzantine customs. The same author, Ibn Khordādhbih, writes that the Russian merchants heading from the Black Sea to the Mediterranean were obliged to pay a tithe to the Byzantine authorities.[227] The tithe on the contents of a slave ship was no negligible sum, and the *Radhaniyya* therefore preferred to stop at Antioch, the port that in the ninth century was closest to the southern border of Byzantium, rather than pass through Constantinople, the largest seaport in that part of the world, which was also a major consumer of slaves.[228]

Another mention of the influence of Byzantine taxes on the Arab market is found in a text written in about 840 by Abū 'Ubaid al-Qāsim ibn Sallām, quoted by Hamilton Gibb. This text reports fiscal regulations, supposedly those of Caliph 'Umar I (634–644), in accordance with which Muslim traders paid 2.5 percent on their merchandise, whereas the *dhimmī* traders paid 5 percent, and foreigners (identified a few lines later as *rūm*) paid 10 percent "because they were taking the same percentage from the Muslim merchants when these entered their territory."[229] But these regulations probably reflect a reality subsequent to 'Umar I's time. In fact, a treaty of 'Umar II (717–720), also translated with commentary by Gibb, specifically bans taxes on trade.[230]

The customs system in seventh- and eighth-century Byzantium allowed the empire not only to control the commercial routes, a control that changed form in the tenth century, but also to preserve something of a monopoly on the slave trade. Patlagean shows how that centralization changed during the reign of Theophilus, or more precisely, in 831–832, when a new type of seal appeared: "The bearer was called imperial or general *kommerkiarios* of a thema,[231] or more often of a city, and above all of a port. In other words, the concessionaire of the public monopoly on silk imports became a collector of customs duties, who had nothing more to do with silk, since he now had general jurisdiction over foreign trade."[232] Oikonomides examines that change within the context of the *kommerkion* in tenth-century Thessalonica, arguing it was a decentralization strategy; it would culminate in the edict of 992 targeting the Venetians.[233] But what were the consequences of the Byzantine economic strategy on the international slave trade?

At first glance, the map I constructed reveals that the principal source of slaves at the time, eastern Europe, was, from the vantage point of the Arab world, the hinterland of Byzantium. That region of the Balkans, where the political situation was unsettled from late antiquity on, acquired an economically strategic position with respect to slavery in the era under study. There were internal Balkan routes for the Byzantine market.[234] For the international market, Byzantium's customs system functioned as an obstruction intended to preserve its commercial hegemony. This system also had consequences in the other three regions through which the slave merchants might pass: Caucasus, Italy, and western Europe.

The eastern boundary that separated the Arab world from the Slavic territories extended from the Black Sea to the Caspian Sea. Three rivers flowed north to south: the Dnieper, the Don, and the Volga. Trade among the Russians, Bulgars on the Volga, and Arabs, attested in the eighth century, intensified in the ninth to tenth centuries.[235] For these two centuries, the Khazars controlled the access of tradespeople on all sides, thanks to the Khazars' position between the eastern bank of the Black Sea and the western bank of the Caspian Sea. Their capital city of Itil at the mouth of the Volga, with its large fairs, attracted merchants from every region.[236] The merchants who passed through Itil (that is, on the Volga-Caspian Sea route) had to pay a tithe to the Khazar princes.[237] In the ninth century, Byzantine control over the Black Sea took the form of a tax to be paid at the port of Trebizond, as attested in the *Life of George of Amastris* by Ignatius the Deacon.[238] That control intensified when the thema of Kherson was founded in 841,[239] and traffic between the Russians and the Arabs was routed to the east as a result.

In the Khazar region of Caucasus, the penetration of the Jews began in about the mid-seventh century, according to Constantin Zuckerman.[240] It intensified following the establishment of a dynasty of Jewish kings in the royal Khazar court in 861.[241] The founding of that dynasty expressed the Khazars' aspiration to remain independent of the two religious blocs surrounding them.[242]

Farther to the east, the Samanids settled in Bukhara in 874. Their first coins, discovered in Kiev in recent times, date back to the reign of Ismāʿīl bn. Ahmad (892–907), thus indicating relations between the Russians and the Muslims of Khorasan.[243] In the ninth century, Byzantium reacted to that un-favorable situation in the Black Sea with Christian diplomacy, exploiting the fact that the "Russians" of Tauric Chersonese were still pagan. The first Christian mission that the Byzantines sent to them dates from 860–861, when Photios was the patriarch of Constantinople.[244]

Although the ships of Arab merchants did not pass through the waters of the Byzantine Empire near the Balkan coasts and Asia Minor, the ports of Italy were open to them. Byzantine slave traffic is very well attested in Italy, especially for the tenth century. As regards the eighth to ninth centuries, the letter from Pope Adrian I to Charlemagne in 776 had to do with the compe-tition between the Byzantines ("Greeks") and Arabs ("Saracens") for the slaves sold in Italy (the *mancipia;* their origin is not indicated).[245] These Byzantines were maritime merchants. The letter of Adrian I consolidated the hegemony of the Byzantine traders by banning the sale of slaves to the Arab ships. Recall that at that date Rome was part of the Byzantine Empire. It is therefore possible that this letter belongs to the context of Byzantine po-litical policies, especially since no religious motive is advanced in it.[246]

In Italy, the Byzantine authorities tried to maintain control over the north-south commercial routes, even when the Franks made inroads be-tween the late eighth and early ninth centuries.[247] To assert their hegemony, the Byzantines made use of Venice. Hence in 814–820 Leo V and the dux of Venice tried to prohibit Venetian merchants from engaging in trade with the Arabs, and in 876 Dux Urso Participacio I banned the purchase of slaves from pirates and the transport of slave merchants.[248]

Byzantine hegemony, which remained strong in Italy, did not prevent Adrian I from turning to Charlemagne at a time prior to the Franks' incur-sions into Italy. In fact, the aforementioned letter was part of a correspon-dence that aimed to restore a political relationship between the pope and the Frankish king.[249] In any case, the Franks had other maritime routes of access: the Mediterranean ports under their domination; the commercial routes that passed through the Frankish territories of western Europe, especially after the victory of Charles Martel and the Frankish conquest of the northern Iberian peninsula that followed; and, in the ninth century, routes in central Europe as well. It was precisely from these ports that the *Radhaniyya* em-barked.[250]

The *Radhaniyya* were not the only Jewish merchants who specialized in the slave trade. In two articles, Alexandre Gieysztor sets out the routes of Jewish merchants generally in central Europe, Germany, Moravia, Hungary, and Poland.[251] Their presence is attested in the Raffelstetten Customs Regulations of 903–906, a document that specifies the total duties on the merchandise required by customs.[252] Charles Verlinden has attempted to reconstitute the *Radhaniyya*'s tenth-century European routes.[253] All this evidence is for the tenth century and clearly identifies the routes connecting northeastern and southwestern Europe. An important commercial stop on that route was Verdun, which Liutprand of Cremona mentions in 986 as a center for castrating slaves on the way to Spain.[254] During the same period, al-Muqaddasī mentions Slavic slaves *(saqaliba)* who were castrated in Spain, then sent to Egypt.[255] The tenth-century *Responsa* by the geonim speak of Jewish merchants who transported castrated slaves.[256] The routes that passed through what is now France led to the Spain of the Umayyads, which provided large markets for *saqaliba*. But other routes took the slaves to Venice, as is apparent in the *Life of Nahum*, which describes the disciples of Methodius abducted in Moravia and sold as slaves in Venice.[257]

The importance of Jewish merchants in the traffic between present-day France and Spain is attested in the mid-ninth century by the commercial privileges regarding the slave trade that Louis the Pious granted a Jewish merchant of Saragossa and two Jews from Lyons (825) and by the writings of Agobard of Lyons in 846 against the Jewish traffic in Christian slaves in France.[258] According to this information, Lyons and Arles served as stops on the route taking the Jewish slave merchants to Spain, and more precisely to Cordova. These were always land and river routes.[259]

The efforts in the ninth century to prevent Arab slave merchants from reaching the ports of western Europe were reinforced by the promulgation of Byzantine and Venetian decrees. The intention of these decrees was primarily political: to limit the grant of aid of all kinds, which the Arab forces had until that time received in wartime. But the decrees also had consequences for trade because they worked to the great advantage of Jewish merchants. Recall that, according to Ibn Khordādhbih, the *Radhaniyya* also traded in weapons.

As early as 593, Gregory I had protested the sale of Christian slaves to Jewish merchants.[260] In a letter to Libertinus, *praetor* of Sicily, Gregory I specifically stated his opposition to a Jewish slave merchant named Nasas who was purchasing Christians. But his letter did not target non-Christian slaves, which explains why eastern Europe (especially the Slavic regions) was before its Christianization the principal source of slaves in Europe.[261] Christians also needed these Jewish merchants as intermediaries, which allowed them to take advantage of the high demand from the Arab markets in Spain. That commercial front, however, was outside the Byzantine influence. I return, therefore, to the eastern Mediterranean, to consider from the Byzantine point of view the map of international slave trade in the first third of the ninth century.

The starting point for the north-south slave traffic was between the Dnieper River and the Adriatic Sea. Byzantium, which extended from these regions to the Mediterranean, in fact blocked maritime traffic between the Balkans and the Arab world from Spain to Iraq, at least where the slave trade was concerned. Byzantium was the principal consumer market for Slavic slaves outside the Arab world. The Byzantines were therefore in competition with the Arabs for that type of merchandise.

The Arab world, then, imported Slavic slaves through routes that circumvented the Byzantine Empire; to the east through Caucasus and the Caspian Sea; to the west by the routes leading from Raffelstetten to Spain via France.[262] The eastern and western parts of the Arab world (Iraq and Spain) thereby procured white slaves. I have cited the customs system of Byzantium to explain the detours taken by the slave merchants. But they also faced taxes in Raffelstetten and Itil. How, therefore, to justify these long detours? I think this is quite simply a matter of dates. The Byzantine ports were already blocking slave traffic in the early ninth century, whereas taxes in Raffelstetten and Itil are attested for the tenth century.[263] In other words, Khazar kings and Bavarian princes were practicing in the tenth century what Byzantium had already been practicing for at least a hundred years.[264]

Iraq and Spain can be considered two different regions from a commercial standpoint, but a third region under Arab domination must also be taken into account: the eastern and central Mediterranean, that is, Syria, Palestine, Egypt, and Ifriqiya. According to Ibn Khordādhbih's description, the *Radhaniyya* passed through these four regions. But to arrive there, they made a long detour, which necessarily raised the price of slaves. As a result, there was not an adequate commercial supply to meet the demand for slaves in these regions (the price of an ordinary slave in tenth-century Egypt was 33 dinars, versus 20 *nomismata* in Byzantium).

It was at that moment, the ninth to tenth century, that Arab piracy came into play. If it was profitable, that alternative for supplying slaves, risky in nature, must have been responding to a sufficiently large market demand in the region, given that the price I mentioned was that for victims of piracy. In this regard, let me point out that there are few mentions extant of Byzantine women being ransomed. The small number of references tallies with the price of female slaves in Arab countries, which was greater than that for male slaves: and in the case of female singers, the price could go even higher.[265]

In the ninth and tenth centuries, Arab piracy threatened all the coastal zones of the eastern Mediterranean, from Egypt to southern Italy and the Adriatic Sea. But not all the pirates were Arabs. Byzantines participated as well, landing on the coasts of Egypt, Syria, and Palestine. Nevertheless, it seems that Byzantine piracy did not reach the same scope as Arab piracy, which covered the entire Aegean Sea, the Ionian Sea, Sicily, and southern Italy. In addition, throughout the ninth century Arab forces from Ifriqiya endeavored to conquer Sicily and southern Italy: Palermo was conquered in 831, Syracuse in 878, and in 872–875 the Arabs reached Dalmatia. The booty from the attacks by Arab pirates arrived at several destinations, usually Egypt and Ifriqiya. Hence Byzantines who were kidnapped by Arab pirates were put up for sale on Arab markets. That phenomenon is attested by the Byzantine hagiographical narratives; the documents of the Genizah; and Arab writers such as Ibn Butlān, who describes the advantages of slaves from every background. The same author mentions Armenian slaves as well.[266] I have already spoken of Arab piracy with respect to the slavery of war captives. Here I shall confine myself to pointing out once again that this Arab threat became an everyday reality on the Byzantine coast, and even in the hinterland, beginning in 827–828, when Arab forces from Spain conquered Crete.

Crete, located between Cyprus and Sicily and between Egypt and the Aegean Sea, of which it marks the boundary, is by virtue of its position the most strategic site in the eastern Mediterranean.[267]

The *Rhodian Sea Law*, though not in the nature of an imperial promulgation, was very important for the commercial traffic in the Byzantine seas around the late seventh to eighth centuries. In fact, that source says nothing about the routes and little about the merchandise, coinciding in that respect with the legal sources of the same period. The *Rhodian Sea Law* focuses on the transfer and maintenance of goods in the boats, and on the responsibility for these goods. Nevertheless, it is possible to conclude that the Byzantine maritime market was very open at the time, despite the pirate attacks, which are mentioned in the text.[268] Although the boats were Byzantine, the merchants were not necessarily so. The commercial routes passed through the islands where the ships made stops,[269] which shows the importance of the islands for maritime trade, especially at a time when pirates were on the attack.

The expatriate Arabs of Spain who conquered Crete in 827 inherited not only a base for conducting raids, which Crete had already been for the Byzantines, but also an island that dominated maritime trade in the eastern Mediterranean.[270] That became obvious in the first half of the tenth century, when Muhammad ibn 'Umar composed the *Faqīh*, a text whose kinship to the Byzantine *Rhodian Sea Law* suggests that the latter was its source.[271] The *Faqīh* was written by a Muslim. Yet the common points between these two sources clearly show that religion had little importance for commercial law. Nevertheless, unlike the Byzantine collection, which has no precise geographical scope (its title is only an allusion to the ancient sea law of Rhodes),[272] the *Faqīh* was composed in Crete by an Arab Cretan. That source therefore reflects the commercial importance of Crete, whose benefit for the local Arab authorities is clear. Like the *Rhodian Sea Law*, the *Faqīh* mentions slaves as merchandise rather than as part of the boat crew, but without indicating their provenance or their destination.[273]

Like Byzantium, Arab Crete did not only block the southern Mediterranean; it also deprived the empire of the use of the Aegean Sea as a domestic waterway.[274] That led to the evacuation of the Aegean isles and even of the coast of Peloponnesus in the tenth century. It was only in 961 that Nicephorus II Phocas succeeded in recovering that Mediterranean base. With that conquest, the Aegean Sea once again became Byzantine. In 965, the same emperor managed to recapture Cyprus and Cilicia; Antioch followed in 969.

The New Politico-Commercial Strategy of Byzantium in the Tenth Century

The conquest of Crete in 961 was part of the great military plan of Nicephorus II Phocas, who reconquered the southern part of Asia Minor for the Byzantine Empire, as well as Cyprus and northern Syria. In addition, the city of Antioch, the Syrian port of such importance for the *Radhaniyya*, also became Byzantine once again. The maritime dominance of Byzantium in the eastern Mediterranean was thus restored in the tenth century. As Ibn Hawqal notes, Byzantine ships easily traveled to Palestine and Egypt.[275] Let me add, to the examples provided by Patlagean,[276] the cases found in hagiographical narratives of Byzantines captured by Arab pirates and sold to Arab countries, especially Egypt and Ifriqiya. The Byzantines who pursued them to ransom the captives embarked from Arab ports (Arab piracy continued well after 961), without fear of being captured themselves. For example, in the *Spiritually Beneficial Tales of Paul of Monembasia*, the monk who travels to Ifriqiya to redeem three brothers belonging to his monastery visits the country's governor with no risk to his freedom.[277] The Byzantine ships that stopped in Arab countries established commercial ties between the Byzantine and Arab ports, as the two journeys reported in the *Life of Nicholas of Sion* (tenth century) attest. In the first, Nicholas leaves Lycia on the boat of a man named Menas and arrives in Askhelon after five days.[278] The ship is coming from Palestine but belongs to a Greek. The second journey, which was supposed to be a pilgrimage to Jerusalem, takes him to Egypt.[279] Then there is the correspondence that the Jewish communities of Egypt maintained with their coreligionists in the Byzantine Empire, especially in the tenth century, as attested in the documents of the Genizah.[280] And it was precisely in that century that the decline of Jewish merchants occurred. The reason may lie in Arab piracy or in the increase of Byzantine commercial channels in the Mediterranean. Ashtor believes that the commercial development of Italian cities began to take over the role previously performed by Jewish merchants.[281] But he too overlooks the Byzantine factor at play on the map, a factor that was particularly decisive for Italy. Let me now turn to examine the trade policy of the Byzantine Empire from the early tenth century onward in its other *mare domesticum:* the Black Sea.

Trade between the Russians and the Byzantines in the North Sea is attested in the mid-ninth century by Ibn Khordādhbih who, in his description of the *Radhaniyya,* devotes a passage to the Russian merchants.[282] The three principal north-south commercial routes were riverways: the Dnieper, the Don, and the Volga.[283] The first two routes ended at the North Sea, while the third continued on to Itil, the Khazar capital on the mouth of the Volga, which Ibn Hawqal calls "the river of the Russians," and to the Caspian Sea. As a result, at the time Ibn Khordādhbih was writing (the first version of the *Kitāb al-Masālik wa'l-mamālik* dates from 846), Russian merchants encountered customhouses on both the Byzantine and the Khazar sides.[284]

This Russian traffic accounts for the Arab and Byzantine coins found in Kiev (on the Dnieper) and in Gnezdovo (on the Volga), which date from the time of Basil I (867–886), Leo VI (886–912), and the reign of the Samanid king Ismā'īl bn. Ahmad (892–907). This proves that the Russians needed coins: they began to mint them themselves only in about the mid-tenth century.[285] Samanid dinars have been found in the area corresponding to the fourth route of the *Radhaniyya* who, according to Ibn Khordādhbih's description, took Slavic slaves behind the Byzantine empire to Transoxiana.

The treaties of 907 and 911 between the Byzantines and the Russians inaugurated a new policy in that region. It went hand in hand with the growth of Russian commercial might in the tenth century. These treaties, as well as that of 944, granted commercial privileges to the Russians, who obtained right of access to Byzantine markets, especially Constantinople.[286] No tax is mentioned, and the Byzantines agreed to lodge Russian merchants and to aid the Russian ships against pirate attacks.[287] There was also a military alliance, as a result of which the Russians participated in Byzantine expeditions. Russian ships also took part in the Byzantine attack on Arab Crete described by Constantine VII Porphyrogenitus.[288] That military alliance, though not permanent, was even more important in the region of the Black Sea.[289]

In 944 a Russo-Byzantine victory was achieved against the Bulgars. And in 969 the Russians destroyed the kingdom of the Khazars.[290] Princess Olga's conversion to Christianity (about the mid-tenth century) was followed by an official journey to Constantinople, which she undertook in 957.[291] It was her son Sviatoslav who in 968 made possible the Byzantine victory over the Bulgars.[292] This does not mean that the relations between the Byzantines and the Russians always remained calm.[293] In 988 Prince Vladimir allowed Basil II to crush Bardas Phocas's rebellion. The Christianization of the Russians has traditionally been attributed to the same prince, who wished to marry Basil II's sister.[294] In the second half of the tenth century, the Russians became the second power in the Black Sea and, in 989, they obtained control of Kherson.[295] Basil, for his part, proceeded to annex Armenia, and, with the end of the Samanid kingdom in 999, the Russo-Byzantine domination of Caucasus was complete.[296]

With respect to the slave trade, the Russians figure as suppliers for the Byzantines in the Russo-Byzantine treaties of the first half of the tenth century.[297] Slaves are in fact the only merchandise mentioned.[298] In *De administrando imperio*, Constantine VII Porphyrogenitus describes the river traffic in slaves by the Russians.[299] The Russian victory over the Khazars also had consequences in that region. According to Ibn Hawqal's description, the Khazars took Russian and Bulgar captives in their raids conducted on the Black Sea. They then sold them as slaves, probably on Arab markets,[300] a description in agreement with that given by Constantine VII concerning the Pechenegs' raids on the Russians.[301] The Russians' victory freed them from that threat and opened markets to the south for which they no longer needed a customs middleman. But during the first half of the tenth century, Russian dominance in the Black Sea came about at the expense of another neighboring kingdom, that of the Bulgars.

I have shown that Byzantium used the treaties it had concluded with the Russians in its international policy during the tenth century primarily against the Bulgars, who were causing disturbances in the empire and who became particularly threatening during the reign of Simeon (893–927). Historians have traditionally seen that war as a reaction against the transfer of Bulgar merchants in 893 from Constantinople to Thessalonica.[302] Theophanes Continuator explains that this measure had been taken by Stylianos Zaoutzes, Leo VI's minister, in favor of two merchants from Hellas.[303]

In the tenth century, the Byzantine authorities found adequate allies in the Black Sea: the Russians. The largest market on that sea was opened to the Russians for political and military reasons, as specified in the treaties. The expulsion of the Bulgar merchants from the Constantinople market followed the same logic.[304] The shift incited major Bulgar opposition, leading to the wars waged by Simeon, after which the Byzantines were forced to once more accept the Bulgar merchants in Constantinople.

The expulsion of the Bulgars, which can be explained by the Byzantine policy in the Black Sea, also gives a glimpse of a commercial and political plan: Byzantium organized the Black Sea and the Aegean Sea by sharing its commercial hegemony in the Black Sea with the Russians and by setting up the Bulgars in the Aegean Sea. Indeed, according to Theophanes Continuator, the motive for their actions was the profit to be made by the Byzantine merchants of Hellas. In fact, Byzantium applied the same policy in the Adriatic-Ionian Sea.

It is clear that Byzantium did everything in its power to assert its commercial hegemony in Italy in the eighth and ninth centuries.[305] That proved to be especially true for the slave trade, as indicated by edicts issued from Byzantium and Venice—and from both at the same time—which tried to limit that traffic. Nevertheless, the prohibition, renewed four times in documents (in 876, 945, 960, and 902), shows that these attempts failed until the mid-tenth century.[306] But why prohibit the Venetian slave traffic?

Among the documents published by Gottlieb Lukas Friedrich Tafel and Georg Martin Thomas are prohibitions targeting trade with Arab merchants and Arab countries in general, especially in wartime.[307] These acts are consistent with Byzantine policy in the eighth to tenth centuries, which obstructed the slave traffic with Arab countries through the use of customhouses. In Italy, Venetian edicts produced the same result by banning Venetians from slave trade with the Arabs. The Arab markets were the destinations of Italian merchants, especially Venetians.[308] But not only were these merchants in competition with the Byzantines, they sometimes sold Byzantines as well.[309] The edicts thus had two objectives: to put an end to the competition in the slave traffic destined for the Byzantine markets, and to stop the slave trade in abducted Byzantines. Byzantium had exactly the same preoccupations during the same period on the eastern front.

Byzantium controlled the commercial traffic on the Adriatic Sea through its customhouse in Corfu, as attested by Liutprand of Cremona.[310] Possibly as a result, the Venetian *placitum* of 960 banned all slave trade between central and eastern Europe conducted by Venetian ships on the Adriatic Sea. The slave traffic did not necessarily pass through that sea, however. The *Radhaniyya*, for example, did not come that way, and the *Life of Elias Spēlaiōtēs* tells us of slave merchants in the villages of Calabria in the second half of the tenth century.[311] Therefore, the Venetian *placitum* of 960 also banned the sale of slaves, even to Jewish merchants. And the same document mentions as well the obligation to ransom captives.[312]

Nevertheless, that series of edicts did not succeed in eliminating the Venetian slave traffic between 876 and 960. At that time, Byzantium changed its strategy. Instead of trying to block Venetian merchants with edicts and customs duties, Byzantium now made use of the Venetians by the same means: it used edicts, hence its legal authority, and customs, its fiscal authority.

The chrysobull, or imperial edict, of Basil II (992), published and studied by Agostini Pertusi, and more recently by Marco Pozza and Giorgio Ravegnani in *Pacta Veneta*, reveals that new policy of the Byzantine emperors, which a century later would produce the chrysobull of Alexius Comnenus (1082).[313] Basil II granted considerable fiscal privileges to the Venetian merchants passing through customs at Abydos: they now paid seventeen *solidi* per boat instead of thirty. That gave them a great advantage over all the other non-Byzantine merchants (the text mentions the Amalfitans, the Jews, and the Lombardians of Bari).[314] As Pertusi explains, this was not the unilateral concession of a privilege but a bilateral accord that considered the Venetians not "a vassal power of the eastern emperor" but "a sovereign state."[315] He shows that this attitude developed during the tenth century as a result of the Venetian victories along the eastern coast of the Adriatic Sea.[316] All the same, the chrysobull explains that the Byzantine emperor could now use the Venetians in his *servitium* (which must be translated as *douleia*). In the late tenth century, that implicitly meant that aid would be granted to the emperor in his wars against the Arabs in Sicily.

To assure himself of the Venetians' aid against the Normans in 1082, Alexius Comnenus granted them an exemption from customs duties in all the chief ports of Syria, Asia Minor, the islands, Greece, Epirus, Macedonia, Thrace, and Constantinople. In addition, a commercial sector was granted them in the capital, consistent with the same policy and in the same manner as for the Russians in the tenth century.[317]

It is therefore clear how the global slave trade and the definitions of the Byzantine institution of slavery evolved as a function of the changes in the medieval geopolitical arena: political, geographical, economic, but also cultural. But what became of the slaves within the empire?

CHAPTER 3

Slavery, a Component of a Medieval Society

The Language of Slavery

Although the terms "slavery" and "slave" have precise meanings in modern languages, the entities to which they refer are always defined by the historiographical perspective and the (civil, social, and economic) dimension within which they were conceived. I have shown that on the Mediterranean geopolitical scene these definitions were dynamic and constantly changing. But the definition of slavery also depends on social structures. Medieval slavery, and more precisely that of the Byzantine world, constitutes an ideal field for examining how the definitions of the slave and of the free person evolved as a function of the modifications occurring in a medieval society, beginning with its language.

The linguistic term currently used to designate the slave, especially in French, has no single equivalent in the Greek language for the era under consideration. Rather, Greek sources provide several terms that can be translated as "slave." That richness of the language raises a first question: what nuances do these terms introduce into the definition of slave, if, that is, differences in meaning exist? Here are the principal terms designating the slave, in Greek alphabetical order:

ἀνδράποδον, *andrapodon* (n.): slave in general; captive reduced to slavery

δοῦλος, δούλη, *doulos* (m.)/*doulē* (f.): slave in general; subordinate, the ruled; servant; a way of referring to oneself when addressing another (the slave of, your slave, and so on)

θεράπαινα, *therapaina:* female slave; female servant

οἰκέτης, οἰκέτις, *oiketēs/oiketis:* slave, literally, "of the house" (domestic) or of the family

οἰκετικὸν πρόσωπον, οἰκετικὸν σῶμα, *oiketikon prosōpon/oiketikon sōma:* literally, faces or bodies of slaves, often used in the plural

παιδίσκη, *paidiskē:* literally, little girl (παιδίσκος, *paidiskos,* little boy);
   slave; a young female slave; a female servant
παῖς, *pais:* literally, "child"; slave; servant
ψυχάριον, *psukharion:* literally, "soul"; slave

This list, though not exhaustive, shows that the meanings of the terms differ from one another and that each term also contains several meanings.[1] These words, moreover, do not designate slaves alone. Consider the word *pais,* for example: it can refer to a slave but also to a servant who is not a slave, or quite simply to a child.[2]

A second question therefore arises: how to identify the slaves in the sources? In other words, how are we to know whether a man is a slave or of free status? In some cases, it is apparent by the context if the source indicates that the person was purchased, sold, emancipated, or captured, for example. Such indications point to the precise criteria by which the slave is legally defined.

In addition to the initial list of terms, there are other words related to the subject (for example, "free person," "freedom," "freedman," "master," "owner"). And since this study covers a period of six centuries, the linguistic evolution in the use of terms and in their meanings must be taken into account. Chronology is therefore an important parameter for defining the various terms. There may also be linguistic variations from one setting to another. The geographical space covered here encompasses regions remote from one another, and terms therefore differ in their use depending on the source. But a source is characterized not only by region but by genre. Hence when the word *doulos* appears in legislation, it almost always translates as "slave," because such texts define their terms on the basis of legal categories, which is not true of, for example, hagiographical works. In addition, some terms are not used in all types of sources. Each source has its own language, and that too must be taken into consideration. The terms are presented below (table 2) based on their frequency of use in various types of Greek sources.

In the first place, it is evident that no type of source uses all the terms: each has its preferred means for designating the slave (the term *doulos* is the exception to this rule). Each type of source selects its words as a function of its own objectives. For example, the word *andrapodon* (a neuter noun) used in the plural *(andrapoda)* designates a large quantity of slaves of both sexes. This use stems from the terminological distinction between the two types of *autokinēta* property:[3] livestock (*tetrapoda,* or "quadrupeds") and slaves. It was

Table 2 Frequency of Occurrence for Terms Designating Slaves, Free Persons, Masters, and Freedmen (in alphabetical order, classified by source)

Term	Public documents	Private documents	Hagiographical literature	Historiographical literature
ἀνδράποδον (andrapodon)	X	–	X	XXX
ἀπελεύθερος/ἀπελευθέρα (apeleutheros/apeleuthera)	XX	X	–	–
ἀπόδουλος/ἀπόδουλη (apodoulos/ē)	–	X	–	X
δεσπότης (despotēs)	XXX	XX	XX	XXX
δουλεία (douleia)	XX	XX	X	X
δοῦλος/δούλη/δούλις (doulos/ē/is)	XXX	XXX	XXX	XX
ἐλευθερία (eleutheria)	XX	X	X	X
ἐλεύθερος/ἐλευθέρα (eleutheros/a)	XXX	XXX	X	X
θεράπων/θεράπαινα (therapōn/aina)	X	–	X	X
κύριος/κύρια (kurios/a)[a]	XX	XX	XXX	X
κατάδουλος (katadoulos)	–	X	X	–
οἰκέτης/οἰκέτις (oiketēs/is)	XXX	X	XXX	X
οἰκετικὸν πρόσωπον/οἰκετικὸν σῶμα (oiketikon prosōpon/oiketikon sōma)	X	XX	–	XX
παιδίον (paidion)	–	–	XX	X
παιδίσκη (paidiskē)	–	X	XX	XX
παῖς (pais)[b]	–	X	XX	X
σύνδουλος (sundoulos)	–	–	XX	–
ψυχάριον (psukharion)	X	XX	–	XX

Note: XXX = very frequent; XX = frequent; X = infrequent; – = no occurrence. The frequency of a term is determined through comparison to the equivalents used in the same type of source and not in relation to the occurrence of the same term in other types of sources: "Very frequent" means that the term is used in more than a quarter of the references, "infrequent" that it is rarely used.

a. This word does not appear in the table when it has the sense of "God" (literally, "the Lord").
b. This word does not appear in the table when it has the sense of "child."

primarily employed by historiographers reporting information on enslaved populations rather than on individual slaves. Nevertheless, the same word was also employed, though rarely, to express metaphorically a form of emotional bondage, for example in the expression "a slave of adultery."[4]

I shall classify references based on meaning, type of source, and date. A first difference can be seen between sources of a documentary nature and literary sources. Documentary sources, whether public (laws in particular) or private, describe in a general manner the duties, rights, and deeds of one person or another. They clarify civil status because their objective is legal. Literary usage, by contrast, does not have to correspond to legal formulations. As a result, the legal category of "slave" need not concern the author of literary works.

In establishing the distribution of terms, I respect this distinction between documentary and literary sources. Documentary sources can be further divided between public documents (legislative for the most part), which concern the empire as a whole, and private documents. What is particular about these private documents is, first, that they were composed with the aim of formalizing an act for a public purpose—that is, they were to serve as proof —and, second, that they were issued by the private individuals directly involved. As for literary sources, these are either hagiographical or historiographical works. Let me now consider the different meanings of the terms used in these four types of sources.

The legal sources prove to be the most enlightening for the relation between the terms used and civil status. As a matter of fact, the terms used in laws designate civil status.

It is clear from the *Novellae* of Justinian, the *Ekloga*, the *Novellae* of Leo VI, and those of the tenth- and eleventh-century emperors that legislators always considered slavery an essential and important subject, since many of these laws concerned slaves. Appendix table A.1 indicates two tendencies in the legal sources regarding the use of words: continuity and change. The terms *doulos* and *oiketēs* were the most frequently used during the entire era, whereas *andrapodon, doulē,* and *therapaina* were still relatively rare. By contrast, the term *apeleutheros/apeleuthera* (the only word to designate a freedman or -woman), very common in Justinian legislation, no longer appeared after the *Ekloga. Eleutheros/eleuthera* took its place. The freedman, who had had a significant place in Roman legislation of the classical and imperial periods,[5] now no longer interested legislators. Does that mean that the freedman ceased to be distinguished from persons who were born free? That seems to be a logical conclusion in view of the occurrence of the term *eugenēs* as well. That adjective and the noun *eugeneia* were used in Roman law to designate the status of one who is "freeborn." From the eighth century on, however, these terms were not used in legislation, thus attesting the disappearance of the legal difference between the statuses of free man, freedman, and freeborn.[6] The term *eugenēs* continued to be used in literary sources in the sense of "well-born," but it did not designate a legal status.[7]

While *apeleutheros* was no longer used in legal sources, two new terms were used for the slave, *oiketikon prosōpon,* which made its appearance with the legislation of Leo VI, and *psukharion,* which appeared in the *Novellae* of the tenth and eleventh centuries and in the *Peira.* That change cannot be explained by the context, since the laws do not distinguish these new terms from others for "slave." Here I touch on the key question, namely, the degree of correspondence between the terms in use in legal sources and the different functions of the slave.

Etymologically, the term *oiketēs* alludes to a domestic function. But nothing in the laws suggests that the *oiketai* played such a role. In fact, some laws use the terms *doulos* and *oiketēs* interchangeably. This confirms that the two terms had the same meaning, at least regarding civil status. In addition, sixth-century *Novellae* use the term *oiketēs* for slaves who worked in the mines,[8] and in the tenth century the same word designates rural slaves.[9] The word *andrapodon,* rarely used throughout the era, was also not linked to a specific usage.[10] In short, if there was any difference whatever among all these terms, it does not appear in the legal sources. As far as the legislators were concerned, all the terms connoted the same civil status. The legal terminology designating slaves simply established a cleavage between them and nonslaves, without any distinctions corresponding to the terms used.

As for the word *douleia,* legal sources use it only to refer to the condition of an enslaved person. The term has the sense of a legal destiny or position—the *tukhē* of the slave (also called *tukhē doulikē,* in contrast to *tukhē eleuthera,* the destiny of a free person). In legal language, then, there is an equivalence, at the level of civil status, between the terms that designate the slave and the word *douleia.*

Unlike the legal sources, hagiographical literature does not define its categories in terms of civil status. The great difficulty with this type of source lies in understanding when the reference is to a slave and why terms designating slavery are used for nonslaves. Hagiographers took an interest in slavery, however, and sometimes used it as a theme in various episodes. In these cases, the characters' civil status is clearly indicated. To differentiate between slaves and free persons in the other cases, I identify the contexts in which the terms are used and the roles to which they refer (appendix tables A.2–A.4) in these literary sources.

Slaves designated as *doulos, oiketēs,* and so on, are always depicted as being under the authority of their master. Sometimes their function is also mentioned, and in most cases this is a domestic function. In each of the various time periods, when the terms are employed without any identification of civil status (appendix table A.4), they consistently have the same connotations as when they are used explicitly for slaves (appendix table A.2). Nevertheless, that is not a sufficient argument for claiming that the author, in using these terms, was describing slaves but without indicating their civil status. In fact, in these cases the author was not interested in civil status but in the social role of these narrative objects, who are for the most part marginal figures.

In appendix tables A.2 and A.4, the same typology appears for the use of the term *doulos,* in the sense of a person under the authority of another and in the sense of "domestic." Beginning in the ninth century, *oiketēs* was also used in these two senses. The words *pais* and *paidiskē,* for their part, almost always designated a person who served in a home, whether a slave or an individual of undetermined civil status. The emphasis placed on the domestic role in hagiographical literature does not mean that there were no other economic functions for slaves during the period in question. It is clear that hagiographers preferred to present slaves as domestic workers because it was in the household that the relation with their masters manifested itself most fully.

It is therefore possible to say that in the hagiographical literature the terms used to designate slaves do not categorize them by their common civil status but by a social status defined in relation to their master's authority, and also by an economic position associated with their function as workers. In addition, the nature of these classifications sometimes resulted in their being grouped with nonslaves. This shows that in Byzantine society during the era concerned, there were nonslaves with the same economic roles as slaves; the literature presents them in similar social positions—that is, as under the authority of a master.[11]

The attribution of some of these terms to persons of free civil status (appendix table A.3), as, for example, in the expressions *o doulos tou theou* (literally, "the slave of God") and *o doulos tou khristou* ("the slave of Christ"), occurred throughout the era.[12] *O therapōn tou theou* began to be used in the ninth century, and *o oiketēs tou theou* somewhat later. From the ninth and tenth centuries onward, *oiketēs* and *therapōn* came to be used in reference to the emperor as well. Normally, they are translated as "servant"—hence "servant of God" or "servant of the emperor." But the word "servant" does not adequately capture the service in question, or rather, the connotation of these expressions extends beyond the meaning of the term "service."[13] The expression *o doulos/oiketēs tou theou* is regularly employed in the literature to designate the saint, whereas *doulos/oiketēs tou basileōs* refers to high officials (military or civilian) in the emperor's service. This was therefore a function corresponding to a social position.

Overall, the word *oiketēs* began to be used in the same sense as *doulos* in the ninth century, and in the ninth to tenth centuries these two terms became synonymous. The same chronological distribution occurs in their use as a social position ("under authority" in appendix tables A.2 and A.4) and in their use to designate a relation to God or the emperor (appendix table A.3). In short, there is a certain correlation in the evolution of these terms within the two contexts: to designate saints and high officials on the one hand and persons subject to a master, including slaves, on the other. In both cases, the terms refer to direct subordinates, either to any master whatever or to God or the emperor.

Hagiographical literature also illuminates the difference between the use of *doulos, oiketēs,* and *pais*. One context in which the term *pais* was used to refer to a free person, though relatively uncommon, was in the expression "*paides* of the heretics."[14] It is clear that these were neither children nor domestics but more likely were servants in the sense of "acolytes" or "disciples."

Unlike most public documents, which were written in Constantinople, private documents have various provenances: Greek papyri from Egypt (the most recent of which date from the seventh to eighth century); documents dispersed throughout Asia Minor (beginning in the tenth century); documents from the Mount Athos archives (beginning in the ninth century); and documents from Patmos and the monasteries of southern Italy (beginning in the eleventh century). The availability of this information from four different regions allows for a regional comparison of the vocabulary.

Private attestations with a legal value (contracts, wills, and other types of declarations) resemble public documents in that they serve a public purpose. They are to be distinguished from documents intended for private use (letters, petitions from private individuals, and so on), which are less likely to identify the civil status of the interested parties. Even private attestations, however, though they specify civil status in the case of slaves, rarely indicate the fact that a person is free. Nevertheless, as legal certifications, they give more details than hagiographical sources on the civil status of the person in question. They shed light on the meaning of *pais*, for example. A papyrus of 569 contains a labor contract whereby a man hires himself out to another.[15] It is obvious in this text that the man is not selling himself (his service is to be remunerated in specified wages—*misthos*). To designate his role and status in the new house, he uses the word *pais*, as well as *upēresia* for service. Another papyrus is a rental agreement dating from 566 between two women, one of whom (the tenant) is a *paidiskē* in another person's house.[16] The legal status of that *paidiskē* is not mentioned, but if she were a slave she could not have signed such a lease. The same meaning appears in a document from the monastery of Saint Elias of Carbone that distinguishes between a slave *(doulē)*, who is emancipated therein, and three *paides*, servants.[17] The economic function that this term designates could therefore be assigned to slaves and to free persons, unlike the word *therapaina* (or *therapainis*), which designates an enslaved female servant.

The word *paidion* is used in the sense of "child"; throughout the era concerned, however, *pais* also continued to designate a child in private documents.[18]

In the labor contract of 569, the author uses the words *pais* and *katadoulos* as equivalents.[19] *Katadoulos* indicates that the person in question has been reduced to the status of a *doulos*. But was this a legal status or a social condition?[20] The word *doulos* is also used for an employee of free status in a private house.[21] Later, *o doulos tou basileōs* came to designate imperial high officials.[22] In both cases, as in the hagiographical sources, the term refers to a relation of social submission.

Unlike *doulos*, the word *oiketēs* is not used in this type of source to designate a slave.[23] The word *doulos* is also employed to refer to oneself in addressing another. That usage appears in a series of papyri from the sixth and seventh centuries.[24] None of the letters are part of a correspondence between friends. They are petitions, complaints, reports, or requests. In all these cases, their content suggests the sender's submission to the addressee. Sometimes the sender was in the service of the recipient as scribe, secretary, or tax collector;[25] sometimes he indicated his social position in the letter as being under the administrative or economic authority of the addressee, also called *despotēs*, master. This meaning of the term *doulos* probably has to do with social dependency. In the sixth and seventh centuries, however, the word in that sense was always used by the speaker: "I am the *doulos/doulē* of [such and

Table 3 Uses of the Terms for Slaves in Private Documents

Term	Papyri of Egypt (6th–7th centuries)	Archives of Athos/Patmos (9th–11th centuries)	Documents of Cappadocia (10th–11th centuries)	Documents of Southern Italy (11th century)
ἀνδράποδον (andrapodon)				
ἀπελεύθερος/ἀπελευθέρα (apeleutheros/ apeleuthera)		freedman/ freedwoman	freedman/ freedwoman	
ἀπόδουλος/ἀπόδουλη (apodoulos/apodoulē)		freedman/ freedwoman		
δοῦλος/δούλη/δοῦλις (doulos/doulē/doulis)	slave; domestic (free)	slave of the emperor (free)	slave	slave
ἐλεύθερος/ἐλευθέρα (eleutheros/eleuthera)	free; freedman	free; exempt from taxes; autonomous	free; exempt from taxes	
θεράπων (therapōn)	slave (dom.)		slave (dom.)	
θεράπαινα/θεραπαινίς (therapaina/ therapeinis)	becomes dom. (free)			
καταδουλος (katadoulos)				
οἰκέτης (oiketēs)				
οἰκετικὸν πρόσωπον/οἰκετικὸν σῶμα (oiketikon prosōpon/oiketikon sōma)	domestic (free)	slave (dom.)	slave (dom.)	
παιδίον (paidion)				
παῖς/παιδίσκη/παιδάριον (pais/paidiskē/ paidiskos)				domestic (free)
σύνδουλος (sundoulos)				
ψυχάριον (psukharion)		slave (caretaker)	slave (rural)	

Note: domestic (abbreviated "dom.") = domestic function (servant) in the home of another; words in parentheses indicate a conclusion inferred by the context.

such a person]." Epitaphs also commonly had the deceased refer to him- or herself as the *doulos/doulē* of God.

Someone who presented himself as the *oiketēs notarios* or *oiketēs nomikos* of another—who was called his *despotēs*—performed the function of secretary, specialized or not, in the master's house.[26] The civil status of these *oiketai* is not mentioned, because there is no reason for it to be. These were persons in the service of another. In the case of the poet Dioscorus of Aphrodite, who presented himself as an *oiketēs nomikos* (specialist in law) in the city of Antinoe, it is clear he was a free person.[27]

Two documents provide another meaning for the word *oiketēs*. The first is a letter explaining that the name of a taxpayer was crossed off the author's tax rolls *(katalogos)* by order of the *comes* (a trusted official of the governor).[28] The term *oiketēs* is used to designate the dependency of the taxpayer—who was therefore of free status—on his protector. The other example is a complaint addressed to a functionary in which the author mentions the measures the residents had taken to defend their lands.[29] The letter explains how the rich used their armed *oiketai*. These may have been slaves or domestics but could also have been dependent peasants whose form of dependency, like that in the first document mentioned, was of a fiscal nature. Hence, in Byzantine Egypt, the word *oiketēs* did not designate the civil status of slave but revealed social relations.

Another term, *oiketika prosōpa*, began to be used to designate slaves in eleventh-century documents. Two wills, composed about thirty years apart —that of Eustathios Boïlas, a Cappadocian magnate, and that of Symbatios Pakourianos, a military leader, both of whom owned many slaves—use exactly the same vocabulary, designating the testators' slaves as *psukharia* and *oiketika prosōpa*.[30]

Symbatios Pakourianos's will makes a distinction between male and female slaves. Note, however, that the word *oikeios* comes from "house" but also has the sense of patrimony or possession ("proper to someone"). *Oiketēs* should therefore not be translated as "domestic."[31]

Finally, the historiographical sources introduce meanings that did not exist elsewhere and make more precise the aspects already mentioned. The use of the terms relating to slaves in this type of source is presented in appendix table A.5, with conclusions regarding *oiketēs, pais, andrapodon,* and *aikhmalōtos.*

The most important insights that the historiographical works provide have to do with the social meanings of the terms *doulos, douleia,* and *douleuō.*

As in the hagiographical sources, the use of "*doulos* of the emperor," for ex-ample, for a person performing a military function is common from the ninth century on. And as in the archival documents of the same era, these words are used for those paying a tribute. In both cases, what was at stake was social subjection.

The term *doulos* is also used to express political submission. The peo-ples subject to the Byzantine emperor or to another sovereign are called his *douloi*. At the same time, there were precise acts for expressing that submis-sion. Take, for example, the description of the Pecheneg by Constantine VII Porphyrogenitus. Their submission to the Byzantine emperor took the form of an agreement stipulating they had to provide a *douleia* wherever the em-peror desired it. This was a military service imposed by the emperor during his wars against the Russians, the Bulgars, and the Turks.[32] Another act of political submission was the payment of taxes. The Venetians, for example, did not want to be the *douloi* of the king of the Franks, which would have meant paying him a tribute; and the residents of the Dalmatian Islands paid a symbolic sum to the governor, signifying thereby their continued submis-sion to the Byzantine emperor.[33] That submission, sometimes called *douleia*, is also designated by the words *doulōsis* and *upotagē*, which mean both "sub-mission" and "subjection."

Nevertheless, along with these meanings of submission, the term *douleia* also contains the sense of pure work or labor. That is the only word that designates both work and the status of slave; the Greek language did not have any nouns formed from the same root as *oiketēs, pais, andrapodon*, or *psukharion* to designate the status, position, or work of the persons so desig-nated. *Douleia* therefore comprised three different concepts: a civil status; a social condition that assigned a social role; and an economic value that was realized in the work, service, or payment entailed by an act of social sub-mission.

In the era under study, these three meanings came to be contained within the word *doulos* and, later, within *oiketēs* as well. It is important for our pur-poses to take into account the different types of sources, since each type of source developed its own language and attached different meanings to the words.

To return to slavery: by what means is it possible to distinguish the work of slaves from the other forms of *douleia?* In terms of their civil status, slaves clearly constituted a delimited group in Byzantine civilization.[34] But was the same true for the other senses of *douleia?* In other words, how, in the three semantic fields at issue (legal, hagiographical, and historiographical), did slaves differ from other *douloi* in their *douleia?*

Alexandre Kazhdan provides an example of the use of the word *douleia* in the twelfth century: residents contracted to be in the service *(thēteia)* of private persons in exchange for wages.[35] According to Kazhdan, in this case the *douleia* was a private service. I have shown that both meanings were already contained within the term *douleia* before the twelfth century. Kazhdan demonstrates in addition that in the twelfth to thirteenth centuries the words *eleutheria* and *douleia* began to be used in a fiscal sense (*eleutheria* to mean "freedom from tax obligations"). David Jacoby defines a fiscal class of "free persons" *(eleutheroi)*, "strangers" *(xenoi)*, or "tax nonentities" *(anepikhnōstoi tō dēmosiō)*—terms that designate peasants not subject to fiscal obligations.[36] Hence the word *douleia* had the sense of being subject to the fisc.

Kazhdan also shows that, just as there was more than one meaning for *douleia* in Byzantium, there was also more than one type of *eleutheria*. But was this still *eleutheria* in the sense of "freedom," or were freedom and slavery opposites only in the case of civil status? In other words, outside the context of civil status, did *douleia* in its other senses still connote "unfreedom"? As it happens, the first difficulty I encountered in attempting to identify slaves in the sources was associated with the question of what was particular about their *douleia.*

I now turn to the place slaves occupied in the social context and to the roles they performed. First, what was the distribution of slaves within Byzantine society? And second, what were their economic and social positions and functions in the different environments in which they could be found?

Slavery and the Other Categories of a Medieval Society

Between the sixth and eleventh centuries, the Byzantine Empire covered a vast and dynamic geographical space. To explore the role of slavery in that space, I must first consider the regions that composed it. I will then be able to demonstrate whether the slaves' tasks varied from one region to another and from one era to another. Because of the particular geopolitical position of Byzantium, the regional makeup of the empire reflected the diversity of the eastern Mediterranean basin. Thus I should be able to situate Byzantine slavery within Mediterranean slavery as a whole.

For the geographical and chronological delimitation of the field, I shall by necessity follow the regional Byzantine sources, primarily those that describe daily life. The richest sources for such a typology are the regional archival documents and the hagiographical narratives. Both place slaves in a physical environment and in a social and economic milieu, which historians and chroniclers rarely do. Legal sources are the least helpful in this regard, since most were written in the capital but applied to the whole empire.

In addition, the geographical distribution of documents is closely linked to their chronological distribution. Syria, for example, like Palestine and Egypt, became poor in Greek documents and hagiographical narratives after the seventh century. The end of that century marked a turning point in the history of the Mediterranean, with the Byzantine Empire's definitive loss of all these regions. Moreover, there are very few examples of these types of sources for the eighth century, particularly because of the iconoclastic crisis—a lacuna that the sources of southern Italy of that era fill to a certain extent. The late ninth century marked another turning point in the history of the Mediterranean. At that time, after the conquests of Basil I, the empire expanded and reclaimed some of its territories, especially in the eastern part of Asia Minor, in the Aegean region, and in eastern Sicily. The Balkans were added during the same period, when they began to be Christianized, but that region produced few of these types of sources. In the tenth to eleventh centuries, a large number of sources originating from northern and southern Greece appeared. At the same time, the number of sources from Asia Minor dropped. In fact, the hagiographical sources that describe Asia Minor deal especially with Cappadocia, Galatia, Paphlagonia, and Lycia; the eastern part of Asia Minor remained poor in sources.

The coast of Asia Minor was part of the Aegean regions. This appears clearly, for example, in the *praktikon* of the monastery of Christodoulos in Patmos, which concerns the *episkepsis* (imperial demesne) of Miletus,[37] as well as in the *Life of Paul of Latros,* which speaks of the region of Miletus and Samos, and in the *Life of Lazarus of Mount Galesios,* which deals with the region of Ephesus. The two Lives, which date from the second half of the tenth century, take place within the same time period as a large number of narratives from southern Greece, whereas those of central Anatolia that have come down to us are set in a different time.

An important factor to consider for the six centuries as a whole, even before taking slaves into account, is the gradual transfer of the center of gravity from the southeast to the northwest, which is reflected in the distribution of sources. By southeast, I mean the provinces of the Near East, Egypt, Palestine, and Syria, but also Cyprus and Asia Minor. Beginning in the ninth century, and increasingly in the tenth to eleventh centuries, even Asia Minor became impoverished in sources, in favor of Greece, the Balkan regions, and southern Italy.

In speaking of social milieus, I make a distinction between the city and the countryside. The terms *kōmē* (village), *khōrion* (rural district), and *proasteion* (suburb) are used to describe the mode of habitation. I also distinguish between the provincial cities and the major cities. Constantinople can be classified as a major city throughout the era, whereas Thessalonica was one only from the ninth century on. Hence changes in the list of sociogeographical milieus are a result not only of geopolitical shifts in the empire but of demographic and urban changes.

In analyzing the milieus in which slaves were placed, I shall also take into account the socioeconomic level of their masters. I shall distinguish well-off persons from those whose total wealth is not specified. But I cannot base my argument solely on the criterion of wealth because that society's elements cannot be classified solely in terms of an economic hierarchy. As a result, I shall also speak of the *arkhontes* and of the *dunatoi*. *Arkhontes* were official agents, whereas *dunatoi*, the "powerful," were those whose wealth was associated with political influence and who possessed a personal and social relation to power. The Pakourianoi exemplified this powerful elite (as did dukes, governors, and strategoi), whereas Boïlas was a mere *arkhōn*. In about the tenth century, the powerful elite become a major presence in the sources, especially documentary sources.[38]

In analyzing the place and economic role that slaves occupied in Byzantine society, I focus on two different milieus, the city and the country.

Slaves in the City: Participation in Artisanal and Economic Urban Life

The Book of the Prefect: *Its Function and Its Arguments*

To examine the place occupied by slaves in artisanal manufacture, the principal—if not the only—source available is the *Book of the Prefect (Eparhikon biblion)*, which dates from the last years of the reign of Leo VI.[39] This source collects the rules governing professional corporations in Constantinople, which were under the authority of the city's prefect.[40] It deals with urban slaves who participated in the city's productive activity and mentions them as artisans and shop foremen.[41] Although these slaves are sometimes depicted as being financially independent, it was actually their masters who used them as workers or gave them business responsibilities.

At first glance, the fact that slaves were entrusted with posts of responsibility in artisanal life appears sufficiently surprising to elicit questions. I cannot address them without situating these slaves in relation to other types of artisanal labor.

In the twenty-five chapters of the *Book of the Prefect*, the trades of *tabell-arios*,[42] notary, silversmith, goldsmith, banker, and moneychanger are all mentioned, along with five different trades related to the marketing and manufacture of silk, plus those of laundress, perfumist, candlemaker, soapmaker, grocer, saddler, butcher, cattle merchant, pig merchant, fishmonger, baker, innkeeper, and construction worker (carpenter, mason, ironsmith, painter). These were not just artisans, but also merchants, suppliers, bankers, and notaries. Not all the urban professions being practiced in Byzantium are mentioned.[43] Nevertheless, this source tells us about the organization of labor in artisanal production generally and about the tasks that slaves performed in it.

There are no general regulations in the *Book of the Prefect* governing all the trades or corporations. Apart from chapter 20, which concerns the deputy prefect, and chapter 22, which contains rules concerning several trades, the text is organized by trade, with certain rules recorded for each one.[44]

The *Book of the Prefect* has no precise rules describing the organization of the different corporations. The artisans making up a specific trade are designated by the collective terms *tekhnē* (trade), *epistēmē* (knowledge), and *sustēma*, or quite simply as "silversmiths," "goldsmiths," and so on. The text speaks of the shop foremen or store managers *(ergasteria, ergaleia)* and of those in charge of the corporations, such as the head of the *tabellarioi*, the chief goldsmith, and so on. These individuals were responsible for the members of their own corporation, whereas general oversight was in the hands of the prefect. The rules in the *Book of the Prefect* do not include all the provisions that would have been necessary to manage the professional corporations of Constantinople, and I would conclude, as a result, that other rules not found in that text also existed.[45]

"Prefect," "foreman," "corporation member," and "worker" are not the only professional categories mentioned in the text. Also noted are "strangers"—to the city *(exotikoi)* and to the empire *(ethnikoi)*—as well as guarantors, whom a person needed to set up a shop or join a corporation. In addition, there are references to wage workers (*misthioi* or *misthōtoi*) and slaves.

Misthioi could be used only as workers under a specific labor contract *(misthosis)* concluded between a *misthios* and the shop foreman who hired him. This form of work differed from that of slaves: slaves could be employed as workers by their masters (without earning wages) and could also become shop foremen.[46] The *Book of the Prefect* mentions another type of worker, one who practiced his trade for wages but whose work was not fixed by a contract: for example, the scribes employed by the *tabellarioi*. In that case, it was the *Book of the Prefect* that fixed the rate of pay.[47] These scribes were not *misthioi* because their work was not done under a fixed-term contract. The *tabellarios* also had to obtain permission from the corporation to hire a scribe.[48] But a scribe could not become the business manager—that is, he could not become a member of the corporation—quite simply because he was not qualified as a notary. Nor could the *misthioi* be shop foremen, because of their terms of employment. It was the rules in the *Book of the Prefect* that made that impossible, by limiting the duration of the *misthosis* to a month at most.[49]

In discussing the production of silk, the *Book of the Prefect* places all sorts of artisanal production workers on the same level: "Any *serikarios* [silk manufacturer] who sells an *oiketēs*, a *misthōtos*, or an *eklektēs* to persons who are strangers to the city or to the empire will have his hand cut off."[50] The sale of these three types of workers would have given outsiders access to Byzantine secrets for manufacturing silk.[51]

In any case, the *misthioi* are mentioned only twice, once in conjunction with the *metaxopratai* (merchants of silk goods) and once within the context of the *serikairioi* (silk manufacturers). And both rules stipulate the same thing: "Anyone who takes a *misthōtos* must make an agreement with him for only one month. He will pay in advance thirty days' wages *(misthos)* at most. Anyone who pays him for a longer duration will lose the excess wages *(misthōma)*."[52] The *metaxopratai* were "prohibited from taking a *misthios* used by another *metaxopratēs* before that *misthios* had worked with the other for the time corresponding to the wage he received. Any offender will suffer the loss of the share of wages that the *misthios* received without having earned it."[53] The *serikarioi*, by contrast, had to pay a fine: "If a *serikarios* takes on a *misthōtos*, knowing he is [the *misthōtos*] of another, and if the *misthōtos* has not yet finished the time for which he was paid, the employer will be subject to a fine equivalent to the *misthos* that the *misthōtos* did not earn for his work."[54] Different rules, then, were applied to different trades, though similar rules might recur. These are the only trades for which norms for wage workers are stipulated, but that does not necessarily mean that no *misthioi* were hired in the other trades. That is one of the characteristic lacunae of the *Book of the Prefect*. The great importance that Constantinople granted to silk and its production may explain why the five silk trades are described in more detail. In such a prestigious field, a skilled worker was valuable and therefore very much in demand.

As for enslaved workers, the *Book of the Prefect* fixes no limits on their use except in banking. Bankers could not entrust a slave with the management of a bank, "which could lead to grave abuses."[55] But this was also a particular case of a general rule: "Bankers cannot yield their place to other persons, even on days of largesse or for a *douleia* to the emperor."[56]

Another trade was closed to slaves: silk finishing. Here the rule specifies that the finisher could not be a slave. The finisher had to so certify by entering his name in the prefect's registers at the time the raw silk was purchased.[57] It is clear that of all the secrets of the silk trade, finishing was the most important. Precautions thus had to be taken so that Byzantine—or even Constantinopolitan—knowledge did not leave the corporations, the only ones authorized to apply it.

The first rule of the bankers' corporation is the only rule in the *Book of the Prefect* that prohibits slaves from being business managers.[58] Because there are no examples of explicit permission being given slaves to become shop foremen, and because in some rules their capacity to do so is presumed, it would seem logical to assume that all the other corporations were open to slaves and that slave foremen belonged to the *sustēmata*. The *Book of the Prefect*, however, tends to distinguish between a shop foreman and a member of a corporation. And though there are rules declaring that slaves can be business managers, there is no direct evidence that they were members of a corporation. Take, for example, the *vestiopratai*—silk clothing merchants. Slave *vestiopratai* are well attested.[59] Nevertheless, the regulations explaining how to be admitted to the corporation and how to obtain permission to acquire a shop do not specify situations in which the applicant is a slave.[60]

The *sustēmata* acted as intermediate bodies between the artisans and the prefect. In setting up a workshop, the artisan had to make a payment to a corporation, and in case of punishment the corporation could impose a fine or order an expulsion.[61] One rule prohibits teaching the trade of soapmaker to a person who does not belong to the corporation, which suggests that the corporation consisted of the group of persons who had the right to practice that trade; but none of the rules relating to slaves as shop foremen specify whether they would also become members of the corporation.[62] These rules indicate only the sum the foremen had to pay to acquire the right to open their shop. Moreover, the rules that apply to both slaves and free persons use a different term than those that apply only to free persons:[63] "setting up a workshop" (εἰς ἐργαστήριον καθεσθῆναι) versus "being admitted to the knowledge" (ἐν τῇ ἐπιστήμῃ καταλεχθῆναι). For example, in the case of *vestiopratai*, anyone setting up a workshop had to pay a fee of ten *nomismata*, whereas to join the corporation *(sustēma)* one had to pay six *nomismata*.[64]

Of the two rules that define the conditions necessary to create a shop, one has to do with free persons, the other with slaves. The first concerns a silver shop, the second a shop of *serikarios*—silk goods manufacturers. Both indicate the guarantee that a shop foreman had to provide. A free person needed the backing of five guarantors, whereas a slave needed only that of his master.[65] That difference can be explained by the fact that a free person could not provide a guarantee for someone else's slave. Moreover, a slave could not present himself as a guarantor, since he had no resources or legal personality. That may have been the legal basis for the capacity given to slaves to set themselves up as shop foremen: since a foreman could not serve as his own guarantor, it was not necessary that he have a legal personality. But the economic and administrative consequences went much further. It was advantageous for a master, in setting up a shop, to declare one of his slaves the foreman rather than bestow the title on himself, because he would thereby not need anyone's backing. That would have resulted, at a social level, in a potential weakening of reciprocal financial relations (of the sort: "I'll be your guarantor if you'll be mine") and would have fostered the growth of a financially independent *oikos* rich enough to have its own slaves and to set up its own shop. In other words, an analysis of the *Book of the Prefect* shows that it was in the interest of a business manager to acquire and use as many slaves as possible.

The custom of permitting a slave to participate in artisanal life as a foreman and even perhaps as a member of a corporation originated in Rome and was adopted with modifications in the *Basilica*.[66] Two Roman institutions allowed the master to make his slave the manager of a business: the *peculium* and the *praepositio*. The institution of the peculium—a property legally held and managed by someone who is under the potestas of another—made it possible to foster economic autonomy not only for slaves but also, for example, for sons who were not *sui juris*. The peculium had a special legal status, a sort of de jure autonomy that allowed the slave or son to become the de facto business manager. Although profits went to the peculium (in effect to the business manager), and expenses were taken from it, the peculium belonged de jure to the slave's owner or, in the case of the son, to the father. Through that institution, masters could encourage their slaves to move toward economic independence, to accumulate a fortune that would then allow them to purchase their freedom. The other mechanism, that of *praepositio* (being in charge), brought the slave in as an *institor* (business agent) for one of his master's properties—a piece of land, a ship, a store, and so on. The *praepositus* slave became a manager, but without recourse to the legal institutions of the peculium; as a result, all expenses were paid by the owner and all profits turned over to him.[67]

The *Book of the Prefect* presents a different system. The initiative for setting up a shop with a slave as its foreman always fell to the slave's master.[68] And according to all the rules that mention slaves as shop foremen, in case of a fine it was neither the master who had to pay nor the slave from his peculium. The punishment was the confiscation of the slave himself. This constitutes proof, it seems to me, that the slave, as shop foreman or as member of a corporation, did not have financial or fiscal responsibility for the affairs of the shop.[69] Therefore, the slaves occupying positions as shop foremen in the *Book of the Prefect* were not placed there through the traditional institution of the peculium. Otherwise, both financial sanctions and the repayment of debts would have been carried out through the *deductio de peculio* and the *naturalis obligatio*.[70] During the era concerned, in fact, the peculium was losing the importance and utility it had previously had.

But if the peculium was not at issue, then the master, in establishing his slave as shop foreman, himself enjoyed all the profits. It was therefore the master who played the active role, because any initiative and any decision rested solely with him.[71] The slave, still being completely dependent on his master's guarantee, could not decide on his own to set up a shop, even though the text sometimes presents it that way.[72] And the master who set up his slave as the business manager when creating the shop enjoyed not only financial advantages but legal ones as well.

Nicolas Oikonomides develops the hypothesis that a person who wanted to set up several shops in different professions (which was prohibited) could use his slaves to that end, with each managing a shop in a different trade.[73] But such a person could also have turned to third parties of free status—relatives, for example. So the question remains: what legal benefit could he draw from the use of slaves?

The *Book of the Prefect* not only contains regulations but also stipulates penalties for violations. The two rules that concern the guarantee given by a master to his slave stipulate that in the case of infringement the master will be subjected to the same penalty as the slave. Yet that was not always so. There were also regulations stipulating different punishments for slaves and for free persons.[74] These cases, one concerning goldsmiths, the other soapmakers, imposed the sanction of confiscation on the guilty slave but a fine when the guilty party was a free person.[75] The master of the confiscated slave, punished by the loss of him, would not be compelled to pay a fine in addition.

Johannes Koder distinguishes among three categories of sanctions: financial sanctions, as in the cases just mentioned; physical punishments; and privative sanctions (what he calls *Ehrenstrafen*, literally "honor sanctions"), such as exile.[76] In most instances, no alternative penalty for slaves is stipulated. The only cases in which a special punishment for slaves is specified or mentioned have to do with financial sanctions. In those cases, the burden fell solely on the guilty party of free status, that is, on one possessing his own economic means. By contrast, mutilation, exile, expulsion, or a ban on practicing the trade could be inflicted on either a slave or a free person.

The problem of the slave's penalty arose, therefore, only in cases in which the accused did not have the means to pay the fine. The sanction could have been the total loss of the shop, but the two rules noted above prove that the lawmaker preferred simply to confiscate the slave. In perpetrating a crime, the only risk the master incurred was that his slave would be confiscated or physically punished (a slave with a hand amputated was no longer worth very much). Since the master had control of the business, it was he who committed a crime through the intermediary of his slave, especially since the slave did not have the ability to defend himself legally.[77] The loss of the slave was sometimes much less serious than the punishment that would have been inflicted on the master were he himself responsible for his business vis-à-vis the prefect. Hence "the goldsmith who accepts delivery of more than one pound [of gold] and who does not immediately declare it to the chief goldsmith, if he is a slave, will be confiscated; if he is of free condition, he will be whipped and will pay a fine of one pound of gold."[78] But a pound of gold, equal to seventy-two *nomismata*, greatly exceeded the price of a slave, by a magnitude of three to four.[79] In other words, it was better to entrust the business officially to one's slave because the worst risk of perpetrating such crimes was loss of the slave.

There was, then, an economic or financial role for which the use of slaves, because of their legal status, proved particularly advantageous. Another aspect of this role had to do with slaves' social status within the shops: *misthioi* could serve only as laborers, whereas slaves could also be shop foremen and have authority over them.[80] In addition, a person who wanted to set up a shop as an investment could not use wage laborers for more than thirty days. He had to have at his disposal enough resources to pay for the shop: namely, ten *nomismata*, plus six *nomismata* to the corporation, and the slave (about twenty *nomismata*). The price of the shop foreman thus constituted a major aspect of the investment, and only slave owners were able to set up such an operation.

It is thus clear that the legal status of slaves and their socioeconomic status did not necessarily coincide, not only because slaves of the rich had a higher standard of living than free persons who were not rich—which was true during every era of the Roman Empire—but also because the legal status of slaves made it advantageous for masters to place them in certain economic positions.

The examples in the *Book of the Prefect* suggest an important question concerning the function of slaves: why did these legal regulations of artisanal life in Constantinople in the early tenth century give artisans a means for perpetrating crimes by using their slaves? This points to the limitations of such a source: no answer to the question will be found in a legal text.

Slaves acquired a high social position thanks to an economic function that they alone could fulfill but that also entailed the risk of being confiscated. The confiscation *(eiskomizō)* of a misbehaving slave, which was actually intended to punish his master, raises the question of the slave's new fate. Another clause may serve as an indication, though it concerns a different crime: it indicates that a slave will be placed among the imperial slaves *(basilikoi douloi)*.[81]

Imperial Slaves

In his study of slaves' roles in the imperial court during the early Roman Empire, Gérard Boulvert makes a distinction between *servi publici* and *servi caesaris*.[82] Only the *servi caesaris* were used by the princeps for an imperial service corps that was personally bound to him, either as property or, after emancipation, in an employer-employee relationship. Their functions were not only domestic; the emperor's freedmen also played administrative roles.[83]

In Byzantium, confiscations supplied slaves for the corps of *douloi basilikoi*.

This term may suggest the expression *doulos tou basileōs,* though the latter did not refer to a slave. Keeping in mind the difference between the *doulos* of the emperor and the imperial slave, I shall try to follow the slave's career once he was brought to the court.

The Roman Empire had a consistent policy of using an unpaid labor force for public works projects, such as mines or agricultural work on fiscal demesnes. Unlike the example given in the *Book of the Prefect,* these slaves had sometimes been born free and later reduced to slavery, either by the justice system as punishment for a crime or by war as captives. Gifts and bequests of slaves made to the emperor by individuals were another source of imperial slaves.[84]

Speros Vryonis's article on the Byzantine mines shows that the mines were not taken out of Byzantine hands after the Arab conquest but continued to operate in Asia Minor and the Balkans.[85] The brief comments Vryonis devotes to labor power allow us to conclude that in the fourth century the authorities continued to inflict the punishment of *damnatio in metallum* for criminals and prisoners of war, while simultaneously using free labor in the mines. At the same time, Jean-Pierre Sodini argues that in the fourth to seventh centuries the number of slaves used in the mines must have dropped, with a concomitant rise in the use of free labor.[86] This tallies with the legal sources, which show that workers of free status were bound to their trades in the state workshops. But all this evidence comes solely from two fourth-century laws, which in fact attest no change in the type of labor used. In other words, it is not possible to conclude that before the fourth century only slave labor was used.

A *Novella* of Justinian that put an end to condemning free persons to slave labor *in metallum* could have resulted in a drop in the use of slave labor.[87] But that was not necessarily the case, since there were two other sources of slaves: those who were confiscated while slaves, and prisoners of war.

The imperial Roman authorities employed slaves not just for work in the mines and on state farms but for the construction of buildings and roads and in fiscal workshops.[88] Imperial workshops *(ergodosia)* where cutters, gold embroiderers, and goldsmiths worked existed alongside factories and armories well after the sixth century, as Oikonomides shows in his commentary on the *Treatise of Philotheus* (899).[89] The use of Muslim prisoners of war as slaves in the imperial shops is attested by al-Muqaddasī in the tenth century.[90] Once again, however, their bondage was on a par with that of workers of free origin, described by Symeon the New Theologian: "The goldsmiths and copperers and line workers. . . . are always at work and barely able to provide for their own bodily needs and those of their dependents. . . . Workers in bronze, and goldsmiths, and artisans, if they do any work for the emperor, receive the fee agreed upon beforehand from the hands of his subordinates and then, like strangers or aliens, return to their homes without having seen the emperor or being aware of any kind of friendship with him."[91] These state workers mentioned by Symeon the New Theologian were bound to serve the emperor as laborers or servants: the word used was *douleontes*. They were used by the emperor in the same way as the fiscal *condicionales* in the fourth to sixth centuries described by Roland Delmaire.[92] But though in the late Roman period these laborers (slaves and nonslaves) belonged to the fisc, in the later era they were designated *basilikoi:* "of the emperor."

Though having Roman origins, the use of slaves continued to develop at the imperial court with the organization of the court in Constantinople.[93] There again, it is the sources from the late Roman Empire that point to the accumulation of slaves at court. Confiscated, imported, and offered as gifts, they probably performed domestic tasks at court.[94] In the fourth to fifth centuries, moreover, some arrived at court as slaves and then went on to perform important functions there.[95] Take the case of eunuchs: a eunuch traditionally held the position of *praepositus sacri cubiculi*,[96] and other positions, including some in the military, were available to eunuchs.[97] Hence true professional careers existed at court, open to slaves from the beginning; but it cannot be proved that such positions were reserved for slaves from the sixth century on.

Novella 38 of Leo VI attests that imperial slaves owned goods, since it grants them permission to bequeath them.[98] These were probably not the slaves who performed humble tasks but rather those who held important positions. In addition, it is certain that very high officials such as Narses did not remain slaves, and that was likely also the case for all the other dignitaries.

An example of the status to which a slave could aspire is provided in the *Life of Stephen the Younger*. A female slave is ready to denounce her mistress to the emperor on condition that she acquire a new social position: as her reward, she will be emancipated and will marry a man of the imperial court.[99]

Even if they were not slaves, holders of high office did not have the right to leave without the emperor's authorization.[100] This attests their personal dependency on the emperor and raises the more general question of the obligation by state officials to remain bound to the court and to fulfill their role there. It is clear that the limitation on freedom of movement linked to socioeconomic position played a role in the definition of unfreedom generally.[101]

I have focused on imperial slaves *(oi basilikoi douloi)* precisely because of the blurry line that existed between their servitude and their freedom. Here I return to the more general topic of slaves who attained a high position in Byzantine society. Imperial slaves were not alone in that respect. In *Novella* 38 of Leo VI, the emperor recommends that other masters in the empire follow his example and give their slaves the right to dispose of their possessions as they wish. Though conceding that slaves owned goods, the law of Leo VI does not give them *dominium de jure* but leaves the slaves' legal capacity to alienate up to the master's consent. But who were these slaves outside the imperial court?

Slaves in the Upper Social Echelons

In the Byzantine era, as in antiquity, the connotations of the term *oikos* extended beyond the limited sense of "house" or "family." Paul Magdalino's article on the structure of the Byzantine *oikos* (especially from the tenth century on) shows that the term referred to a socioeconomic unit bound to a person or institution.[102] That unit was composed of slaves and of freemen (known as *anthrōpoi*) personally bound to the master. As Magdalino demonstrates, the existence of the *oikos* depended on the person (or master) in that if he died without an heir, these personal relationships came to an end. Three wills—of Boïlas and of the Pakourianoi, husband and wife—have particular importance here because of the place they reserve for slaves. Large numbers of slaves held a permanent place in the *oikoi* of the powerful. A study of the structure of the *oikos* will thus complement the insights uncovered in the *Book of the Prefect* regarding the use of slaves.

The Pakourianoi belonged to the Constantinopolitan aristocracy. The first will is that of Symbatios Pakourianos, signed in 1090; the second is that of his widow, Kalē Diabatenē, signed in 1098 after she entered monastic life under the name Sister Mary.[103] This couple was descended from three aristocratic families: the Pakourianoi, the Basilakioi, and the Diabetenoi.[104] The Pakourianoi, who appear in the sources for the first time in 988, were a Georgian or Armenian family who occupied high military positions; the most famous among them was Gregory Pakourianos (second half of the eleventh century).[105] Kalē was the daughter of Basilakios the Kouropalatos and Zoē Diabatenē.[106] The Basilakioi were a family of Armenian or Paphlagonian origin who were close to the circles of power. The Diabatenoi, a family that included the dux of Edessa and the governor of Mesembria, were high dignitaries of Armenian origin. Some Diabatenoi left seals with titles such as *sebastos* or *protokouropalatos*. On both sides of the family were high dignitaries (military and administrative) who, in the tenth to twelfth centuries, belonged to the social elite and to the entourage of emperors: Symbatios Pakourianos mentions in his will horses and clothing given him by the emperor. As a couple, Symbatios and Kalē, who lived in Constantinople, owned the lands of four villages in Thessaly, one of which, Radolibos, was bequeathed to the monastery of Iviron. The relations with that monastery can be explained by the family's origin: Iviron, literally "of the Iberians," was a monastery of Georgians.

The number of people bound to the *oikos* of the Pakourianoi exceeded thirty-one and included eighteen freedmen. The figures are not precise because only the wife's will enumerates them individually.

Another example of the Byzantine *oikos* appears in the will of the *protospatharios* Eustathios Boïlas, signed in 1059. Boïlas was a native of Cappadocia. Because of constraining circumstances, he was obliged to take a journey with his family lasting a week and a half. At the end of that trip, he arrived among people who were "strangers by their faith and their language" (that is, they did not speak Greek and were not Christians, or at least not Chalcedonians), probably Armenians. Boïlas mentions six villages *(khōria)* in his document. He bequeaths his demesnes to his daughters and to the churches he built. He mentions that he gave three villages in usufruct to his "master" Michael, who had demanded them. This detail points to a real conflict between Boïlas and Michael.[107] Boïlas held a much lower rank than the Pakourianoi. He was not living in an urban environment: unlike his *kurioi*, he lived on his demesnes. He was also not among the "powerful," as were the Pakourianoi, yet he had no fewer slaves than they.

These wills, it is true, can hardly be said to have emerged from the artisanal milieu depicted in the *Book of the Prefect*. They do not provide precise information on the positions in which slaves were placed (their weapons—*armata*—indicate that slaves may have served as private soldiers or guards) or on their careers in the service of their master. The case of the *oikos* of Theognostos, a *protospatharios* and military leader in the territories of Anatolia, who is described in the *Life of Andrew the Fool*, provides more information.[108] Having purchased Andrew as a slave, he educates him (seeing to it that Andrew learns to read and write) so that Andrew can become his *notarios*. Then Theognostos entrusts Andrew with the affairs of his *oikos*, which includes a large number of slaves. A hierarchy among slaves within the *oikos* was a known phenomenon in Roman society. The *servus vicarius*, for example, was the overseer of other slaves and was placed above his subordinates in the house or on the master's demesne in the countryside. Such a function is not found explicitly in the Byzantine sources. The case of Andrew the Fool, however, shows that some slaves were elevated to a higher position than others in their master's *oikos*. But Andrew was no ordinary slave.

The case cited by the *Peira*, of slaves who participated in the military actions of their masters, and Kekaumenos's recommendation that slaves be integrated into private military operations, both show that slaves were not restricted to domestic labor.[109] That they—or rather, their masters—had a chance to be integrated into every socioeconomic stratum is clear from legislation on "industrial" organization (ninth–tenth centuries); from the opportunities afforded slaves to participate in the private management of economic, financial, and military matters; and from the structure of the Byzantine *oikos*. Let me point out, however, that these aspects are revealed only in sources from the ninth century on.

Slaves in the Countryside

Social Elements

Information on the entire era under study attests the presence of slaves in the rural areas. But being part of a peasant society did not necessarily entail having an agricultural role. The place of slaves in the socioeconomic distribution of social groups in the Byzantine countryside—from the coloni of the late empire to residents of village communities to peasants, magnates, and *paroikoi*—still remains to be studied.

In fact, the role of slaves in the rural areas has been underestimated by scholars studying slavery and by the majority of specialists on the Byzantine countryside.[110] The scant attention given to slavery is even more noticeable in the two major theories on the social structures of the Byzantine countryside, those of Georges Ostrogorsky and Paul Lemerle. According to both authors, slaves constituted an agricultural labor force but played no other role in rural society. Lemerle focuses his attention on farming and sees slavery as a characteristic part of the ancient economy. Slave laborers, according to him, were replaced in the seventh to eighth centuries by peasants who settled in the empire.[111] Ostrogorsky concedes the importance of slaves as an agricultural labor force but, since he is primarily interested in the ownership of land and the transfer of ownership, excludes slaves from the social structures he is studying.[112]

As I consider the place of slavery in the countryside, one question will arise repeatedly: given the demographic changes over a period of six hundred years in geographical regions remote from the empire and in border territories, is it possible to speak of "Byzantine countryside" in the singular? Documentary sources of great diversity—chronological as well as geographical—will provide the response and will indicate the place of slavery. Here is a first list:

— the papyri of Egypt from the sixth to seventh centuries relating to the countryside;[113]
— the *Rural Code (Nomos georgikos),* a collection of regulations of rural life, probably from the eighth century;
— the imperial *Novellae* concerning the land;[114]
— the documents conserved in the archives of the monasteries of Athos and Patmos, which deal with the categories of persons constituting the countryside;
— the various treatises on taxation, and especially the cadastres;
— the wills of peasants and of persons owning real estate, such as Boïlas's will and other private wills from southern Italy held at the monastery of Saint Elias of Carbone, as well as the *typika* that mention real property.[115]

I propose to do a comparative study focusing on the two sorts of documents used in studying slaves: those that mention them and those that do not. For documents that mention slaves, the question will be what role they grant to the category of slaves when compared with the other categories indicated. For the documents that make no mention of slavery, I shall attempt to explain that absence and what it may signify. The problem of the *paroikoi* and the *douloparoikoi* will also arise at this point.

The categories I propose are large landowners, small landowners, monasteries, tenants, wage-earning nonowner peasants, slaves, and the imperial authorities.[116] Once I have established a typology of slaves in the Byzantine countryside on the basis of these categories, I shall consider that typology in the light of the literary sources dealing with the same chronological and geographical spaces.

In table 4, I present the most important documents for the Byzantine countryside and the categories they attest. But this information needs to be further refined and considered in more detail. For example, slaves cannot be placed in the same category as their owner. A distinction must therefore be made between nonfarmer-owners, farmer-owners, nonfarming tenants, and tenant farmers. But the typology of the Byzantine countryside makes it difficult to distinguish between peasant owners and tenants precisely because property rents were paid as general fiscal obligations.[117]

To have a complete array, a third category has to be added: the persons to whom these fiscal obligations were paid. Since I am interested primarily in slavery, I shall group the tenants together with the small landowners who paid their taxes to a third party. In this case, the third party was the de facto owner in the eyes of the public authorities because he oversaw tax payments on the land. In that way, I delineate a category of dependent peasants in the countryside that corresponded to the coloni of the late Roman era and, from the ninth century on, to the Byzantine *paroikoi*.[118]

Slaves in the Sources

Slavery and the dependent peasantry in the Byzantine countryside each represented one form of unfreedom. The freedom of dependent peasants, whether they were coloni, *paroikoi*, tenants, or owners who paid their taxes to a third party or to the fisc through a third party, was restricted by financial obligations.[119] The dependency of the peasant, whether tenant or owner, was determined by the status of the plot of land in question. Hence a peasant could own two properties for which he paid taxes, one directly to the fisc, the other to a third party; or he could be simultaneously the owner of one property and a tenant on another.[120] Dependency in the Byzantine countryside can therefore be understood in terms of the obligations associated with the land and the social relations determined by these obligations.

The sources indicate that slaves and dependent peasants belonged to two distinct categories. In addition, different kinds of sources attest different aspects of these groups in the Byzantine countryside. Hence a will relating to a piece of property may mention the owner's lands and slaves but not any *paroikoi* or *misthioi* who might be present there. By contrast, a cadastre listing taxpayers, both owners and tenants, will exclude the agricultural labor force. The absence of slaves from the fiscal registers of the cadastres, for example, does not prove that they were absent from the environments referred to.

Slaves were viewed as part of the rural property and, at the same time, as a

Table 4 Social Positions in the Byzantine Countryside

Reference	Region and date	Mode of habitation/ type of property	Social positions
Nov. Just. 32	Thrace (6th century)		—small *geōrgoi*, owners who become the tenants of their creditors —cattle, slaves
Nov. Just. 7, praef. *Nov. Just.* 120	(6th century)		—church/monastery owners —rural slaves —coloni *(geōrgoi)*
Papyri of Egypt	Egypt (6–7th centuries)	—*kōmē*	—small landowners —tenants —magnates responsible for payment of taxes *geōrgoi* (coloni) —slaves —wage workers
Rural Code (Nomos geōrgikos)	(end of 7th–8th century)	—*khōrios*	—landowning farmers *(geōrgoi)* —rural slave —rural wage workers *(misthioi)*
Archives of Athos (acts)	Macedonia Thessaly (late 9th–11th century)	—*khōrioi* —*proasteia* —*ktēsis* (uninhabited *proasteia* or *agridia)*	—monastery owners —large owners who live in Constantinople —taxpaying *paroikoi* —small landowners (lands sold)
Dölger, *Der Traktat des Cold. Marc. Gr.* 173	(10th–12th centuries)[a]	—*khōrios/ktēsis* —*agridia/proasteia* —*episkepsis* (imperial demesne)	—small landowners (of *agridia)* —midsize landowners who live elsewhere and whose *proasteia* are farmed by slaves and by *misthioi*

Source	Date/Period	Land categories	Social/economic description
Schilbach, *Le Traité fiscal du Paris. Suppl. gr. 676*	(10th–11th centuries)		-*paroikoi* (*zeugaratoi, boïladoi, aktēmones*—taxation categories)
Svoronos, *Les Novelles des empereurs macédoniens. Concernant la terre et les Stratiotes*	(10th century)	-*ktēsis* (*agroi, topoi, proasteia*)	-ban on the sale and lease of land; -*geōrgoi*: small landowners; -*dunatoi*: "powerful elite" who obtain the lands of the poor (*penētes*) and as a result increase the work for slaves (*oiketai*) and wage workers; -monasteries—accumulation of properties, cattle, slaves (*oiketai*)
Karayannopulos, *Le traité Zavorda*	(late 11th–early 12th centuries)[a]	-fiscal categories of lands in the villages	-nearby village landowners and types of landholding, property, ownership, and payments on the land
Lemerle, *Boïlas, test.*	Cappadocia-Anatolikon (1059)	-*khōrioi*; -*proasteia*	-large landowners; -slaves (*oiketai/psukharia* + livestock); -a mention of renting out land (the value of one of the lands bequeathed is mentioned in a *pakton*, or land lease)
Patmos (act)	Region of Miletus (insular, coastal) (second half of the 11th century)	-*proasteia* (and *episkepsis*); -uninhabited and uncultivated lands	-large landowner (imperial, monastic); -*paroikoi*-taxpaying tenants; -wage workers (*misthioi*); -slaves ("who are dead")
MM, *Chios* (acts)	Region of Chios (mid-11th century)	-lands (*ktēmata*)	-large landowner (imperial, monastic); -*paroikoi*

continued

Table 4 *(continued)*

Reference	Region and date	Mode of habitation/ type of property	Social positions
Svoronos, *Le cadastre de Thèbes*	Hellas (Boeotia/Euboea/ Attica) (second half of 11th century)	–lands in *khôrioi* –*proasteia*	–midsize landowners (who own other lands); some are dignitaries (*proedria, spatharies*), some live in the cities (hence *proasteia*)
Robinson, *Carbone*	Southern Italy (Basilicata) (11th century)		–monasteries –midsize landowners –small landowners
Gautier, *Le typikon du sébaste Grégoire Pakourianos*	Thrace (11th century)	–inalienable lands (*ktêmata*) –*khôrioi* –*proasteia* –*agridia* –*paroikotopia*	–monasteries –*paroikoi* –*misthioi* –*kinêta* –*autokinêta*
Ferrari, no. 37	Italy (11th century)		–owners –slaves

[a] In *Die ländliche Steuergemeinde des Byzantinischen Reichen im X. Jahrhundert* (pp. 4ff.), Dölger dates this treatise to between 912 and 970. Oikonomides believes that both the Marciana and Zavorda treatises were probably composed in the early twelfth century; Oikonomides, *Fiscalité et exemption fiscale à Byzance (IXe–XIe siècles)*, pp. 44–45.

rural labor force. The farm *misthioi* were solely labor power, whereas the small landowners and tenants could be farm operators, laborers, and also—in paying their taxes to a third party or to the fisc through a third party—dependent peasants. To move forward in this classification, then, it is indispensable to recognize that the forms of unfreedom in the Byzantine countryside were always defined as a function of other social actors and of the peasantry's relations with them. For example, I shall link the fact that a certain plot of land was cultivated by slaves to the relation between the owner's economic level, his mode of habitation, and his ability to rent out that land. This method will allow me to show why slaves might be present in one source but absent in another.

Slaves appear in a text either as farm workers—where they are mentioned alongside hired farm workers (the *misthioi*)—or as property, thereby indicating their owners' economic standing, in which case they are mentioned with the lands and livestock. By contrast, they are completely absent when the context is fiscal: for example, in a treatise on taxation, an act of exemption, or something similar. The treatise on taxation found in the Biblioteca Marciana in Venice, known as the *Marciana Treatise,* mentions slaves only in the context of how rich the landowners were. As far as the text's objective is concerned, the mention is completely superfluous.

The *paroikoi* appear primarily in a fiscal context—hence in treatises on taxation, acts of exemption, and so on. For example, the mention of the *paroikoi* from the village of Radolibos in the will of the landowner (Mary Pakouriana) can be attributed to her desire to offer them a total exemption in the year following her death. But when she bequeaths the lands in Radolibos, she, like her husband, does so without mentioning the *paroikoi.*[121]

It is therefore possible to identify three different socioeconomic aspects of the countryside recorded in the sources: first, the relation between the owner and the land, which depends on the owner's wealth and also determines the type of property; second, the fiscal context, that is, the control of the imperial authorities over the relation between the owner and the land; and third, the farming method, the means by which the owner makes the land productive.

It appears at first glance that for the interested parties in the Byzantine countryside—that is, the imperial authorities, the powerful elite *(dunatoi),* the monasteries or bishoprics, and the small landowners—the question of slavery was a marginal issue, entailing only the third aspect. The exploitation or use of slaves in the Byzantine countryside is not fully recorded in the sources, however: slaves in the countryside performed not only agricultural but also domestic tasks, and sometimes both at once.[122]

Mode of Habitation and Farming Methods

From the Egyptian context of the sixth and seventh centuries, it is clear that the countryside comprised vast tracts that were controlled by powerful families.[123] Sometimes peasants who lived in the *kōmai* either owned some part of this land or rented it. In any event, the magnates who oversaw taxation in the rural areas were not interested in whether the land was owned by the peasants or rented[124] or whether the peasants used means other than their own labor for working the land—for example, wage workers, slaves, or livestock.

I shall not attempt to determine the type of habitation at issue based on whether the magnates lived on their demesnes or not, or how large the demesnes were. The size of the demesne is relevant, however, for the question of how slave labor was used, since a peasant responsible—whether as owner or tenant—for a plot of land measuring a few tens of *modioi* would need far fewer workers to farm that land than would an owner of a large demesne. Roger Bagnall's depiction of the Egyptian village, composed of small plots of land, makes clear why each plot needed only a few slaves.[125] That depiction tallies with Izabela Biezunska-Malowist's thesis that slavery assumed much less importance in Roman Egypt than elsewhere in the Roman Empire.[126]

The case of Egypt demonstrates that the type of property and the farming method were closely linked. That appears clearly later in the *Marciana Treatise:*

Agros is one thing, *agridion* another. *Agros* is any space completely under cultivation, whereas *agridion* is a claim on a large demesne, whose cultivation is also partial; which also has a farmed part; it is therefore called *agridion* because of its modesty, just as a *polidion* (small city) is distinguished from a *polis* (city). *Agridia* come about because villagers *(khōritai)* do not remain in the center of the village, or because they, unlike others, do not possess so-called interior gardens, and as a result they transfer their residences to a parcel of land, which they cultivate and where they settle. Similarly, fathers of many children, when they die, leave to some what they owned in the village and to others what they owned outside it. Thus those who have received their patrimonial inheritance outside the village, unable to dwell and live far from it, move there and, improving the land, make it into an *agridion.* Still others, rich in livestock and slaves or bothered by bad neighbors, unable to dwell in the center of the village, move to a portion of land, and similarly, by improving it, do the same thing. And if we were to look, we would find many starting points for the development of the *agridia.*

The *proasteia* originate in the same way, but are nevertheless distinct, in that their owners do not live on site but establish their own dependents there: slaves, wage workers, and others. And so it is for the *agridia* and *proasteia* included in the dependency of the village.[127]

This passage not only explains the difference between *agridion* and *proasteion*—that is, between a plot of land occupied by its owner and another that is not—but also describes the creation of the large demesnes. Economics was the determining factor. Slaves, who are omnipresent in this description, marked their owner's high economic level and at the same time constituted the force by which he increased his wealth. These were farm workers, then. As such, they could be set up by their master on a *proasteion,* exactly like farmers who worked for wages—*misthioi.* The agricultural labor force was thus linked to the type of property.

The *Life of Philaretos* provides a different example. Philaretos falls from wealth into poverty. His living situation deteriorates, reduced from a *proasteion*—the vast lands he loses—to the *agridion* around his house, which he will farm on his own. The loss of his slaves is part of the same context: his slaves are both an indicator of wealth and an agricultural labor force.[128] Another, much earlier example (second half of the sixth century), which associates the agricultural demesne with the presence of slaves, this time in the region of Amida, is provided in the *Lives of Thomas and Stephen* related by John of Ephesus. Like Philaretos, Thomas, who is so rich that he is in the habit of washing his face and hands ten times a day, owns a demesne *(ousia)* and male and female slaves.[129] According to the *Life of Leo Luke of Sicily,* the Sicilian countryside had a population of small peasants—called "simple"—who lived on and worked the land; so did the countryside of Calabria described in the *Life of Elias Spēlaiōtēs.*[130]

The *Marciana Treatise* reveals the existence of slaves completely by chance: their mention is unnecessary because the text deals with the different categories of tax payments on the land. In this context, only the difference between an *agridion* and a *proasteion* is important, not how they came into existence: the text need only note that the owner did not reside on the *proasteion,* for example. But if that treatise had not mentioned slaves, we might have wrongly concluded that slaves in the Byzantine countryside were not employed as farm labor. Another attestation to the presence of slaves as agricultural labor is found in the eleventh century, in the *Peira*. Here a field *(agros)* in usufruct is mentioned, along with the slaves "who are there" (ἐν αὐτῷ).[131]

Similarly, *misthioi* are mentioned when the farming method is at issue, and livestock when the matter at hand is the type of property—and therefore the owner's economic level. Like the *Peira*, the *Rural Code* mentions owners, slaves, and wage workers, whereas the *paroikoi* are completely absent from the *Marciana Treatise*. In fact, the texts—treatises on taxation, cadastres, or private documents—that speak of *paroikoi* almost never mention slaves,[132] and the sources that refer to slaves do not mention *paroikoi*.

Let me begin, then, with the type of habitation, that is, with the distinction between the small and large properties, which is also a socioeconomic distinction. For the large properties, the problem that has long attracted scholars and that preoccupied emperors in the tenth century was the increase in power of the *dunatoi*.

Changes in the Byzantine Countryside in the Tenth and Eleventh Centuries

The historical scholarship has viewed the Byzantine countryside schematically in terms of the struggle pitting the "powerful" against the "poor" for the ownership of the land. That binary view was in fact that of the public authorities. But the authorities themselves played a role: hence they constituted a third factor. Moreover, social factors outside the purview of the authorities also existed.

Tenth-century legislation established the definition of the group constituting the powerful elite *(dunatoi)*, those who obtained their power from the state, whether laypeople or ecclesiastics.[133] But did the distinction between that group and other landowners correspond to the two forms of property in existence? It is clear that in the vast majority of private documents referring to the tenth- and eleventh-century Byzantine countryside, the individuals and monasteries mentioned had attained such a high socioeconomic level that the property could not have been an *agridion*. But it would be incongruous to call all these individuals and institutions *dunatoi*. Take, for example, the *Cadastre of Thebes:* it is true that the *proasteia* mentioned in the region of continental Hellas belonged to dignitaries, but these were mere *arkhontes*, and the properties were only a few tens of *modioi*.[134] Can these dignitaries really be placed in the same category as landowners such as the Pakourianoi,[135]

Michael Attaliate,[136] Michael Andronikos,[137] or the monasteries of Mount Athos? Hence two different criteria are important: the dimensions of the property and the owner's position or degree of power.

Theophanes the Confessor, Theodore Studites, Boïlas, the widow Danielis, and the individuals cited in the *Life of Elizabeth of Heraclea,* the *Life of Michael Maleinos,* and the *Cadastre of Thebes* were all ninth- to eleventh-century dignitaries who could be classified as *arkhontes* and who owned *proasteia* on which they did not necessarily live.[138] But they did not reside far from them, unlike those who could be called the "landed powerful." Philaretos, a characteristic example of a large landowner from the first half of the ninth century, cannot be considered a *dunatos* in the sense defined in the legislation of the time. Similarly, Boïlas, a *protospathorios,* owned vast properties, but he lived on these demesnes. In addition, he was under the influence and control of his *authentai,* the dux Michael and his son Basil, who according to Lemerle lived in Edessa, far from the lands they were fighting over with Boïlas.[139] Michael and Basil were in fact *dunatoi.*

The type of property is therefore to be defined in terms of the owner's relation to the plot of land, including the distance that separated him from it. That was both a geographical distance and a social distance from the emperor and, as a result, a distance from political influence.[140] Like the *dunatoi,* the *arkhontes* were official agents, but unlike them they were not within the sphere of political influence.

One social stratum, the *dunatoi,* who were close to power and possessed vast properties far from their residences, thus came to occupy an increasingly important place in documents throughout the eleventh century.[141] One of the characteristics that distinguished this group was that they benefited from tax exemptions. These might consist of exemptions from fiscal obligations on the land or of authorizations to place *paroikoi* on it. The large landowners could actually rent out their lands for a sum lower than the taxes that might fall due on them. To keep all the small landowners from leaving their own lands to become *paroikoi* on the large demesnes, therefore, the state attempted to limit the number of *paroikoi,* even on lands that were not tax-exempt. But that measure was not always effective. The documents speak of imperial investigations whose aim was to find the peasants who had fled their own lands to settle illegally on private land as *paroikoi* exempted *(ateleis)* from tax obligations. These investigations had to be completed before the thirty-year statute of limitations.[142] Ostrogorsky defined such peasants as *paroikoi* "of the fisc" *(dēmosiarioi)* because they had been registered on lands subject to the fisc.[143]

To turn now to the farming method: the small landowners living in the villages used slave labor. That is attested by the *Rural Code,* by hagiography, and in the tenth century by the *Marciana Treatise.*[144] As for the "powerful," they offered rented lands to *paroikoi,* who thereby became their dependent peasants, but the *paroikoi's* farming methods did not matter to them. That explains why slaves are completely absent from the documents that mention the *paroikoi.* Slaves, like wage workers, were of no concern to tax agents, in cadastres, or in grants of tax exemption for the lands. Similarly, the absence of livestock *(ktēne)* in these documents does not prove that they were not used in farming the land. Most of these documents concern small plots of land—a few tens of *modioi* per *paroikos* according to the cadastre of Radolibos.[145]

Oikonomides has attempted to explain the sense of the term *douloparoikos,* widespread in the sources between the tenth and thirteenth centuries. Adopting Robert Browning's idea of the *servi casati,*[146] Oikonomides develops the theory that the *douloparoikoi* were slaves settled *(casati)* on public lands as freedmen.[147] That custom is said to have originated in Italy. Browning bases his theory on the Byzantine state's need to use small farmers subject to the public authorities and on the possibility that slaves could have been used with such an aim in view. But that theory is at variance with the way the term was used: it appears only in documents that offer a tax exemption for installing such *douloparoikoi.*[148] If the chief purpose of emancipation had been to create persons "subject to the state," the state would have kept them for itself. If these had been private slaves, the owners would not have needed such exemptions. In addition, in all the documents concerned, there is no indication of a qualitative distinction between the *paroikoi* and the *douloparoikoi.* This clearly demonstrates that the public authorities did not distinguish between the two either for purposes of taxation or in the designation of economic status.

The definition of *douloparoikoi* therefore remains open to other interpretations. In addition, the term is frequently found in documents of the eleventh to thirteenth centuries, that is, after the struggle against the "powerful" was long over. The outlook of the public authorities in the tenth century must be distinguished from that prevailing in the eleventh century and after.

Social Changes and Geographical Changes

As far as the geographical distribution of sources on the Byzantine countryside is concerned, it is the documents from Greece that mention the *paroikoi;*

by contrast, they are completely absent from the sources from Asia Minor.[149] The *typikon* of Gregory Pakourianos (1083), which mentions "lands inhabited by *paroikoi*" that he gave to the monastery, is the only document that mentions *misthioi* as well as *paroikoi*.[150] The fact that slaves are not mentioned in this document appears to prove that they were absent from the lands given to the monastery.[151] Since these were still border lands (in Thrace, but in the region of Philippopolis), the following question arises: did the presence of slaves vary by region? The documents from Macedonia and northern Thrace are at variance with those from Asia Minor.

The only document that mentions both *paroikoi* and slaves in an agrarian context is the one describing a gift to Andronikos Doukas taken from an imperial demesne.[152] It was on the Aegean coast of Asia Minor, situated close to the Aegean and mainland Greece. "The slaves are all dead," says the text, in the same sentence that mentions livestock.[153] "Slaves" would seem to refer to farmers.

Thus far, I have primarily examined the small landowners and the powerful of the eleventh century, those who received large plots of land, who lived far from them, and who received permission to install tenants, exempted from taxes or not. But what about the large landowners who were not exempted? And especially, how were their lands cultivated? I am thinking especially of the landowners described in the *Marciana Treatise* and of others for whom there is a great deal of information from the ninth century on.[154]

According to the *Marciana Treatise,* these owners possessed vast properties that were cultivated "by slaves, *misthioi,* or by other labor forces" that the text does not specify. The same labor forces were also employed by monasteries before the eleventh century.[155] There are few extant sources that specifically describe the cultivation of the land. Even the hagiographical narratives set in the countryside do not provide a great deal of information,[156] giving few details about wage labor and tenants. But on the basis of the indications available, it is possible to conclude that the labor force in these *proasteia* was provided by wage labor and slaves in the seventh and eighth centuries, as it would be in the ninth and tenth centuries.

For the eleventh century, the case of Boïlas is very instructive. He had lands in Asia Minor "a week and a half's journey from Cappadocia," in eastern Anatolikon, perhaps Armenia.[157] His lands comprised six *khōrioi*. Boïlas had to hand over three of these to his *authentai,* which indicates the nature of their relationship. Boïlas, himself a *protospatharios,* cannot be considered one of the eleventh-century powerful elite—especially since he received nothing from the emperor, neither lands nor exemptions. One land lease *(pakton)* is mentioned, but *paroikoi* are completely absent from this document. My main question is therefore: how were these large demesnes farmed? When Boïlas drew up his will, he had already bequeathed most of his property to his two daughters. He bequeathed the rest to the two churches he had built and to his emancipated slaves.[158] Most scholars are persuaded that these were domestic slaves because they are called *oiketika prosōpa* and because they were born in Boïlas's *oikos* and then freed. I shall not dispute that plausible hypothesis, since all of them had been freed by the time the will was drawn up.[159] But this explanation, even if true, does not provide information on the agricultural labor force and thus does not contradict the idea that Boïlas also had unemancipated slaves. To glean that information, it is necessary to focus on the part of the document that concerns the lands. It lists all the properties bequeathed to the daughters, which included lands *(proasteia)*, livestock, and *psukharia*.[160] Are we to conclude that these *psukharia* were slaves working on demesnes? Such an explanation would tally well with similar references from Boïlas's socioeconomic milieu.[161] All the individuals in these references were *arkhontes*, that is, dignitaries in the armed forces or the administration, large landowners who lived in the countryside. The only evidence about their labor force concerns slaves. It must not be forgotten that in Boïlas's case this is a will, which nevertheless does not mention *paroikoi*. Once again Asia Minor, which can be called traditional, stands in contrast to the Balkans.

It is noteworthy that in the hagiographical narratives, figures such as Michael Maleinos, Elizabeth of Heraclea, Theophanes the Confessor, and others sold their properties and distributed the money, an act of piety that may have reflected a social trend of the times. Because that act was always accompanied by the dividing up of livestock and the emancipation of slaves, who in fact received *legata*, it is very likely that some slaves in the countryside were used for rural tasks.[162] What became of these slaves once they were freed?

Freedmen in Society

The Legal Act of Emancipation

With regard to the place of slaves in the socioeconomic distribution of social groups (*misthioi*, other wage earners, tenants, and so on), the question arises whether that place changed once the slave was freed. In other words, where were freedmen situated in the typology of Byzantine society, and what does their role say about the status of slaves?

Along with the institution of slavery, the Byzantine state inherited from the Roman Empire the act of emancipation, the obverse of enslavement. The two acts, one imposing the status of slave and the other restoring one's legal freedom, marked the delimitation between two groups, slaves and free persons, in the society in question. But one act does not necessarily entail the other. In other words, only the act of enslavement is necessary to define a delimited group of slaves in society. The obverse act makes membership in that group reversible. That was the raison d'être for the act of emancipation. But just because both acts were part of the legacy of Roman law does not mean the two were necessarily retained in Byzantium or that they took the same form as before. A glimpse at the sources, however, reveals that the act of emancipation continued to be in force throughout the era studied.

The laws propose specific formulas for emancipating slaves. In addition, they describe all the possible social circumstances under which that act was desirable or necessary.

There were three means by which a master could free his slave: he could declare him a *freedman (eleutheros)* in public or in a church or before three witnesses who could attest the act in writing;[163] he could mention the slave in his will;[164] or he could have the slave baptized.[165]

A master who wanted to marry his slave had to free her so that they would have the same status. In that case, the female slave not only became *eleuthera* but also received the legal status of freeborn *(eugenēs)*. Their children also became freeborn.[166] To marry a slave *(doulē)* of another, a man had to buy and free her;[167] but if the marriage was dissolved, the slave, though remaining *eugenēs*, could not marry again without her former husband's consent.[168]

A master who wanted to free a slave in his will had to indicate so in writing in his own hand before witnesses; the slave became a freedman *(eleutheros)* and could also inherit from his master.[169] A *Novella* of Leo VI shows that the master who made use of such a method of emancipation had to give the slave the opportunity to draw up his own will, even if the slave did not know of his future emancipation.[170] From that time on, therefore, masters were permitted, even advised, to let their slaves draw up wills.[171]

The employer-employee relationship between the master and his freedman is attested in Roman legislation.[172] In Byzantine legislation, however, that relationship is not specifically stipulated within the context of emancipation.[173] In any event, the freedman became *eleutheros* but not *eugenēs* and could therefore be returned to slavery if he inflicted harm on his employer or the employer's family.[174] A *Novella* of Justinian stipulated that the freedman would receive Roman citizenship but stated that his dependency would continue.[175] The freedman *(eleutheros)* could not testify for or against his master *(despotēs autou)*.[176] A *Novella* of Leo VI indicates that this dependency continued to exist in the tenth century.[177] The *Novella* notes as well that the children of freedmen, who received the status of *eugenēs*, succeeded their parents in the state of dependency.

Two types of emancipation documents are available: specific acts of emancipation; and wills that mention the author's wish to free some of his slaves. The four formulas of emancipation that have come down to us contain one key sentence: "So-and-so frees So-and-so at such and such a date." The formulas also specify that the document is to be given to the freedman to serve as proof of his new status as a free person.[178] Hence, in the *Spiritually Beneficial Tales of Paul of Monembasia*, the slave steals his act of emancipation before being freed.[179] Speaking allegorically, the author of the *Life of Athanasia of Aegina* recounts that the saint received "the document of her emancipation."[180] By contrast, a will, which was generally a much longer document, was not given to each freedman. But even wills drawn up after the act of emancipation take care to include a declaration using the same formula as the act of emancipation: "So-and-so is emancipated and no one can deprive him of his freedom."[181] It is therefore clear that the aim of these wills was to prove the status of the freedman. This underscores the fact that, for lack of such proof, the freedman ran the risk of once again losing his freedom.

And it was not only freedmen who faced such a risk. Two sixth-century papyri are concerned with providing such a document to certify a woman's free status.[182] The two papyri, which are not in the same hand, contain the same text.[183] The document is written in first-person singular.[184] The author, whose name is not known, certifies that a woman named Martha, living in his house, possesses "free" status *(eleuthera)* and was never a slave *(doulē)*. In fact, that person had been born in the author's house. She was the granddaughter of two servants who came to work in the house of the author's father. Martha was afraid of losing her freedom, since that is what happened to her cousin Sophia. The author recounts that Sophia and her sons, by a father whose identity is unknown, were reduced to slavery *(eis douleian)*. He does not mention where they lived, who enslaved them, or under what circumstances, but he states that their status was that of *eleutheroi* and that their enslavement was thus illegal.

If Martha had been a freed slave, she would not have needed such a document, because she would have had her act of emancipation. In the same document, the author emphasizes that the certification is necessary because those close to the person were no longer available. He is the only one to bear witness to the free status of the woman concerned because she was born in his father's house. Apart from the author, only his son knew her story well. And it was this son who was threatening her, probably in order to seize everything she owned.[185]

This case, then, is apparently the story of a free person threatened with losing her status. To prevent that, her employer supplied her with a legal document attesting that status.[186] What is important in this case is that the danger of Martha losing her free status stemmed from the circumstance that she was born in the author's house and lived there; that is, she was neither a member of the family nor a *misthia,* which meant she lacked a work contract.[187] Her grandparents arrived at the author's house to work for wages for the author's father. The circumstances conspired to suggest that she was a slave. In other words, since her socioeconomic status corresponded to that of a slave, she could be deprived of her civil status and possessions unless she had legal certification. That is exactly what this document offered her.[188]

Another example from Byzantine Egypt concerns a man who wanted to liberate his wife—she had been captured and reduced to slavery—by proving her free status.[189] To this end, he went to the bishop of Alexandria, who could attest the wife's free status, perhaps because he had married the couple.

Throughout the entire era under study, whatever the formula for emancipation, a legal document had to attest the act.[190] The deed of emancipation or another document could serve as proof, provided it was kept either at the freedman's house or in a public place. Beginning in the sixth century, emancipation could occur in a church, but that did not prevent the freedman from receiving a written document, as shown by the formula from Byzantine Italy composed for such circumstances.[191] Boïlas's will was intended to be kept in the church that was its beneficiary. And the emancipation act graffiti from a village in Cappadocia, which is not a will, indicates the free status of the two slaves in question.[192]

The Social Status of the Freedman

The formulas and acts of emancipation serve solely to indicate the specific dates on which certain individuals would become persons of free status. According to these formulas, the former slave "is free to go where he or she will"—a phrase that is repeated in all the acts of emancipation identified above.[193] Nevertheless, as the laws explain, the relationship between the master and his slave did not end once the slave had been freed. The laws mention the freedman's dependency on the man he continued to call his "master." But acts of emancipation do not provide any information on what happened afterward. That is precisely why wills are particularly useful—they were sometimes drawn up a certain time after the author had emancipated his slaves.

Two questions remain to be answered: What was the relationship between the master and the freedman? And why did the master free his slaves before his death rather than in his will?

Formulas of emancipation, which very rarely mention the peculium,[194] create the impression that the slave was freed in an economic void, receiving no money or goods. The wills and other documents that mention slaves who had already been freed, and which were therefore drawn up after the act of emancipation, indicate rather that freedmen were not deprived of income: they received *legata* in the master's will. And this also attests that the freedman remained with his master. The property given to the freedman was transmitted at the time the master died, that is, when the personal relationship between him and the freedman came to an end. In seeking to discover what happened between emancipation and that moment, I shall consider the property given to the freedman as a criterion for defining the relationship between him and his master. That criterion functioned differently in the city and in the country.[195]

All the slaves emancipated in the countryside for which there is information in private documents received ownership of some of the master's land.[196] In general, the gift was made at the time of the master's death. By contrast, the devout persons in the ninth to tenth centuries who distributed their property granted the *legata* at the time of emancipation. In such cases, this too was the moment at which the personal relationship with the master was broken off. In Boïlas's will, the freedmen were already living on the properties intended for them.[197] The will simply provides them with legal confirmation of ownership. A document from Lavra presents the case of a sale of land to a monastery. The sellers specify that the land sold does not include the plot intended for their freedman, who was thus already emancipated but did not yet have ownership of the plot.[198] Documents from different regions attest that this was the rule in the rural areas of Italy, Greece, and Asia Minor.[199]

At issue in all these documents are resources for the freedmen. The master made provisions for their future without him because his heirs would not inherit them as property. But why did he not make such provisions earlier—at the time of emancipation, for example? In fact, a *Novella* of Leo VI shows that any inheritance bequeathed to a freedman returned after his death to his master's family.[200] That may be the reason why Boïlas states that the lands bequeathed to his freedmen, which were considerable, would remain "completely free" in perpetuity.[201] Regarding his freedmen—probably all his former domestic slaves, who would receive plots of land—Boïlas notes that they "will lose them and fall back into slavery if they leave the right Orthodox faith."[202] This was not a real threat that would have left the freedmen dependent on Boïlas's daughters, since all his heirs were threatened in the same way. Nevertheless, a clause that gives his heirs permission to use his freedmen as wage labor indicates the relationship between these freedmen and Boïlas's daughters.[203] Once more, this was an economic relationship between an employer and an employee.

The wills of the Pakourianoi reveal a different type of relationship. In his will, Symbatios Pakourianos frees all his male slaves, giving them their clothing, litter, peculium, horses, weapons, and 20 *pholleis* apiece.[204] His female slaves he bequeaths to his wife. She also had her own slaves, men and women, and she in turn freed them along with the slaves inherited from her husband.[205] Sister Mary mentions in her will that she had already freed all her slaves, which her husband had not done during his lifetime.[206] She indicates that upon her death her freedmen would receive clothes, litter, and peculium, which means that they did not receive them upon emancipation. In addition, she had arranged that for a year after her death, wheat and wine from her lands would be distributed to the freedmen. The inheritance set aside for her freedmen, which included small items, livestock, and clothing, proved to be greater than that which her husband bequeathed to his slaves. The fact that they are mentioned in the will long after they were all freed means that they remained in the same *oikos* after emancipation.

Unlike Boïlas, the Pakourianoi did not have children to perpetuate their relations with their freedmen. But the bond between the mistress and her freedmen is well attested in Sister Mary's will. This document also reveals the other relationships of the Pakourianoi with persons in their *oikos*, designated *anthrōpoi mou*, "my men" or "my people."[207] These relationships must be taken into account if we are to understand the place of freedmen in the Pakourianoi's milieu.

In his study of the structure of the aristocratic *oikos*, Paul Magdalino shows that this unit was composed not only of slaves but also of free men in the service of the master (his *anthrōpoi*).[208] This type of relationship, personal in nature (we might call it "man-to-man" if that term were not so fraught) indicates a social dependency reminiscent of the Roman institution of patronage. But unlike in that institution, the term *anthrōpoi* included all persons fulfilling functions in the service of their *authentēs* in or outside his *oikos*. According to the documents that mention them, in the tenth to eleventh centuries these were men bound to the powerful elite—to the Pakourianoi and the Diabatenoi, for example.[209] The case of Boïlas shows that these were not necessarily persons who lived in the *oikos* of their "master" (the appropriate translation for *authentēs*, a term that also designates one's own parents). Lemerle identifies Boïlas's *authentai*, whom Boïlas calls "my *kurioi*," as the Apokapēs family.[210] Were the slaves and freedmen in service within the same *oikos* included in this social relationship, which came into existence in Byzantine society in the tenth century?

In his will, Symbatios Pakourianos mentions each of his *anthrōpoi* individually: "[So-and-so], *anthrōpos mou*, receives . . ." Conversely, he groups all his male slaves together, emancipating them upon his death. His widow mentions in her will what she is bequeathing first to her relatives, then to each of her *anthrōpoi*, all male, and to each of her freedmen and -women, whom she designates as "*apodoulos/apodoulē mou.*"[211] After enumerating them individually, she then refers to them collectively as *anthrōpoi mou*, which her husband did not do. This term also includes the freedmen who remained in the mistress's service until her death, as she explicitly says: "All my *anthrōpoi*, great and small, free and slave, male and female." This phrase encompasses all those who were in her dependency and who remained so even after leaving her *oikos*, to enter a monastery, for example.[212] It is true that the term *anthrōpoi* does not refer to freed slaves in her husband's will, but that is because his slaves had not been freed at the time the document was drawn up but would be so only on the author's death. That is the difference between the two wills where the slaves were concerned.

The *anthrōpoi* of Sister Mary therefore included men and women, emancipated or free from birth. In the mid-eleventh century, Kekaumenos gave the following advice in his *Stratēgikon:* "You must have at your disposal enough resources for you: your family, slaves and free, who must ride on horseback with you and go into battle."[213] This is not just advice. The *Peira* cites a case in which slaves participated in a military mission of their master.[214] And Nicephorus Bryennios similarly describes Michael Mavrix's private militia, which counted "a host of slaves."[215]

Boïlas's freedmen, then, like those mentioned in the documents of Saint Elias of Carbone and of Lavra, remained in a relationship with the master, living near him on a plot of land that would become theirs upon his death.[216] At the same time, after emancipation, they could have an employer-employee relationship with him, as indicated in Boïlas's will. These were not *misthioi* in either case, because the master set up his freedmen near him or his family and without a work contract.[217]

After his emancipation, therefore, the slave was not left to his own fate. The two wills of the Pakourianoi point to the same situation. There, the freedmen remained in the *oikos* as part of the master's *anthrōpoi*. As such, they could pass into the service of the children. That was the case for Stephanos, the *anthrōpos* of Sister Mary, a personal servant she had received from her parents.[218]

Only the slaves Symbatios Pakourianos bequeathed to his wife continued to have dealings with her; his *anthrōpoi*—who according to his will were not slaves—did not. This shows that the *anthrōpoi* were in the exclusive service of an individual and his children. In Gregory Pakourianos's *typikon*, the author's subordinate, termed his *anthrōpos*, is mentioned in the same capacity as his loved ones.[219]

After Boïlas's death, the freedmen's relation of dependency continued with his daughters. Symbatios and Mary Pakourianoi, by contrast, not having had any children, had to terminate the service of their *anthrōpoi* in their wills. Such an act is mentioned in the hagiographical narratives as well. For example, Theodore, a military leader close to the emperor, draws up a will in the emperor's presence before going after the dragon that had abducted his mother; in it he specifies that his slaves will be emancipated.[220] Theodore also had no children.

But does not the fact that the slave remained under the protection of his master suggest a need on the slave's part? That is the situation recounted in the *Spiritually Beneficial Tales of Paul of Monembasia*, in which the slave steals his act of emancipation, refuses to work, but still remains in his mistress's house.[221] Contrary to what we might expect, the freedman does not leave the house once he has the document, since that *oikos* provides him with the material conditions for his existence. In tenth-century Peloponnesus (the setting from the *Spiritually Beneficial Tales of Paul of Monembasia* as well), a man who was discovered in an "open" place of the countryside was immediately considered a fugitive slave.[222] This indicates that freedmen remained in the homes of their former masters. In all the known cases, gifts of property were made only as bequests, not before the master's death. This kept the freedmen economically dependent on the master.

All the documents cited, which concerned the rural areas, show that it was the land that bound the freedman to his master. Here a difference arises between the country and the city. The two types of social relations—an employee in the service of his master versus the *anthrōpos* of someone—are known to us through documents from the rural areas and from Constantinople. But these were, in fact, two different social environments. Boïlas had his own *authentai*, with whom he disputed the possession of three villages. It was his *authentai*, not he, who had the same status as Pakourianos.[223] But Boïlas and the Pakourianoi also lived in different geographical locales. As we saw, Asia Minor was more traditional, so to speak, in the use of rural slaves. Boïlas, a native of Cappadocia, settled in eastern Asia Minor and used slaves on his estates. In contrast, the Pakouianoi, who lived in Constantinople, used both their slaves and "their men" at home and possessed villages in Macedonia.[224]

The *typikon* of Gregory Pakourianos shows that the dependents of such an individual could be his own direct subordinates in the army.[225] In the same manner, Symbatios Pakourianos and his father-in-law, Basilakios Diabatenos, held the position of *kouropalatos* and had their own subordinates. Michael Apokapēs, whom Lemerle identifies as Boïlas's *authentēs*, was dux of Edessa, and Boïlas probably served as his *protospatharios*. These were all *dunatoi*, who could acquire their *anthrōpoi* as a result of their social position as *authentēs*. But someone like Boïlas, however rich he might be, had only his slaves from whom to form his *anthrōpoi* and those of his heirs.

The Use of Freedmen by the State

I have already considered slaves in the imperial service and the high position they could attain, especially once they were freed. But in the case of freedmen, I focused primarily on the private domain. There was another category of freedmen, however, alongside the slaves who came into the possession of the imperial authorities.

These were, in the first place, prisoners of war, some of whom were exchanged. Traditionally, these prisoners were considered the property of the state. They could thus be sold, and the money turned over to the fisc, or they could be otherwise put to use, depending on public needs. Arab prisoners in the tenth century, for example, were emancipated and set up as taxpaying subjects in the border regions. Their loyalty was guaranteed by their conversion to Christianity and then their marriage to a woman born in the empire.

The state also received slaves as bequests. The wealthy widow Danielis, for example, is said to have bequeathed her vast demesnes, which included three thousand slaves, to the emperor. He chose to free the slaves and sent them to a border region, the thema of Longobardia.[226] Although that story may be legend and the number of slaves appears unlikely, what matters is the use the imperial authorities made of the slaves bequeathed to them and the mass emancipation of said slaves.

In the tenth century, the state preferred to use its slaves as freedmen and to set them up where it needed them, in border regions particularly. By virtue of being freed, these slaves were placed directly under public authority, with no need for an intermediary. In addition, they became subject to taxes or military service, which was also a fiscal obligation. The state thus drew a direct benefit from its emancipation of slaves. But the slaves were not the only ones so treated. The forced displacement of entire populations as a political strategy was common in Byzantium after the sixth century.[227] From that standpoint, emancipation by the state was simply the act that transformed potential subjects into actual ones.

But what was the relationship between the emancipation of slaves by the state and that by private landowners? Private emancipation too served to turn the slaves of individuals into their "people," whether they were set up on their own lands or put into service in their *oikoi*. In either case, the owner did not give them property until his death, thus preventing them from leaving.

Thus whether the master was the state or an individual, and whether the setting was the countryside or the city, the relation between the master and the emancipated slave was the same. The state made better use of slaves when it emancipated them. Private owners followed that example.

Emancipation as a Christian Act

Two saint's Lives recount the histories of well-known freedmen: Andrew the Fool and Elias the Younger. Andrew, who is deemed mentally ill, is sent by his master to the Church of Saint Anastasia in Constantinople to be cured. After three months, during which his condition did not improve, he is freed and can now display his mad behavior throughout the city.[228] Unlike the examples previously discussed, Andrew the Fool does not remain with his master: to live out his sainthood, he has to dwell apart from any social framework. That is why he is emancipated. Elias the Younger is also a freedman. His emancipation is rather unusual in that he leaves his master's house to travel to the Holy Land.[229] In both narratives, it is the hero's destiny as a saint that places him outside the freedman's usual context. That destiny is revealed to each of them in a dream.[230] On the path to sainthood, emancipation is an instrument and a phase rather than a goal. Unlike Andrew the Fool, who remains in Constantinople after his emancipation, Elias the Younger has to leave Africa to go to Jerusalem and never again sees the house where he was a slave or his former master. But these two cases, which belong to hagiography, remain exceptions, because the slaves, in order to realize their destiny as saints, must first break away from their masters' milieu.

There is further evidence about freedmen in the Lives of Matrona of Perge, Michael Maleinos, Elizabeth of Heraclea, Nilus of Rossano, Theophanes the Confessor, and Theodore Studites.[231] For example, Anastasia, a wealthy woman living in Constantinople who owns demesnes, frees her slaves before entering a monastery and gives them houses.[232] But in all these cases, slaves are mentioned only at the time of their emancipation, when their master or mistress, entering a new spiritual life, breaks off the relationship with them. They find themselves in the same situation as the slaves emancipated in wills.

I have demonstrated in this chapter that slave ownership was not limited to those placed at the highest echelons of society or to the wealthy. Traditionally, the scholarship has considered medieval slaves primarily as domestics, but I have shown that they figured in the artisanal and agricultural labor force and thus fulfilled the same functions as wage workers. Similarly, the presence of *paroikoi*—dependent Byzantine peasants—in the documents of the time, particularly from the ninth century on, does not mean that they replaced slaves as a new type of "unfree" persons. Their unfreedom, based on their fiscal status, was completely different from that of slaves. As for domestic functions, what is now called a "house" does not correspond to the medieval notion of the Byzantine *oikos* and its components. That unit was not limited to habitation but formed an economically autonomous family unit that also included dependents, both male and female. These subordinates of the master of the *oikos* were grouped under a new term, "my people," whose dependency, whether in an urban or rural environment, was economic. Slaves could also become the "people" of their master in being freed. After emancipation, they remained bound to their master by an economic dependency and continued to be part of the same *oikos*. That economic organization required slaves and created a social need for a slave market. It is now necessary to examine the idea of slavery in culture and in the mind-set of the civilization under study.

CHAPTER 4

Evolution of the Concept of Unfreedom

The Byzantine Church and the Idea of Slavery

Slavery in the Doctrine of the Church Fathers

"There is neither Jew nor Greek, there is neither bond nor free, there is neither male nor female: for ye are all one in Christ Jesus" (Gal. 3:28).[1] In taking as my starting point the idea of equality in Christ as expressed in the New Testament, I wish to show that the subject of slavery preoccupied the church fathers from the beginning of the Christian era. Peter Garnsey has discussed slavery with reference to Paul, Ambrose, and Augustine.[2] In addition, Jennifer Glancy has analyzed the image of the slave generally in Christian thought of the first and second centuries,[3] and Peter Gruszka has studied the attitude of the Cappadocian fathers toward the institution of slavery.[4] Beginning with Gruszka's work, I shall analyze the attitude toward slavery in daily life rather than the philosophical questions, then approach the more general question of spiritual slavery. Gruszka distinguishes the various components of fourth-century Cappadocian society: elites (aristocracy, clergy, dignitaries) and peasants, wage earners, and soldiers on the one hand, and slaves on the other.[5] In his view, what he calls "the question of slavery" constituted the principal problem of the era, both social and moral.[6] He examines the attitudes toward the institution of slavery expressed in the writings of Gregory of Nazianzus, Basil of Caesarea, and Gregory of Nyssa, comparing them to the view of John Chrysostom.

From Paul to the fourth-century Cappadocian fathers, Christian commentators took little interest in the institution of slavery.[7] There is nothing surprising about that since Paul paved the way for the notion that slavery was one social condition among others established by God, thus discouraging any debate on social equality.[8] The inequality in question was that between

131

free and slave, but also that between male and female, rich and poor, or any other inequality existing among Christians as a whole. In the Epistle to Philemon, Paul returns the fugitive slave Onesimus to his master (Philem. 10–17); in the Epistle to the Ephesians, the slave's duties to his master are compared to those of a child to his parents, and Paul urges the slave to "be obedient to them that are your masters according to the flesh, with fear and trembling, in singleness of your heart, as unto Christ" (Eph. 6:5).[9] Similarly, he enjoins masters to show consideration toward their slaves (Col. 4:1).

Gruszka shows clearly how the attitude, doctrinal as it were, toward slavery formed in the fourth century, conditioned by two factors: on the one hand, the social milieu of the church fathers and the questions that arose in their environment; and on the other, their individual reflections, their personalities. The first factor suggests why the subject of slavery was not treated earlier by the church fathers. In the second and third centuries, the most prominent theological centers were in Africa and Egypt; church fathers such as Clement, Tertullian, Cyprian, Origen, and others emerged from them. Palestine, Syria, and Cappadocia became important in the fourth century, and all remained a rich source of patristic literature until the sixth century. None of the other regions managed to become central, though major personalities originated there.

As it happens, Africa and certainly Egypt never seem to have experienced slavery on a large scale—as the hagiographical literature also shows for the late Roman era and up to the early eighth century, when the Byzantine Empire lost these provinces.[10] The social typology was very different in the eastern Mediterranean basin, in Syria, Palestine, and especially Asia Minor. Slavery was a strong presence in these regions and therefore attracted the attention of such writers as Gregory of Nazianzus, himself a slaveholder, and Basil of Caesarea, who dealt with particular problems concerning slaves and slave owners.[11] In other words, the institution of slavery received doctrinal attention in fourth-century Cappadocia not because it was the "problem of the era" but because the milieu called for it. Gruszka argues that slavery was becoming the problem of the era because it was the problem of the milieu. But slavery remained merely one problem among others, if that. *Pace* Gruszka, slavery was never problematic outside the church and was rarely so even within it. Nevertheless, the institution of slavery raised particular questions, fundamental or secondary, where the church was concerned. Since these questions appeared only in the works of the Cappadocian fathers, there is every reason to examine their specificity.

It is likely that some of the many slaves in this milieu were Christians.[12]

And the slave's relation to the church was not in the hands of the master alone. It is clear that the decision to be baptized lay within the slave's freedom of choice. Hence the relation between the slave and the master also became the church's affair, or more precisely, that of the local bishop, who protected the slaves in his diocese. Gruszka cites a case in which Basil of Caesarea intervened to protect the Christian slaves of a certain Kalisthenes.[13]

But the church also protected the master. The anathema of the third canon of the Council of Gangra (343), for example, was directed against those who urged slaves to leave their masters.[14] Things became even more complicated if a slave wanted to join the clergy. Even before the law of asylum, established by Justinian legislation, went into effect,[15] there were known cases of slaves who were ordained and who even became bishops without their owners' agreement. Consider the famous case of Simplicia's slave, reported by Basil of Caesarea and Gregory of Nazianzus. A rich woman, Simplicia, asked that her slave's ordination be rendered null and void. She threatened to initiate legal proceedings against Basil of Caesarea and sent her slaves to intimidate him.[16] In this instance, the ordination had taken place without anyone knowing that the future bishop was a slave. Moreover, Gregory of Nazianzus claimed that had he been informed beforehand, the ordination would not have taken place without the owner's consent.[17] But that was the whole problem: how could he have known? In any event, the ordination of the person in question was respected, and he also retained his slave status. But his two statuses were in conflict where authority, responsibility, submission, and the law were concerned.

In an article devoted to the problem of the slave's ordination in Byzantium, Stavros Perentidis attempts to show that a slave could not be ordained because the very sacrament of ordination freed the slave.[18] It seems to me that such a hypothesis cannot be accepted for the era concerned: no entity but the state could delegate the capacity to free the slave by sacrament, and there is no source available indicating it did so.[19]

Gregory of Nazianzus places the emphasis more particularly on the personal aspect, which Gruszka calls the "spiritual" aspect. Gregory considers the case of slaves working on his patrimonial demesnes, who were members of a *familia rustica*. He wrote that slaves had to be respected as human beings.[20] He was not alone. In fact, the idea that everyone had a specific social role to fulfill within a totality harkened back to Paul. As a slave owner, however, Gregory of Nazianzus took a more personal position, and he demonstrated that position by freeing his slaves in his will.[21] But any humanitarian interpretation of his attitude needs to be qualified, since he did not go so far as to free all his slaves before his death and because the wishes expressed in his will may have been determined by the absence of any direct heirs on his part.[22] But was the emancipation of one's slaves always perceived as a devout act? The Lives of saints provide evidence in response to that question.

Emancipation and Ownership

The act of emancipation must be examined from two sides, the slave's and the master's. The slave becomes a free person, whereas the master gives up his property. In hagiographical narratives, the act of emancipation was often part of the saint's renunciation of all earthly goods.[23]

The decision to give up one's possessions was not new. In the hagiographical literature of the late period of the Roman Empire, it occurred repeatedly as an act of piety. In general, the hagiographical narratives made such a gesture on the part of the wealthy a preliminary step to the path of sainthood. Thus, in the *Life of Melania the Younger* and the *Life of Symeon the Fool*, the two heroes have to give up their wealth to begin their spiritual lives.[24] The problem of ownership was resolved either by bequeathing the property to a loved one or by selling it and distributing the money to the poor. Slaves were property and as such met the same fate as material goods, receiving no special treatment; they were either left to the devout person's family or sold with the fields and belongings. There are two distinct ideas here. One is that ownership binds the person to material life while preventing spiritual development, the other that charity is expressed as the distribution of money: property was thus converted into money for the poor. We might find it surprising that Melania the Younger wants to sell her slaves to give money to the poor, precisely because we might have expected her to free them as an act of charity. But in the fifth century, that phenomenon was not widespread. At the time, it was ownership that was harmful, not slavery.[25]

A different perspective is evident in the *Life of Matrona of Perge*. Athanasia, a well-off woman from Constantinople, "attends to her slaves before entering a monastery."[26] She frees some of them, giving them houses and lands so that they can earn a living, and finds a place in a monastery for others. Being a good mistress and freeing one's slaves by giving them the wherewithal to earn their living is thus attested already for the fifth and sixth centuries. But a geographical difference is at issue: the *Life of Melania the Younger*, the *Life of Marcellus Acemetes*, and the *Life of Symeon the Fool* come from Palestine, Syria, and Cyprus, respectively, whereas the *Life of Matrona of Perge* and the other narratives that mention emancipation were composed in Constantinople and Asia Minor.[27] It is interesting to note the difference between the *Life of Melania the Younger* in its Greek and Latin versions, in which she wants to sell her slaves, and the version of Palladius, in which she frees her eight thousand slaves.[28] In Palladius's version Melania wants to free all her slaves. But apart from the eight thousand she emancipates, her slaves refuse, and she sells them all to her brother for three *nomismata*. On this point, Palladius's account converges with the Greek and Latin versions, in which the slaves who do not want to be sold are persuaded by Melania's brother-in-law to proclaim that they do not belong to her. Here again, the author came from Asia Minor, in this case Bithynia.[29]

Christian formulas of emancipation, such as "it is the will of God that all men be free. . . . God created all men free and it was war that made them slaves," were not found everywhere.[30] The idea that there were originally no slaves was expressed by John Chrysostom: God, in creating man, made him not a slave but free; sin, war, and greed made man a slave.[31] The same attitude is found in the writings of Ambrose and Augustine. In trying to explain why there are slaves, both conclude that slavery is not a condition of "nature" but the consequence of foolishness (Ambrose) or human sin (Augustine).[32] Contrary to Aristotle, they use the term *natura* to signify not the optimal order of the world created by humans and for humankind but rather the laws created by God.[33] In other words, the institution of slavery is a consequence of human behavior. Slavery is not an essential part of man's existence but a punishment for his sins. Hence it is conceived not as a misfortune befalling human beings but as just and divine punishment. It is clear that such a definition does not call slavery into question. I believe, moreover, that it coincides perfectly with the definition of slavery in the law of the sixth-century state, especially that proposed in the *Digesta:* by natural law all men are free, it is wars that make them slaves.[34] But the state and the church define "natural law" differently: one proposes that war, a human act, is the origin or cause of the institution of slavery, whereas the other proposes it is sin, also a human act. John Chrysostom, linking the two, declares that war is a sin.[35]

The Place of Slavery in the Christian "Order of the World"

Given these views, it is not surprising that slavery was not perceived as a harmful phenomenon. That tallies with the fact that bishops and monasteries owned slaves during the entire period. In addition, ecclesiastical sources emphasize the master's responsibility toward his slaves, which also accords with the church's attitude toward the "prostitution" of slaves.[36] The *Nomocanon 14 titulorum* (Canon law of fourteen titles) speaks of people who prostituted female slaves or reduced freedwomen to slavery. The canon prohibited the practice and stipulated penalties in case of violation.[37] But the prostitution of slaves, both male and female, continued.

A canon attributed to the patriarch Nicephorus, though probably of later date, adds that a master who prostitutes his *doulē* or *doulos* must marry off the slave or risk excommunication.[38] Masters thus had a moral responsibility for their slaves. The relationship was similar to that between a parent and a child. It is clear that this attitude was consistent with the social order and not revolutionary. In sources prior to the tenth century, then, slaves and masters fulfilled social roles established by God, a point of view found in the hagiographical sources. Symeon the Fool, for example, explains to a master why one must not beat one's "companions in slavery" *(sundouloi).*[39] At the same time, Theodore of Sykeon, intent on preserving the social order, exhorts slaves to fulfill their duties toward their masters.[40] As the author of the *Life of Mary the Younger* writes: "We use slaves like our own hands and legs, and we accomplish things by using them."[41] In fact, the cleavage apparent in that type of source does not correspond to the cleavage between slave and free, but that between slave and master. That cleavage differs from the one I have primarily focused on thus far. Why did the other cleavage, that between slave and free, not attract the attention of authors who formulated Christian doctrine in their writings?

Let me set aside the slave for a moment and consider what type of cleavages interested ecclesiastical writers—church fathers and hagiographers—in their works. There were two: the first distinguished between Christians and non-Christians, the second between Christians and God. Both cleavages occupy a place in the world constructed by Augustine: the *Civitas Dei* excludes all non-Christians (the damned) and places only faithful Christians in a relationship with God.

The church fathers addressed the cleavage between Christians and non-Christians in all the philosophical and theological controversies from early Christianity on, attempting to establish a clear delimitation between the two groups, initially with respect to pagans and Jews and then in relation to all the heresies that emerged in the third to sixth centuries. It is obvious that God was also at the heart of all these debates, where the nature of Christ was a fundamental issue. It was the definition of God that divided the world between "true Christians" (the orthodox) and others. The two aspects of that cleavage, that having to do with infidels and that concerning heretics, continued to exist in Byzantium throughout its history. For the most part, however, it attracted the attention of ecclesiastical authors between the second and sixth centuries. It was during that period that the definition of the cleavage was established, for at that time the empire lost its troublesome Monophysite regions.

If every slave in the Byzantine world had been non-Christian and every free person Christian, the cleavage between Christians and non-Christians would have corresponded to that between free and slave. Christianity, however, was by definition a religion open to all, including slaves. The fourth- to fifth-century church fathers thus preferred to develop the idea of slavery as a punishment for human beings' misdeeds.

In addition, since the determining factor for dividing Christians from non-Christians, or the orthodox from non-Christians, was the definition of God, the cleavage was theological. And that cleavage had little to do with the idea of slavery or the life of the slave. That was not the case for the second type of cleavage that concerned Christian authors: that between believers and God. As a matter of fact, it would be inaccurate to speak of a cleavage. In the world of Christians, it was in relation to God that all believers defined themselves and in relation to him that they had duties to perform (though of course saints, angels, and other spiritual elements were also part of that world). And the term *theos* was not the only one that designated God: there was also the expression *o kurios*, with the article *o* always included. In modern languages, it is translated as "the Lord"—literally, "the master"—parallel to the Hebrew term *Adonai*, which is derived from the word *Adon*, "master."[42] In Greek as well, the same word, *kurios*, designates both master and God. The Latin word *dominus* corresponds to the two Greek words *kurios* and *despotēs*, and also designates both God or a master, generally an owner. God is *"o kurios"* because he is the master of the entire world, and human beings owe him total obedience. The idea of moral slavery followed as a result.

In a chapter titled "Slavery as Metaphor," Garnsey shows that this idea preoccupied the church fathers. In trying to construct a unified schema of the different writings, he concludes his analysis with the model of Augustine: we are all slaves of God, the master of the *oikos* ("the household master"). Nevertheless, there are good slaves (good Christians) and bad slaves (bad Christians or unbelievers). Good slaves are superior to bad because their slavery is moral, their obedience morally grounded.[43] The idea of moral slavery does not entail differences between the slave and the free person, since both must perform the task that God conferred on them. What creates the face-to-face relation between God and believers is obedience. And obedience is an act or a position with social consequences.[44]

Let me leave aside for the moment the question of who the slave owed obedience to in the first place: his earthly master or his heavenly master. Such a conflict could not come about in the era of the church fathers since, in their view, slaves' social duties were also their duties toward God. That conflict would occur later, in the tenth and eleventh centuries. The key point is that it was obedience that defined believers in relation to *o kurios*—God. In the earthly parallel, slaves owed their obedience not to free persons in general but to their own masters. Hence the cleavage best corresponding to the Christian mentality that formed in the second to fourth centuries was the one between slave and master. Of course, Christianity did not invent religious obedience. Nevertheless, having adopted a monotheistic model, Christianity proposed a religious concept according to which everyone had a single heavenly master, the same for all. That model resembled the earthly relationship between a slave and his master, since, under Roman law, a slave could have only one master.[45] That parallelism explains the use of the words *kurios* and *doulos,* which, in the religious context of the empire, had previously been used only for the Jewish religion. It was the Septuagint that introduced the word *kurios* for God, translating the Hebrew tetragrammaton in the Old Testament that represents the "sacred name of God."[46]

The Christian religion introduced a perspective that saw the slave not in relation to the free person but in relation to his master, that is, not within a civil but within a social dimension.[47] In addition, the duty to properly fulfill one's social role applied to both the master and the slave. The master had to be lenient and not cruel toward his slaves. What happened when the slave was Christian and the master was not? Such a conflict was subject to regulation by imperial legislation as early as the fourth century.[48] The slave as individual, however, did not attract the attentions of writers of that period. But were the slaves at issue always Christian? It was within the context of the new notion of unfreedom in the medieval geopolitical space that the question of the slave's religion arose.

The Christian Identity of the Byzantine Slave

The Christian Slave and Baptism

I have shown that the Christian religion did not particularly encourage the emancipation of slaves. In fact, in hagiographical narratives prior to the ninth century, the act of emancipation is not recounted from the point of view of the freedman but from that of the master. The identification of church and state introduced a new perspective in the civil arena, one that gave Christians the advantage over non-Christians. Slaves could become free through manumission in a church, a form of emancipation added in the fourth century to those stipulated in Roman law, namely, wills and declarations before five witnesses.[49] *Manumissio in ecclesia* in its fifth-century version was an act granted by the master but performed in a church by the bishop or, in later formulations, by a priest.[50]

It is clear that *manumissio in ecclesia* was used primarily by Christian masters and that they wanted their slaves to be Christian as well—otherwise, why do it in a church? But did that act have religious consequences for the slave? The formulas used do not mention whether the slave became Christian. Fabrizio Fabbrini believes that the act was preceded or followed by the slave's baptism.[51] That seems logical, but there is no evidence of mandatory baptism.[52] I believe, however, that neither the laws nor the formulas mention the act of baptism because the slave may have been a Christian before the emancipation took place. That accords with the evidence from late antiquity regarding Christian masters who owned Christian slaves. Within the context of the assimilation of church and state, the law establishing *manumissio in ecclesia*—the first version of which, now lost, dates to 313–316—made the office of bishop a state position, just as it gave religious buildings an administrative function. Along the same lines, *Novella* 142 of Justinian gave bishops and magistrates the power to free a castrated slave without his master's permission.[53] Similarly, a law of Theodosius II, adopted and elaborated by Leo I, granted free status to the slave prostituted by her master if she appeared before a magistrate or bishop.[54] Bishops were thus considered representatives of public authority. The slave's religion is not mentioned in the laws that speak of *manumissio in ecclesia* and remained a matter unrelated to emancipation. That changed in the eighth century with the legislation of the so-called Isaurian emperors.

The *Ekloga* introduced a new form of emancipation, whereby the master or a person from his family "received the slave after baptism by immersion."[55] I call that act "emancipation by baptism," which, unlike *manumissio in ecclesia*, is specifically designated for cases in which the master was Christian and the slave non-Christian. Whereas the *Ekloga* includes *manumissio in ecclesia* in the clause dealing with the other means of emancipation—in public or before five witnesses, in a will or signed document—it mentions emancipation by baptism, which has no legislative precedents, separately.[56] In addition, the *Prochiros Nomos* (between 870 and 879) shows that this act created a kinship between master and freedman, which translated into a ban on marriage between the two parties participating in the baptism.[57] That new possibility of emancipation can be explained historically by the wars of the seventh and eighth centuries. Through that measure, the state opened an avenue by which non-Christian captives could become integrated into Byzantine society in both the private and public sector.[58]

The equivalence posited between the stranger, the enemy, the potential slave, and the non-Christian, which became widespread in the sixth century, was no longer valid after the ninth century, an era when Byzantium took Slavic captives who were sometimes Christians. Several hagiographical works depict slaves for whom no act of baptism, initiated either by the master or, secretly, by the slave, is mentioned. These slaves were often members of the community of believers. But it is difficult to know whether they became Christian before being reduced to slavery or after.[59] Thaddaeus, for example, who was originally pagan, was already baptized when he became a slave,[60] whereas the author of the *Life of Andrew the Fool* does not mention his Christian origin, considering it self-evident.[61]

The story of the slave child in the *Spiritually Beneficial Tales of Paul of Monembasia* (second half of the tenth century) illustrates that, at the time it was written, slaves were assumed to be Christian. That child "of Scythian origin" received communion at the age of twelve with all the other children because his master had no doubt that he was originally Christian.[62] The child himself knew very well that he had not been baptized, but that did not prevent him from acting like a Christian. When the master discovered the truth, he hastened to have the child baptized by the priest, an act that did not bring about his emancipation, however.[63] The master did not doubt his foreign-born slave's Christian identity, which confirms, it seems to me, that hagiographers of the time were depicting slaves who were Christians, or at least, if they were not so, who behaved as if they were.[64] The slave, who was a practicing Christian, must have been aware of the importance of baptism, but in this case the initiative for baptizing him fell to his master.

Quasi-Marital Unions and Christian Marriage

Another important aspect of the slave's Christian identity was domestic life as a couple. According to the definitions of classical Roman law, a marriage (Latin *matrimonium*, Greek *gamos*) was a contract between two free persons that set the conditions of their married life in the aim of procreation. By that definition, slaves could not be married because they had no legal personality. Such a contract would have had no meaning, since they did not have property of their own; that is, they could have nothing in their potestas because they had no potestas. In addition, the child of a slave mother belonged solely to the mother's master, and the mother had no potestas of her own.[65] Hence under Roman law things were very clear. The two definitions of potestas, both the right to own and the right to have a legal personality, were consistent in positing the slave's civil status in negative terms.

Matters relating to marriage began to change in the late Roman era. Until recently, the general opinion has been that the Christianization of the Roman Empire and the new ideology of marriage it introduced caused that shift. The works of Joëlle Beaucamp and Judith Evans Grubbs make clear, however, that these changes had non-Christian roots in the imperial ideology of the late era of the Roman Empire.[66] In any event, the domestic unions of slaves were still not governed by laws pertaining to marriage. I would argue that legal definitions were the cause of that situation. Grubbs's book is very instructive on the subject, since it describes all the possibilities of quasi-marital unions between persons of different status: a free woman with her own slave, with the slave of another or of the emperor, with her own freedman or someone else's, and a free man with a slave or a freedwoman.[67] The author shows clearly that in the fourth century these relationships attracted the attention of legislators, who tried to put an end to "mixed unions" of this kind. But these were actually "liaisons," that is, cohabitation, and solely "mixed liaisons" with the problems they raised. The only law that truly concerned marriage was the one that resolved the problem of a marriage between a free person and a person who had presented himself as free but was in fact a slave. In that case, problems arose relating to the status of the children and of the dowry. In any event, this type of marriage, not being legitimate, was immediately dissolved.

The subject of sexual relations and illegitimate marriage between slaves and free persons (most often between masters and their female slaves) preoccupied legislators a great deal throughout that period, which proves that this type of union was quite common, if not very well regarded. None of the cases considered was a Christian union.[68]

But what about Christian marriage *(gamos)* between two slaves? According to the 1095 *Novella* of Alexius Comnenus, a master preferred to have his slaves marry in a non-Christian ceremony because Christian marriage could have led to the slaves' emancipation. The *Novella* banned the practice, assuring the master that the slave he allowed to marry would remain his property.[69] It does not explain why such an act might have led to emancipation. The first supposition is that slaves were emancipated by baptism, a necessary preliminary to Christian marriage. But as I have shown, there was not necessarily a causal relation between the baptism of slaves and *manumissio in ecclesia,* and in any case, according to the *Ekloga,* emancipation by baptism required the master's consent.[70] The *Novella* explains that, since slaves and masters experience the same baptism, they must also have the same type of marriage.[71] It is therefore clear that in the eleventh century, the legislator assumed that all slaves were baptized and that this act did not lead to their emancipation. Note that the *Nomocanon 14 titulorum* prohibited slave couples joined outside the church from taking communion.[72]

In the *Life of Basil the Younger,* one of the main characters is Theodora, a slave woman in the house of Primikarios, where Basil is taken in. She is placed in the service of the saint.[73] In the fantastic account of Theodora's journey to the hereafter, she is accused by attacking demons of having led a life of fornication. But the angels who accompany her explain to the demons that she lived with a man outside Christian marriage and gave him children because, being a slave, she could not marry him.[74] It is their master who joined them. It is clear in this narrative that Theodora represents not only a good Christian but also a person who has led a very elevated spiritual life. But if slaves were already baptized, why deprive them of Christian marriage?

The *Peira* presents a legal complaint made by freedmen against their former master to impel him to emancipate members of their family who were still slaves.[75] The jurist explains why the judge could not accept that complaint. There is no mention of whether this was a Christian marriage. But the example shows that, in the eleventh century, masters encountered problems when selling members of a family of slaves, because the masters could not separate married slaves or have their unions dissolved. A Christian marriage would have made such a dissolution impossible. In addition, in the same clause, the *Peira* determined that when a family of slaves was divided between two owners, the master who owned the majority could claim the rest.[76] This, it seems, explains why masters did not encourage Christian marriages between their slaves.

That tendency can be detected earlier, in the legislation of Leo VI, who wanted to resolve the problem of slave couples joined in any union whatsoever when one was then emancipated while the other remained a slave.[77] It is not surprising that legislation encouraged their union. But in this case, it was primarily contingent on the master's wish to leave them in the same status. *Novella* 100 of Leo VI deals with the marriage of two persons who do not have the same civil status, especially a union between a slave and a free person.[78] It is therefore clear that unions between slaves began to occur within the framework of a legal institution. Note that, in the legislation of Leo VI as in that of Irene, the term *gamos* is used when the union includes at least one free person.[79] Hence, before the tenth century, there was no *gamos* between two slaves. In addition, according to the *Novella* of Alexius Comnenus, Christian marriages *(gamos)* between slaves existed well before the *Novella* was composed in 1095. That *Novella* banned any other form of union between slaves, imposing Christian marriage as the only legitimate conjugal union and thus completing the institutional framework for the marital lives of slaves in keeping with the process begun by Leo VI.

The question arises whether the *Novella* of Alexius Comnenus was the expression of an imperial policy that favored the church at the expense of private owners. It is true that the second part of the *Novella*, whose content is identical to the first, is addressed to the archbishop of Thessalonica, Theodoulos. But the *Novella*—and the marriage of slaves is not its only subject—speaks as well, even primarily, of Bulgar slaves, and is therefore addressed to Theodoulos because his region was the most affected by it, or perhaps because Theodoulos had initiated it. In fact, as Köpstein remarks, the *Novella* in no way changed the legal status of married slaves, since it clearly stated that Christian marriage was no argument in favor of emancipation.[80]

Unlike the classic institution of Roman marriage, Christian marriage had the particularity of being indissoluble except under special circumstances. It is clear from the *Novella* of Alexis Comnenus that masters presided over marriage unions between their own slaves.[81] How could a master hold onto a slave who was bound in an indissoluble marriage to someone else's slave, especially if cases like the one described in the *Peira* could lead to legal action being taken against the master?[82] It would have been preferable to avoid Christian marriage completely. The *Novella* of 1095 obliged masters to consent to the Christian unions of their slaves: slaves to whom Christian marriage was not granted would be freed.[83]

Thanks to imperial legislation, then, neither baptism nor Christian marriage was a threat to the master-slave relationship. The law of asylum seems to have constituted the only means the slave had to overcome the difficulties that his master imposed on his personal life.

The Law of Asylum: Evolution, Practice, and Rationale

A conflict between the interests of the church and those of private owners erupted when the slave wanted to leave the *oikos* altogether and become a member of the clergy. Unlike baptism, such a course of action would have been difficult to carry out in secret, because the law of the empire would have automatically considered the slave a runaway. It was Justinian's law of asylum that granted the church permission to accept such a slave. The indications relating to slaves were only part of the institution of asylum, which comprised several laws dating back to the late fourth century.[84] The law of asylum also made provisions for the protection of other people who sought to evade obligations, whether penal (criminals, convicts), fiscal, or social (curials, procurators, coloni, and so forth).[85]

Canon 7 of the Council of Sardica (346–347) advised bishops to intervene in favor of the unfortunate, those who had suffered unjust violence, widows, orphans, those subject to deportation, and those under the weight of a legal judgment.[86] Slaves were not mentioned. Theodore Balsamon's commentary on canons 8 and 16 of the Council of Carthage (401) interprets them as a complaint from the church to which Justinian replied with the promulgation of the law of asylum.[87] But these two canons speak only of *manumissio in ecclesia,* which Balsamon interprets as the law of asylum.[88] In fact, the Council of Chalcedon (451) stated that asylum would not be granted to fugitive slaves; according to its fourth canon, the slave who entered a monastery without his master's consent would be sent back.[89] All of which proves, it seems, that the initiative behind the law of asylum was not the church but the public authorities.

Before the sixth century, slaves' capacity to pursue the monastic life was contingent on their masters' consent. That condition changed with the legislation of Justinian. Two *Novellae* are at issue: the first dealt with a slave who fled his master to become a monk;[90] the second with a slave who wanted to become a cleric.[91] In both cases, the church obtained permission to accept them, provided they had not committed any crime apart from flight.[92] Masters could reclaim them within a year in the case of slaves who had become clerics, and within the first three years for slaves who had become monks, if the masters proved that the refugees had harmed them. In both cases, the statute of limitations was comparatively short.[93]

The church was in this case perceived as an autonomous entity that offered a refuge outside the delimitations defined by the law. That refuge, however, remained temporary in that the status of the person in question changed only within the asylum, in this case to prevent the church from being used as a "way station toward emancipation."

The law of asylum as it was promulgated under Justinian offered the slave the opportunity to join the religious life as a member of the clergy, and gave the church the power to end his condition of slavery. Although emancipation was indispensable for the ordination of slaves, the same was not true for monks. The higoumene could not free slaves who had fled and taken refuge in his monastery. He could only "liberate [them] by abduction" *(anarpazesthōsan eis eleutherian)*, which shows that their civil status did not change outside the monastery.[94]

In the case of a slave who became a member of the clergy, the law granted the church the legal power to free him.[95] But if the emancipation of a slave consecrated as a bishop, for example, was valid only inside the church, why would the church move forward with that act? The answer is found in the aforementioned case of the slave of Simplicia who was ordained a bishop without his owner's consent. That slave was not emancipated, both because the case occurred prior to the law of asylum and because his status as a slave was unknown. But despite Simplicia's fierce opposition, the ordination could not be rendered void. Moreover, as a bishop, the slave was responsible for his bishopric's possessions. That role also entailed legal responsibilities and legal representation outside the church—two things for which the bishop had to have free status. Finally, his status as a slave would have raised the problem of legitimacy, since the bishopric's possessions were being managed by a person who was not legally master of himself.[96] Probably for that reason, Justinian granted the slave who had been ordained not only free status but also the status of a freeborn *(eugenēs, ingenuus)*. In case of a conflict between the former master and the church, the freedman would be completely independent. All the same, if the freedman should happen to leave his position, he would once again become, as in the case of the monk, the slave of his former master. Hence the status of freeborn was acknowledged to be reversible.

In addition to giving slaves the power to conduct a spiritual Christian life without their masters' consent, the law of asylum protected them from possible abuses by their masters. For example, in the *Life of Hypatios* and the *Life of Theodore of Sykeon,* fugitive slaves were acquired by the monastery.[97] The law of asylum did not require as a preliminary condition that the slave be Christian; it thereby had the effect of encouraging the flight to monasteries of both Christian and non-Christian slaves. As a result, it constituted a threat to slave owners.

As for the slave who had committed a crime, originally that law did not grant him asylum—as it explicitly stated.[98] Nevertheless, by a synodal decision of 1050, even a slave sentenced to death could be accepted into the church.[99] This decision affirmed that he would remain a slave and would now belong to the church.[100] Bishops and other members of the clergy were prohibited, however, from selling him outside the church. All the same, the sale of a slave inside the church, by one "individual owner" to another, was authorized. At issue here was the protection the law of asylum gave to murderers. In prohibiting the sale of the slave outside the church, the church protected him by virtue of its ecclesiastical legal autonomy. Nevertheless, the slave kept his civil status and his social position as a slave. It is not known, however, how the state judged that decision. Constantine VII established asylum for any murderer.[101] An interesting case describing asylum for murderers in the eleventh century is recounted by Nicetas Stethatos in the *Life of Symeon the New Theologian.* A "Western" bishop unintentionally kills a child. As "penance," he weighs himself down with chains and presents himself at the monastery of Saint Symeon, where he goes on to serve the other monks with a great deal of humility.[102] Although this is a bishop who killed unintentionally, the case attests to the type of refuge offered by the church.[103] In any event, the law of asylum concerned only persons who found themselves outside the authority of the church. The church, however, also owned slaves.

Indeed, in addition to fulfilling its spiritual role, the church was one of the largest—if not the largest—landowners throughout the era under study. But what we understand by the term "church" was composed of different autonomous entities, such as monasteries and bishoprics. (All the same, the notion of "the church" in general existed in legislation.) When the *Novellae* of Justinian dealt with the land owned by the monasteries, what was at issue was the "private" property of each monastery or bishopric. That property consisted not only of immovables *(akinēta)* but also of movables *(kinēta)* and of livestock and rural slaves *(autokinēta)*, which the *Novellae* prohibited monasteries from alienating.[104]

In using the term "private" in opposition to "public," I need to clarify that in the late Roman Empire that term did not have its current sense. Take, for example, the state lands given to the church. These were public lands, but the church received them in a private capacity. That is, they belonged privately to a bishopric or monastery, but they retained a public character because the bishop or the higoumene held them only by *possessio* and not by *dominium*. That is, he could not transmit the property.[105] The *Novellae* of Justinian also prohibited alienating rural slaves living on the demesnes of monasteries.[106] These were slaves given with the land.

It is not surprising that slaves were the private property of bishops, inherited by their families, purchased, or received as gifts. I have shown that the church, throughout the era concerned, did not establish any general rule opposing slave ownership.[107] Several cases can be cited, including the synodal decree of the Armenian church at the Council of Dvin (527), which prohibited priests—for moral reasons—from purchasing female slaves, thus attesting to the use of slaves not only by bishops but also by priests.[108] The bishops' slaves *(pueri languentes)* who participated in the Council of Ephesus in 431 provide another example.[109] In addition, there were freed slaves who became the heads of ecclesiastical dioceses, as indicated in the will of Gregory of Nazianzus.[110]

The slaves of wealthy devout persons who chose the monastic life constitute another case. Their owners had the following options: leave the slaves and their other possessions to their family; sell the slaves and distribute the money to the poor; free their slaves; or take their slaves along to the monastery.

In the first two options, the slaves were considered movable property, whereas in the third, they were viewed as human beings. The fourth possibility—take them to the monastery—is attested especially in the hagiographical narratives but also in archival documents. These sources do not tell us, however, whether the slaves were introduced into the monastery as slaves or as free persons.

This question is important for understanding their status in the monastery. When a rich woman brought her slaves with her to the monastery, for example, did they answer to her or were they her equals?[111] There is no indication in the sources that they were emancipated beforehand, though that possibility appears the most logical. Hagiographers had little interest in these aspects. In fact, the act of bringing one's slave into the monastery was considered part of the master's or mistress's responsibility for the slave's spiritual life and not as the manifestation of a position on slavery. In the *Life of Tribunus*, related by John of Ephesus (second half of the sixth century), the saint enters a monastery and keeps his slaves. They continue to serve him, and he sends them on Christian missions.[112] Another revealing case is the papyrus *P. Köln* 3.157, in which the monk Viktor frees his slave. That case proves that there was no contradiction between being a monk and being a slave owner.[113]

These references complement the sources that mention monasteries as owners of slaves. In the early ninth century, the reform of Theodore Studites sought to put an end to the phenomenon. In his writings and in his will, he mentions several times the presence of slaves in the monasteries. He set an example by freeing his own slaves before entering monastic life, claiming that their use in monasteries was not desirable and was even prohibited.[114] After that, saints who entered a monastery no longer took their slaves with them.[115] The documents that have come down to us from the archives of Athos and Patmos do not make explicit mention of slaves, though some seem to suggest their presence. Hence a document of Lavra dating from 1030 singles out a monk who entered that monastery, bringing with him his three "subordinates" *(upourgoi)*.[116] Another document of 1065 specifies that Lavra received *kinēta* and *autokinēta*, which the editors understand simply as livestock.[117] Still another, of 1089, mentions a person who wanted to bring three of his beardless *oiketai* (children or eunuchs?) with him to the monastery.[118] And despite the reform of Theodore Studites, slaves continued to be present on church properties, and the law of asylum was instrumental in perpetuating that situation.

Asylum gave the church exclusive permission not only to offer refuge but also to take in men who otherwise could not have legally left their duties behind. Patlagean shows that the term "asylum" defined a space corresponding to the land area of each religious establishment.[119] In that way, "the boundaries of the asylum were in practice indistinguishable from those of the demesne" and "imperial decisions thereby set up conditions favorable for the growth of the monastery," both in terms of land area and in the number of men.[120]

The nature of the asylum was thus determined by its limits. The state granted permission to every Christian establishment to offer the slaves who found refuge there a new local status, which the state recognized. In other words, the imperial authorities considered the institution of the church an autonomous structure as well as a structure that could be defined as civil, in the sense that the status of the possessions and persons held inside, which were recognized by the public authorities, differed from their status outside the ecclesiastical institutions. This applied not only to civil status, as was the case for slaves or convicts, but also to the fiscal and social statuses of coloni or curials. Note that married women and men had to have their spouse's permission to enter a monastery in the sixth century, as also in the tenth century.[121] In the ninth or tenth century, Athanasia of Aegina first had to persuade her husband to allow her to enter a monastery, just as Melania the Younger had had to do in the fifth.

But did asylum truly change the status of the person who sought refuge there? Slaves could become monks, but asylum obliged them to remain bound to the establishment. Nor could coloni and curials leave the asylum. In other words, though their position may have changed, their situation was still restrictive, because they now became dependent on the establishment offering them asylum. It may have been for that reason that hagiographical narratives and private and public documents remain silent on the civil status of slaves once they arrived at a monastery. That status had no importance inside the monastery, where other relations of subordination existed. In fact, the other monks also could not leave the monastery without the higoumene's permission.[122] Consider, by way of example, Athanasia, who is accompanied everywhere by seven eunuchs and three women who serve her. These three remain with her when she enters the monastery of Matrona of Perge.[123] During the same period, John of Ephesus related that Thomas the Armenian built two monasteries, one for him, his sons, his male slaves, and the persons "bound to him," the other for his wife and the women who were with her.[124] In his *Epitaphium Sanctae Paulae*, Jerome speaks of the social organization inside the monastery that Paula founded for women (she founded another for men): "The many virgins she had gathered from various provinces, both *nobiles* and of ordinary or humble origins, were divided, courtesy of her, into three branches or monasteries; separated only for work and meals, they came together again for psalmodies and prayers."[125] In addition, Jerome relates that "a *nobilis* was not allowed to have a woman from her house as a companion, for fear that, in memory of the actions of the past and of a spirited childhood, she did not awaken her earlier wildness and refresh her memory of it through frequent chatter."[126] It is therefore clear that the women who followed their mistresses to a monastery kept their social status, because they continued to serve their mistress or, in the case of Paula's monastery, other mistresses.[127]

In the *Spiritually Beneficial Tales of Paul of Monembasia,* a monk purchases a

child and rears him, bringing him into his monastery. When the child is abducted by Arab pirates and sold in Africa, the higoumene tells the monk that
he should bring the child back because he is the child's *kurios*.[128] I do not
mean to suggest that the child became the slave of the monk who purchased
him, though that was possible according to the law of the empire. I mean
that the child had become his purchaser's subordinate, and when the monk
lost him, he sought as much to save him as to recover his purchase.[129] These
cases complement references to monks with personal servants inside the
monastery.[130]

The state thus allowed one social relation of unfreedom to come to an end
while allowing another to be created. In the case of slaves, it also had to permit a change in civil status, but always within a fixed framework where civil
status had no meaning. It could permit such a change because the state's own
power remained unaffected. Conversely, the change had major consequences
for private owners.

The state, in promulgating the law of asylum, allowed the church to enter
into a rivalry for slaves with their private owners. It did not matter to the
owners whether slaves who sought refuge in a monastery became monks of
free status or remained slaves. The only important thing for them was that
they lost their fugitive slaves. That risk already existed in the sixth century,
when the law of asylum promulgated by Justinian gave any slave the opportunity to flee his master and enter a monastery. The consequences are indicated in a "chrysobull of Justinian for the Great Church of Constantinople,"
whose authenticity is not assured.[131] This text attests that such a large number of slaves were exploiting the law of asylum that they had become uncon-
trollable.[132]

As for the masters, they tried to find their slaves. *In Praise of Theodore
Tyron*, written in the late fifth century by Chrysippos of Jerusalem, recounts
that the saint prevented slaves from escaping by using invisible ropes.[133] If
the master of a runaway slave spent the night on the saint's grave, the saint
would reveal the fugitive's hiding place in a dream. Masters sometimes came
into conflict with the church. Take the example of four fugitive slaves who
found asylum in the monastery of Hypatios.[134] In this case, the slaves became
monks, and their master, who tried to recapture them, did not accept that
state of affairs. Similarly, fugitive slaves and coloni *(geōrgoi)* found refuge at
the monastery of Theodore of Sykeon.[135] Nevertheless, though these slaves
were cruelly treated by their masters, the higoumene—in this case, the saint
—returned them to their owners, whom he lectured on how to treat slaves. If
that did not help, he himself purchased the slaves. The author does not spec-

ify what happened if their masters did not wish to sell them or what their status was in the monastery once they had been purchased.[136] The case of Theodore Sykeon was not unique and proves that the law of asylum was not applied immediately and that the church sometimes preferred to throw its lot in with the masters, even though it had the authority to do the opposite. Seventh-century hagiography indicates that the church took the side of the owners. Theodore of Sykeon's social role was to transform the master into a man who was kind to his slave, but also to transform the slave so that he would perform his duties, especially the labor he owed his master.[137] Similarly, Mary the Younger pays for broken or lost objects so that the slaves responsible will not be beaten by their masters. She herself never beats her slaves.[138]

All these cases also prove that slaves did escape and that they knew the church could offer them shelter. These escapes are attested by the *Synaxarion of Constantinople* in a supplement to Joseph the Hymnographer's entry on Theodore the Revelator *(fanerōtēs)*. In that supplement, a man goes to the tomb of Saint Theodore (probably Theodore the Recruit) so that the saint will show him where his fugitive slave is.[139] Another saint whose specialty was to uncover fugitive slaves and thieves was John the Soldier Saint.[140] Slave flights were probably the reason behind certain new laws. In the late ninth and early tenth centuries, imperial legislation tried to put an end to the law of asylum for slaves, making their masters' consent a preliminary condition for their acceptance in monasteries and in the church generally.[141] Hence *Novella* 10 of Leo VI explains that the slave who flees a good master does wrong, and one who flees a bad master cannot be a monk because he should have stayed and suffered, all the while thinking of the suffering of Christ. Thus in the tenth century the imperial authorities began to protect the owners, an action in keeping with their fight against the powerful elites—which included the monasteries—during the same period. The author of the entry on Joseph the Hymnographer in the *Synaxarion of Constantinople* probably borrowed from Chrysippos of Jerusalem's *In Praise of Theodore Tyron* the miracle of a fugitive slave's hiding place being revealed in a dream to a master who had fallen asleep on the saint's grave. (Note, however, that this miracle does not appear in the *Life of Joseph the Hymnographer*.)[142] But all these attempts did not succeed in stopping the flight of slaves, who are the only ones, apart from criminals, to be mentioned in the law of asylum in the ninth and tenth centuries. Coloni, curials, and decurions, who had been included in the law in the sixth century, are no longer mentioned.

It is clear from the late-tenth-century narratives that flights of slaves were common. That phenomenon intensified to such a point that the intervention of public authorities became necessary. Hence Constantine VII promulgated a *Novella* on the subject of fugitive slaves, who were to be returned to their masters.[143] The imperial authorities also began watching the roads in search of persons who "looked like slaves" and returned them to their owners.[144] Was the objective of these slaves to take advantage of the law of asylum and seek refuge in the church, where they could attain a higher social and economic standard of living? The available evidence is not sufficient to confirm such an interpretation, though it remains a plausible hypothesis. The road taken by Luke the Younger, on which he meets only fugitive slaves, leads him from Peloponnesus to Bithynia, and his aim is the monastic life.[145] Athos and the monasteries of Bithynia were also located on that route.[146] In addition, when Luke enters the monastery, the higoumene questions him exactly as he was supposed to do according to the *Novella* of Justinian, but Luke persistently refuses to give the higoumene information about his earlier life.[147] Another flight of a son is that of Nikon Metanoeite (Nikon "Repent Ye"), who is pursued by his father. The father arrives at the monastery and begs for his son's return.[148] It is true that nothing obliged fugitive slaves to seek refuge in the church. But that was the only place that could legally offer it to them. The church affirmed in the eleventh century that slaves who found asylum there would belong to the church forever. In the case at issue, it is true, a slave had committed a murder and was therefore guilty of a crime against the public authorities. But the same argument could be made about the fugitive slave, since flight was also a crime against the state.

From the owners' point of view, the failure of Leo VI's imperial legislation to achieve its objective of controlling the church's absorption of runaway slaves left owners with no means for recovering them. To circumvent that risk, they could keep their slaves as far from the church as possible.[149] They could also offer them better conditions than would the church by freeing them and setting them up as *anthrōpoi* in their *oikoi* with a share of their inheritance. That is what Boïlas did for his domestic slaves in the eastern part of Asia Minor in the eleventh century. Anthimos may have done the same in Cappadocia.[150]

Like freedmen in the private domain, slaves who took refuge in the church and were "liberated by abduction" received a new status in order to remain there. They could not leave because the church could not or even would not grant them free status—which would have allowed them to leave legally—outside its framework. It was also impossible to grant freedom to the slaves the church received as property, with lands, for example. The church could not free them because they were inalienable property. From that standpoint, there was no difference between the slaves given to the church and those who found refuge there.

From the point of view of slaves, then, it was probably preferable to be emancipated while remaining in their familiar environment, sure of their master, rather than face an unknown future in the church, one that might improve their standard of living but that did not make them free legally or socially. Take, for example, the story of the slave in the *Spiritually Beneficial Tales of Paul of Monembasia* who steals his act of emancipation from his mistress but never leaves the house.[151] Emancipation simply allows him to stop working.

The Slave as Human Being: A Change in Mentality

Evolution in the Image of the Slave

In saints' Lives of the sixth and seventh centuries, slaves are almost always represented as narrative objects. They have no name, no inner life, and they almost never speak. In several cases, they are accompanied by their master—when they are taken to be cured, for example. Having no identity of his own, the slave was bound to his master. Sometimes a slave is presented in a negative bit part: for example, when Peter the customs officer sells himself and becomes a slave, he is beaten by the other slaves at his master's house for his good character.[152] Peter is very devout, whereas the slaves by birth, those who did not choose their status, are portrayed negatively. Similarly, Symeon the Fool is wrongly accused of having raped a slave woman, who is also described in negative terms.[153] Many other cases exist. For example, though the four slaves who flee and go to the monastery of Saint Hypatios are given active roles in the narrative,[154] that is solely to create a conflict between the slave, their owner, and the former consul Monaxios over the law of asylum. Hence the law of asylum is represented from the points of view of the owners and of the church and not from the slaves' perspective, and emancipation is presented from the standpoint of the devout masters and not that of the freedmen.

Beginning in the ninth century and increasingly in the tenth to eleventh centuries, narratives depicted different aspects of slavery. Although slaves during that period remained narrative objects in other works—and even in the same ones—slavery was now sometimes shown from the slave's own viewpoint. The two most important Lives in this regard are those of Andrew the Fool and Basil the Younger. The former is the story of a slave of "Scythian" origin acquired by a powerful man (a *protospatharios* and military leader) and reared in his house. Andrew reaches a very high position in his master's house but, after having a vision in which Christ asks him to become a fool *(salos)* for him, Andrew decides that if he is to fulfill his vocation, he must be free.[155] To compel his master to emancipate him, he commits senseless acts.[156] But the master, who loves him a great deal and does not want to be separated from him, sends him for treatment to a church with a reputation for curing madness. After a period of three months, during which Andrew's mental state does not improve, the master signs a document for his emancipation, and Andrew begins his spiritual life by walking free in the city of Constantinople and imitating the madness of Saint Symeon the Fool.[157] The narrative, dated to the mid-tenth century by the editor, Lennard Rydén, is told completely from the point of view of the slave, which is to say of the saint himself.[158]

The *Life of Basil the Younger,* dating from the second half of the tenth century, does not relate the life of a slave saint, though Basil does find himself deprived of his freedom and thrown into prison.[159] But the saint is not the only main character in this work. There is also the author, a disciple of Basil, and Theodora, the saint's servant. Theodora is the slave of a powerful man in the house where Basil is residing.[160] Her master makes her available to Basil as a personal servant. But she achieves such a high spiritual level that the author casts her as the central character in describing the hereafter in the second half of the narrative. Theodora tells the author everything that happened after she left her earthly life. In the company of angels, she journeys beyond the grave, passing through "checkpoints" where demons interrogate her, trying to keep her from attaining paradise after forty days.[161] Note that the part of the narrative describing the journey of the slave Theodora to the hereafter may be the work of a second, later hand.[162] Unlike the *Life of Andrew the Fool,* the slave in this case is not freed but remains a slave in her earthly life.[163] Her status is not relevant for the account of her travels in the hereafter. All the same, that status provides her with extenuating circumstances regarding her actions in earthly life.[164] Once again, she is not judged as a good or bad slave, that question being completely beside the point, but as a good or bad person, that is, as a good or bad Christian.[165]

It is obvious that in these narratives the slave is considered a person with her own thoughts, ideas, and views. Nevertheless, in the *Life of Basil the Younger*, the author also presents slaves from the master's point of view.[166] These two outlooks do not seem to be in contradiction. Moreover, in the *Life of Andrew the Fool*, in which the slave is the hero, neither slave ownership nor the master's duties are disputed. On the contrary, it is the slave's duties toward his master that are called into question.[167] Before dealing with the fundamental issue raised by that view, which may have represented a new trend, let me examine how the slave is presented. I begin with madness, the mad slave, an element that is repeated in several of these narratives and that sheds particular light on the way the slave was perceived.

In the *Life of Andrew the Fool*, the author distinguishes two stages in the hero's madness. In the first stage, his vocation is to become a fool for Christ. In the second, madness becomes the instrument for his emancipation. Madness, and especially that of a slave, is a fairly common theme in Byzantine hagiographical literature. There are in fact two different types of madness, distinguished by different Greek terms: one is a state of mental illness, or *mania*, the person so afflicted being called *afrōn* or *maniakos*. The other is folly for Christ, which is thus deliberate, the person being designated by the term *salos*. Within the hagiographical context, the first of these two types is represented by the sick who are healed by the saint (they may be possessed by a demon),[168] the second by the "holy *salos*." The holy *salos*, bound directly to Christ, rejects the social and mental order of the earthly world (the word *salos* is normally translated into English as "fool"). But the symptoms are the same in both cases, and those who witness their manifestations cannot know what type of folly is at issue. Holy fools keep their sanctity hidden: for example, they go to pray in the church in secret and, conversely, behave provocatively at church when in public view.[169] Folly for Christ is nevertheless presented as a simulated folly inasmuch as the *salos* does not lose his sanity, and all his acts of folly are intentional.

All the cases in which the slave becomes mentally ill belong to the first type: the slave is truly sick. The master then takes the slave to the saint or invites the saint to his house to heal the slave.[170] The slave's literary role in this case is completely passive. Unlike what might occur with other types of illnesses, the slave cannot initiate contact with the saint. In addition, the state of illness has grave consequences, making the slave completely useless in the performance of tasks. The psychological condition of a mentally ill slave therefore coincides with the representation of the slave as a narrative object.

In addition to turning to the healer saint, the master may bring the slave who suffers from a mental illness into a place of treatment. The cure for mental illness practiced by the Saint Anastasia Church in Constantinople is mentioned in the *Life of Andrew the Fool* and in the *Life of Basil the Younger*.[171] Moreover, the slave who suffers from a mental illness may manifest a refusal to fulfill his social duties. The cure returns the slave to his position and obligations. Hence, for example, Theodore of Sykeon, in healing a slave possessed by a demon, restores her ability to do her work.[172] If the slave is not cured, his master may free him, though caring for him is considered characteristic of a good master.[173] As a result, the slave who wants to be free may play the fool in hopes that his master will grow tired of him. That was exactly Andrew's plan.

In Byzantine literature, the fool for Christ is the only one who simulates a mental illness. Slaves who wanted to be freed to leave their environment thus had a motivation for feigning madness. But that view does not tally with the passive literary image of the slave. In other words, to present the slave as a fake fool, the hagiographer must make a saint of him—an unthinkable perspective in the hagiographical literature of the fifth to seventh centuries because it contradicted the perception of the slave in society.

Thus the case of Andrew the Fool was a great innovation. Unlike what took place in the narratives of the sixth to eighth centuries, he does not choose to become a holy fool, with the series of radical changes in social and everyday life entailed by such sainthood. Instead, he is chosen by Christ and in a dream. Yet it is the slave who, by his own initiative, plays the fool to be emancipated by his master. And these two types of folly are very distinct in the narrative: the slave does not begin to commit senseless acts for Christ before being free of his earthly master because he cannot serve two masters at once.[174] To seek the origins of such a change in mentality, it may be helpful to examine the literary models of slave heroes that were available to Byzantine literature.

The Literary Models

In the Byzantine hagiography of late antiquity, the slave was generally restricted to a passive role. Of course, the roots of that literature do not lie solely in Greek literature. But it is that literature that would have to be examined to learn whether slaves always appeared in bit parts. Such a pursuit lies beyond the scope of this book. Nevertheless, I shall take into account the image of the slave in the literary tradition before advancing the hypothesis that, in the tenth century, a change in mentality transformed the perception of slaves. Henri Wallon undertakes such an inquiry in his work on ancient slavery, in which he carefully gathers the references to slavery provided by classical literature.[175] Wallon, however, is not interested in the representation of the slave as an individual, the aspect I would like to examine.

William Fitzgerald and Vittorio Citti have studied the representation of the slave in Greek and Roman literature, demonstrating that the slave is presented as a passive agent.[176] As counterexamples, let me cite the character of Carion in Aristophanes' *Plutus (Wealth)* and the role of slaves in the comedies of Plautus. But as Kathleen McCarthy shows, even in comedies the "fictive" image of the slave is fashioned to assert or legitimate the master's power.[177] In fact, in Greek and Latin comedies, the master-slave relationship is always exploited as a comic situation. In describing the thrashing of slaves as comical, the authors completely ignore not only the slave's suffering but even the possibility that he could be suffering.[178] The same is true in Aristophanes: even though Xanthias and Carion are part of the family, "the slave can have only purely material concerns; eating, drinking, not fatiguing himself, avoiding blows, which establishes a contrast, often comical, between his world and that in which the flaws of demagogues and Sophists, or relations with Sparta, or the comparative merits of the tragic poets are discussed."[179] Hence, on the matter of the literary image of slaves, fifth- to seventh-century hagiographers were altogether in the literary tradition of their predecessors from the classical to the late Roman era. I refer, of course, to the majority of the works. There are also exceptions.[180]

I shall single out two literary examples of famous slaves from the imperial Roman era, whose influence on Byzantine literature must be taken into consideration: the fabulist Aesop and the biblical Joseph.[181]

I shall not concern myself with the question of Aesop's historical reality, since I am speaking of him as a literary character. References to his existence as a historical character, however, can be found in Herodotus, Heraclides, and Plutarch. Of these authors, only Herodotus mentions that he was a slave.[182] Several Lives have come down to us, prototypes for which are found in the papyri of the second century A.D.[183] Ben Edwin Perry and, more recently, Grammatiki Karla have studied the manuscript tradition of these narratives.[184]

Papyri from second-century Egypt contain abridged and incomplete versions of the *Life of Aesop*.[185] The oldest extant manuscript dates from the late tenth or eleventh century and comes from Grottaferrata *(Vita G)*; it is now in the Morgan Library in New York. According to the manuscript tradition described by Perry, that version has the same origin as a shorter one from the eleventh century, which survives only in a single manuscript from the thirteenth century, the *Vita W.* Both contain the *Life of Aesop* and his fables in their entirety; they prove that interest in his life and work experienced a renaissance in Byzantium in the tenth to eleventh centuries.[186] Ioannes-Theophanes Papademetriou has shown the great importance that the *Life of Aesop* had in Byzantium.[187] Unlike in every other work, the hero in this case is a slave. The narrative itself depicts the difficulties of a slave's life from Aesop's point of view, and the character does not correspond to the stereotype of the submissive slave. For example, he defends another beaten slave, which brings to mind the biblical episode in which Moses rises up to protect an abused slave (Exod. 2:11–12).[188] In another instance, Aesop questions an order from his master.[189]

Another prototype of the slave hero is the story of Joseph in Genesis. That Hebrew narrative entered the corpus of Greek literature through the Septuagint. But unlike more learned examples, the Old Testament—along with the New Testament, with its significance for Christians—became among the best-known texts of the early Christian Middle Ages. And the story of Joseph's slavery (Gen. 37–48) as well as the slavery of the people of Israel in Egypt are part of that text. In contrast to the previous examples, Joseph is a free person who is sold into slavery in his youth. From the legal point of view, his state of slavery is not legitimate: he is born free and is sold by his brothers without his father's knowledge. Once he is reduced to slavery, his surroundings change completely. He arrives in Egypt, where he is purchased by Potiphar. At that time, his enslavement becomes legitimate from the Egyptian point of view, since he is bought from traders. All these legal arguments are obviously not of concern in the biblical text, in which Joseph's slavery serves two purposes: from a historical standpoint, it opens the route to Egypt for the Hebrews; from a moral standpoint, it makes Joseph pay for his sin of pride. These two objectives were achieved when Jacob's descendants, the people of Israel, found themselves in a condition of collective slavery in Egypt. Joseph's role is to bring them to that point.

The Greek tradition of Joseph's story includes the romance *Joseph and Aseneth*. The original of this literary narrative, composed in Greek in Alexandria, dates back to the early second century A.D.[190] The first part of the romance relates how Aseneth, the daughter of Pentephrese, adviser to the pharaoh and priest of Heliopolis, becomes infatuated with Joseph, the pharaoh's vicar, and converts to Judaism to marry him.[191] The second part deals with the conflict between the pharaoh's son, who is Aseneth's suitor, and Joseph. The first time Joseph's slavery is mentioned is when Aseneth initially refuses to marry him.[192] The question of the narrative's origin has greatly preoccupied modern scholarship. The debate focuses on whether it had a Jewish or a Christian author and to what milieu he belonged. According to Marc Philonenko, the author was an Egyptian who converted to Judaism.[193] Christoph Burchard also leans toward a Jewish author. He notes in this regard the conflict between the pharaoh's son and Joseph. To take his revenge on Joseph, the pharaoh's son persuades Dan and Gad, Joseph's brothers by Bilha and Zilpa, respectively, to rebel against Joseph. The pharaoh's son uses the argument that they were born of slave mothers: "I heard your brother Joseph tell Pharaoh, my father, 'Dan and Gad are the children of slaves *(paidiskōn)* and are not my brothers. I will await the death of my father and will crush them with their whole family, so that they will not be our coheirs, for they are children of slaves and it is they who sold me to the Ishmaelites.'"[194] But according to the Old Testament, nothing distinguished the sons of Bilha and Zilpa from those of Leah and Rachel. They were all Jacob's children and hence of free status, just as Ishmael, as the son of Abraham, was free even though his mother was the slave Hagar. The same Jewish law existed at the time of the Second Temple: unlike in Roman law, free status came from the father.[195] In ancient Hebraic law, in late Babylonian law, and in Islamic law, the slave mother of his master's child possessed a special status—she could not be sold, for example—which suggests a legal approach common to the Semitic peoples.[196] One of the Byzantine names for the Arabs, in addition to "Saracens," was "Hagarenes" *(Agārenoi),* that is, "sons of Hagar." That designation, pejorative no doubt, stems from the fact that the descendants of Hagar were, in the eyes of the Byzantines—but not of the Arabs or Jews—slaves. The other designation, "Ishmaelites," used by the Byzantines and the Jews, referred to their descent from Ishmael but also evoked the sale of Joseph as a slave into Egypt by the "Ishmaelites" (Gen. 37:28). In any event, the story of Joseph and Aseneth became popular in Byzantium probably in the ninth to tenth centuries, during the literary renaissance.[197]

The model of the Joseph story is thus different from the examples of classical Greek literature. Nevertheless, it was aspects of this story that were adopted as a literary model by Byzantine hagiography in the ninth to tenth centuries, especially the detail of a free person who is abducted and reduced to slavery in a strange land and who at the same time has a mission in that land or even a destiny as a slave.

Joseph's Slavery as Model

The example that first comes to mind is the *Life of Elias the Younger* from the mid-tenth century: abducted twice during raids of Arab pirates, Elias is sold as a slave into Africa to a master with an important political position.[198] There he relives episodes from the biblical story of Joseph, especially the attempted seduction by his master's wife and his imprisonment.[199] The same element of the saint's seduction is found in the *Life of Elias Spēlaiōtēs*, also from tenth-century Byzantine Italy, in which the "new Egyptian" seduces the "new Joseph."[200] As in the story of Joseph, the husband unjustly throws the saint into prison, but in this case for reasons unrelated to his wife's attempted seduction of the saint.[201] In addition, the false accusation against Elias for having stolen sacred vessels evokes Joseph's accusation of Benjamin (Gen. 44:1–17).[202] The same theme of a charge of seduction, this time against the woman, is recounted in the *Life of Mary the Younger.* The saint is accused of having committed adultery with a slave, "like the Egyptian woman and Joseph."[203] Then there is Fantinos the Younger, who like Joseph is thrown into a cellar and is saved by God "just as Israel was saved from Egypt."[204] All these cases prove that the story of Joseph was circulating in the tenth century.

In the *Life of Elias the Younger,* Joseph's name is explicitly mentioned as the model for the saint (Elias is even called "the new Joseph").[205] But in this narrative, the saint's innocence is revealed, and his master frees him. He then goes on a Christian mission.[206] The case of Elias is not unique among Byzantine hagiographical narratives. On the contrary, the theme of the abduction of Christians by the Arabs from their own lands to be sold into slavery was widespread: it appeared in the *Spiritually Beneficial Tales of Paul of Monembasia* from the second half of the tenth century; in the *Life of Theoctiste of Lesbos* in the early tenth century; in the *Life of Nilus of Rossano* from the first half of the eleventh century; and in the *Life of Nikon Metanoeite* from the mid-eleventh century.

The work that seemingly paved the way for that theme was the *Life of Joseph the Hymnographer.* Originally from Sicily, the saint died in about 886, becoming the hero of the narrative composed by a contemporary shortly after his death. This was not just a case of the first Byzantine Saint Joseph. The narrative also contains remarks that evoke his biblical namesake, such as "Joseph, whom God's love did not prevent from honoring his parents and brothers."[207] Nevertheless, though Joseph the Hymnographer was the first to have had a Life recounting the story of his abduction, he does not fall into slavery. His boat is seized by the Arabs of Crete, and he is cast into prison, where, like his biblical predecessor, he becomes the prisoners' leader.[208] Then he is liberated by a man who redeems him, but his true liberator, as in the story of Joseph, is God.[209] The last episode associated with the story of Joseph the Hymnographer must not be overlooked: in the *Synaxarion of Constantinople,* Saint Theodore the Revelator *(fanerōtēs)* does not discover the hiding place of a fugitive slave because he is "taken" by the soul of Joseph the Hymnographer.[210] That scene is not found in any version of the Life itself.[211]

The narratives containing the theme of the abduction of Byzantines by Arabs and their sale into slavery belong to one of two types: either it is the hero himself who has such an experience, or it is other, sometimes very minor, characters. The *Spiritually Beneficial Tales of Paul of Monembasia,* the narratives of Nicholas of Myra, as well as the *Life of Nilus of Rossano* and the *Life of Nikon Metanoeite* all mention cases of innocent persons who fall victim to abduction and are then sold into slavery in the Arab territories.[212] In these texts it is the secondary characters who are reduced to slavery, and they are sometimes liberated by the hero. By contrast, in the *Life of Theoctiste of Lesbos,* it is the saint herself who is abducted from her island by the Arabs of Crete. Having managed to escape during a stop in Paros, she recounts her captivity to the author.[213] Similarly, in the *Life of Joseph the Hymnographer,* as in the *Life of Elias the Younger,* it is the saint who experiences misfortunes: abduction, exile, life in prison, and slavery are all recounted from the hero's point of view.

The historical backdrop for all these works is the taking of Crete from Spain by Arab forces in 827–828. They held it until 961, when Nicephorus II Phocas recaptured the island. The Arab presence supplanted Byzantine hegemony in the Mediterranean and introduced difficulties in maritime relationships within the empire between Asia Minor, the islands, Peloponnesus, and Byzantine Italy. The series of raids in all these regions during that period was a new element of everyday life in Byzantium. Hence it was the political atmosphere of the time that introduced the motif into hagiographical literature. A good example is the *Life of Theoctiste of Lesbos,* whose author presents himself as a Byzantine officer named Nicetas. He adopts the model from the *Life of Mary of Egypt,* but the episode of the saint's captivity is totally absent from the other story.[214] That episode was probably created to show the difficult situation of the civilian population in the cities.[215] Nicetas recounts in the first person how he was sent by the emperor to join Admiral Himerios, who had been charged with a mission among the Arabs of Crete. The Arabs were responsible for the saint's abduction.[216] The work thus serves its author's political aim.

This new literary trend presented the Christian captive or slave as a real person endowed with his or her own thoughts and words, unlike older representations of the slave. It manifested itself even more clearly in cases in which the hero becomes a captive or slave. But in contrast to the older narratives, the characters who have fallen into slavery in the aforementioned works were all born free and lost their freedom following an Arab attack. From the Byzantine point of view, these were therefore free persons, and their condition of slavery, again from the point of view of Byzantine law, was illegitimate. Their status as free persons accords with their literary description as human beings. Authors were slow to present slaves as heroes.

A literary character based on the free Byzantines who were abducted by the Arabs has three options: he can escape, be ransomed and return to Byzantium, or be sold as a slave. Needless to say, he can be sold and then redeemed, or he can be sold and then escape. The possibility that such a person might be liberated by an exchange of prisoners of war organized by the public authorities does not exist in the hagiographical literature, however. In fact, the raids by the Arabs of Crete, who were independent of the other Arab forces, had a solely economic aim: to earn money by ransoming or selling the persons abducted rather than to conquer the Byzantine Empire.

In any case, the author had few models for presenting a hero saint in that setting. For a secondary literary character, the condition of involuntary slavery or a private redemption was possible. In the *Spiritually Beneficial Tales of Paul of Monembasia,* for example, the enslaved monk comes to gain the favor of the governor of Africa thanks to the miracles he performs. He is then returned at no charge to the person who comes to redeem him.[217]

In the case of the hero, either the author does not present him as a slave, and in that case he escapes of his own volition or by a miracle, or he represents slavery as a Christian mission. In the latter case, the mission is not chosen by the saint himself. Given the political situation, it is divine destiny that imposes it on him through the intermediary of his enslaved condition. Hence in the *Life of Elias the Younger* the saint is alerted to his fate in a childhood dream: he will be taken by the Arabs and sold as a slave, and he will use his enslavement to spread the Christian faith where it is needed.[218] But that theme of the devout Christian in Arab territory, as developed by hagiographers, also had a moral aim. Among the dangers that Byzantines faced was not only the abduction of their free inhabitants but also the conversion of these prisoners to Islam. Hence Nikon Metanoeite takes an expedition to Crete to bring renegades back to the Christian faith.[219] With the motif of abduction and enslavement as a Christian destiny, the hagiographers provided the captured Christian Byzantines with an exemplary model intended to persuade them that their misfortune, especially their unanticipated state of slavery, had a spiritual aim, so that they would resist being converted to Islam.

The hero's enslavement accords very well with the idea that his trajectory toward sainthood is not voluntary but is imposed by God's design. In fact, this is the case not only for saints who are abducted by Arab pirates. In the ninth to eleventh centuries, many more saints were depicted as choosing neither their holy life nor its mode of expression. The late Roman model of the martyr did return, adapted to the political circumstances of the time, especially in the hagiography of the iconoclastic period; but in other narratives of the ninth and tenth centuries, the new trend was to depict persons who are almost forced to follow the path of sainthood. Note the difference between the sainthood of Theoctiste of Lesbos and that of her model, Mary of Egypt. Theoctiste's fate is imposed on her, whereas Mary decides on her own to leave her world and go out into the desert.

I have indicated that, in the narratives set in the Mediterranean of the ninth to eleventh centuries, the enslaved saints are Byzantines and are always born free. In fact, that type of slavery was already represented in the seventh century in the *Life of John of Cyprus,* written by Leontius of Neapolis. But in that case, the person who becomes a slave acts of his own will: he sells himself to distribute money to the poor.[220] Because his slavery is totally voluntary, it does not represent the situation of most slaves. By contrast, the new trend marked a change in mentality: literary depictions of slavery took an interest in the point of view of the slave, who became the subject of the narrative. That change in the perception of the slave is attested as well in language. Hence the term *psukharion* ("small soul") to designate a slave became increasingly common in the Byzantine sources of the ninth to eleventh centuries, whereas the words *sōma* and *sōmation* ("body" and "little body") became rarer.[221]

This new conception in the hagiographical literature resulted from the political and demographic situation in the Mediterranean basin of Byzantium. The evolution in the free status of Byzantines reduced to slavery by the Arabs was accompanied by a development in their literary representation as heroes and also entailed a new literary portrayal of enslavement. Conversely, the authors of the *Life of Basil the Younger* and the *Life of Andrew the Fool* took as heroes a slave not in Arab territory but in Byzantium, and not a free-born person who was enslaved but one whose original status was obscure.[222] The hypothesis that needs to be examined is whether the case of free Byzantines who had fallen into slavery can account for the spectacular metamorphosis in mentalities, which culminated in the transformation of a slave-object into a slave-subject; in other words, whether the fact that slavery was for the first time represented from the point of view of Byzantines of free status enslaved by the enemy also changed how slaves living within the empire were perceived.

The Image of the Slave's Progress toward Sainthood

Unlike the Byzantines enslaved by the Arabs, Andrew the Fool is of Slavic origin, which already marks a real departure.[223] But the case of Andrew the Fool is not unique. Another example, the *Life of Thaddaeus,* has come down to us in its Slavonic version.[224] It recounts the story of a pagan slave "at the time of Leo the lawbreaker." The slave is baptized by his master, then freed after the master's death to enter a monastery and to lead a spiritual life, a trajectory that culminates in a dispute with the emperor.[225] That narrative is probably based on the case of Thaddaeus the Confessor, who was the slave of Theodore Studites.[226] But no Greek version has survived except the one in the *Synaxarion of Constantinople.*[227] It is this text that mentions him as Theodore Studites's Scythian slave. The *Synaxarion* attributes a role to him in the struggle against the iconoclastic emperor (both Michael II and Theophilus are named);[228] in that version, the emperor tries to compel the saint to tread on a cross, and when he refuses he is thrown into prison and tortured. But the Slavonic Life does not include that scene or the detail that Thaddaeus belongs to Theodore Studites. In it the saint fights with the emperor ("Leo"), then endures torture. The question has arisen whether a Greek version predating the Slavonic one existed. Dimitri Afinogenov proposes a date of between 821 and 826 for the original Greek Life.[229]

Hence Andrew the Fool was not the only Slavic slave to have become a saint. Thaddaeus may even have served as a model for the author of the *Life of Andrew the Fool.* The two narratives must be differentiated, however. The *Life of Andrew the Fool,* whose literary quality makes it one of the most appealing works of Byzantine hagiography, bears little resemblance to the laconic *Life of Thaddaeus.*[230] For my purposes, it is altogether a secondary matter that the *Life of Thaddaeus* is about a real person. The same is true regarding the real existence of Andrew the Fool. What is significant is that slaves were chosen to drive the plot of two literary narratives, which are therefore told from the slave's point of view.

Note that during the same period, between the late ninth and the eleventh centuries, two new slave types came to be represented in Byzantine hagiographical literature. On the one hand, a free Byzantine, born Christian, falls into Arab captivity and is then sold as a slave. On the other, the non-Christian "Scythian" slave—Slavic, Bulgar, or Russian, in other words—is purchased by a Byzantine master who baptizes him. These two types, moreover, refer to two different geopolitical contexts: the Mediterranean setting (the narratives mention Sicily, Byzantine Italy, Peloponnesus, and the Greek isles) and the region of Constantinople and the Balkans. The point at which they meet is Greece, and it is therefore not surprising to find both models in the *Spiritually Beneficial Tales of Paul of Monembasia.*[231] Each of the two literary motifs has the slave play the role of the hero, and especially of the saint. The appearance of one motif cannot be explained by the existence of the other, however.

The common point between the slaves Andrew the Fool and Thaddaeus, despite the difference in their type of sainthood, is that to pursue their path in Christ, they must first be freed. Emancipation arises as a necessity. But why is it not possible for a saint to be a slave? Aesop was both a fabulist and a slave. Similarly, the voluntary slavery of the customs officer in Leontius of Neapolis's *Life of John of Cyprus* and the missionary slavery of Elias the Younger (his is not voluntary) are part of the mission of the devout character, who can be simultaneously the slave of an earthly master and of the heavenly master. In fact, as I have shown through the writings of the church fathers, in being a good slave of an earthly master, a person fulfills his duties toward his heavenly master.

By contrast, Andrew's and Thaddaeus's paths of sainthood require, first and foremost, their fidelity to God. In these two narratives, the author depicts a conflict of loyalty associated with their mission. In the *Life of Andrew the Fool,* the conflict is illustrated by another episode, in which a slave discovers the sainthood of Andrew, who has kept it secret.[232] As a good slave, he immediately goes to his master to reveal the secret. But Christ himself prevents him from doing so by sealing his mouth shut. To remain faithful to Christ, he is compelled to compromise his fidelity toward his earthly master. Within the context of the story, this episode is no accident. The author emphasizes that the slave's discovery of Andrew's sainthood was intentional and guided by Christ.[233] The same theme is also evoked in reference to another slave, a eunuch. Andrew refuses the dates offered him by this eunuch because the eunuch sins by sleeping with his master. Epiphanios, the saint's confidant, explains to him that the eunuch is a slave and must therefore obey his master. Andrew replies that slaves must disobey their masters when the orders are not moral.[234]

In all these examples, the slave characters are male. The only female slave who achieves a high spiritual level is Theodora in the *Life of Basil the Younger*. She is not obliged to renounce her earthly servitude to become a person of great piety, though she now serves a spiritual master: Saint Basil the Younger. Her earthly servitude coincides with her spiritual servitude, as the author recounts in the first person. But that is not sufficient when one becomes a saint, hence *o doulos tou theou*, literally, "the slave of God." Note that in Andrew's vision, Christ does not tell him that he must emancipate himself; that is Andrew's own conclusion. Fidelity toward his corporeal master cannot coexist with fidelity toward his spiritual master. It is the latter that takes precedence. I use the term "corporeal master" and not "earthly master" here because I believe that in Andrew's case, his earthly master is precisely Christ and not the master who purchased him. In other words, because his heavenly master is also his master on earth, Andrew can have no other.

Hence the evolution in the image of the slave as an individual went hand in hand with an interruption in his submission to his earthly master. In fact, there was a social conflict here that went beyond the master-slave relationship, and of which God and the emperor were also a part. I thus return to the term *o doulos tou*.

The Slave, the Free Person, and the Public Authorities

"To Be the Doulos*"*

The expression *o doulos tou theou* was used throughout the period. An evolution began in the ninth to tenth centuries, when the two expressions *o doulos tou* and *o oiketēs tou* came to be used in reference to the emperor as well. Normally, these terms are translated into English as "the servant": hence "the servant of God" or "the servant of the emperor." But the word "servant" does not indicate the kind of service involved. Unlike *doulos tou theou,* which expresses a private devotion, the expressions *o doulos/o oiketēs tou theou* (with the article therefore) are used in Byzantine literature almost exclusively to designate the saint. In the same way, *o doulos/o oiketēs tou basileōs* designate the emperor's high military or civilian officials, whose title or high position indicates a service they must provide him.[235] The service of the servants of God was not so clearly defined. The saint earned that title not only through his mode of life but also through his virtue.[236] As *the* servant of God, he was qualified to perform miracles. In this capacity he was even solicited to perform them. In fact, a person's ability to bring about miracles meant that he was truly *the doulos* of God.[237] Can the capacity to perform miracles, or their performance itself, be seen as a service to God? It was rather a function, or more precisely, *the* function of the saint, just as the service that a high dignitary provided the emperor constituted his function. But in both cases, it was a function assigned by social position. High officials were directly subject to the emperor and were his intermediaries, just as saints were the intermediaries of God. Like the slave's function, that of *o doulos tou theou* or *o doulos tou basileōs* resulted from a direct and personal subordination to God or to the emperor, but, unlike in the slave's case, these social positions were perceived as privileges.[238]

The correlation between the earthly—imperial—model and the heavenly model was not new. In adopting Christianity, Constantine I also adopted a heavenly model that corresponded to his earthly model: a single emperor on earth was equivalent to a single *kurios* in heaven. The emperor's subjects had to become the faithful of the only God; conversely, God's subjects were faithful to only one emperor.

When the empire's existence was in danger in the seventh century, the heavenly model came to the aid of emperors. They then used icons to assert their own authority, as Averil Cameron demonstrates: "If we look more closely at the imperial symbols of the late sixth and early seventh centuries it will be clear at once that they are, above all, symbols of authority. If Justinian had tried and hoped, Heraclius succeeded in placing the emperor at the very heart of the religious as well as the political loyalties of his subjects. As the Persian Chosroes II in 626 appeared as the wicked Holophernes, so the Byzantine Heraclius became David."[239]

In the sixth and seventh centuries, the emperor became *imago Christi*,[240] and he used that association with Christ to prove and impose his authority, a gesture that also evoked King David. But in the iconoclastic era he went even further, opposing all other *imagines Christi*.[241] Without joining the debate on the reason behind iconoclasm, I shall examine the consequences for slavery of that political crisis.

With the saints of the iconoclastic era, the hagiographical literature on martyrs from the late Roman Empire was reborn in a new context. The central question was the rivalry between obedience to the emperor and obedience to God. The saint was of course obliged to submit to God. One of the terms designating the proponents of images was "icono-*douloi*," not only because they venerated icons but also, I would argue, because, having been forced by the crisis to choose between subordination to the emperor and subordination to the icon of Christ, they chose the icon.[242] When the iconoclastic crisis ended in the ninth century, the ultimate subordination to heavenly authority prevailed, and it was clear that the emperor was now only *o doulos tou Christou*, the *doulos* of Christ.[243]

Between the Doulos *and the Slave*

Although it was one thing to be *the doulos* and another to be a slave, in both cases there was a relationship between *doulos* and *kurios*. By contrast, those who were not subject to any political authority were called *autonomoi* and *autodespotai*, the latter term being the opposite of *doulos*. *Douleia*, as a relation of submission to a person, was always expressed as a tribute, military service, or some other service.[244] That service, whether or not it was attached to an office, always remained unremunerated.

I have distinguished between the relations the public authorities had with the slaves under them and the relations between private owners and their slaves. But the public authorities, by their legislative power, also controlled the private slaves. Hence, in promulgating the law of asylum in its sixth-century version, the imperial authorities opted to weaken the master-slave relationship in favor of the church-slave relationship. Toward the end of the tenth century, the imperial authorities imposed a sales tax that military leaders had to pay on prisoners who became their private slaves.[245] To examine how the public authorities intervened in master-slave relations, I return to the Roman legacy of the Byzantine Empire.

The ecclesiastical sources, patristic and hagiographical, saw the question of slavery from the angle of the cleavage between slave and master and not in terms of the cleavage between slave and free person. That viewpoint was based on the heavenly model portrayed by these writers. Modern scholarship has always granted a determining role to Christianity in the many social changes and developments that occurred during the late Roman era. In recent years, however, it has had a tendency to invoke a catalyst that was not necessarily Christian but rather political and, more precisely, imperial.[246] That imperial role can also be seen in the cleavage between master and slave. It was widespread in Christian literature and appeared as the only cleavage involving the slave; at the same time, the slave is also found in the imperial sources, especially legal texts. The legislation of Hadrian was the first to grant a significant place to the slave. Most characteristically, the slave for the first time earned the right to lodge a complaint—in very special cases, it should be added—against his own master.[247] The same emperor's legislation dealt with cruelty against slaves and made the crime of castration equivalent to homicide, and Antonin the Pious made the murder of a slave a crime as serious as the homicide of a free person.[248] In fact, not only did the legislation involve the public authorities in relations between master and slave, which had previously remained outside its purview, but it also began to protect the slave. Justinian I, in eliminating the need, on the part of a slave making a claim for free status, to have an intermediary to gain access to the justice system, brought the slave even closer to the public authorities.[249] Hence, from the second century on, the public authorities intervened in the master-slave relationship, judged private before that time, transforming it into a tripartite relationship.

The case of eunuchs exemplifies the political dimension of the state's emancipation of slaves belonging to individuals, as practiced in the late empire, especially during the fourth to fifth centuries. In Roman law, castration had always been prohibited, at least since the legislation of Domitian.[250] The penalties became increasingly harsh, as indicated by the sanctions imposed up to the Justinian era.[251] I believe that therein lies the origin of the tripartite relationship.[252] The legislation of Constantine I and that of Leo I called for a castrated slave to be confiscated.[253] The later legislation of Leo I offered asylum and freedom to the castrated slave who took refuge in the imperial court.[254] The time of that legislation corresponds perfectly to the beginning of the use of eunuchs in the imperial court of Constantinople.[255]

This example shows that it was during the late era of the Roman Empire that private slaves became a matter of interest for the imperial powers. It was through legislation that the public authorities transformed the situation of eunuchs. In other words, it was only because the slave had a civil status that legislators—that is, the public authorities—could change the social relationships in which the slave participated.

The public authorities had the power to change the slave's status by intervening in and modifying the relation between slave and master. The master therefore had only one option for preserving that relation of submission: set his slaves back in his *oikos* as social dependents. But that transformation also required their emancipation, since in Byzantium that form of dependence was defined in economic terms. In the countryside, for example, fiscal obligations linked to land ownership defined relations of social dependency. That implied that the dependent person had the ability to own property; as a result, he was also a taxpayer and had the civil status of a free man.

An analysis of the legislation on freedmen indicates that no legislator since Justinian had been concerned with the status of that group.[256] Of course, many *Novellae* refer to emancipation, but only from the slave's side, that is, prior to the act itself. Linguistically speaking, the word *eleutherizō* appears, but *apeleutheros* is totally absent. (That is true of the *Novellae* but not of the compilations of previous laws, which cannot provide evidence of any change.) This absence is particularly striking, given that a large number of laws concerning slavery were promulgated throughout the era and that Roman law had paid a great deal of attention to the freedman. The degeneration of the specific status of the *apeleutheros* in the Byzantine era and the collapse of the distinction between *apeleutheros* and *eugenēs* as it had existed in Roman law show that this special status was no longer applicable.[257]

As for the term *doulos,* one of its meanings had to do with social submission. The submission of *douloi* to their masters and at the same time to the emperor could prove problematic, in exactly the same way that the submission and loyalty of saints were compromised by the conflict between being *o doulos tou theou* and being a *doulos* of an earthly master (the emperor was the equivalent of God on earth). In the late Roman era, the slave's submission to his master was also the expression of his submission before God. Recall the anathema that the Council of Gangra proclaimed in 343 against those who, on the pretext of Christianity, incited slaves to leave their masters.[258] But a century later, the church understood the benefit it could draw from such an incitement. In the sixth century, the pretext was recognized and legitimated. In the mid-tenth century, the slave was even encouraged to reject the authority of his master, not to enter the ranks of the church but to live outside any religious order, like Andrew the Fool, who was led away by Christ to become his *doulos*. The role the author assigned to Christ in this narrative is precisely that of the person anathematized by the Council of Gangra.[259]

All these cases show that the person in question was, first and foremost, subject to supreme authority, either heavenly or earthly, and that the relation of loyalty to his private master was undermined by that authority. One of the consequences was that the public authorities were provided with an opportunity to use private slaves for their own purposes. Hence, in the early ninth century, Nicephorus I tried to destroy his adversary, the Constantinopolitan aristocracy, by inciting slaves to denounce their masters.[260] That course of action ran completely counter to the Roman tradition, which had required the slave's total submission and fidelity to his master. In *The Civil Wars*, Appian recounts that, because of the triumviral proscriptions spearheaded by Octavius, men began to fear being betrayed even by their wives, their children, their freedmen, and their slaves. Slaves, taking advantage of the political situation, became a real threat to their masters, whom they took the initiative to denounce.[261] But in the ninth century, it was the emperor himself who incited slaves to turn against their masters.

A parallel case can be found in the *Life of Stephen the Younger*. It concerns a slave who is persuaded by the iconoclastic emperor Constantine V to denounce her mistress.[262] It is true that such a move was in keeping with the political circumstances of the iconoclastic era. Nevertheless, the date of the work's composition corresponds to the era of Emperor Nicephorus I. The hagiographical narrative thus attests to the imperial use made of private slaves in this regard.[263] In addition, that same narrative shows what motivated the slave: her reward would be an act of emancipation, a marriage, and a position in the imperial court.

In this story, the slave is not tortured to denounce her mistress, as was the case in the Roman era.[264] She bears witness against her because it is her duty to the emperor. In the eleventh century, the *Peira* is very clear on that subject: "Compared to the emperor's power, the authority of the *pater familias* is nothing," which also meant that the slave was obliged to denounce her master, her *sundoulos*, of her own accord.[265]

The new perception of the slave as an individual was also that of the public authorities. Instead of being considered private property, he or she was now considered a human being. The status of slaves occupies an important place in the legislation of Leo VI. Of his 113 *Novellae*, nine deal specifically with changes in the status of the slave as individual. Their subjects include conjugal life, marriage, family, the law of asylum, the right to draw up a will, and the right to bear witness.[266] Many of these questions concern slaves in their capacity as Christians. That legislation thus accords perfectly with the new perspective in literature during the same era. On the question of marriage, the legislation offers new possibilities for mixed unions between slaves and free persons.[267] I have already mentioned the *Novella* of Alexius Comnenus, which obliged owners to unite slaves only in Christian marriage.[268] Religion appears as a motivation or as a pretext on the part of the public authorities to intervene in relations that until then had been judged private. Legislation was the means they used.

Hence it was the imperial authorities who controlled the relation between master and slave. They could do so because slavery was an institution of *ius civile*. I have shown in this book that slavery was a dynamic institution, in that definitions of it were constantly being modified by the public authorities. The other aspect of the institution also needs to be examined, namely, the situation of the free Byzantine who was reduced to slavery by his own state.

The Public Authorities and the Free Person

One of the state's means for procuring slave labor from the classical Roman era on was penal slavery *(servi poenae)*. The penalties of *damnatio in metallum, damnatio in sulpurarium,* and *damnatio in opus salinarum* provided slaves for the ore and sulfur mines and for the saltworks. Under such conditions, slavery was often imposed in perpetuity with no prospect of emancipation, and the convict's property was confiscated, in accordance with classical Roman law.[269] Another type of penalty, which also reduced the convict to slavery, was *damnatio ad bestias* and *ad gladium*.[270]

These penalties changed in the fourth to sixth centuries, with the suppression of convictions *ad gladium* by Constantine in 324 and, in the West, by Honorius in 404.[271] In 536, slavery as a penalty was abolished by Justinian.[272] That ban was part of *Novella* 22, which deals with Christian marriage. As was the case for captives, the *Novella* states that the marital status of the couple had to remain in force. In the case of *damnatio in metallum,* that meant that the state had to eliminate penal slavery; otherwise, if one of the spouses was reduced to slavery by the state, the marriage would be annulled. What other punishment was to be inflicted on the convict? The *Novella* does not specify. Because under the Roman penal system, prisons held only those awaiting or currently on trial, the public authorities had to set in place a different penal system to replace the penalty of slavery.[273]

In an article devoted to penal mutilation, Patlagean shows that the system of corporal punishments described in the *Ekloga* offered a means for the poor to pay with their bodies if they did not have the financial means to pay a fine.[274] In addition, penal mutilation was inflicted for crimes against the state, and it ultimately replaced capital punishment as well. Patlagean demonstrates that this penal system dated back to the reign of Justinian and can even be discerned in earlier historiography.[275] There is every reason to suppose that the development of penal mutilation was linked to the abolition of slavery as punishment. In fact, as in the case of corporal punishment, slavery was not a punishment inflicted on just any culprit. In the age of the Severi, jurists made the distinction between the *honestiores* and the *humiliores*. It was only the *humiliores* who were sanctioned through slavery; the *honestiores* could pay a fine.[276] In addition, slavery was at first inflicted as a *form* of capital punishment, only later taking its place. Corporal punishment followed the same pattern, "leading the public authorities and society jointly toward a state of law in which penal mutilation gained ground over capital punishment."[277]

Hence the abolition of penal slavery in 536 led the imperial authorities to adopt a new penal system. Again there was a Christian catalyst: on the one hand, the strengthening of Christian marriage, and on the other the penal codification of sexual crimes. That advance on the part of the public authorities also resulted in changes in another of the modalities for becoming a slave, by being sold.

According to the *Digesta*, the act of selling oneself into slavery was a legitimate act provided that the person who sold himself was of legal age, set at age twenty.[278] It was the person's market value that may have motivated such an act. Hence he could sell himself to pay off his debts or because he needed money.[279] Nevertheless, that act, which contradicts everything we know about modern slavery, was not transparent within Roman society either. In fact, according to classical Roman law, the status of freeborn—*ingenuus*—was irreversible. If a person of that status was reduced to slavery, the act was illegal, and he could always reclaim his freedom, if he was in a position to prove it, by appealing to the justice system.[280] For the most part, that possibility protected free persons from abduction and the resulting enslavement. Once a slave, that person could have no recourse to justice because he had no legal identity; he needed an intermediary of free status. Because of the need for a third party, the process was not easy, especially in the case of a child sold by his father.

According to these definitions, a person could sell himself and then demand his freedom, thereby committing fraud. That was exactly the reason for the amendment that prohibited a person sold into slavery from reclaiming his freedom if he had received money for the sale. The aim, of course, was to protect the purchaser. Buckland shows that this was a legislative evolution, apparently dating back to the second century A.D., that is summarized in the *Digesta*.[281] One of the results of that amendment was to grant legitimacy to the act of selling oneself. The sale of oneself is mentioned as a legal act for the first time in a constitution of Constantine dating to 323.[282] That does not mean that the act was prohibited prior to that time.[283] In any event, the person who sold himself without then reclaiming his freedom actually became a slave.[284] But free status, considered a personal characteristic, was defended by the law, and thus by the public authorities. The problem arose primarily if a person with the status of freeborn did not possess his own legal identity. Such was the case for children.

Classical Roman law did not explicitly prohibit the sale of children, who were under the potestas of their father. That also meant, at least de jure, that the father "owned" his child by virtue of *ius vitae necisque*.[285] In 294, Diocletian and Maximian prohibited parents from selling their children, but evidently their legislation did not put an end to the phenomenon.[286] Third-century jurists explained that the freeborn child who was sold could reclaim his status as a freeborn, thus suggesting that the act of selling one's children was not considered altogether legitimate.[287] In 313, Constantine considered the act valid, explaining that it had been so previously.[288] There is evidence of children being sold by their parents, especially from the fourth century on.[289] *Novella* 33 of Valentinian explains that the act was intended to save the lives of children who would otherwise have died.[290]

One result of this legitimation of the selling of children and other free persons was a degeneration in the status of the freeborn *(ingenuus, eugenēs)*. Whereas in the Roman Classical Age that status was a personal characteristic, granted solely by birth and irreversible, that was no longer the case beginning in the fourth century, when the public authorities recognized as legitimate the renunciation of that characteristic. The imperial authorities thus made the personal characteristic a legal status. That worked in the other direction as well: the status of freeborn could now be attributed to a slave. Hence, when a master freed a slave to marry her, she and her children automatically became free and possessed freeborn status.[291] That was also true under the law of asylum, whereby a slave became a cleric.[292]

There were practical reasons for that change. Hence, for example, a constitution of 322 mentioned that persons in the provinces had the habit of selling their children because of poverty.[293] To prevent such a situation, the constitution exempted such persons from their fiscal obligations. The case of proxenetism, the sale of a child for purposes of prostitution, was included within the same context.[294] The legislation of Justinian limited the financial use of children, banning creditors from taking the children of their debtors and reducing them to slavery.[295] The same legislation also prohibited parents from abandoning their children, so that they would not be reduced to slavery by a third party who might find them and who, according to classical law, could raise them free or slave as he wished.[296] Nevertheless, these *Novellae* did not prohibit parents from selling their children. They stated that children could not become slaves against the will of their parents. The same policy was applied to slaves: the legislation of Justinian prohibited creditors from taking the slaves of debtors *against the will* of their masters and affirmed that slaves abandoned by their masters would be free.[297]

At first sight, the public authorities in the late Roman era made the delimitation between slave and free person more dynamic, in that the free or freeborn person could legitimately lose his status by his own will or by that of his parents. But in fact these means had not been prohibited previously, and that is what compelled the public authorities to limit such acts, which were becoming increasingly frequent, especially in the eastern provinces.[298] The characteristic of being freeborn became a definition controlled by the public authorities, a reversible civil status, and thus lost its meaning.[299] The adjective *eugenēs* as well as the substantive *eugeneia*—the status of being freeborn—were no longer used in legislation after the eighth century. Henceforth they meant simply "of good birth."

The act of selling oneself was finally prohibited in the early tenth century by the legislation of Leo VI, which defined the sale of oneself as a senseless act *(parafrosunē)*.[300] The emperor, however, allowed the person who wanted to marry someone of slave status to sell himself to his intended's master if that master did not want to sell his slave.[301] On this question, Islamic law did not allow a Muslim to be reduced to slavery and therefore prohibited him from selling himself.[302] The evolution in Byzantine legislation expressed an analogous perspective.

Cases of children being sold into slavery are attested in the legislation of Alexius Comnenus. The *Novella* of 1095, already mentioned regarding Christian marriage between slaves, contains another article that deals with the case of children born of free parents and then sold or abducted.[303] The *Novella* mentions Bulgar parents who, because of the famine, sold their children, as well as Byzantines who abducted Bulgar children. It is true that the *Novella* does not prohibit these acts; rather, it determines that anyone who could prove he was "born of free parents" would receive the status of free, and the master could not prevent it. Because this was a foreign population, Köpstein is persuaded that these acts were also prohibited in the empire. That seems logical, though such a prohibition has not come down to us in the Byzantine *Novellae*, apart from the *Novella* of Leo VI mentioned above.[304] In my understanding, the *Novella* of 1095 was a measure that, in giving Bulgar children the same status as children born in the empire, protected them from being enslaved as a result of their parents' actions or as a result of actions taken by the Byzantines.

That imperial policy has often been understood within the context of the tenth century as a way to encourage emancipation in order to form a stratum of freedmen subject to the public authorities: in short, new subjects capable of backing the authorities in their struggle against the powerful elite. But by 1095, that struggle was long over. Such legislation must be considered within a much broader context than that of the tenth century: the public authorities continually modified the definition of slavery from the second to the eleventh century, and always in the same direction.

At first sight, the legislation of Leo VI and of Alexius Comnenus reinstated the classical Roman status of freeborn. But in reality, it did quite the opposite. Byzantine law took even more distance from its Roman origins by making personal power over one's own children, one's own slaves, one's own body, and one's own birth an affair of the state.

Classical Roman law dealt with the sale of oneself only in cases of fraud. Such an act, done in good faith, was either unthinkable or considered outside *ius civile*, because the person was the owner of himself. The law had to protect only persons of freeborn status who were reduced to slavery against their will and, in the case of children, without their knowledge. That was no longer the case under the empire: in the fourth to seventh centuries, the state, accepting the fact that the person could sell himself and his own children, conceded that it was a matter of concern for the public authorities; in the tenth to eleventh centuries, the authorities became further involved, prohibiting such acts. And that meant, in reality, that the person of free status was no longer the owner of himself.

Conclusion: Slavery, Freedom, and Unfreedom

Through legal, ecclesiastical, historiographical, legendary, hagiographical, and other sources, I have followed medieval slavery in its evolution over six centuries in the eastern Mediterranean, from late antiquity to the Middle Ages. Byzantium occupies the center of this configuration not only because of its geopolitical position but also because it transmitted the Roman world's legacy of slavery and of other institutions to the medieval world.

After the sixth century, however, the Mediterranean was no longer what it had been under the Roman Empire. The new geopolitical map entailed, among other things, a change in the perception of the free person. Residents of the empire identified themselves primarily as Christians. With the strengthening of Christian marriage in the age of Justinian, the dissolution of captives' marriages was no longer permitted, and the church elaborated the notion of a religious duty to redeem Christian captives from the "Barbarian" enemy. The term "Barbarian," in coming to designate non-Christians, acquired a new meaning. The continual wars against the Arabs, new rivals of Byzantium on the Mediterranean scene, and the threat they represented weighed heavy on the empire's existence, contributing as well to the development of the free Byzantine Christian's identity. That identity implied a responsibility and even a duty on the part of the community—which in the eighth century became the state—to redeem the captive. Hence legislation regulated the status of the Byzantine captive while stipulating that he would maintain his civil status in the empire, regardless of the situation in which he found himself.

Because of the political circumstances, the delimitation between the free person and the slave came to be very dynamic in the medieval Mediterranean. The definition of the person of free status was linked to his religious identity, to his community, and to his state.

That dynamism within the medieval geopolitical space means that it is very difficult to make the de jure and the de facto definitions of the slave and the free person coincide. I have therefore tried to discern these definitions at work in the economic field. In comparing the situation of slaves to that of other groups in the same society, I have been able to show that slaves did not possess any defining characteristics proper to them. They appear in all the documents studied as an artisanal and agricultural labor force, playing the same roles as wage workers. At the same time, they represent only one form of unfreedom. Unfreedom, however, has a specific character that extends far beyond the political and economic fields. It was that realization that led me to consider the social dimension of unfreedom as mentality, beginning with its expression as a Christian identity.

The social relationship between slave and master corresponded perfectly to the global Christian perspective developed by the church and the state in late antiquity, in which a single God, designated by the word *o kurios* ("the Lord"), was master of the whole world. Social submission constituted the cornerstone of that outlook. The submission of slaves was only one example: the slave was obliged to fulfill the social duties entailed by his status because they were also his duties toward God.

The ninth to eleventh centuries witnessed the advent of a new attitude. The slave was perceived as an individual, and slavery was portrayed from his point of view. That perspective went hand in hand with the idea that the slave ought ultimately to submit to God and not to his earthly master. In other words, the slave-God relation grew stronger at the expense of the slave-master relation. The slave was perceived as an individual because the intermediary role of the master was weakening. But I could not situate the slave within that tripartite relation of slave-master-God without simultaneously considering the place of the emperor, the equivalent of God on earth.

The change in the perception of the slave expressed, first and foremost, the point of view of the public authorities. The shift in his status from private property to human being was linked to the transmutation of private into public that marked the medieval era as a whole. Private property was only one example. In order to profit from real property, the imperial authorities became involved in relations that had been outside their influence in the Roman Classical Era. They thus changed the landowner-property relation into a tripartite relation. They acted in the same manner with respect to the ownership of human beings. By intervening in the master-slave relation, the imperial authorities raised the question of the status of slaves, of whether they were private subjects or imperial subjects.

But the public authorities could not in fact recognize private subjects, and were ready to subjugate them. They therefore manipulated slavery by modifying civil definitions at the expense of the private master's potestas. That action had consequences both for the master-slave relation and for the father-child relation. As the Byzantine jurists stated in the eleventh century: "Compared to the emperor's power, the authority of the *pater familias* is nothing." The public authorities could not have acted otherwise because they were constructed from and at the expense of private potestates or, in other words, at the expense of personal freedoms. That process meant, notably, that slaves could no longer be defined as the res of another. In that case, it turned out to be easy for the public authorities to modify the definitions of slaves, since these were civil definitions. The evolution of ancient slavery thus appears to be, more than anything, the history of the growth of public power.

The definition of slavery is not a contractual definition of freedom or of "free persons." Its evolution is consistent with changes in the political, social, and religious arenas. Historians have sought in vain to apply the modern concept of freedom to societies in which it remained unknown. Unfreedom and freedom are not civil definitions but social relationships. That also explains why in modern society, though slavery as an institution—in the sense of one person being the property of another—no longer exists, and though every person is free by civil definition, unfreedom is found everywhere. Only a medieval civilization such as Byzantium, which evolved from the ancient world and had to adapt to a politically, geographically, socially, and economically dynamic Mediterranean space, can show us so clearly that slavery has nothing to do with freedom, and vice versa.

APPENDIXES

ABBREVIATIONS

NOTES

BIBLIOGRAPHY

INDEX

APPENDIX A

Terminology

Legal Sources

Table A.1 below shows the different uses of the terms designating a slave, a free person, or a freedman, based on the legal definition. I distinguish compilations of laws (common throughout the period) from newly promulgated laws (especially the *Novellae*). Only new laws are presented here, along with legal decisions: unlike the compilations of ancient laws, these provide direct information on the use of the terms during the period when they were created.

First and foremost, it is necessary to examine the distinction between *doulos* and *doulē*, between *oiketēs* and *oiketis*, and between *therapōn* and *therapaina*. In fact, in distinguishing between a male and a female slave, the laws do not respect the gender difference articulated by language. In general, they use masculine terms to designate female as well as male slaves. For that reason, uses of *doulē* and of *therapaina* are restricted to laws that specifically concern female slaves. These laws also attest that *doulē* is the terminological equivalent of *doulos,* whereas *therapaina* is the equivalent of *oiketēs*.[1] The word *oiketis* is rarely if ever used in the legal sources. Note as well that *therapōn,* like *pais* and *paidiskē,* is not used within the context of slavery.

Hagiographical Sources

As literary figures, characters in saints' Lives are part of a narrative history that places them in a setting and gives them a role or what could be called a literary function. The two criteria of civil status and literary role may thus serve as parameters for the analysis of hagiographical sources. But since the terminological and chronological parameters also had to be taken into account, more than one table was required to display the four criteria. I have opted to divide the data into three tables, each of which presents the different uses of terms corresponding to a given civil status: one for terms used for

Table A.1 Frequency of Occurrence for Terms Designating Slaves, Free Persons, and Freedmen in the Legal Sources (in alphabetical order)

Term	6th–7th centuries	8th–9th centuries	10th–11th centuries
ἀνδράποδον (andrapodon)	X	X	X
ἀπελεύθερος/ἀπελευθέρα (apeleutheros/apeleuthera)	XX	X	—
ἀπόδουλος/ἀποδούλη (apodoulos/apodoulē)	—	—	XX
δουλεία/τύχη δουλική (douleia/tuche doulikē)	XX	XX	XX
δούλη (doulē)	X	X	X
δοῦλος (doulos)	XX	XXX	XXX
ἐλευθερία (eleutheria)	XXX	XXX	XXX
ἐλεύθερος/ἐλευθέρα (eleutheros/eleuthera)	XXX	XXX	XXX
εὐγενής/εὐγενές (eugenēs)	XX	X	—
θεράπαινα (therapaina)	X	X	X
θεράπων (therapōn)	—	—	—
κατάδουλος (katadoulos)	—	—	—
οἰκέτης (oiketēs)	XX	XXX	XXX
οἰκέτις (oiketis)	—	—	—
οἰκετικὸν πρόσωπον (oikettikon prosōpon)	—	X	X
παιδίσκη/παῖς (paidiskē/pais)[a]	—	—	—
σύνδουλος (sundoulos)	—	—	X
ψυχάριον (psukharion)	—	—	XX

Note: XXX = very frequent; XX frequent; X = infrequent; - = no occurrences. The frequency of a term is determined in relation to the occurrence of equivalent terms in the laws of the same period, "very frequent" for when the term is used in more than a quarter of the references, "infrequent" for when it is rarely used.

[a] This term does not appear in the table when it has the sense of "child."

Table A.2 Civil Status of Slave Attested for the Term in Hagiographical Sources (in alphabetical order)

Term	6th–7th centuries	8th–9th centuries	10th–11th centuries
δοῦλος/δούλη/δοῦλις *(doulos/doulē/doulis)*	under authority domestic secretary other function	under authority domestic	under authority
θεράπαινα *(therapaina)* θεράπων *(therapōn)*[a] οἰκέτης/οἰκέτις *(oiketēs/oiketis)*		domestic domestic	domestic under authority domestic
παῖς/παιδίσκη *(pais/paidiskē)* σύνδουλος *(sundoulos)*	domestic domestic	domestic domestic	domestic domestic

Note: "under authority" = under the authority of another with no mention of function; "domestic" = domestic function (servant) in the home of another; "other function" = another function in the home of another, such as secretary, caretaker, and so on. In the narratives set in town, there are two types of slaves: those who are mentioned as being domestics and those whose function is not indicated. Domestic slaves as well as nondomestic ones were, of course, under their master's authority. In the narratives set in the countryside, a slave's role is rarely described. Saints' Lives almost never take an interest in the slave's function.

[a] The semantic distinction between *therapōn* and *therapaina* appears clearly in these tables. These are not really the same term, despite their common etymology.

Table A.3   Civil Status of Freeman Attested for the Term in Hagiographical Sources (in alphabetical order)

Term	6th–7th centuries	8th–9th centuries	10th–11th centuries
δοῦλος/δούλη (doulos/doulē)	of God[a]	of God	of God
θεράπαινα (therapaina)			
θεράπων (therapōn)		of God	of God
			of the emperor[b]
οἰκέτης (oiketēs)			of God
		of the emperor	of the emperor
παῖς/παιδίσκη (pais/paidiskē)[c]			
σύνδουλος (sundoulos)			

[a] *tou theou.*

[b] *tou basileōs.*

[c] The use of *pais* and *paidion* to designate a (free) child was very common throughout the period, and therefore I do not include it in the present tables.

Table A.4   No Attestation of Civil Status for the Term in Hagiographical Sources (in alphabetical order)

Term	6th–7th centuries	8th–9th centuries	10th–11th centuries
δοῦλος/δούλη/δούλις (doulos/doulē/doulis)	under authority domestic	under authority domestic	under authority domestic
θεράπαινα (therapaina)			
θεράπων (therapōn)			
οἰκέτης/οἰκέτις (oiketēs/oiketis)		under authority	under authority domestic
παῖς/παιδίσκη (pais/paidiskē)	domestic	domestic	domestic
σύνδουλος (sundoulos)			

slaves (table A.2); a second for free persons (table A.3); and a third for cases in which no indication of civil status is associated with the term (table A.4).[2] The frequency of occurrence for the different terms does not seem to be as significant for saints' Lives as for public documents.

Historiographical Sources

As table A.5 shows below, in historiographical works the words *oiketēs* and *doulos* are used in the same way to designate any kind of slave, in contrast to *pais/paidiskē*, which always refers to a domestic (civil status is sometimes not specified). Unlike in the other types of sources, in these works the term *andrapodon* occurs very frequently. That word traditionally designated the slave captured in war or during a military expedition. Similarly, the verb *andrapodizō* continued to be used throughout the era to designate the capture of slaves. Within that context, it should also be recognized that there was another, equally common term to designate captives during the entire period concerned and in all types of sources. This was *aikhmalōtos (αἰχμά-λωτος)*, or prisoner of war; the verb form *aikhmalōtizō (αἰχμαλωτίζω)* referred to the act of taking into captivity. These terms are related only indirectly to slavery.[3]

The Word *Sklavos*

Having demonstrated the wealth of terms relating to slavery in the Greek language of the sixth to eleventh centuries, I shall add a few words on the term *sklavos*, the source of the word "slave" in modern European languages (with the exception of the Slavic languages).

Helga Köpstein argues that the word *sklavos (σκλάβος)*, which designates a "Slav" in Greek, was not used in the sense of "slave" in Byzantium before the twelfth to thirteenth centuries.[4] Indeed, I have not found any instances of *sklavoi* used to mean "slaves" in the sources I examined.[5] Henry Kahane and Renée Kahane, however, have produced a survey on the typology of the word that is critical of prior research on the subject.[6] They show that by the sixth century the word already meant "Slav" in Byzantium. The sense of "slave" entered in part through the Arabic language and appeared in a Greek text for the first time in southern Italy in 1088.[7] Nevertheless, it is likely that, in tenth- and eleventh-century Greek, such words, especially those designating ethnic or geographical origin, were used in spoken language but did not

Table A.5   Terms for Slaves in Historiographical Works (in alphabetical order)

Term	6th–7th centuries	8th–9th centuries	10th–11th centuries
ἀνδράποδον *(andrapodon)*	captive	captive	captive slave
ἀπόδουλος/ἀποδούλη *(apodoulos/apodoulē)*[a]	—	freedman/ freedwoman	freedman/ freedwoman
δοῦλος/δούλη/δούλις *(doulos/doulē/doulis)*	slave	slave of the emperor	slave of the emperor under authority
οἰκέτης/οἰκέτις *(oiketēs/ oiketis)*	slave	slave	slave
οἰκετικὸν πρόσωπον *(oiketikon prosōpon)*	—	—	domestic slave
οἰκετικὸν ἀνδράποδον/ οἰκετικὸν σῶμα *(oiketikon andrapodon/oiketikon sōma)*	—	—	slave
παῖς/παιδίσκη *(pais/ paidiskē)*[b]	domestic	domestic	domestic slave
ψυχάριον *(psukharion)*	—	—	slave

Note: "domestic" = domestic function (servant) in the home of another; "under authority" = under the authority of another with no mention of function.

[a] This term was not very common in the historiographical sources. It is presented in this table because it was more commonly used to designate a freedman than in the other types of sources. By contrast, the word *apeleutheros*, which traditionally designated such a person in the legal sources, is absent from these works.

[b] In addition to *pais*, the historiographical sources also use the word *paidion/paidarion* for a child.

appear in writing. This is demonstrated, for example, in the work of Constantine Porphryogenitus, who writes that in vernacular Greek *(dialektos)*, the word *serbloi (σέρβλοι)* designated slaves *(douloi)*, and that this word was applied to the Serbs *(serbloi)* because they had become the *douloi* of the emperor.[8] Because there is not a great deal of information available on the vernacular before the twelfth century, other equivalent terms cannot be found, and sometimes the origin of a term is not clear.[9]

Legal Sources

I have assembled the imperial regulations dealing with Byzantine slavery and those that changed a person's status. I indicate the legal issue under consideration and include a brief summary of the regulation. For a complete list of references concerning slavery in the *Peira*, see Köpstein's indispensable study "Sklaven in der 'Peira,'" pp. 29–33.

Table B.1 Imperial Regulations Dealing with Slavery (in chronological order)

Source	Century or year	Subject	Summary
Nov. Just. 1	535	will	emancipation by will and the status of the freedman
Nov. Just. 7, praef., 7.1–3	535	real properties of the church	prohibition on alienating church property, including rural slaves
Nov. Just. 5.2, 10	535	law of asylum	slave who flees to a monastery and becomes a monk
Nov. Just. 18.11	535	concubinage/marriage	a master who marries his slave
Nov. Just. 32	535	creditors in the countryside of Thrace	creditors must return property confiscated from the peasants, including slaves
Nov. Just. 22.7	536	marriage of captives	marriage is not dissolved if a spouse is taken into captivity
Nov. Just. 22.8	536	enslavement as punishment	the state's punishment of *damnare in metallum* will no longer be imposed
Nov. Just. 22.9	536	marriage of a freedman	the marriage of a freedman reduced to slavery is dissolved
Nov. Just. 22.10	536	marriage	marriage between slave and free person is not valid
Nov. Just. 22.11	536	marriage	the slave married to her master will be free
Nov. Just. 22.12, 153	536	abandoned slave or child	will be free
Nov. Just. 22.37	536	marriage	a freedwoman cannot marry a freedman without the consent of her master
Nov. Just. 78.1–4	539	emancipation	the status of the freedman
Nov. Just. 90.6	539	testimony	a freedman who testifies and who is accused of being a slave must prove he is of free status
Nov. Just. 119.2	544	will	a minor may emancipate his slaves as soon as he can draw up a will
Nov. Just. 120.1	544	real properties of the church	prohibition on the church from alienating rural slaves
Nov. Just. 123.5, 17	546	law of asylum	the slave who becomes a member of the clergy, with or without the consent of his master, becomes a slave once more when he leaves his position

Source	Date	Category	Description
Nov. Just. 134.7	556	creditors	prohibition on the creditor from taking the debtor's children to work for wages or in service (*doulikos*) and from hiring them out to another (and taking the children's wages)
Nov. Just. 142	558	castration	the castrated slave will be emancipated
Imp. Justiniani Novellae quae vocantur (vol. 1, pt. 1, pp. x–xii)	6th c.	law of asylum	penalizes wrongful enslavement, slave mistreatment, and the unjustified petition for asylum by the slave
Nov. Post. Just., coll. 1, no. 7 (Justin) (=*Nov. Just.* 144)	572	Christian slave of a Samaritan	the slave of a Samaritan master who becomes Christian is emancipated
Leges navales 15	7th–8th c.	transport of slave	a slave as merchandise on a boat is the captain's responsibility
Leges rusticae 45	7th–8th c.	rural slave	a slave who kills an animal; his master must reimburse the owner
Leges rusticae 46	7th–8th c.	rural slave	a slave who steals an animal is responsible for the lost animal and will be hanged
Leges rusticae 47	7th–8th c.	rural slave	a slave who steals animals; his master must reimburse the owner, and the slave will be hanged
Leges rusticae 71	7th–8th c.	herdsman slave of another	neither the slave nor his master is responsible for the livestock of another if the master was not informed
Leges rusticae 72	7th–8th c.	herdsman slave of another	his master is responsible for the livestock of another if the master was informed
Ekloga 10.2	741	creditors	those who hire the children of debtors must cancel the debt
Ekloga 17.12	741	slave who steals	if his master does not wish to keep him, he will give him to the person from whom the slave stole
Ekloga 17.16	741	abduction of a free person	the kidnapper is punished by having his hand cut off
Ekloga 17.17	741	theft of a slave	punishment is the return of the slave with a second one, or with his value
Ekloga 17.21–22	741	sexual relations	anyone who sleeps with the female slave of his wife or of another must pay the slave's owner 36 *nomismata*

continued

Table B.1 (continued)

Source	Century or year	Subject	Summary
Ekloga 17.42	741	slave/master	the slave who provides his master (or a wife who provides her husband) with drink will be put to death if the master becomes drunk and dies
Ekloga 17.49	741	slave/master	the master who beats his slave to death "without due cause" will be charged with homicide
Ekloga 8.1.1	741	emancipation	the means by which one emancipates a slave
Ekloga 8.2	741	captive	a captive purchased from the enemy is considered free and pays his value to his purchaser or works for wages
Ekloga 8.4.1	741	captive	a captive who behaves well toward the state is emancipated even if he was a slave beforehand
Ekloga 8.4.2	741	captive	a prisoner of war who flees and returns will be reduced to slavery for five years and will be emancipated if he behaves well toward the state
Ekloga privata aucta 9.5	8th c.	captive	a captive purchased from the enemy is considered free and pays his value to his purchaser or will work in his house for wages
App. Eklo. 4.4 (*CJ* 9.11)	8th c.	sexual relations between a mistress and her slave	the woman will be put to death, the slave burned
App. Eklo. 8.1–3	8th c.	Christian slave	Christian slave belonging to a Samaritan, a Jew, a pagan, or a heretic will be freed
App. Eklo. 8.6	8th c.	Christian slave	emancipated Christian slave will not be reduced to slavery
Leges militares (*version A*) 22	8th c.	deserters	deserting soldiers are reduced to slavery
Leges militares (*version B*) 48	8th c.	captives	are not part of the booty and will be taken to the emperor or kept by the strategos for a possible prisoner-of-war exchange

	797–802		
Nov. Irene, p. 26		marriage	prohibition on marriage or conjugal relations with a female slave
Eparch. bib. 2.8 (éd. Nicole, 2.8–2.9)	–912	slave/free goldsmiths	prohibition on purchasing more than one pound of gold
Eparch. bib. 2.9 (éd. Nicole, 2.10)	–912	slave silversmith	must have his master as guarantor to set up a workshop
Eparch. bib. 3.1	–912	banker	shall not set up any of his slaves to run the bank in his place
Eparch. bib. 4.2	–912	slave/free *vestiopratai*	must inform the prefect in the case of expensive articles
Eparch. bib. 6.7	–912	slave *metaxopratai*	his master will be his guarantor
Eparch. bib. 7.5	–912	silk finisher	when purchasing silk, he must prove that he is not a slave
Eparch. bib. 8.7	–912	silk manufacturers, slaves and *misthōtoi*	prohibited from selling silk outside the city
Eparch. bib. 8.13	–912	slave silk manufacturer	must have his master as guarantor to set up a workshop
Eparch. bib. 11.1	–912	candlemaker	prohibited from using a slave to sell candles outside the workshop
Eparch. bib. 12.9	–912	slave soapmaker	if he uses illegal scales, he will be confiscated and made an imperial slave
Nov. Leo. 9	–912	law of asylum	the slave who has become a cleric without his master's knowledge will be returned to the master
Nov. Leo. 10	–912	law of asylum	the slave who has become a monk without the master's knowledge will be returned to the master
Nov. Leo. 11	–912	law of asylum	the slave who has become a bishop without his master's knowledge will be returned to the master
Nov. Leo. 29	–912	sexual relations	the child of a slave born in the home of a third party returns to the slave's owner
Nov. Leo. 33	–912	marriage of captive	prohibition on the wives of captives contracting a union with another man
Nov. Leo. 36	–912	inheritance of captive	the captive's son will be his heir

Table B.1 *(continued)*

Source	Century or year	Subject	Summary
Nov. Leo. 37	–912	freedman/will	the slave emancipated by a will has the right to draw up his own will, even if he does not know of the measure taken on his behalf
Nov. Leo. 38	–912	slaves of the emperor	slaves of the emperor may dispose of their belongings and private masters may follow the imperial example
Nov. Leo. 40	–912	slaves of captives	captives have the right to draw up a will; the slaves of captives who die without an heir are not turned over to the fisc but are emancipated
Nov. Leo. 49	–912	slave as witness	slaves are not allowed to be witnesses
Nov. Leo. 59	–912	the act of selling oneself	prohibition on a man selling himself
Nov. Leo. 60	–912	castration	prohibition on castration: the castrated slave will be freed
Nov. Leo. 66	–912	selling the slave of another	someone who sells the slave of another pays him twice the slave's value
Nov. Leo. 67	–912	slavery as punishment	someone who goes over to the enemy two times will be sold into slavery for three years; someone who goes over three times will be sold into slavery in perpetuity
Nov. Leo. 100	–912	marriage	between a slave and a free person: the person can work for wages in the house of the slave's master
Nov. Leo. 101	–912	marriage	between two slaves when one is emancipated, as in *Nov. Leo.* 100
Svoronos, nov. 3 (Romanus I)	934	powerful/poor owners	definition of the *dunatoi* and prohibition on acquiring possessions from the poor (mention of slaves as well as hired workers who farm the land)

Source	Date	Subject	Description
Nov. Post. Just., coll. 3, nov. 13 (Constantine VII)	945–959	fugitive slave	must be returned to his master, who will pay the person who returns his slave a sum fixed by the law
Svoronos, nov. 8 (Nicephorus Phocas)	963/964	real properties owned by monasteries	limitation on the establishment of new monasteries and prohibition on donations of lands to the monasteries and to religious foundations (including rural slaves)
Nov. Post. Just., coll. 3, nov. 25 (John I Tzimisces)	972–975	selling war captives	military leaders must pay a tax upon selling their prisoners of war
Nov. Post. Just., coll. 4, nov. 35 (Alexius Comnenus)	1095	the freeborn slave will be emancipated	the slave, upon proving he was born free, will be emancipated, and his master cannot prevent it (an example concerning Bulgar slaves)
Nov. Post. Just., coll. 4, nov. 35 (Alexius Comnenus)	1095	Christian marriage of slaves	masters prefer to marry their slaves in a non-Christian ceremony, which is henceforth prohibited; slaves who are united in Christian marriage will remain slaves

Note: A minus sign (−) preceding the date = terminus ante quem.

APPENDIX C

Prices

I have gathered together the information on the price of slaves and on prices in general unearthed over the course of my research. I have compared this information to that appearing in other studies on prices.[1]

Table C.1 Prices of Slaves and Other Merchandise, Wages

Source	Century or year	Location or milieu	Price	Merchandise/payment
P. Stras. 1404	5th–6th	Egypt	4 *nom.*	a black slave sold by Ethiopian traders
P. Cair. Masp. 67312	6th	Egypt	12 *nom.*	annual payment to a freedwoman
P. Cair. Masp. 67312	6th	Egypt	6 *nom.*	inheritance to a freedman
CJ 6.43.3.1 (= *CJ* 7.7.1.5)	530–531	Constantinople	20 *solidi* 30 *solidi* 50 *solidi* 30 *solidi* 60 *solidi* 70 *solidi*	slave slave, eunuch over ten years old slave with a profession *notarius* slave physician or midwife slave slave, eunuch over ten years old who has a profession
Life of John of Cyprus 21	6th	Cyprus	50 *nom.*	slave
Miracles of Artemios 36	7th	Egypt	8–12 *nom.*	doctor's fee to cure a sick child
Leges rusticae 62	7th–8th	rural	12 *folles*	compensation for the loss of a day of work in the fields by the thief of a yoke
Ecloga 17.22	8th	Constantinople	36 *nom.*	anyone who sleeps with the female slave of another person must pay him
Theoph., A. M. 6302 (p. 487)	9th	Constantinople	2 *nom.*	tax for an imported slave passing through the empire

Source	Century	Place	Amount	Description
Proch. Nom. 10.5 (*Dig.* 24.1.5.5)	9th	Constantinople	5–10 *nom.*	the husband who sells his wife's slave must compensate the wife for the slave's loss
Proch. Nom. 14.5	9th	Constantinople	10 *nom.*	slave
Oikonomides, *Patmiacus* 171 (fol. 516)	10th	Constantinople	6–10 *nom.*	price of a workshop
Eparch. bib. 1.19	10th	Constantinople	2 *keratia* per 1. *nom.* (1/12)	salary of a *tabellarios*
Eparch. bib. 4.5–6	10th	Constantinople	10 *nom.*	fee to establish a *vestioprate* (silk clothing merchant) workshop
			6 *nom.*	fee to join the corporation of the *vestiopratai*
Nov. Leo. 100	10th	Constantinople	2 *nom.*	the wage for a year of work for someone who wants to marry another person's slave and who is unable to purchase her
Treaty of Aleppo (969)	10th	Constantinople–Syria	30 *nom.* 20 *nom.* 15 *nom.*	price of a male refugee price of a female refugee price of a child
Life of Auxentios, by Symeon Metaphrastes, PG 114:1384A	10th	Constantinople	3 *folles*	the wage for a day of work in a workshop
Life of Nicholas of Sion 58	10th	Lycia	80 *nom.*	to build a church
Spiritually Beneficial Tales of Paul of Monembasia 2.5	10th	Peloponnesus	1 *nom.*	to steal a document
Spiritually Beneficial Tales of Paul of Monembasia 8.3	10th	Peloponnesus	100 *nom.*	to ransom three people

continued

Table C.1 (continued)

Source	Century or year	Location or milieu	Price	Merchandise/payment
Laurentian Chronicle, p. 75	10th	Kiev	5–10 *nom.*	a slave who had taken refuge among the Greeks is ransomed by the Russians
Life of Nilus of Rossano 70–72	11th	Sicily	100 *nom.*	to redeem three people
Iviron I 16	1010	Thessaly	15 *nom.*	the price of a piece of land sold to redeem a son abducted by pirates
RP, *Syntagma*, 5:48–49 (Grumel, *Reg. pat.* vol. 1, pt. 2–3, no. 887, p. 376)	1050	Asia Minor	24 *nom.*	price of a murderer slave sold to a bishop
Lemerle, *Boilas, test.*	1059	eastern part of Asia Minor	3–15 *nom.*	inheritance to various persons (including freedmen)
			400 *nom.*[a]	the slave Zoe
Robinson, *Carbone* 10 (59)	1076	Basilicata	10 *nom.*	inheritance
Iviron II 47	1098	Constantinople	30 *nom.*	inheritance to certain freedmen
Documents of the Genizah on the purchase of captives sold to Alexandria	11th	Egypt	100 dinars (*zebuvim*)	for three slaves (in most cases)
T.-S., loan 28, fol. 1 (*Mann II*, 1:354–356)	11th	Egypt	5000 dinars	a ransom for 200 persons (25 dinars per person)

Note: The gold *solidus*, or *nomisma* (abbreviated *nom.*) was divided into 12 *milliarisia* (E. Schilbach, *Byzantinische Metrologie*, pp. 169ff. and 185ff.; see also Morrison, "Monnaie et prix à Byzance du Ve au VIIe siècle"); a *milliarision* was divided into 2 *kreatia*; a *kreation* was divided into 12 *folles* or *oboli*.

[a] The exorbitance of that price is noted by the commentator (Lemerle, *Boilas, test.*, p. 34 n. 27) and can only be explained as an error (either by the copyist, the writer, or the testator).

Abbreviations

For complete bibliographical references to the papyrological, legal, and other collections, see entries under the corresponding rubric.

AASS	*Acta Sanctorum*
AB	*Analecta Bollandiana*
ACO	*Acta Conciliorum Oecumenicorum*
Amm.	Ammianus Marcellinus, *Rerum gestarum libri*
Annales ESC	*Annales économies, sociétés, civilisations*
Annales HSS	*Annales histoire, sciences sociales*
App. Eklo.	*Appendix Eclogae*
BAR	British Archaeological Reports
Basilic.	*Basilicorum libri LX*
BBA	Berliner byzantinische Arbeiten
BCH	*Bulletin de correspondance hellénique*
BBS	Berliner byzantinische Studien
BGA	Bibliotheca Geographorum Arabicorum, ed. De Goeje, 8 vols. in 7 parts (Leiden: Brill, 1938–1939; 1st ed. 1870–1894)
BHG	Halkin, *Bibliotheca hagiographica graeca*, 3rd ed.
BHL	*Bibliotheca hagiographica latina antiquae mediae aetatis*
BMGS	*Byzantine and Modern Greek Studies*
BollBadGr	*Bolletino della Badia Greca di Grottaferrata*
BS	*Byzantinoslavica*
BS/EB	*Byzantine Studies/Études byzantines*
ByzF	*Byzantinische Forschungen*
BZ	*Byzantinische Zeitschrift*
CahCM	*Cahiers de civilisation médiévale*
CChr	Corpus Christianorum, Brepols
CFHB	Corpus fontium historiae byzantinae
CJ	*Codex Justiniani*, in *CJC*, Vol. 2
CJC	*Corpus Juris Civilis*

Const. Porph.
De adminis. Constantine Porphyrogenitus, *De administrando imperio*
Const. Porph.
De cerimon. Constantine Porphyrogenitus, *De cerimoniis aulae byzantinae*
CSHB Corpus scriptorum historiae byzantinae, Bonn
CTh *Codex Theodosianus*
Dig. *Digesta*, in *CJC*, Vol. 1
Dölger, *Reg.* *Regesten des Kaiserurkunden des*
     oströmischen Reiches von 565–1453
DOP *Dumbarton Oaks Papers*
Ekloga *Ecloga. Das Gesetzbuch Leons III. Und*
     Konstantinos' V.
EFR École française de Rome
EHESS École des hautes études en sciences sociales
Ency. of Islam *Encyclopedia of Islam* (Leiden: Brill, 1960–)
EO *Échos d'Orient*
Eparch. bib. *Das Eparchenbuch Leons des Weisen*
EPHE École pratique des hautes études
Epit. Leg. *Epitom Legum*
Erytheia *Erytheia Rivista de Estudios Bizantinos y Neogriegos*
Evag., *HE* Evagrius, *Historia ecclesiastica*
Ferrari Ferrari, "Fomulari notarili inediti dell'età bizantina"
Font. min. *Fontes minores*
ForByzRecht Forschungen zur Byzantinischen Rechts-geschichte
Gai. *Inst.* Gaius, *Institutiones*
Gli ebrei nell'alto *Gli ebrei nell'alto medioevo. 30 marzo–5 aprile 1978*, 2 vols.,
   medioevo   *SettStu* 26/1–2 (Spoleto, 1980)
GOrThR *The Greek Orthodox Theological Review*
Grumel, *Reg. pat.* *Les regestes des actes du patriarcat de Constantinople*
Hefele-Leclercq, Hefele-Leclercq, *Histoire des conciles*
   Conciles
Inst. Just. *Institutiones Justiniani*, in *CJC*, Vol. 1
Iviron I *Actes d'Iviron*, Vol. 1, in *Archives de l'Athos*, Vol. 14
Iviron II *Actes d'Iviron*, Vol. 2, in *Archives de l'Athos*, Vol. 16
JHS *Journal of Hellenic Studies*
JÖB *Jarhbuch der Österreichischen Byzantistik* (and before 1969,
     Jahrbuch der Österreichischen byzantinischen Gesellschaft)
Jones, *LRE* Jones, *The Latter Roman Empire 284–602*
JRS *Journal of Roman Studies*
Kekaumenos Kekaumenos, Στρατηγικόν
Lavra I *Actes de Lavra*, Vol. 1, in *Archives de l'Athos*, Vol. 5
Lemerle, *Boïlas*, Lemerle, ed., *Le testament d'Eustathios Boïlas (avril 1059)*
   test.

Mann I	Mann, *The Jews in Egypt and in Palestine under the Fatimid Caliphs: A Contribution to Their Political and Communal History Based Chiefly on Genizah Material hitherto Unpublished*
Mann II	Mann, *Texts and Studies in Jewish History and Literature*
Mansi	Mansi, *Sacrorum conciliorum nova et amplissima collectio*
Mercati e mercanti nell'alto medioevo	*Mercati e mercanti nell'alto medioevo: l'area nell'alto medioevo euro-asiatica e l'area mediterranea. 23–29 aprile 1992, SettStu 40 (Spoleto, 1993).*
MGH	Monumenta Germanie historica
MM	Miklosich-Müller, *Acta et diplomata graeca medii aevi sacra et profana*
MM, *Chios*	*Diplomata et acta monasterii S. Mariae, dicti Neamone, in insula Chio,* in MM, Vol. 5, pp. 1–13
MM, *Patmos*	*Diplomata et acta monasterii Sancti Ioannis Theologi in insula Patmo e tabulario coenobii,* in MM, Vol. 6
MS. *Adler*	Collection of Mr. Elkan N. *Adler* (documents of the Genizah published in Mann I–II)
Nov. Irene	*Die Novellen des Kaiserin Eirene*
Nov. Just.	*Novellae Justiniani,* in *CJC,* Vol. 3
Nov. Leo.	*Les Novelles de Léon le Sage*
Nov. Post. Just.	*Novellae et Aureae Bullae imperatorum post Justinianum,* in Zepos, *JGR,* Vol. 1
Nov. Val.	*Liber legum novellarum divi Valentiniani Augusti*
ODB	*The Oxford Dictionary of Byzantium,* ed. Kazhdan, 3 vols. (Oxford, 1991)
OrChr	Orientalia christiana
OrChrAn	*Orientalia christiana analecta*
OrChrP	*Orientalia christiana periodica*
P & P	*Past and Present: A Journal of Historical Studies*
P. Cair. Masp.	Maspero, *Papyrus grecs d'époque byzantine, Catalogue général des antiquités égyptiennes du Musée du Caire*
P. Köln	*Kölner Papyri*
P. Lond.	*Greek Papyri in the British Museum*
P. Oxy.	*The Oxyrhynchus Papyri*
P. Nessana II	Casson-Hettich, *Excavations at Nessana,* Vol. 2
P. Nessana III	Kraemer, *Excavations at Nessana*
P.S. I	*Papiri greci e latini (Publicazioni della Societa italiana per la ricerca dei papiri greci e latini in Egitto)*
P. Str.	*Griechische Papyrus der kaiserlichen Universitäts—und Landesbibliothek zu Strasburg*
Patmos I	Ἔγγραφα Πάτμου, Vol. 1, Αὐτοκρατορικά
Patmos II	Ἔγγραφα Πάτμου, Vol. 2, Δημοσίων Λειτουργῶν
Patria Const.	Πάτρια Κωνσταντινουπόλεως

PG	Patrologiae cursus completus. Series graeca, ed. Migne, 161 vols. in 166 parts (Paris, 1857–1866)
Pitra, *Juris eccl.*	Pitra, *Juris ecclesaistici Graecorum historia et monumenta* Patrologiae cursus completus. Series latina, ed. Migne, 221 vols. in 222 parts (Paris, 1844–1880)
PLRE	Jones-Martindale-Morris, *The Prosopography of the Later Roman Empire*
PO	Patrologiae Orientalis, ed. Graffin and Nau (Paris, 1904–)
Proc., *BG*	Procopius Caesariensis, *De bello gothico*
Proc., *BP*	Procopius Caesariensis, *De bello persico*
Proch. Nom.	*Prochiros Nomos*
RE	Paulys-Wissowa-Kroll, *Realencyclopädie der classischen Altertumswissenschaft* (Stuttgart, 1893–)
REB	*Revue des études byzantines*
Robinson, Carbone	Robinson, ed., *History and Cartulary of the Greek Monastery of St. Elias and St. Anastasius of Carbone*
RH	*Revue historique*
RP, *Syntagma*	Rhalles and Potles, Σύνταγμα τῶν θειῶν καὶ τῶν ἱερῶν κανονῶν
RSBN	*Rivista di studi bizantini e neoellenici*
RSBS	*Rivista di studi bizantini e slavi*
Sathas, *MB*	Sathas, Μεσαιωνικῆς Βιβλιοθήκης
SC	Sources chrétiennes
SChH	*Studies in Church History*
SB	Preisigke, *Sammelbuch griechischer Urkunden aus Aegypten*
Sebeos	*The Armenian History attributed to Sebeos*
SettStu	*Settimane di Studio del Centro Italiano di Studi sull'alto medioevo*
SubsHag	Subsidia Hagiographica, Société des Bollandistes
Svoronos, *Nov. Mac.*	Svoronos, *Les Novelles des empereurs macédoniens. Concernant la terre et les Stratiotes*
Synax. Const.	*Synaxarium Ecclesiae Constantinopolitanae: Propylaeum ad Acta sanctorum Novembris*, ed. Delehaye
T.-S.	*Taylor-Schechter Collection* (documents of the Genizah published in Mann I–II)
Tafel-Thomas	*Urkunden zur Ältern Handels-und Staatsgeschichte der Republik Venedig*
Theoph.	Theophanes, *Chronographia*
Theoph. Cont.	*Theophanes Continuatus*
TM	*Travaux et Mémoires*
VizVrem	*Vizantijskij vremennik*
VizVrem (BX)	*Vizantijiskij vremennik (Βυζαντινὰ Χρονικὰ)*
Xenophon	*Actes de Xenophon*, in *Archives de l'Athos*, Vol. 15
Zepos, *JGR*	Zepos, *Jus Graecoromanum*
Zos.	Zosimus, *Histoire nouvelle*

Notes

Introduction

1. In "Fernand Braudel, l'Antiquité et l'histoire ancienne," interview conducted by Jean Andreau and Roland Étienne, *Quaderni di Storia* 24 (July–December 1986): 5–21, quoted in Jean Andreau, "Vingt ans après *L'économie antique* de M. I. Finley. Présentation du dossier de *L'économie antique*," p. 960. [Unless otherwise noted, quoted passages are my translation—Trans.]

1. Theoretical Approaches

1. A. Hadjinicolaou-Marava, *Recherches sur la vie des esclaves dans le monde byzantin* (1950). In this chapter I shall indicate the year of publication for each work cited to situate the scholarship on slavery within its historiographical context. For the same reason, the works will be cited in chronological order.

2. The most important of these are: A. Kazhdan, "Slaves and *Misthioi* in Byzantium, Ninth to Eleventh Centuries" (1951; in Russian); M. J. Sjuzjumov, "Occupations and Commerce in Constantinople in the Early Tenth Century" (1951; in Russian); R. Browning, "Slavery in the Byzantine Empire" (1958; in Russian); P. A. Yannopoulos, *La société profane dans l'Empire byzantin des VIIe, VIIIe et IXe siècles* (1975), part 3, "Les personnes privées de liberté (esclaves)"; C. Verlinden, *L'esclavage dans l'Europe médiévale*, Vol. 2: *Italie—Colonies italiennes du Levant—Levant latin—Empire byzantin* (1977); and the studies of Helga Köpstein cited below.

3. H. Köpstein, "Die byzantinische Sklaverei in der Historiographie der letzten 125 Jahre" (1964); H. Köpstein, "Einige Aspekte des byzantinischen und bulgarischen Sklavenhandels im X. Jahrhundret. Zur Novelle des Joannes Tzimiskes über Sklavenhandelszoll" (1966); H. Köpstein, *Zur Sklaverei im Ausgehenden Byzanz: Philologisch-historische Untersuchung* (1966); H. Köpstein, "Zur Sklaverei in byzantinischer Zeit" (1967); H. Köpstein, "Zur Novelle des Alexios Komnenos zum Sklavenstatus (1095)" (1976); H. Köpstein, "Zum Bedeutungswandel von ΣΚΛΑΒΟΣ/SCLAVUS" (1979); H. Köpstein,

"Sklaverei in Byzanz" (1981); H. Köpstein, "Zum Fortleben des Wortes doulos und anderer Bezeichungun für den Sklaven im Mittel- und Neugriechischen" (1981); H. Köpstein, "Sklaven in der 'Peira'" (1994).

4. In using the plural form, I wish to emphasize that, in spite of the term "Greco-Roman antiquity," which covers more than a thousand years, I will distinguish among the different societies.

5. R. MacMullen, "Late Roman Slavery" (1987).

6. And even in Italy: "The further away from Rome, the smaller appears the impact of slave labor in manufacture and the less inventive and pervasive its deployment" (ibid., p. 244).

7. Ibid., p. 248.

8. "In the countryside, villages and smaller, poorer towns of the provinces, I would suppose they amounted to only a few percent at any point in the first four and a half centuries of the era, while in the middle-sized or larger cities the picture we have seems to accord with a figure approaching 25 percent" (ibid., p. 245).

9. Yannopoulos, *La société profane dans l'Empire byzantin*, pp. 278 and 305.

10. P. Garnsey and R. Saller, *The Roman Empire: Economy, Society, Culture* (1987), chap. 5, "The Land"; A. Cameron, *The Later Roman Empire, A.D. 284–430* (1993), pp. 118–121; A. Cameron, *The Mediterranean World in Late Antiquity, A.D. 395–600* (1993), pp. 81–87; P. Garnsey and C. R. Whittaker, "Rural Life in the Later Roman Empire," in *The Cambridge Ancient History*, Vol. 13 (1987), pp. 277–311. While still situating themselves within the economic dimension, Garnsey and Whittaker support the idea that slaves were used as tenant farmers, quasi coloni. In fact, it is not slavery but the economic organization of the late Roman Empire that is central in their analysis. In positing the continued productive labor of slaves, they reject the theory of the general decline of the late empire's economy. Logically, then, these authors refer exclusively to the role of slaves in agriculture. All the same, slaves were not involved solely in agriculture, as their writings might suggest.

11. M. Bloch, "Comment et pourquoi finit l'esclavage antique" (1947); P. Bonnassie, "Survie et extinction du régime esclavagiste dans l'Occident du haut Moyen Âge" (1985).

12. Bonnassie, "Survie et extinction du régime esclavagiste," p. 329.

13. Especially in K. Marx, *The German Ideology* (1845–1846), pp. 89ff.

14. That is, in contrast to the situation of "the conquering barbarian people," for whom only war can produce the need for new means of production.

15. Marx, *The German Ideology*, p. 93.

16. For Marx, "determinism" simply means that historical development rests on material conditions. He does not say that it is always the *same* conditions that determine such a development. On the contrary, he demonstrates that different societies react in different ways depending on the particular political situation. It is the causes of their reactions that are determined. Here is what he says, for example, about the end of slavery in antiquity: "From this necessity of

producing, which very soon asserts itself, it follows . . . that the form of community adapted by the settling conquerors must correspond to the stage of development of the productive forces they find in existence; or, if this is not the case from the start, it must change according to the productive forces. This, too, explains the fact, which people profess to have noticed everywhere in the period following the migration of the peoples, namely that the slave was master, and that the conquerors very soon took over language, culture and manners from the conquered" (ibid., p. 94, [translation slightly modified—Trans.]). I do not wish to address this explanation, which, it must be said, remains completely marginal in Marx's theories. I am merely seeking to understand Marx's perception of slavery, not the decline of the Roman Empire or the historical development that produced capitalism.

17. Hence, in *The Class Struggle in the Ancient Greek World* (1981), G. E. M. de Ste. Croix groups slaves, serfs, debt bondsmen, and coloni under the single term "unfree labour."

18. Bloch, "Comment et pourquoi finit l'esclavage antique," pp. 276–279; M. Bloch, *La société féodale*, pp. 355–370.

19. "Of course, the master had not stopped feeding, lodging, and clothing slaves, who were constantly at his disposal and who helped him work his fields. But they were less and less adequate to the task; it was now tenant farmers, whose lands were placed under the sphere of influence of the principal demesne, who were asked to perform, in the form of obligatory service, the bulk of the labor necessary for his property. Some were no doubt peasants, already accustomed to living under the domination of a powerful landowner, or who gradually came to be so; others had only recently settled on the new parcels of land. In abandoning a part of his landed property, the large landowner thereby assured himself the manpower required for the rest. Many of these newly arrived tenant farmers, as we have seen, were slaves. They continued to toil for the master; but they were no longer kept by him, any more than a present-day employer keeps his employees. The land that had been transferred over to them— subject to rents, moreover, which are not of concern to us here—was something like their wages, on which they had to live" (Bloch, "Comment et pourquoi finit l'esclavage antique," pp. 264–265).

20. M. Bloch, "Liberté et servitude personnelles au Moyen Âge, particulièrement en France" (1933).

21. "We see, however, that all conditions favorable to [the] elimination [of slavery] were combined in Sabina in the second half of the eighth century. It is then that the access to freedom by enfeoffed slaves *(servi residentes)* on tenancies began to break down the legal barrier separating free coloni from the most well-off unfree laborers. The practice of establishing prebendary slaves on smaller parcels carved from the communal lands moved in the same direction. It played a role in attenuating social differences between *servi residentes* and *servi manuales*. It created the best conditions for their being jointly accepted within the body of free tenant farmers" (P. Toubert, *Les structures du Latium*

médiéval. Le Latium méridional et la Sabine du IXe à la fin du XIIe siècle [1973], p. 478).

22. J. P. Poly and E. Bournazel, *La mutation féodale, Xe–XIIe siècles* (1980), p. 211.

23. P. Dockès, *La libération médiévale* (1979). Slaves reacted to that collapse by engaging in social struggle. Here Dockès, though speaking in Marxist terms, opposes the "ideological" thesis that political changes emerge from the struggle of "unfree producers."

24. Bonnassie, "Survie et extinction du régime esclavagiste."

25. G. Duby, *La société aux XIe et XIIe siècles dans la région mâconaise* (1971); G. Duby, *Guerriers et paysans, VIIe–XIIe siècles, premier essor de l'économie européenne* (1973); G. Duby, "Servage," in *Encyclopaedia universalis* (1989–1990), 20:934–936; D. Barthélemy, "Qu'est-ce que le servage en France au XIe siècle?" (1992).

26. I will have occasion to return several times to the work of Helga Köpstein, who views the matter differently.

27. They came to have a greater presence beginning in the tenth century, especially in archival documents. The term literally means "resident" or "dwelling nearby," but their origin remains obscure.

28. On the identification of the *paroikoi* with the coloni of late antiquity, see H. Köpstein, "Paroiken in frühen Byzanz: Zu Problemen von Terminus und Status" (1992). Köpstein shows that there was in fact no development linking the two in the ninth to eleventh centuries.

29. G. Ostrogorsky, *Quelques problèmes d'histoire de la paysannerie byzantine* (1956), pp. 29ff.; D. M. Gorecki, "A Farmer Community of the Byzantine Middle Ages: Historiography and Legal Analysis of Sources" (1982); D. M. Gorecki, "The Slavic Theory in Russian Pre-revolutionary Historiography of the Byzantine Farmer Community" (1986).

30. This is the favorite theme of the historians cited above who analyze the Byzantine countryside. The legislative sources are collected in N. Svoronos, *Les Novelles des empereurs macédoniens: Concernant la terre et les stratiotes* (1994).

31. Browning, "Slavery in the Byzantine Empire"; N. Oikonomides, "Οἱ Βυζαντινοὶ δουλοπάροικοι" (1983).

32. That population was one of the sources for the supply of slaves, acquired by war and piracy, in the Arab world.

33. The Zanj uprisings in Iraq in 694 and again between 868 and 883, described by historians of the time, attest to the agricultural use of slaves on rice, cotton, and sugarcane plantations *(Ency. of Islam,* s.v. "al-Zandj," 11:444–446 [A. Popovic], based on Al-Tabarī, *Ta'rīkh al-rusul wa'l-mulūk* 3:1742–1787; 1835–2103); A. Popovic, *La révolte des esclaves en Iraq aux IIIe–IXe siècles;* B. Lewis, *Race and Slavery in the Middle East,* pp. 31–34, 62ff. For the special character of military slaves in Islam, see D. Pipes, *Slave Soldiers and Islam: The Genesis of a Military System.* For the sociopolitical explanation of the phenomenon, see P. Crone, *Slaves on Horses: The Evolution of the Islamic Polity,* esp. chaps. 9–10.

34. I am not speaking of military functions traditionally performed by slaves as oarsmen, but of slaves as soldiers. The most representative example is the re-

cruitment of twenty thousand slaves by Augustus to fight against Sextus Pompeius. To manage this, Augustus first had to emancipate them (Suetonius, *Divus Augustus* 16), even though he used them as oarsmen. Dio Cassius (48.49.1) does not mention their emancipation (see also 50.11). P. Vidal-Naquet and P. Ducrey note the same phenomenon in Athens (P. Vidal-Naquet, "Les esclaves grecs étaient-ils une classe?" p. 90; P. Ducrey, *Guerre et guerriers dans la Grèce antique*, p. 218). See, by way of comparison, Pausanias's description of the battle of Marathon, where "slaves fought for the first time." The Athenians buried slaves in a separate tomb with the Boeotians (Pausanias 1.32-3). In their war against Mummius (147 b.c.), the Achaeans emancipated slaves to make them soldiers, "imitating the decision of Miltiade and the Athenians before the Marathon crisis" (Pausanias 7.15.7; 16.7).

35. There were cases, however, when Persian, Slav, and Arab captives became part of the Byzantine army. They were probably emancipated for that purpose.

36. For a definition of a slave-owning society based on the percentage of slaves within it, see K. Hopkins, *Conquerors and Slaves*, chap. 2, "The Growth and Practice of Slavery in Roman Times."

37. See Köpstein, *Zur Sklaverei im Ausgehenden Byzanz* as well as her other works.

38. Verlinden, *L'esclavage dans l'Europe médiévale*, 2:978–998. See also Michael McCormick's recent book, *Origins of the European Economy: Communications and Commerce, a.d. 300–900* (2001).

39. Verlinden, *L'esclavage dans l'Europe médiévale*, 1:95–110.

40. Bonnassie, "Survie et extinction du régime esclavagiste," pp. 309–310. The following passage shows that Bonnassie's perspective differs from Verlinden's: "As for the economic analysis, it is shortsighted; although we are spared none of the variations in the market price of slaves, the very concept of a slave mode of production is ignored. In fact, C. Verlinden's vast undertaking represents no advance in relation to the sorts of questions formulated by Marc Bloch. On the contrary, it tends to obscure the problems by treating within a single approach the two very different types of slavery that medieval Europe possessed: the rural slavery of the late Middle Ages (the dominant mode of production bequeathed by antiquity); and the commercial slavery of the early modern age, an urban slavery with an artisanal or domestic aim, which was a marginal phenomenon having little effect beyond the major ports of the Mediterranean basin."

41. Verlinden, *L'esclavage dans l'Europe médiévale*, 2:978–980.

42. J. Heers, *Esclaves et domestiques au Moyen-Âge dans le monde méditerranéen* (1981).

43. I do not mean to suggest, however, that I have no interest in studying the economic functions of Byzantine slaves. I shall later show that the lack of a single economic status for Byzantine slaves had social consequences.

44. Vidal-Naquet, "Les esclaves grecs étaient-ils une classe?"

45. In the articles in J. P. Vernant and P. Vidal-Naquet, eds., *Travail et esclavage en Grèce ancienne* (1988).

46. M. I. Finley, *Ancient Slavery and Modern Ideology* (1980).

47. Finley cites three conditions necessary for the creation of a slave society (ibid., chap. 2: "The Emergence of a Slave Society," esp. pp. 84–97): "My argument is that, logically, the demand for slaves precedes the supply. The Romans captured many tens of thousands of men, women and children during the Italian and Punic wars because the demand for slaves already existed, not the other way round. Existence of a sufficient demand requires at least three necessary conditions. The first, in a world which was overwhelmingly agrarian, is private ownership of land, with sufficient concentration in some hands to need extra-familial labour for the permanent work-force. The second is a sufficient development of commodity production and markets (for the present discussion it does not matter whether the market is a distant one, an export-market in the popular sense, or a nearby urban centre). Hypothetically, helots and other forms of dependent labour can be employed in non–commodity-producing societies, but not slaves, who must be imported regularly, in quantity, and therefore paid for. The third is a negative condition, the unavailability of an internal labour supply, compelling the employers of labour to turn to outsiders. All these conditions must exist at the same time, as they did in Athens and other Greek communities in the sixth century B.C. and in Rome by the third century B.C. at the latest" (ibid., p. 86). By the same reasoning, I may add, "in the New World."

48. After setting his three conditions, Finley has to search for at least one that no longer existed in the late period of the Roman Empire to explain the "replacement" of the slave system (ibid., chap. 4, "The Decline of Ancient Slavery," esp. pp. 123–149). See J. Andreau's critique "Originalité de l'historiographie finleyenne, et remarques sur les classes sociales" (1982); and J. M. Carrié, "Esclavage antique et idéologie moderne dans *Ancient Slavery and Modern Ideology*" (1982).

49. M. I. Finley, *Economy and Society in Ancient Greece* (1982), p. 115.

50. H. Wallon, *Histoire de l'esclavage dans l'Antiquité* (1847).

51. I will not comment here on the moral (or, for Finley, ideological) element in Wallon; there is no reason to insist on the interpretation presented in the final chapter, which attempts to explain the decline of ancient slavery in terms of Christianity. It is not altogether true that Wallon, who was greatly criticized by Finley *(Ancient Slavery and Modern Ideology,* chap. 1, esp. pp. 12–17 and 32–39), analyzes classical societies in light of what he sees in slave-owning societies of his own time. His moral explanation—that slavery destroys society morally and then economically—was as irrelevant for the Caribbean as it was for Greece. Such an interpretation no longer has currency.

52. Nonetheless, let me point out that Wallon was writing in a society where slavery coexisted with what he called "free labor," that is, wage labor, whereas when Finley was writing slavery no longer existed. In addition, I cannot reject the idea of an economic cleavage while continuing to speak of a social cleavage without mentioning M. I. Rostovzeff's thesis. In his *Social and Economic History of the Roman Empire* (1926), Rostovzeff rejects the economic explanation of the decline of the Roman Empire. In opposing the notion of "precapitalist

societies" (which has since been replaced by that of "preindustrial societies"), he cites social causes. In chapter 12 ("The Decay of Ancient Civilization"), he concludes: "The evolution of the ancient world has a lesson and a warning for us. Our civilization will not last unless it be a civilization not of one class, but of the masses" (pp. 486–487). Although Rostovzeff is speaking not of slaves but of the poor, there is an echo here of Wallon's reasoning.

53. J. P. Vernant, "La lutte des classes" (1965), p. 77; P. Vidal-Naquet, "Réflexion sur l'historiographie grecque de l'esclavage" (1973), pp. 100–102.

54. A. Testart, "L'esclavage comme institution" (1998).

55. Vernant, "La lutte des classes" (1965), p. 77. Vidal-Naquet: "The slave made the social game possible, not because he assured material labor as a whole (that will never be the case), but because his status as anticitizen, absolute stranger, allowed the status of citizen to develop; because the slave trade and trade in general, the monetary economy, allowed an altogether extraordinary number of Athenians to be citizens" ("Les esclaves grecs étaient-ils une classe?" pp. 89–90). It is interesting to note that although Bonnassie sees slavery in terms of economics, he shares the same point of view: "A telling argument: beggars, the destitute, are, to be sure, situated on the lowest rung of the social ladder; hence the solicitude with which the clergy surrounds them. Where are the slaves, then? Outside society" (Bonnassie, "Survie et extinction du régime esclavagiste," p. 324).

56. O. Patterson, *Slavery and Social Death: A Comparative Study* (1982).

57. That point of view has been rendered null and void by the works of Jean-Michel Carrié.

58. Although Byzantine law emerged from Roman law, it is necessary to distinguish between the two. That distinction will be explained subsequently, particularly in relation to the institution of slavery.

59. *Inst. Just.* 1.3, in R. W. Lee, *The Elements of Roman Law, with a Translation of the Institutes of Justinian*, p. 54 [Latin terms in parentheses appear in Lee's translation; those italicized in brackets are Y. Rotman's intercalations—Trans.]. In the version from the Justinian era:

De iure personarum:

Summa itaque divisio de iure personarum haec est quod omnes homines aut liberi sunt aut servi. 1. Et libertas quidem est, ex qua etiam liberi vocantur, naturalis facultas eius quod cuique facere libet, nisi si quid aut vi aut iure prohibetur. 2. Servitus autem est constitutio iuris gentium, qua quis dominio alieno contra naturam subicitur. 3. Servi autem ex eo appellati sunt, quod imperatores captivos vendere iubent ac per hoc servare nec occidere solent, qui etiam mancipia dicti sunt, quod ab hostibus manu capiuntur. 4. Servi autem aut nascuntur aut fiunt. Nascuntur ex ancillis nostris; fiunt aut iure gentium, id est ex captivate, aut iure civili, cum homo liber maior viginti annis ad pretium participandum sese venumdari passus est. In servorum condicione nulla differentia est. 5. In liberis multae differentiae sunt. Aut enim ingenui sunt aut libertini. (See also *Dig.* 1.5.4.)

60. By virtue of the distinction among three types of law: first, "natural law" *(ius*

naturale or *nature),* the order existing without the intervention of man-made law; second, "the law of peoples" or "of people" *(ius gentium),* the norms of private law that Roman legislators believed valid among all peoples; and third, "civil law" *(ius civile),* the law of the state or of the Roman Empire.

61. *Inst. Just.* 1.8.
62. *Inst. Just.* 1.5.
63. Does it not also confuse the present-day terms "freedom" and "equality"?
64. M. Gordon, *Slavery in the Modern World,* pp. 43–44.
65. *CJ* 9.11; *App. Eklo.* 4.4; J. Beaucamp, *Le statut de la femme à Byzance (IVe–VIIe siècles),* 1:181–182.
66. See the example of the mobility of slaves in medieval Icelandic society by virtue of their ability to become emancipated (R. Boyer, *L'Islande médiévale,* pp. 53–55).
67. As demonstrated in the articles collected in the issue of *Journal des africanistes* titled *L'ombre portée de l'esclavage. Avatars contemporains de l'oppression sociale,* edited by R. Botte (70, nos. 1–2 [2000]).
68. K. Bradley, *Slavery and Society at Rome* (1994). See also Patterson, *Slavery and Social Death.*
69. That is an ethnocentric perspective that biases reflection. The model seems so inherent in our society that we have a tendency to generalize it to all societies. Nevertheless, even in contemporary societies, civil, social, and economic statuses are far from coextensive.
70. For a methodological example, see G. Condominas, ed., *Formes extrêmes de dépendance, contribution à l'étude de l'esclavage en Asie du Sud-Est* (1998), especially the articles by H. Stern, E. T. Magnnon, A. Gurreiro, P. Beaujard, M. A. Martin, H. Sok, L. F. F. R. Thomaz, B. Milcent, J. P. Dimenichiani, B. D. Ramiaramana, B. Brac de la Perrière, and A. Doré.
71. Ibid.
72. In rejecting the idea that coloni replaced slaves as "a new form of forced labor," I am following J. M. Carrié's "Le 'Colonat du Bas-Empire': Un mythe historiographique" (1982); J. M. Carrié, "Un roman des origines: Les généalogies du 'Colonat du Bas-Empire'" (1983); and J. M. Carrié, "'Colonato del Basso Impero': La resistenza del mito" (1997).

2. Medieval Slavery in a New Geopolitical Space

1. *Dig.* 1.5.5.2; *Proch. Nom.* 34.5–7.
2. *Proch. Nom.* 34.5–7. There were several terms for designating a free man. But unlike the words relating to a slave, they defined different legal statuses, as indicated in the *Inst. Just.* (1.3), "De iure personarum," and then in the *Prochiros Nomos* (34.3). There were no legal categories for *douloi,* as there were for *eleutheroi:* (1) *eleutheros/a (liber/a);* (2) *apeleutheros/a (libertus/a);* (3) *eugenēs (ingenuus/a).* The word *apeleutheros* referred to someone with the status of an emancipated slave (it is translated here as "freedman"), *eugenēs* to a man who

was born free ("freeborn"). Nevertheless, *eleutheros,* a freeman in general, was also used for an emancipated slave. Legally, *freeborn* was a different status from *freedman.* In cases where no distinction was made between these two statuses, the law generally spoke of *eleutheros,* in the *Novellae* of Leo VI for example, when it was not necessary to specify whether one was *freeborn.* As a result, *eleutheros,* translated here as *free,* designated the status of an emancipated person falling within the status of a *free person.*

3. *Nov. Just.* 18.1; *App. Eklo.* 10.2. According to classical Roman law, the status of the child after birth was independent of its mother's status. Changes in the law were introduced by Justinian.

4. *CJ* 9.11; *App. Eklo.* 4.4.

5. *Nov. Leo.* 59.

6. *Nov. Leo.* 100.

7. W. W. Buckland, *The Roman Law of Slavery,* pp. 420–422; *CTh* 4.8.6.

8. *CJ* 9.20.7; *Ekloga* 17.16; *Proch. Nom.* 39.5, 39.22.

9. *Nov. Just.* 134.7; 153; *Nov. Post. Just.,* coll. 4, nov. 35.

10. *Proch. Nom.* 34.2–3.

11. For the moment I shall apply the term "Byzantine population" only to inhabitants born in Byzantium and shall not address the question of whether, for example, a slave imported from a foreign country belonged to that population.

12. On this question I rely on the following sources, cited in chronological order: A. A. Vasiliev, *Byzance et les Arabes;* M. Canard, "Deux épisodes des relations diplomatiques arabo-byzantines au Xe siècle"; M. Canard, "Quelques 'à-côtés' de l'histoire des relations entre Byzance et les Arabes"; H. Kennedy, "Byzantine-Arab Diplomacy in the Near East from the Islamic Conquests to the Mid-eleventh Century"; R. Khouri, "'Ανεπίσημες ἀνταλλαγές, ἐξαγορές καί ἀπελευθερώσεις Βυζαντινῶν καί 'Αράβων αἰχμαλώτων"; A. Tibi, "Byzantine-Fatimid Relations in the Reign of al-Mu'izz Li-Din Allah (R. 953–957 A.D.) as Reflected in Primary Arabic Sources"; D. Letsios, "Die Kriegsgefangenschaft nach Auffassung der Byzantiner"; C. Verlinden, "Guerre et traite comme sources de l'esclavage dans l'empire byzantin aux IXe et Xe siècles"; T. G. Kolias, "Kriegsgefangene, Sklavenhandel und die Privilegien des Soldaten: Die Aussage der Novelle von Ioannes Tzimisikes"; M. Campagnolo-Pothitou, "Les échanges de prisonniers entre Byzance et l'Islam aux IXe et Xe siècles"; A. Kolia-Dermitzaki, "Some Remarks on the Fate of Prisoners of War in Byzantium (Ninth–Tenth Centuries)."

13. Campagnolo-Pothitou, "Les échanges de prisonniers entre Byzance et l'Islam"; Khouri, "'Ανεπίσημες ἀνταλλαγές, ἐξαγορές καί ἀπελευθερώσεις Βυζαντινῶν καί 'Αράβων αἰχμαλώτων."

14. *Inst. Just.* 1.3. The status of captured Romans is addressed at length in Buckland, *Roman Law of Slavery,* pp. 291–317 (though not a recent work, a more extensive and exhaustive study of the Roman legal institution of slavery could hardly be hoped for; it remains irreplaceable). See also M. Kaser, *Das römische Privatrecht,* 1:290–291.

15. This was the case only for a Roman held captive in an enemy country. Romans captured by pirates, bandits, or during a civil war retained their free status (Buckland, *Roman Law of Slavery*, pp. 291–292). See also *Dig.* 28.1.13, "qui a latronibus capti sunt, cum liberi manent, possunt facere testamentum," in contrast to *Dig.* 28.1.12, which refers to those captured *in hostium potestate* but nevertheless allows heirs to inherit from such Romans who die in captivity.

16. The property he had assigned to his own slave or to his son by *actio de peculio* before being taken captive did not fall into that category. In fact, the subject of the peculium belonging to the captive's slave or son was an object of debate among third-century jurists (Buckland, *Roman Law of Slavery*, pp. 294–295).

17. *Dig.* 49.15.12.4; 15.8; Buckland, *Roman Law of Slavery*, pp. 295–298.

18. The Romans sometimes asked that their captured citizens be returned, however. See J. Kolendo, "Les Romains prisonniers de guerre des Barbares au Ier et au IIe siècle." The only reference given by Dio Cassius is the treaty of 172. The return of Roman captives was requested from the Quadi (Dio Cassius 72.13). P. Ducrey indicates two other examples in the treaties the Romans concluded with their defeated enemies, especially with the kings of Macedonia and Syria, from whom they demanded the return of their prisoners and refugees. These treaties contain no reciprocity clause (P. Ducrey, *Guerre et guerriers dans la Grèce antique*, p. 242). In addition, the fate of these Romans returned by the enemy is unknown.

19. Malchus, frag. 6.2 (in Blockley, *The Fragmentary Classicising Historians of the Later Roman Empire*); frag. 4 (L. R. Cresci, ed., *Malco di Filadelfia Frammenti*, p. 77). Cresci writes that Heraclius was probably made *Magister Militum per Thracias* by Zeno (Cresci, ed., *Malco di Filadelfia Frammenti*, p. 176).

20. Buckland, *Roman Law of Slavery*, pp. 304–317 and 597; E. Lévy, "Captivus redemptus"; L. Amirante, *Prigionia di guerra: Riscatto e postliminium;* R. Mentxaka, "Sobre la existencia de un *ius pignoris* del redentor sobre el cautivo redimido en el derecho romano clasico"; A. Maffi, *Ricerche sur postliminium;* M. F. Cursi, *La struttura del 'Postliminium' nella repubblica et nel principato.* See also Kaser, *Das römische Privatrecht*, 1:291 and 2:129–132.

21. Provided that the state applied the *ius postliminii* on his behalf. On this subject, historians often mention the fate of Hannibal's captives in Cannae, whom Rome refused to ransom, as well as the case of Attilius Regulus. The *postliminium* was created, in fact, for Romans who fell outside the *limes* of the Roman *ius civile* and not specifically for Romans captured at war. As for captured slaves, in returning to the empire they once more became the slaves of their former masters.

22. M. Melluso, *La schiavitù nell'età giustinianea*, pp. 18–23.

23. See esp. Mentxaka, "Sobre la existencia de un *ius pignoris* del redentor"; and *CJ* 8.50.3.

24. Mentxaka, "Sobre la existencia de un *ius pignoris* del redentor," p. 331; *Dig.* 49.15.12; Buckland, *Roman Law of Slavery*, pp. 304–317; Kaser, *Das römische Privatrecht*, 1:291; 2:129–130; *Dig.* 49.15.5ff.

25. M. V. Sanna, *Nuove ricerche in tema di postliminium e redemptio ab hostibus.*

26. *Dig.* 49.15.2. All the same, Trajan returned the weapons captured by the Daci in 100 (Dio Cassius 68.9.3). During the war against the Germanic tribes in A.D. 9, many Romans were captured. Some were then redeemed by their families. That act, writes Dio, was permitted at the time provided that the persons so ransomed remained outside Italy (Dio Cassius, 56.22.4, following Kolendo, "Les Romains prisonniers de guerre des Barbares").

27. See the analysis in P. Dockès, *La libération médiévale,* pp. 10–14.

28. *CJ* 8.50.15.

29. Roman law recognized the restoration of such a person's free status by postliminium as soon as his ransom price was reimbursed. That status was then attributed to him retroactively from the moment he was captured. And yet, for any other scenario, there seems to have been a reluctance to impose different laws or Roman jurisprudence. The works that clearly explain the legal problematic in this regard are Maffi, *Ricerche sur postliminium,* part 4; Cursi, *La struttura del 'Postliminium' nella repubblica et nel principato,* chaps. 9–10; and Mentxaka, "Sobre la existencia de un *ius pignoris* del redentor." Maffi and Cursi show the legal evolution of the matter and critique earlier studies. Historians speak almost exclusively of the captive who had the money to ransom himself from his purchaser. That was in fact the only case that attracted the attention of Roman jurists. Mentxaka explains precisely that if the person did not have the means, he became de facto a slave.

30. *CTh* 5.7.2 (*CJ* 8.50.20). See Amirante, *Prigionia di guerra,* pp. 253ff.

31. Note that the process was not considered *manumissio,* and the liberated captive regained his original status.

32. But Olympiodorus, frag. 7, indicates that, during the siege of Rome by Alaric, many slaves fled ("especially those of Barbarian origin").

33. Ambrose, *De officiis* 15.70–71. For cases where the Vandals' captives were redeemed by Western bishops, see J. Gaudemet, *L'Église dans l'Empire romain (IVe–Ve siècles),* p. 310 n. 6.

34. "As for these men, therefore, I preferred to return them to you free rather than keep the gold. That host of prisoners, that procession, gleams brighter than the beauty of goblets. It is for this purpose that the Redeemer's gold ought to be put to use, that is, to redeem men in peril." Nevertheless, "the Eucharistic goblet must not leave the church in that form, for fear that the sacred chalice service will be put to impious uses. That is why, within the church, sacred vessels that had not been consecrated were first sought out; they were then shattered and finally melted down, divided up into small pieces and distributed to the indigent *(egentibus);* they also served as ransom for prisoners" (Ambrose, *De officiis* 28.136–143, M. Testard translation) [my translation from the French—Trans.].

35. Amm., 18.2; Zos. 3.4. Eunapius (frag. 19) attributes the initiative to Vadomar, king of the Alamans, who asked that his son, a hostage of the Romans, be returned.

36. *Nov. Just.* 120.9, originally promulgated for the church of Jerusalem.
37. *Nov. Just.* 131.11.
38. *P. Cair. Masp.,* 3.67312. On the abduction of free persons in Egypt in the sixth century, see papyrus *SB* 3.6097. For other sources regarding the redemption of captives as an act of charity, see Amirante, *Prigionia di guerra*, chaps. 9–10.
39. Proc., *BP* 2.5. Nevertheless, Procopius indicates that the initiative came from the Persian king and that the bishop Candidus rejected it on the pretext that he did not have enough money. Khosrow, in love with a captive Christian girl, whom he married, had the captives returned before receiving the total sum of two *centenaria*. Theophanes relates that Emperor Maurice refused all offers from the king of the Avars to ransom Byzantine prisoners (Theoph. A. M. 6092, pp. 279–280). As a result, the Byzantines became enraged against Maurice, who, according to Theophanes, had to repent because, not having ransomed the prisoners, "he sinned against God" (Theoph. A. M. 6092–6093, pp. 279–285). Note, however, that unlike Procopius, who lived in the sixth century, Theophanes was writing at a time when the redemption of prisoners of war was customary. For the ransom of the captives in Gaul during the same period, see W. Klingshirn, "Charity and Power: Caesarius of Arles and the Ransoming of Captives in Sub-Roman Gaul," which identifies the bishop's personal motives behind the act of redemption.
40. *The Talmud of Babylonia* (Baba Batra 1.3; Neusner, ed., 22A:8) makes the ransoming of captives *(Pidyon Shevuym)* a "mitzvah raba" (great precept) for which public money, even that intended for the construction of a synagogue, could be used.
41. In *The Manumission of Slaves in Early Christianity* (chap. 4), J. A. Harrill shows that, between the first and third centuries, public cash boxes in synagogues and churches raised funds for the collective emancipation of private slaves.
42. *Nov. Just.* 22.7 (*cf. Nov. Just.* 117.11, which establishes an indeterminate waiting period for a spouse in captivity). In application of that method, the *Novella* voided the right of the husband to the dowry if he wanted to dissolve the marriage. Hence the dissolution of marriage was possible only for the person who gave up nuptial property rights.
43. Note that the law prohibiting the enslavement of a free person by the state *(Nov. Just.* 22.8) was part of the same *Novella*.
44. G. Greatrex, *Rome and Persia at War, 502–532;* E. Chrysos, "Some Aspects of Roman-Persian Legal Relations."
45. S. Lieu, "Captives, Refugees, and Exiles: A Study of Cross-Frontier Civilian Movements and Contacts between Rome and Persia from Valerian to Jovian."
46. Proc., *BP* 2.14.
47. Sebeos, chap. 33 (112).
48. Proc., *BP* 2.26.
49. In works by fifth- and sixth-century historians and in Greatrex, *Rome and Persia at War, 502–532;* and Chrysos, "Some Aspects of Roman-Persian Legal Relations."

50. Proc., *BP* 1.13; Theoph. A. M. 6080 (p. 261).
51. Proc., *BP* 1.7.
52. Priscus, frag. 2.
53. Ibid.
54. Menander Protector, frag. 23.8–9.
55. Sebeos, chap. 38 (126); 29 (128); Theoph. A. M. 6114 (p. 308).
56. I use the word "citizen" to designate civilian residents of the empire who had reached legal age and enjoyed free status.
57. As Buckland says, quoting Otto Karlova: "A war ends either by surrender of the enemy—*deditio*—or by a treaty of *amicitia*" (Buckland, *The Roman Law of Slavery*, p. 306).
58. Ibid., p. 292. The reason was the same in both cases: the abduction by pirates or bandits was considered an act of theft, whereas war (and hence capture during wartime) was a lawful act. For a definition of banditry in Roman law, see B. D. Shaw, "Bandits in the Roman Empire," pp. 6–7 and 21–22. Shaw provides a social definition of the phenomenon and points to its presence in the Roman world. Piracy became a threat for the Roman state only in the first century B.C. (pp. 39–40).
59. In "Piracy under the Principate and the Ideology of Imperial Eradication," D. Braund shows that piracy was not completely eliminated under the principate and that it was imperial ideology that led Roman historians to present it as such (see *Res Gestae Divi Augusti* 25, where Augustus claims to have personally rid the sea of pirates through a war that was actually a civil war against Sextus Pompeius). As Benjamin Isaac shows, acts of banditry were still present in Palestine, Arabia, and Syria in the first to third centuries (see also Priscus, frag. 4). The Roman authorities aimed to eliminate them (B. Isaac, "Bandits in Judaea and Arabia"). See also P. de Souza, *Piracy in the Graeco-Roman World*, chap. 6.
60. Attested for the Saracens even in the sixth century; Proc., *BP* 1.17; Malalas, log. 18.35 (L. Dindorf, ed., p. 447). The Saracens later sold those captured during the repression of the Samaritan revolt in the Persian Empire and in India.
61. *Ekloga* 8.2: "If someone purchases from the enemies an [originally] free captive and establishes him in his *oikos*, and if the captive has the means to pay the value agreed upon between them, let him be released as free. But if he does not have the means, let his purchaser keep him as a wage earner until the agreed-upon value is reached; the auditors will obviously fix what must be paid as a wage each year to the man thus purchased."
62. Unlike the constitution of Honorius, which sets a period of five years of labor for the captive to ransom himself, the *Ekloga* fixes neither a time frame nor a price.
63. Campagnolo-Pothitou, "Les échanges de prisonniers entre Byzance et l'Islam." The author chooses to base her argument on the writings of al-Maqrīzī (1363–1442), explaining that they conserve information lost from *al-Tanbīh* by al-Masʿūdī (893–956), which has come down to us with several lacunae as a result of the deterioration of the two known manuscripts

(Campagnolo-Pothitou, "Les échanges de prisonniers entre Byzance et l'Islam," pp. 10–11). See also the exchanges of prisoners between the Byzantines and the Arabs, reported by al-Masʿūdī and translated by M. Canard in Vasiliev, *Byzance et les Arabes*, 2, pt. 2:405–408.

64. A. J. Toynbee, *Constantine Porphyrogenitus and His World*, pp. 390–393; A. Kolia-Dermitzaki, "Some Remarks on the Fate of Prisoners of War," pp. 614–620, and, for the exchanges in Sicily, pp. 603–604.

65. Theoph. A. M. 6261 (p. 444).

66. According to the editor, L. Burgmann, it was published in March 741 rather than in 727 (*Ecloga. Das Gesetzbuch III. und Konstantinos' V,* pp. 10–12). N. Van der Wal and J. H. A. Lokin agree *(Historiae Iuris Graeco-romani delineatio. Les sources du droit byzantin de 300 à 1453*, p. 72).

67. The manuscript tradition links this collection to the *Ecloga privata* (the legislative manual of Leo III).

68. *Leges militares (version B)*, p. 48.

69. The collection contains rules dating back to the sixth century: P. Verri, *Le leggi penali militari dell'impero bizantino nell'alto medioevo*, pp. 13ff.; Van der Wal and Lokin, *Historiae Iuris Graeco-romani*, pp. 73–74; *ODB* 3:1492, s. v. "Nomos Stratiotikos." In any case, rule 48 in the Korzenszky edition (*Laurentinian Codex* 75.6), which is not found in the manuscript edited by W. Ashburner *(Leges militares [version A])*, must have been written after the promulgation of the *Ecloga*.

70. Al-Masʿūdī, *Murūj al-dhahab wa-maʿadin al-jawhar* 8.75–76 (*The Meadows of Gold*, p. 320), quoted in Campagnolo-Pothitou, "Les échanges de prisonniers entre Byzance et l'Islam," pp. 22–23.

71. Al-Balādhurī, *Kitāb Futūh al-Buldān (History of Muslim Conquests)*, p. 133 (pp. 112–113 in the new edition by F. Sezgin), cited in Campagnolo-Pothitou, "Les échanges de prisonniers entre Byzance et l'Islam," p. 23.

72. By being liberated, ransomed, or enslaved (R. Guemara, "La libération et le rachat des captifs. Une lecture musulmane"); Campagnolo-Pothitou, "Les échanges de prisonniers entre Byzance et l'Islam," pp. 8–10; *Koran,* "Muhammad," sura 47:4–10: "When you meet the unbelievers in the battlefield strike off their heads and, when you have laid them low, bind your captives firmly. Then grant them their freedom or take a ransom *(fidā)* from them."

73. Campagnolo-Pothitou, "Les échanges de prisonniers entre Byzance et l'Islam," pp. 8–10. The paragraph that speaks of the charity *(birr)* of liberating the slave does not mention the *fidā (Koran,* "The Cow," sura 2:177) even though, in the French translation, Denise Masson renders it as "ransom." See also M. Khadduri, *War and Peace in the Law of Islam*, chap. 11, "Spoils of War."

74. For a comparison, see Yvonne Friedman, *Encounter between Enemies: Captivity and Ransom in the Latin Kingdom of Jerusalem*. The crusaders were aware of their Arab adversaries' custom of exchanging prisoners.

75. Al-Masʿūdī, *Kitāb al-Tanbīh wa'l-ishrāf* p. 188 (B. C. de Vaux translation, *Le livre de l'avertissement et de la révision*, p. 254.), cited in Campagnolo-Pothitou, "Les échanges de prisonniers entre Byzance et l'Islam," p. 21.

76. In "La libération et le rachat des captifs," Guemara bases his argument on the Koran and shows that there were no public exchanges stipulated by Islamic law.

77. Scholars sometimes confuse these slaves with ransomed prisoners of war. See N. Stratos's interpretation of the treaties of 659 and 685 in *Byzantium in the Seventh Century*, 3:188 and n. 693, 4:48.

78. There are also treaties that give the total figure. Theoph. A. M. 6150 (p. 347); A. M. 6176 (p. 361); A. M. 6178 (p. 363).

79. Slaves belonging to a tribute are not found in the treaties between the Persians and the Byzantines, which tallies well with the fate of captives among the Persians.

80. According to al-Tabarī in 802 or 803 and al-Masʿūdī in about 806; M. Canard, "La prise d'Héraclée et les relations entre Hârûn al-Rashîd et l'empereur Nicéphore Ier."

81. M. Canard ("Quelques 'à-côtés' de l'histoire des relations") and H. Kennedy ("Byzantine-Arab Diplomacy in the Near East from the Islamic Conquests to the Mid-eleventh Century," p. 135) show that such relations already existed in the seventh century.

82. *Ekloga* 8.4.2; *Leges militares (version A)*, 22.

83. Menander Protector, frag. 6.1ff.

84. That was also true in the treaties of 574 (ibid., frag. 18.2–4) and 576 (frag. 20.2).

85. R. C. Blockley, *The History of Menander the Guardsman: Introductory Essay, Text*, p. 257 n. 55.

86. Menander Protector, frag. 6.1.

87. Unlike the fate of Hun refugees: their king demanded them back from the Romans and then crucified them (Priscus, frag. 2). For other accords dealing with the Roman refugees, see Priscus, frag. 9–11, 14–15, and 41.

88. Menander Protector, frag. 6; Theoph. A. M. 6305 (pp. 497–498) for the Bulgar-Byzantine treaty of 812.

89. *Digenis Akritas* (Grottaferrata version), 1.30ff.

90. Ibid., 2.50ff. The same theme is also found in the Arabic literature.

91. Const. Porph., *De cerimon.* 2.49 (p. 695). Cretan captives who declined to convert were tortured by Nicetas *(Theoph. Cont.* 5.61).

92. Note that, in the story of Digenis Akritas, the emir falls in love with a Christian woman (whom he had kidnapped) and converts to marry her. Here the romantic character of the narrative makes its appearance.

93. *Life of Athanasia of Aegina* 2.

94. A. M. Talbot, who comments on this narrative, adopts Kazhdan's interpretation that the edict was promulgated by Theophilus in 832 (A. M. Talbot, *Holy Women of Byzantium: Ten Saints' Lives in English Translation*, p. 143 n. 22). The edict is cited by Dölger (Dölger, *Reg.* 1, no. 422).

95. Al-Masʿūdī, *Murūj al-dhahab wa-maʿadin al-jawhar* (2.60). Other cases, already attested in the ninth century, are cited by Canard ("Quelques 'à-côtés' de l'histoire des relations," p. 109), who does not necessarily see them as captives.

96. Canard, "Quelques 'à-côtés' de l'histoire des relations," pp. 106–108; Canard, "Deux épisodes des relations diplomatiques arabo-byzantines au Xe siècle," pp. 54ff; Vasiliev, *Byzance et les Arabes*, 1:196–197; Guemara, "La libération et le rachat des captifs."

97. Vasiliev, *Byzance et les Arabes*, 2, pt. 1:181ff.

98. *Theoph. Cont.* 6.21; Leo of Tripoli is called Rašīq am Wardāmī in the Arabic sources. He was also nicknamed Gulām Zurāfā. Vasiliev believes that this nickname indicates that Leo was originally the slave of someone named Zurafa (Vasiliev, *Byzance et les Arabes*, 2, pt. 1:163 and n. 2). For Damian the governor of Tarsus (Damyana in Arabic), see ibid., 2, pt. 1:212ff.

99. Neither Byzantine nor Arab sources specify that Andronikus Doukas converted to Islam.

100. Theoph. A. M. 6274 (pp. 455–456).

101. Abū al-Faraj al-Isbahānī, *Kitāb al-Aghānī* 5.175ff., as cited by Canard, "Quelques 'à-côtés' de l'histoire des relations," pp. 106–107.

102. The roots of this evolution date back, of course, to Constantine I. For the course of action he took to change the institution of marriage, the standard reference is J. Evans Grubbs, *Law and Family in Late Antiquity: The Emperor Constantine's Marriage Legislation.*

103. Menander Protector, frag. 16.1.

104. Proc., *BP* 2.19. Note that Justinian then sent these captives to Italy to fight against the Goths. Hence prisoners had been put to military use at an earlier date. In another instance, Justinian II sent Slavic captives to the Arab border (Nikephoros, Patriarch of Constantinople, *Short History* 38). Conversion is not mentioned in either case.

105. The fourth exchange on al-Mas'ūdī's list, translated in Vasiliev, *Byzance et les Arabes*, 1:336–337; Campagnolo-Pothitou's "Les échanges de prisonniers entre Byzance et l'Islam" (p. 17 n. 94) cites al-Maqrīzī on this matter.

106. Canard provides a list of special delegates sent by the Arab caliphs and the Byzantine emperors on a mission to exchange captives (Canard, "Quelques 'à-côtés' de l'histoire des relations").

107. *Nov. Just.* 37.7, 144.2 (*Nov. Post. Just.*, coll. 1, nov. 7). That legislative course of action dates back to the fourth century, where only Jewish masters and Christian slaves were at issue (Buckland, *The Roman Law of Slavery*, pp. 605–607).

108. These *Novellae* are repeated in the *App. Eklo.* 8.1–3, which broadens the prohibition to heretics. See also the eighth canon of Nicaea II (RP, *Syntagma*, 2:583).

109. According to the *fiqh*, Arab jurisprudence; *Ency. of Islam*, 1:24–26, s.v. "'Abd" (R. Brunschvig).

110. The importation of Muslim slaves from Africa to the Arab world occurred after the era under study. See B. Lewis, *Race and Slavery in the Middle East*, pp. 11ff.; M. Gordon, *Slavery in the Arab World*, pp. 23ff.

111. V. Beševliev, *Die protobulgarischen Inschriften*, no. 41 (pp. 190ff). See Kolia-Dermitzaki, "Some Remarks on the Fate of Prisoners of War," p. 607 n. 98.

For the dating of the treaty to 816, see W. Treadgold, "The Bulgars' Treaty with the Byzantines in 816," which also cites the *Life of Nicetas of Medicium* 45.

112. *Life of Luke the Younger* 24, 32–34.

113. *Life of Blaise of Amorion* 8.

114. Ibid., 9.

115. *Life of Fantinos the Younger* 61.

116. *Life of Nikon Metanoeite* 57.

117. Ibid., 70.

118. *Life of Gregory the Decapolite* 10.

119. Kolia-Dermitzaki ("Some Remarks on the Fate of Prisoners of War," pp. 606–612) describes the mission of Leōn Choirosphaktēs, sent to the Bulgars by Leo VI to ransom Byzantine prisoners. A great number of letters were sent from Leōn Choirosphaktēs to Simeon (see G. Kolias, *Léon Choerosphactès, magistre, proconsul et patrice*, pp. 1ff.). Michael McCormick, basing his argument on the Slavonic Lives of the brothers Constantine-Cyril and Methodius, shows that on two occasions the saints return Byzantines captured by the Russians and the Slavs (*Origins of the European Economy: Communication and Commerce, A.D. 300–900*, pp. 188, 190).

120. Theoph. A. M. 6624 (p. 410). T. S. Noonan explains the common interests of the Byzantines and Khazars on the international scene ("Byzantium and the Khazars: A Special Relationship?"; and "The Khazar-Byzantine World of the Crimea in the Early Middle Ages: The Religious Dimension"). Noonan points out, however, that their interests were not always the same.

121. In *Sheviya and Pedut: Captivity and Ransom in Mediterranean Jewish Society* (pp. 22ff.), E. Bashab explains the development of the custom of putting out a cash box to collect ransom money for captives *(kupa le-pidyon shevuym)*.

122. Y. Friedman, "The 'Great Precept' of Ransom: The Jewish Perspective."

123. *Genizah* is the name of the room in a synagogue where books and documents written in Hebrew are kept. Because they are written in Hebrew and bear the name of God, they cannot be destroyed. They are therefore hidden away in that storage space. The root of the word *Genizah* means "to conceal forever." The Cairo Genizah, discovered in the old synagogue of Al-Fustāt in the nineteenth century, is the most famous and contains more than two hundred thousand pages of books and documents dating from the late ninth century.

124. *T.-S.* 10 J 27², Mann I, vol. 2, supp. chap. 2, pp. 347–349. The "mitzvah" of redeeming captives in the Talmud of Babylonia became a major religious duty in the twelfth century with the rules of Maimonides (1138–1204) (Bashab, *Sheviya and Pedut*, p. 23 n. 13). "Gaon" (pl. "geonim") was an honorific title given to the head of a Talmudic academy in the Babylonia of the post-Talmudic era.

125. *Nov. Post. Just.*, coll. 3, nov. 25.

126. H. Köpstein, "Einige Aspekte des byzantinischen und bulgarischen Sklavenhandels im X. Jahrhundert: Zur Novelle des Joannes Tzimiskes über

Sklavenhandelszoll"; Kolias, "Kriegsgefangene, Sklavenhandel und die Privilegien des Soldaten."

127. Hence the rule of the *Leges militares (version B)*, 48, promulgated with the *Ekloga*—namely, that prisoners of war were not part of the booty and had to be held for an exchange—was not applied in the tenth century to the Bulgar captives. In fact, the taking of captives and their enslavement seem to have been the general rule in the Balkans until the eleventh century.

128. An overview of Bulgaro-Byzantine political and religious relations and of the events that preceded the Bulgars' conversion is provided in R. Browning, *Byzantium and Bulgaria: A Comparative Study across the Early Medieval Frontier*, pp. 54–55, 144ff.; and in G. Cankova-Petkova, "Contributions au sujet de la conversion des Bulgares au christianisme."

129. For another case of political submission—that of the Serbs—to the Byzantine emperor in the tenth century, see the description of Constantine VII (Const. Porph., *De adminis.* 32).

130. Const. Porph., *De adminis.* 8 and 28–30.

131. In her article "Nommer les Russes en grec, 1081–1204," Patlagean shows that the term "Scythians" had not an ethnic meaning but a geographical, cultural, and political-historical one. That is, as in antiquity and late antiquity, those designated "Scythians" were peoples from the Black Sea hinterland, who were perceived as Barbarians by the empire. Hence, in the tenth century, the Russians were called *Rhōs* in a political context that considered them a known and non-Barbarian political entity. In other words, the author's intent determined which term was used. In the hagiographical sources, the term "Scythians" refers to the Barbarians of the northeast (the Balkans, eastern Europe) and adds a cultural sense of "non-Christian." "The Scythians are not Christians," said the author of the *Spiritually Beneficial Tales of Paul of Monembasia* (9) in the tenth century. During the period of concern here, the name "Scythians" was attributed to the Russians, the Pechenegs, the Serbs, and also the Bulgars (though the Bulgars were often called by their ethnic name). For the Bulgars called "Scythians," see the story of the abduction of Blaise of Amorion by the "Scythians," who take him to Bulgaria (*Life of Blaise of Amorion* 8). See also the use of "Scythians" and "Bulgars" as synonyms in *Life of Luke the Younger* 24 and 32–34.

132. S. Assaf, "Slaves and Slave Trade among the Jews in the Middle Ages," pp. 91ff. The *Responsa* (plural form of *responsum*) is the name for a Halachic jurisprudential system dealing with ritual, ethical, and civil aspects and using a procedure whereby questions are asked of rabbinical authorities, sometimes by very remote communities, so that they may receive guidance on Halachic problems. The Halacha is the body of Jewish law.

133. The term in Hebrew is *Ben-horin* ("free"); S. Assaf, *The Responsa of the Geonim in the Manuscripts of the Genizah*, pp. 88, 91–92, 95.

134. Even non-Jewish slaves could not be used on the Sabbath. But it was prefera-

ble to use Jewish slaves in the kitchen so as not to make the wine *neseh* (according to Jewish law, wine must not be touched by a non-Jew).

135. Even against a slave's will (Assaf, "Slaves and Slave Trade among the Jews in the Middle Ages," pp. 94–95); S. D. Goiten, *A Mediterranean Society: The Jewish Communities of the Arab World as Portrayed in the Documents of the Cairo Genizah,* 1:136–147 (for wills especially) and 5:148–150. For emancipation encouraged by the geonim, see Assaf, "Slaves and Slave Trade among the Jews in the Middle Ages," pp. 101ff.

136. H. Ahrweiler, *Byzance et la mer: La marine de guerre, la politique et les institutions maritimes de Byzance aux VIIe–XVe siècles,* pp. 93ff.

137. V. Christides, *The Conquest of Crete by the Arabs (ca. 824): A Turning Point in the Struggle between Byzantium and Islam,* pp. 81ff.

138. The sack of Thessalonica is described in Ioannes Kaminiates, *De expugnatione Thessalonicae* (esp. 35ff.); Vasiliev, *Byzance et les Arabes,* 2, pt.1:166ff.; and Christides, *The Conquest of Crete by the Arabs,* pp. 159–161. But Kazhdan calls into question the authenticity of Kaminiates' text ("Some Questions Addressed to the Scholars Who Believe in the Authenticity of Kaminiates' 'Capture of Thessalonica'").

139. Vasiliev, *Byzance et les Arabes,* 2, pt.1:11–12.

140. *Life of Luke the Younger* 2.

141. Ibid., 24, 32–34.

142. Al-Balādhurī, *Kitāb Futūh al-Buldān,* p. 133 (pp. 112–113 in the F. Sezgin edition); Christides (*The Conquest of Crete by the Arabs,* pp. 163–165) provides a list of references in the Arabic sources that speak of it.

143. Michael the Syrian, *Chronique* 12.21 (3:100), J. B. Chabot translation [my translation from the French—Trans.].

144. Ibn Hawqal, *Kitāb Sūrat al-ard (Configuration of the Earth),* BGA ed., p. 205, J. H. Kramers and G. Wiet translation, 1:19 [my translation from the French—Trans.].

145. *T.-S.* Loan 28, folio 1 (Mann II, 1:354–356, commentary by Jacob Mann, pp. 348–349).

146. *Sylloge Tacticorum* 50 (following Kolia-Dermitzaki, "Some Remarks on the Fate of Prisoners of War," pp. 585–586); Hārūn bn. Yahyā recounts the story of his captivity (between 880 and 890 or 912–913) in a passage cited in Ibn Rusta's *Kitāb al-A'laq al-nafīsa,* BGA ed., pp. 199–127. A translation of the passage describing Constantinople is provided in Vasiliev, *Byzance et les Arabes,* 2, pt. 2:382–394. The best-known description is that of the poet Abū Firās in his *Rūmiyyāt* (Byzantine poems), written during his imprisonment in Constantinople between 962 and 966. See also L. Simeonova, "In the Depths of Tenth-century Byzantine Ceremonial: The Treatment of Arab Prisoners-of-War at Imperial Banquets." Simeonova points out that only illustrious prisoners received such treatment. And see Kolia-Dermitzaki, "Some Remarks on the Fate of Prisoners of War," pp. 599–606.

147. *Leonis Imperatoris Tactica* 16.9–11. Athina Kolia-Dermitzaki estimates that between 50 percent and 70 percent of captives were sold ("Some Remarks on the Fate of Prisoners of War," pp. 604–605). For the use of captives in artisanal production, which exploited their knowledge, see S. Patoura, Οἱ αἰχμάλωτοι ὡς παράγοντες ἐπικοινωνίας καὶ πληροφόρησης (4ος–10ος αἱ..).

148. Vasiliev, *Byzance et les Arabes*, 1:201, based on al-Ṭabarī, *Ta'rīkh al-rusul wa'l-mulūk*, 3:1353 and app. p. 314. See also Y. Ragib, "Les esclaves publics aux premiers siècles de l'Islam."

149. *Leonis Imperatoris Tactica* 18.138.

150. Vasiliev, *Byzance et les Arabes*, 1:223, based on al-Ṭabarī, *Ta'rīkh al-rusul wa'l-mulūk*, 3:1426.

151. *Alf Layla wa-Layla*, night 874 in the Habicht and Fleischer edition, 11:24ff. In the tenth century, the term "sultan" meant "power, authority" or "holder of power, authority" (*Ency. of Islam*, 9:849, s.v. "sultān" [J. H. Kramers and C. E. Bosworth]). The Mahdi edition of the most ancient sources does not contain that night.

152. Tibi, "Byzantine-Fatimid Relations," esp. appendices 3–7 (pp. 103–107), which present other episodes involving Byzantine attacks.

153. Yaḥyā Ibn Saʿīd Al-Antāq, PO 18, pt. 5:730 (chap. p. 98).

154. Al-Muqaddasī, *Aḥsan al-taqāsīm fī maʿrifat al-aqālīm (The Best Divisions for Knowledge of the Regions)* 194–195 (pp. 209–210 in the A. Miquel French translation; p. 184 in the B. A. Collins English translation).

155. *Théodore Tyron, Miracle of the Dragon* 2. For that saint, see N. Oikonomides, "Le dédoublement de saint Théodore et les villes d'Euchaïta et d'Echaneia."

156. A few examples: *Life of Luke the Younger* 2; *Spiritually Beneficial Tales of Paul of Monembasia* 8 (for Calabria); *Life of Leo Luke of Sicily* 4ff., in which the Sicilian peasants flee into the mountains of Calabria because of the Arab attacks; *Life of Athanasia of Aegina* 1, in which the saint loses her husband during the Arab attacks on the island; *Life of Theoctiste of Lesbos* 15, in which the heroine leaves her city for her sister's village and is abducted by the pirates of Crete; *Life of Elias the Younger*, 3–4ff.; *Life of Nikon Metanoeite* 20, 23; *Life of Theodora of Thessalonica* 6, in which Theodora's family leaves the island of Aegina and moves to Thessalonica because of the attacks by the Arabs, who take captives and kill residents, including Theodora's brother.

157. Methodius, *In Praise of Nicholas of Myra* 42–43.

158. *Three Miracles of Nicholas of Myra* 8ff. These scenes involving piracy by the Arabs of Crete helped Kazhdan to date the narratives (A. Kazhdan, "Hagiographical Notes," *Byzantion* 54 [1984]: 176–181).

159. *Life of Nilus of Rossano* 68–69; *Spiritually Beneficial Tales of Paul of Monembasia* 8.

160. *Iviron I* 16 (of 1010).

161. *Life of Nilus of Rossano* 70–72. See G. da Costa-Louillet's note "Saints de Sicile et d'Italie méridionale," p. 152 n. 2. We find the same motif in the story told by Procopius, in which Khosrow's marriage to a Christian captive from the

city of Sura makes it possible to redeem other captives (Proc., *BP* 2.5). Note that in all the sources specifying the price and the number of persons, it is always three persons ransomed for a hundred *nomismata*, which corresponds to the evidence in the documents of the Genizah.

162. A. Mez, *The Renaissance of Islam*, pp. 160–163.

163. *Life of Theoctiste of Lesbos* 15.

164. *Life of Joseph the Hymnographer* 6ff.

165. *Life of Elias the Younger* 4ff.

166. *T.-S.* 13 J 14^{20} (Mann I, no. 12, 1:87).

167. *T.-S.* 13 J 20^{25} (Mann I, no. 13, 1:88).

168. *MS. Adler*, 2804, fol. 7 verso (Mann I, no. 15, 1:89–90).

169. *T.-S.* 13 J 34 (Mann I, 2:344–346, supp. chap. 2); D. Jacoby, "What Do We Learn about Byzantine Asia Minor from the Documents of the Cairo Genizah?" p. 90.

170. *T.-S.* 24.29 (Mann II, 1:367–370).

171. *T.-S.* 10 J 27^8 (Mann I, 2:363–365, supp. chap. 2).

172. *T.- S.* 13 J 94 (S. Assaf, *Texts and Studies in Jewish History*, pp. 108–113).

173. S. D. Goitein, "Autographs of Yehuda Halevi," pp. 397ff.

174. Abraham Ibn Daud, *The Book of Traditions (Sefer Ha-Qabbalah)*, ed. G. D. Cohen. See Cohen's "The Story of the Four Captives," in which he argues that Ibn Daud used known literary elements to create a fictive history.

175. *Nov. Leo.* 40.

176. From the third century on, a slave who was the heir of a person who died in captivity could inherit if the testator had made his will prior to his captivity (*Dig.* 38.1.12, "servus heres scriptus ab eo, qui in hostium potestate decesserit, liber et heres erit"). There, in a word, is the explanation for why a Roman captured by the enemy was considered a slave: being within the enemy's potestas, he had no potestas of his own. Note the version of the law in the *Basilica:* "The captive's last will is considered as if he were not a captive" (*Basilic.* 35.1.13). Unfortunately, the scholia of that law have not come down to us.

177. *Nov. Leo.* 36. The permission granted in the third century to inherit from a person who died in captivity was limited to wills prepared before the person was taken into captivity. Note that the *Ekloga* does not deal with all the consequences resulting from the change it introduced. Unlike in the *Novellae* of Justinian, the status of slaves occupied an important place in the *Novellae* of Leo VI. Of the 113 *Novellae*, more than a quarter had to do with changes in the status of the slave as individual.

178. Olympiodorus, frag. 7.

179. Proc., *BP* 1.20. For Justinian's policy in that region in 530, see I. Shahid, *Byzantium and the Arabs in the Sixth Century*, 1, pt. 1:144ff.; I. Shahid, "Byzantium and Kinda." The Himyarite kingdom had strategic importance not only for Ethiopia but also for the commercial pathways between the Arabian Gulf and the Persian Gulf on the route to India (Cosmas Indicopleustes, *Christian Topography* 2.50, also mentions the war conducted by the Ethiopian king to

capture this kingdom; ibid., 2.56). See also "Homeritae" in *RE* 8, pt. 2.2182–2188.

180. Proc., *BP* 1.15.

181. *Life of Nikon Metanoeite* 20.

182. Byzantium sometimes returned its Arab prisoners in exchange for Christian relics and icons. The best-known example is the "holy image or holy face, the Mandylion." In 942–943, the Byzantines proposed to exchange their Arab prisoners to recover that image, which was located in the church of Edessa; PO 18, pt. 5:730 (chap. 93); Theoph. A. M. 6118 (p. 327); E. Patlagean, "L'entrée de la Sainte Face d'Edesse à Constantinople en 944"; A. Cameron, "The Mandylion and Byzantine Iconoclasm."

183. Theoph. A. M., 6305 (pp. 497–498).

184. *Laurentian Chronicle*, in *The Russian Primary Chronicle*, pp. 65ff.; I. Sorlin, "Les traités de Byzance avec la Russie au Xe siècle," pp. 329–336.

185. Ibn al-ʿAdīm, *Zubdat al-Halab fī taʾrīh Halab*, ed. S. Dahhân (Damascus, 1951), 1:163–169; French translation by M. Canard, *Histoire de la dynastie des Hamdanides de Jazîra et de Syrie*, pp. 831–835; Latin version in *Ex Camaleddini annalibus halemensibus* (in *Excerpta ex Historiis Arabum* 3).

186. According to Theophanes, the Arabs used the episode as a pretext to attack the Byzantines; Theoph. A. M. 6208 (p. 387).

187. *Life of Luke the Younger* 4–7.

188. *Nov. Post. Just.*, coll. 3, nov. 13.

189. Translation in Canard, *Histoire de la dynastie des Hamdanides*. Note that the prices are slightly different in the version of the *Ex Camaleddini annalibus halemensibus* (in *Excerpta ex Historiis Arabum* 3): thirty-six dinars for a male slave, twenty dinars for a female, and sixteen for a child.

190. *Laurentian Chronicle*, p. 67.

191. Ibid., p. 65 (as in the treaty of 944, ibid., p. 77). The same treaty specifies that some of the Russians were Christians and others were not, which is important for the question of oaths. For these treaties and for the Russian ones of the time, see H. Ahrweiler, "Les relations entre les Byzantins et les Russes au IXe siècle."

192. *Life of Nahum*, pp. 287–288.

193. The Russo-Byzantine and Arab-Byzantine treaties not only speak of slaves but also deal with the case of thieves and murderers who flee abroad, stipulating that each party had to return them.

194. *Nov. Post. Just.*, coll. 3, nov. 25. The *Novella* of Alexius Comnenus of 1095 attests to the practice of private abductions by the Byzantines to procure slaves, especially Bulgars (*Nov. Post. Just.*, coll. 4, nov. 35).

195. Cosmas Indicopleustes, a sixth-century Egyptian trader, describes his personal travels in his *Christian Topography*. These travels led him to the Arabian Gulf and to the Persian Gulf, as far as the mouth of the sea (2.29–30). He describes the eastern traffic between Egypt, India, China, and Ethiopia (2.43–64) and mentions the slave trade (2:64).

196. *P. Str.* 1404, edited with commentary in F. Preisigike, "Ein Sklavenkauf des 6. Jahrhunderts. P. gr. Str. Inv. Nr. 1404."

197. According to two appraisals, in 530 and 531, *CJ* 6.43.3.1; 7.7.1.5.

198. Later laws of the fourth to fifth centuries concerning castration targeted the dux of Mesopotamia (*CJ* 4.42.1) and the Eastern prefect (*CJ* 4.42.1; cf. *PLRE* 2:1179; *CJ* 12.5.4; *PLRE*, 2:930). See Proc., *BP* 1.15.31, for the Persian-Armenian origin of Narses; Proc. *BG* 4.3; *BP* 2.15, for the importation of eunuchs from the Abasgi and Lazi Caucasian peoples; and *Dig.* 39.4.16.7 for the third-century tax on luxury goods, including on the *spadones Indici*, "the Indian eunuchs."

199. Theoph. A. M. 6101 (p. 297).

200. Michael McCormick, however, supports the idea of a much earlier decline of Roman Mediterranean commerce, which in his view was linked to a general decline in the empire's economy (*Origins of the European Economy*, part 1, "The End of the World"). For a different point of view, see P. Horden and N. Purcell, *The Corrupting Sea: A Study of Mediterranean History*, pp. 153–172. Horden and Purcell show a continuity in commercial communication. I shall not join the debate here on the decline of Mediterranean traffic in the seventh to eighth centuries. I would simply like to show how the map of international traffic changed as a function of geopolitical shifts and what role Byzantium played in that change.

201. Arabic names are cited here in the standard Latin transliteration.

202. A. Gieysztor, "Les Juifs et leurs activités économiques en Europe orientale"; E. Ashtor, "Gli Ebrei nel commercio mediterraneo nell'alto medioevo (sec. X–XI)."

203. Ibn Khordādhbih, *Kitāb al-Masālik wa'l-mamālik*, p. 153 (129) ff.

204. The map provided in McCormick (*Origins of the European Economy*, p. 762) is limited to Europe between 700 and 900.

205. Horden and Purcell, *The Corrupting Sea*, chap. 2.

206. McCormick, *Origins of the European Economy*; M. McCormick, "New Light on the 'Dark Ages': How the Slave Trade Fuelled the Carolingian Economy."

207. When using the term "Russia," I refer to the regions extending from the Baltic Sea to the Black Sea and the Ural Mountains.

208. B. Lewis, *Race and Color in Islam*, pp. 28–38; Gordon, *Slavery in the Arab World*, pp. 49ff. and chap. 5.

209. *Ency. of Islam*, 8:872–881, s.v. "Al-Saqāliba" (P. Guichard and M. Meouak).

210. H. Köpstein, "Zum Bedeutungswandel von ΣΚΛΑΒΟΣ/SCLAVUS"; H. Kahane and R. Kahane, "Notes on the Linguistic History of 'sclavus.'"

211. M. Espéronnier, "Les échanges commerciaux entre le monde musulman et les pays slaves d'après les sources musulmanes médiévales," pp. 17–18 (and n. 2). Byzantine, Arab, and Samanid coins, for the most part from the ninth and tenth centuries—though there are also coins from the eighth and eleventh centuries and even Byzantine coins from the sixth and seventh—were found at the following archaeological sites: Gorodische near Novgorod (E. Nosov,

"Rjurikovo, Gorodišche et Novgorod," pp. 148 and 152), Timerevo on the Volga (V. Sedyh, "Timerevo—Un centre proto-urbain sur la grande voie de la Volga," pp. 175–178, with Western coins), Gnezdovo (T. Puškina, "Les trouvailles monétaires de Gnezdovo: Un marqueur des relations commerciales"), and Kiev (G. Ivakin, "Kiev aux VIIIe–Xe siècles," pp. 231– 232). For the total number of tenth- to eleventh-century dirhams in the finds of Russia, see T. S. Noonan, "The Impact of the Islamic Trade upon Urban- ization in the Rus' Lands: The Tenth and Early Eleventh Centuries"; and T. S. Noonan, "Khazaria as an Intermediary between Islam and Eastern Europe in the Second Half of the Ninth Century: The Numismatic Perspective."

212. S. Assaf, "Slaves and Slave Trade among the Jews in the Middle Ages"; M. Gil, "The Radhanite Merchants and the Land of Radhan"; E. Ashtor, "Aperçus sur les Radhanites"; Ashtor, "Gli Ebrei nel commercio mediterraneo"; C. Cahen, "Y a-t-il eu des Radhanites?"; Gieysztor, "Les juifs et leurs activités économiques en Europe orientale"; and C. Verlinden, "Les Radaniya: Intermédiaries commerciaux entre les mondes germano-slave et gréco-arabe."

213. Ashtor, "Gli Ebrei nel commercio mediterraneo," pp. 458–460.

214. According to the *Responsa* of the geonim.

215. *Ency. of Islam*," 8:363–364, s.v. "Al-Rādhāniyya" (C. Pellat).

216. I leave aside the question of which was the most convenient conveyance for slaves, boats or caravans: Gieysztor, "Les Juifs et leurs activités économiques en Europe orientale," p. 506; J. Ferluga, "Mercati e mercanti fra mar Nero e Adriatico: Il commercio nei Balcani dal VII all'XI secolo," pp. 452–455. In any case, the *Radhaniyya* used both modes of transport. Note as well that the wa- terways were not accessible all year long and that it is therefore probable that the traders traveled by land during the winter.

217. *Patria Const.* 2.64. For the Byzantine spice market, see Patlagean, "Byzance et les marchés du grand commerce," pp. 596–597. J. Koder ("Maritime Trade and the Food Supply for Constantinople in the Middle Ages") does not mention spices as being among the goods that the Byzantine ships brought to Constan- tinople.

218. H. Antoniadis-Bibicou, *Recherches sur les douanes à Byzance. L'"octava," le "kommerkion" et les commerciaires*, pp. 157ff.; M. Hendy, *Studies in the Byzantine Monetary Economy, c. 300–1450*, pp. 630–634; N. Oikonomides, "Silk Trade and Production in Byzantium from the Sixth to the Ninth Century: The Seals of Kommerkiarioi"; N. Oikonomides, "Le kommerkion d'Abydos, Thessalonique et le commerce bulgare au IXe siècle."

219. *Leges navales; Lex rhodia*, ed. W. Ashburner. Its linguistic kinship to the *Ekloga* has been widely noted. For dating, see Van der Wal and Lokin, *Historiae Iuris Graeco-romani delineatio*, p. 73; D. Letsios, "Sea Trade as Illustrated in the 'Rhodian Sea Law' with Special Reference to the Reception of Its Norms in the Arabic Ecloga." See also Koder, "Maritime Trade and the Food Supply," p. 115 and n. 37.

220. *Leges navales* 15.

221. Published in Oikonomides, "Silk Trade and Production in Byzantium," pp. 51–53 and nn. 109–116.

222. Ibid., pp. 51–53 (appendix 2: "A Giant Sale of Slaves in 694/95").

223. Hendy, *Studies in the Byzantine Monetary Economy*, pp. 630–634. A new seal has been published by S. Bendall ("Slaves or Soldiers?"). According to Bendall, that discovery, dating to 693–694 (close to the time of the Byzantine defeat in 692–693), tends to confirm Oikonomides's interpretation.

224. Theoph. A. M. 6293 (p. 475).

225. C. Mango and R. Scott, *The Chronicle of Theophanes Confessor: Byzantine and Near Eastern History A.D. 284–813* (pp. 653–654 n. 4); and N. Oikonomides, "Le kommerkion d'Abydos, Thessalonique et le commerce bulgare au IXe siècle" (p. 242). Both works mention the letter from Theodore Studites to Irene (*Theodori Studitae Epistulae* 7). This letter provides many details on these measures. Theodore Studites speaks of the taxes on The Straits that navigators from the east, west, and north had until then been "throttled" into paying. Oikonomides interprets these taxes as *kommerkia*.

226. Theoph. A. M. 6302 (p. 486).

227. Ibn Khordādhbih, *Kitāb al-Masālik wa'l-mamālik*, p. 155 (130).

228. The tenth-century slave market of Constantinople is described in the *Patria Const.* 2.64.

229. H. Gibb," Arab-Byzantine Relations under the Umayyad Caliphate," p. 230.

230. Gibb, "The Fiscal Rescript of 'Umar II," p. 7 (xiv).

231. The organization of the empire into themata, military and administrative units whose origin dates back to the seventh century (and perhaps even to the reign of Emperor Maurice, between 582 and 602), to a certain extent replaced the old system of Roman provinces.

232. Patlagean, "Byzance et les marchés du grand commerce," pp. 620–621, which follows Oikonomides's analysis ("Silk Trade and Production in Byzantium") of the *apothēkai* concessions.

233. Oikonomides, "Le kommerkion d'Abydos"; Oikonomides, "Le marchand byzantin."

234. J. Ferluga, "Der byzantinische Handel auf der Balkanhalbinsel vom VII. bis zum Anfang des XIII. Jahrhunderts"; Ferluga, "Mercati et mercanti fra mar Nero e Adriatico"; A. Gieysztor, "Les marchés et les marchandises entre le Danube et la Volga aux VIIIe–XIe siècles," pp. 513–514. See the route reconstructed from the numismatic evidence in McCormick, *Origins of the European Economy*, pp. 375–379, and the routes between central Europe and Constantinople in the ninth century (pp. 548ff.). The journey between Thessalonica and Belgrade took eight days (Const. Porph., *De adminis.* 42).

235. Espéronnier, "Les échanges commerciaux entre le monde musulman et les pays slaves." The most important information dates from the ninth to tenth century. See T. S. Noonan, "Volga Bulgharia's Tenth-century Trade with Samanid Central Asia."

236. Ibn Fadlān, *Voyage chez les Bulgares de la Volga,* pp. 66–71. M. Espéronnier, "Villes et commerce: La Khazarie et la Bulgarie de la Volga, d'après les textes arabes et persans des IXe et Xe siècles," pp. 413–416. Espéronnier also points out the commercial role of the other two Khazar cities, Balandjar and Samandar. The author notes that the sources speak of foreign (Arab and Russian) merchants who passed through these cities, rather than of Khazar merchants.

237. Ibn Khordādhbih, *Kitāb al-Masālik wa'l-mamālik,* p. 155 (130); Ibn Hawqal, *Kitāb Sūrat al-ard,* BGA ed., p. 392; Ibn Fadlān, *Voyage chez les bulgares de la Volga,* p. 71. For an overview, see T. S. Noonan, "Les Khazars et le commerce oriental." For the relations between the Khazars and the Arabs based on the numismatic and historiographical evidence, see Noonan, "Khazaria as an Intermediary between Islam and Eastern Europe."

238. In "Byzance et les marchés du grand commerce" (pp. 603–604), Patlagean explains the commercial position of Trebizond; *Life of George of Amastris* 33.

239. In "Short Notes: Two Notes on the Early History of the Thema of Cherson" (pp. 210–215), C. Zuckerman dates it to 841 rather than 837 (Dölger, *Reg.* 1, no. 431).

240. After the fall of the Sassanid Empire; C. Zuckerman, "On the Date of the Khazars' Conversion to Judaism and the Chronology of the Kings of the Rus Oleg and Igor," p. 241.

241. Ibid., pp. 241–250; P. B. Golden, "Khazaria and Judaism."

242. It also set them up as a third empire (D. Shapira, "Two Names of the First Khazar Jewish Beg").

243. G. Ivakin, "Kiev aux VIIIe–Xe siècles," p. 232; Noonan, "Khazaria as an Intermediary between Islam and Eastern Europe," pp. 202–204. Noonan points to the economic growth of the Bulgars on the Volga resulting from the trade with the Samanids ("Volga Bulgharia's Tenth-century Trade") that accompanied their Islamization (see Shapira, "Two Names of the First Khazar Jewish Beg," p. 235). For the Khazar economy, see Noonan, "What Does Historical Numismatics Suggest about the History of Khazaria in the Ninth Century?"

244. Before Kiev was conquered by the Russians (Ahrweiler, "Les relations entre les Byzantins et les Russes"). Byzantium imposed the same policy in Crimea during the same period, with the agreement of the Khazars (Noonan, "The Khazar-Byzantine World of the Crimea in the Early Middle Ages").

245. MGH, *Epistolae,* vol. 8; *Codex Carolinus,* no. 59 (pp. 584–585). For the presence of Arab traders in Carolingian Europe, see M. McCormick, "Voyageurs, monnaies et esclaves," especially the map of the diffusion of Arab and Byzantine coins (p. 44).

246. For the importance of the Byzantium-West routes in general, see M. McCormick, "Byzantium on the Move: Imagining a Communications History."

247. The Franks arrived at the Adriatic Sea but were obliged to leave in 811–812 (Const. Porph. *De adminis.,* 28; Dölger, *Reg.* 1, no. 385). Nevertheless, they

maintained indirect contact through their Lombardian route, and, like the Byzantines, they made use of Venice (McCormick, *Origins of the European Economy*, pp. 759–767).

248. Tafel-Thomas 1:3 (no. 3), p. 5 (no. 7).

249. E. Patlagean, "Variations impériales sur le thème romain," pp. 38ff.

250. Ibn Khordādhbih mentions *Firanja* as the *Radhaniyya*'s starting point. Gil ("The Radhanite Merchants and the Land of Radhan," pp. 310ff.) believes that *Firanja* was Lombardy. McCormick (*Origins of the European Economy*, p. 691) thinks the port was Venice ("New Light on the 'Dark Ages'"). Because Ibn Khordādhbih also mentions *Firanja* as the starting point for the land route, and because his description specifically includes the "king of *Firanja*," I believe rather that it designates the "country of the Franks." In fact, Jewish merchants bringing slaves to Arles on the Rhone are also mentioned by Agobard of Lyons (*Agobardi Lugdunensis Opera omnia*, no. 6).

251. Gieysztor, "Les juifs et leurs activités économiques en Europe orientale"; Gieysztor, "Les marchés et les marchandises entre le Danube et la Volga."

252. MGH, *Capitularia Regum Francorum*, ed. A. Boretius and V. Krause, vol. 2, no. 253 (pp. 249–252); H. Dopsch, "Raffelstettener Zollordung," in *Lexikon des Mittelalters* 7:397. Raffelstetten is near present-day Linz, which attests to the importance of the route on the Danube between eastern and western Europe (for this route, see also McCormick, *Origins of the European Economy*, pp. 553–557).

253. C. Verlinden, "La traite des esclaves. Un grand commerce international au Xe siècle."

254. "Antapodosis" 6.6, in *Liudprandi Cremonensis Opera omnia*. He describes the castration of slaves by traders who made a very large profit on them ("Verdunenses mercatores ob immensum lucrum facere et in Hispaniam ducere solent").

255. Al-Muqaddasī, *Description de l'Occident musulman au IVe–Xe siècle*, p. 56.

256. Assaf, "Slaves and Slave Trade among the Jews in the Middle Ages," pp. 100–102 and nn. 62–63. I should note that the Jewish prohibition on castration (ibid.; Assaf, *The Responsa of the Geonim in the Manuscripts of the Genizah*, p. 192) explains why Jewish merchants needed intermediaries to perform it. Nevertheless, it is not known who performed castration in Verdun and why it was done there.

257. *Life of Nahum*, pp. 287–288. See the route connecting central Europe to the Adriatic described by McCormick, *Origins of the European Economy*, pp. 369ff. ("The Amber Trail").

258. A letter sent to Louis the Pious; *Agobardi Lugdunensis Opera omnia*, no. 11 (pp. 189–195), "De insolentia Iudeorum (ad Ludovicum)." For the Jewish merchants who received privileges in France, see Ashtor, "Aperçus sur les Radhanites," pp. 250–251.

259. As for the sea routes linking Muslim Spain to northern Europe, al-Ghzāl (Yahyā bn. Hakam al-Bakrī), the emir's envoy from Cordova to Constantino-

ple between 822 and 852, describes the sea routes of Arab merchants who circumvented western Europe in order to disembark in the ports of the Baltic
Sea. In "Les échanges commerciaux entre le monde musulman et les pays
slaves" (p. 20 n. 18), Espéronnier cites the account given by R. Dozy,
Recherches sur l'histoire et la littérature d'Espagne pendant le Moyen Âge (Paris
and Leiden, 1881), 2:267–278. That description, along with the circumstances
presented (al-Ghazāl's embassy to the Normans) is probably imaginary (*Ency.
of Islam* 2:1038, s. v. "Al-Ghazāl, Yaḥyā b. Hakam al-Bakrī," [A. Huic
Miranda]).

260. *Gregorii I Papae Registrum epistolarum, Libri I–VII,* ed. P. Ewald and L. M.
Hartmann, MGH, *Epistolate I,* 3.37.

261. See the writings of Agobard of Lyons on this subject: *Agobardi Lugdunensis
Opera omnia,* no. 6 ("De baptismo maniciporum Iudaeorum").

262. Merchants of Bavarian *(Bawari)* and Slavic *(Sclavi)* slaves were exempted
from the tax of one-twelfth the price of each slave at Raffelstetten.

263. Ibn Hawqal and Ibn Fadlān wrote in the second half of the tenth century.
Carolingian toll stations are attested for the ninth century (McCormick, *Origins of the European Economy,* pp. 640–652), but without any mention of the
special tax on slaves.

264. It is clear that the importation of slaves was subject to the *kommerkia* before
Irene's tax exemptions and Nicephorus I's special tax.

265. The document *Ms. Adler* 2804 verso (Mann I, no. 14, 1:88–39), conserved in
the Cairo Genizah, attests to the redemption of a Byzantine Jewish woman.
For the prices of slaves in the Arab countries, see Y. Ragib, "Les marchés aux
esclaves en terre d'Islam," pp. 757ff.; A. Cheikh-Moussa, "Figures de l'esclave
chanteuse à l'époque abbasside," pp. 45–60; E. Ashtor, *Histoire des prix et des
salaires dans l'Orient médiéval,* pp. 58–59.

266. Mez, *The Renaissance of Islam,* pp. 160–163. For the presence of Armenians in
the Mediterranean, see *Life of Lazarus of Mount Galesios* 9, quoted in
Patlagean, "Byzance et les marchés du grand commerce," p. 598.

267. For a comparison with the position of Cyprus, see R. J. H. Jenkins, "Cyprus
between Byzantium and Islam, A.D. 688–965"; and A. Cameron, "Cyprus at
the time of the Arab Conquests."

268. *Leges navales* 15.

269. Ibid.

270. V. Christides, *The Conquest of Crete by the Arabs (ca. 834): A Turning Point in
the Struggles between Byzantium and Islam.*

271. V. Christides, "Raid and Trade in the Eastern Mediterranean: A Treatise by
Muhammad b. ʿUmar, the *Faqih* from Occupied Moslem Crete, and the
Rhodian Sea Law, Two Parallel Texts." See the exhaustive study of Hassan S.
Khalilieh, *Islamic Maritime Law. An Introduction.*

272. For the Roman *Lex Rhodia,* see *Dig.* 14.2 ("De lege Rhodia de iactu"). For the
evolution of Roman sea law and its Greek origins, see J. Rougé, *Recherches sur
l'organisation du commerce maritime en Méditerranée sous l'Empire romain,*
pp. 397–413. For maritime loans in Roman law, see J. Andreau, *Banque et*

affaires dans le monde romain, IVe siècle av. J. C.–IIIe siècle apr. J.-C., pp. 108–112.

273. Christides, "Raid and Trade in the Eastern Mediterranean," pp. 77–78. Hassan S. Khalilieh, *Islamic Maritime Law. An Introduction,* pp. 101–102. For the crew and the dimensions of the boats, see McCormick, *Origins of the European Economy,* pp. 402–430.

274. E. Malamut, *Les îles de l'Empire byzantin, VIIIe–XIIe siècles,* 2:535ff.

275. Ibn Hawqal, *Kitāb Sūrat al-ard,* BGA ed., p. 205, trans. J. H. Kramers and G. Wiet *(Configurations de la terre),* 1:19.

276. Patlagean, "Byzance et les marchés du grand commerce," pp. 611–612. Patlagean shows how that maritime commerce allowed Byzantium to become a strong presence in the eastern Mediterranean.

277. *Spiritually Beneficial Tales of Paul of Monembasia* 8.

278. *Life of Nicholas of Sion* 8–9.

279. Ibid., 29–32.

280. *T.-S.* 16.251 (Mann I, no. 18, 1:92–93), a letter from the Jewish community of Alexandria to the community of Mastaura (in Lydia), asking for money to ransom its members abducted by Arab pirates and sold to Alexandria. The *Ketubah,* composed in Mastaura in 1022, is also conserved in the Genizah (*T.-S.* 16.374, Mann I, no. 19, 1:94–96). See M. T. Reinach, "Un contrat de mariage du temps de Basile le Bulgaroctone"; D. Jacoby, "What Do We Learn about Byzantine Asia Minor?" pp. 84ff.

281. Ashtor, "Gli Ebrei nel commercio mediterraneo."

282. Ibn Khordādhbih, *Kitāb al-Masālik wa'l-mamālik,* p. 154 (130).

283. The first two routes have been studied in J. Shepard, "Constantinople—Gateway to the North: The Russians."

284. Ibn Khordādhbih, *Kitāb al-Masālik wa'l-mamālik,* p. 154 (130); in 922, Ibn Fadlan (p. 71) attests to the tithe paid for each slave ship to the king of the Khazars.

285. In the ninth century, before Kiev was conquered by the Russians, it was the Russians of Tauric Chersonese who faced an obstruction in the Black Sea (Ahrweiler, "Les relations entre les Byzantins et les Russes").

286. All three treaties are described in the *Laurentian Chronicle,* pp. 65–75, translated into French with commentary by I. Sorlin in "Les traités de Byzance avec la Russie au Xe siècle," pp. 329–336, 447–452.

287. For foreign merchants and their accommodations in the capital, see Jacoby, "The Byzantine Outsider in Trade," pp. 132–134.

288. Const. Porph., *De cerimon.* 2.44.

289. In 944, the Russians again attacked Byzantium, a war that led to the treaty of 944 (Sorlin, "Les traités de Byzance avec la Russie," pp. 452–455).

290. Ibn Hawqal, *Kitāb Sūrat al-ard,* BGA ed., p. 392; and, on the same date, the destruction by the Russians of "al-Bulghar." Was this the principal city of the Volga and Kama Bulgars?

291. Ioannes Scylitzes, *Synopsis historiarum,* p. 240; C. Zuckerman, "Le voyage d'Olga et la première ambassade espagnole à Constantinople."

292. For Russo-Byzantine relations in the second half of the tenth century, I have followed A. Poppe, "The Political Background to the Baptism of Rus': Byzantine-Russian Relations between 986–989."

293. Consider Sviatoslav's attacks of 970, which the Byzantines succeeded in repelling. The Russian attack and the Byzantine victory are also described in *Life of Basil the Younger* (in *Moscou gr. 249*), fol. 136 verso.

294. Yaḥyā Ibn Saʻīd Al-Antāk, PO 23, pt. 3:422–424; Poppe, "The Political Background to the Baptism of Rus,'" pp. 205–210.

295. Yaḥyā Ibn Saʻīd Al-Antāk, PO 23:432–433; *Leonis Diaconi Historiae* 10.10. The taking of Kherson by the Russians has traditionally been explained by Basil II's refusal to give his sister Anna in marriage to Vladimir as promised. Poppe ("The Political Background to the Baptism of Rus,'" pp. 198ff.) argues that "the 'Cherson problem' remains the key question in the interpretation of Byzantine-Russian relations around the time of the conversion of Rus' to Christianity." He presents a different interpretation of the events, claiming that the Russians' expedition against Kherson was not directed against Byzantium but rather supported Basil II in his policy against the partisans of Bardas Phocas (pp. 211ff.). At the time, the Russian control of Kherson, which began in 989, was presented as part of Byzantine policy.

296. For the rise and fall of the Samanids, see *Ency. of Islam*, 8:1025–1031, s.v. "Sāmānids" (C. E. Bosworth).

297. *Laurentian Chronicle*, pp. 68, 75; Sorlin, "Les traités de Byzance avec la Russie," pp. 458–459.

298. In the treaty of 944, payment is to be made in silk; Sorlin finds an equivalence between silk and gold in the treaty ("Les traités de Byzance avec la Russie," pp. 458–459).

299. Const. Porph., *De adminis.* 9. See I. Sorlin, "Voies commerciales, villes et peuplement de la Rôsia au Xe siècle d'après le *De administrando imperio* de Constantin Porphyrogénète."

300. Ibn Hawqal, *Kitāb Ṣūrat al-arḍ*, BGA ed., pp. 392, 394.

301. Const. Porph., *De adminis.* 4.

302. *Theoph. Cont.* 6.9 (p. 357); 6.3 (p. 354), following Patlagean, "Byzance et les marchés du grand commerce," p. 622.

303. Note that, during the same year, Vladimir, the eldest son of Boris Michael, returned to paganism. It was also Leo VI, the signatory of the treaties with the Russians in 907 and 911, who, in about 911–912, promulgated the *Book of the Prefect*.

304. See also *Eparch. bib.* 9.6, where the presence of Bulgars ("and other foreigners") may have led to financial problems for a shop in Constantinople.

305. I have not mentioned, however, the importance of the Dalmatian Islands for navigation in the Adriatic (J. Ferluga, "Les îles dalmates dans l'Empire byzantin"; J. Ferluga, "Navigation et commerce dans l'Adriatique aux VIIe et VIIIe siècle") or the Byzantine-Venetian response to the arrival of the Arabs in that sea in 872–875, namely, Basil I's creation of the thema of Dalmatia.

306. Tafel-Thomas, 1:5 (no. 7); p. 16 (no. 12); p. 17 (no. 13); *Pacta Veneta: I trattai con Bisanzio 992–1198*, no. 1.

307. Tafel-Thomas, 1:3 (no. 3); pp. 25–30 (no.14).

308. For the new position of Venice at that time, see McCormick, *Origins of the European Economy*, pp. 523ff.

309. *Life of Nahum*, pp. 287–288. For the slave merchants passing through Moravia, see Gieysztor, "Les juifs et leurs activités économiques"; Ashtor, "Gli Ebrei nel commercio mediterraneo," pp. 508–509 (also for the ninth century); and Ashtor, "Aperçus sur les Radhanites," pp. 260–263. Blaise of Amorion, whose Life dates from the first half of the tenth century, is captured when he returns to Rome and is then sold in Bulgaria (*Life of Blaise of Amorion* 8; for his route, see Malamut, *Sur la route des saints byzantins*, pp. 258–260) (it is still not known who abducted him). The decree of 876 (Tafel-Thomas, 1:5, no. 7) explicitly targeted profit-hungry Venetian merchants who purchased slaves abducted by pirates and bandits in order to market them.

310. Patlagean, "Byzance et les marchés du grand commerce," p. 622 and n. 121; "Relatio de Legatione Constantinopolitana" 65, *Liudprandi Cremonensis Opera omnia* 65.

311. *Life of Elias Spēlaiōtēs I* 18 (*Life of Elias Spēlaiōtēs II* 12). The saint criticizes the merchant for his activities, but the merchant, who does not repudiate them, finally meets his death.

312. Tafel-Thomas, 1:17 (no. 13).

313. *Pacta Veneta: I trattati con Bisanzio 992–1198*, no. 1 (of 992, pp. 21–25 n. 2; of 1082, pp. 35–45); A. Pertusi, "La crisoballa del 992."

314. See the different interpretation of David Jacoby ("The Byzantine Outsider in Trade," pp. 133–134), who argues that the Byzantines wanted to keep their monopoly over the silk market (for the chrysobull of 1082 and the continuation of that imperial policy, see ibid., pp. 134ff.). See also L. Ralph-Johannes, *Handel und Politik. Zwischen dem byzantinischen Reich und den italienischen Kommunen Venedig, Pisa und Genua in der Epoche der Komnenen und der Angeloi (1081–1204)*, pp. 1–8.

315. In Pertusi's words, "Venezia e Bisanzio nel secolo XI," p. 131.

316. Ibid., pp. 127ff.

317. *Pacta Veneta: I trattati con Bisanzio 992–1198*, no. 2 (of 1082, pp. 35–45). Ralph-Johannes, *Handel und Politik*, pp. 8–16.

3. Slavery, a Component of a Medieval Society

1. For the word *sklavos*, see appendix 1.

2. It is necessary to distinguish between the servant, one who serves in general, and the domestic, a person who performs specific tasks in the house.

3. Roman law distinguishes among three types of property: *kinēta* (movable), *akinēta* (immovable), and *autokinēta* (able to move on its own).

4. *Andrapodon tēs moikheias*, used in reference to Constantine V (*Life of Stephen*

the Younger 23), or *doulos epitumias,* "slave of greed," a rhetorical usage known since Plato (J. A. Harrill, *The Manumission of Slaves in Early Christianity,* pp. 165–167).

5. He remained dependent on his master after emancipation. In fact the master, who became the freedman's employer, could return him to slavery.

6. See the definition of "freeborn" in *Inst. Jus.* 1.4–5, where the various statuses of free persons are defined. "Freeborn" was a civil status and did not necessarily refer to the fact of having been born free: *eugeneia* could in certain cases be granted to a person who was born a slave.

7. More often in the literary sources.

8. *Nov. Just.* 22.8; these were not persons who were already enslaved and were taken to the mines to work, but rather free men reduced to slavery, who therefore could not have had any prior domestic role.

9. N. Svoronos, *Nov. Mac.* nov. 3 and 8.

10. A *Novella* from the sixth century refers to a rural slave as *andrapodon,* adding the qualifiers *agroikikon* and *geōrgikon* (*Nov. Just.* 7, praef., 7.1, 7.3, 120.1, praef.).

11. During the entire period under study, the words *therapaina* and *sundoulos* also indicated a domestic role, but, unlike the other terms, they were generally used only in that sense. They did not occur frequently.

12. The civil status of these characters is evident because they are important in the narrative and the author describes them in detail, not necessarily because their legal status is explicitly mentioned.

13. See A. Kazhdan and M. McCormick, "The Social World of the Byzantine Court," pp. 189–195.

14. *Life of Stephen the Younger* 27; *Life of Andrew the Fool* 36.

15. *P. Stras.* 1.40.

16. *P.S. I* 6.709. For this document and the words *paidiskē* and *pais,* see J. Beaucamp, *Le statut de la femme à Byzance (IVe–VIIe siècles),* 2:58 n. 38.

17. Robinson, *Carbone* 4.53 (of 1049).

18. In the papyri of Cairo (Maspero), *pais* and *paidion* designate a child, but *paidarion* does not (*P. Cair. Masp.* 1.67005, 1.67028, 1.67032, 1.67077, and 1.67089 verso). Nevertheless, in the papyri of Oxyrhynchus of the same period (sixth century), the word *paidion* is used in place of *pais* for a child and in place of *paidarion* for an employee or servant (*P. Oxy.* 16.1829, 16.1842, 16.1868, 16.1872, 16.1874, 16.1913, 16.1921, 16.1940, 16.2046).

19. *P. Stras.* 1.40.

20. It is clear from the context—and the editor also explains—that the *katadoulos* became a wage laborer for a fixed period of time (at issue is the institution of the *paramonē*). R. Taubenschlag, *The Law of Greco-Roman Egypt in the Light of the Papyri,* p. 375.

21. *P. Cair. Masp.* 2.67166.

22. *Iviron II* 52.

23. In an emancipation act graffito from tenth-century Cappadocia (N. Thierry, "Libelle d'affranchissement des esclaves à Zelve, Xe siècle"), the word *uketas* is almost effaced. Only the ending *"-tas"* can be deciphered with certainty. In addition, the author uses the word *douloi* on the following line to refer to his freed slaves.

24. *P. Oxy.* 16.1837, 16.1855, 16.1860, 16.1866, 16.1939.

25. As in a document from Mount Athos: *Iviron II* 52 (early twelfth century).

26. For example, Menas, secretary of Apion, in *P. Oxy.* 16 (1896, 1898, 1976, 1983).

27. *P. Cair. Masp.* 2.67131 verso. For the figure of Dioscorus the Aphrodite, see J. L. Fournet, *Hellénisme dans l'Égypte du VIe siècle. La bibliothèque et l'oeuvre de Dioscore d'Aphrodité*, 1:317ff.

28. *P. Cair. Masp.* 2.67200.

29. Ibid., 1.67089[B].

30. Lemerle, *Boïlas, test.* (composed in April 1059); *Iviron II* 44 (composed in January 1090).

31. But P. Chantraine links *oiketēs* to the verb *oiketeuō*, which means "reside" (*Dictionnaire étymologique de la langue grecque. Histoire des mots*, 2:781–782, s.v. *"oikos"*).

32. Const. Porph., *De adminis.* 8.

33. Ibid., 28–30; in the last two cases, this was a text from the emperor.

34. By virtue of their legal definition.

35. A. Kazhdan, "The Concept of Freedom *(eleutheria)* and Slavery *(douleia)* in Byzantium."

36. D. Jacoby, "Une classe fiscale à Byzance et en Romanie latine: Les inconnus du fisc, éleuthères ou étrangers."

37. For the lands belonging to the Saint John the Theologian monastery in Patmos on other Aegean islands, see N. Oikonomides, *Fiscalité et exemption fiscale à Byzance (IXe–XIe siècles)*, pp. 230ff. For that *episkepsis*, see ibid., p. 78.

38. For a definition of the powerful elite dating back to the fifth century, see Patlagean, *Pauvreté économique et pauvreté sociale à Byzance, IVe–VIIe siècles*, pp. 289ff.

39. J. Koder, the most recent editor, dates it to 912 (*Das Eparchenbuch Leons des Weisen*, pp. 31–32). It is particularly worth mentioning that this is the only text that reveals the place of slaves in artisanal manufacture.

40. The word "guilds" could also be used here. On the development of the function of the prefect of Constantinople in late antiquity, see G. Dagron, *Naissance d'une capitale. Constantinople et ses institutions de 330 à 451*, chap. 7 ("Proconsulat et préfecture urbaine, de Rome à Constantinople"), esp. pp. 227ff.

41. *Eparch. bib.* 2.8, 2.9, 3.1, 4.2, 6.7, 8.7, 8.13, 11.1.

42. *Tabellarioi*: official secretaries or notaries. See H. Saradi-Mendelovici, *Le notariat byzantin du IXe au XVe siècle.*

43. See also J. P. Sodini, "L'artisanat urbain à l'époque paléochrétienne (IVe–VIIe siècles)"; N. Oikonomides, "Quelques boutiques de Constantinople au Xe siècle"; P. Yannopoulos, *La société profane dans l'Empire byzantin*, pp. 157ff.

44. It is not clear whether these rules applied to one corporation only or whether the different corporations had the same rules.

45. For example, the *Book of the Prefect* tells how to set up a workshop only for certain trades. Koder shows that it is not possible to say whether other rules that have not come down to us were initially part of the text and have since disappeared (J. Koder, "Delikt und Strafe im Eparchenbuch: Aspekte des mittelalterlichen Korporationswesens in Konstantinopel," p. 114).

46. *Eparch. bib.* 2.9, 8.13.

47. Their wages were indexed to what the notary earned: 2 *keratia* per *nomisma* (*Eparch. bib.* 1.19), that is, one-twelfth the notary's wage (E. Schilbach, *Byzantinische Metrologie*, pp. 185–186).

48. *Eparch. bib.* 1.24.

49. On this subject, see A. Kazhdan, "Slaves and *Misthioi* in Byzantium, Ninth to Eleventh Centuries"; and A. Kazhdan, "The Corporations and Government Workshops of Constantinople in the Ninth and Tenth Centuries." On the question of the organization of artisanal labor, Kazhdan takes issue with M. J. Sjuzjumov's "Occupations and Commerce in Constantinople in the Early Tenth Century."

50. *Eparch. bib.* 8.7. The *eklektēs* probably had a specific role in the manufacture of silk. Koder translates it as "sorter" (*Titrierer* in German); Koder, *Das Eparchenbuch Leons des Weisen*, p. 105.

51. The rule does not mention that anyone who sold a free man was guilty of another crime, for which the same sanction is stipulated (*Ekloga* 17.16; *Proch. Nom.* 39.5).

52. *Eparch. bib.* 6.2 (for the *metaxopratai*); *Eparch bib.* 8.12 (for the *serikarioi*).

53. *Eparch. bib.* 6.3.

54. Ibid., 8.10.

55. Ibid., 3.1. Slaves' participation in financial life was widespread in the Roman era: J. Andreau, *Banque et affaires dans le monde romain, IVe siècle av. J.-C.–IIIe siècle apr. J.-C.,* pp. 125–135, 153–170 (for slaves as assayers).

56. *Eparch. bib.* 3.6.

57. Ibid., 7.3, 7.5.

58. The rule regarding silk finishers (ibid., 7.3) does not do so explicitly.

59. Ibid., 4.2.

60. Ibid., 4.5, 4.6.

61. Ibid., 8.13, 12.1, 19.4.

62. Ibid., 12.1.

63. Ibid., 2.9, 8.13.

64. Ibid., 4.5–6.

65. Ibid., 2.9, 8.13, as noted in Sjuzjumov, "Occupations and Commerce in Constantinople," p. 15.

66. *Dig.* 47.22.3; *Basilic.* 60.32.3.
67. Gai. *Inst.* 4.71; *Dig.* 14.3; Buckland, *The Roman Law of Slavery*, pp. 187ff. For an overview of these systems, see Andreau, *Banque et affaires dans le monde romain*, pp. 125–135.
68. *Eparch. bib.* 6.7, which describes the master as the initiator.
69. *Cf.* the participation of slaves in urban artisanal life in Egypt during the Roman era: I. Biezunska-Malowist, *L'esclavage dans l'Égypte gréco-romaine. Seconde partie: Période romaine*, pp. 84ff. "In Roman Egypt, the practice of a trade was taxed at a fixed per capita rate. Several receipts indicate that slaves paid that tax. That is not absolute proof that the slaves in question worked for themselves. In fact, apprenticeship contracts show that the artisan was sometimes responsible for paying the artisanal tax for his apprentice. In addition, this was a per capita tax imposed on all who practiced an artisanal trade, whether for others or for themselves. Other documents attest, however, that slave artisans were sometimes hired out by their masters to third parties, for whom they worked, and they sometimes even practiced their trade in an independent manner, outside the master's house, though that was rather rare" (ibid., pp. 87–88; bibliography, p. 87 n. 53; list of papyri concerned, p. 88 n. 54). That tax *(chrysargyre)*, attested by Zosimus (Zos. 2.38), differs from the outlay that corporations required of their new members (Patlagean, *Pauvreté économique et pauvreté sociale*, p. 173).
70. Buckland, *The Roman Law of Slavery*, p. 222; M. Morabito, *Les réalités de l'esclavage d'après le Digeste*, pp. 103–111. The *naturalis obligatio* held the slave himself responsible (and hence protected his master from any obligation regarding his slave's acts), whereas the *deductio de peculio* allowed the slave's debts to be paid from the peculium (and thus protected creditors).
71. *Eparch. bib.* 6.7.
72. Ibid., 2.9, 8.13. Note that the price of a workshop, according to the *Patmiacus 171 (fol. 516)* published by Oikonomides ("Quelques boutiques de Constantinople au Xe siècle"), was quite high, 6–10 *nomismata* (compared to 10 *nomismata* in the *Book of the Prefect* for the workshop of a silk clothing merchant, *Eparch. bib.* 4.6); and the slave could not become an owner or a tenant on his own behalf.
73. Oikonomides, "Quelques boutiques de Constantinople au Xe siècle," pp. 355–356.
74. *Eparch. bib.* 2.8, 12.9.
75. There are more details on enslaved goldsmiths in the *Life of Theophanes the Confessor* (7).
76. Koder, "Delikt und Strafe in Eparchenbuch," pp. 119–125, 128–131.
77. *Eparch. bib.* 11.1. In this case, candlemakers sent their slaves or apprentices to sell their merchandise where such sale was prohibited. The rule stated that the act had to be punished. But a master could escape being charged simply by setting up his slave as the shop foreman.
78. *Eparch. bib.* 2.8.

79. Schilbach, *Byzantinische Metrologie*, pp. 169–174.
80. That also explains why, in the *Book of the Prefect, misthioi* occupy a marginal place when compared to slaves.
81. *Eparch. bib.* 2.8, 12.9.
82. G. Boulvert, *Esclaves et affranchis impériaux sous le Haut-Empire Romain. Rôle politique et administratif.*
83. Beginning in the era of the Antonii and increasingly under the Severi, emperors preferred to entrust the management of important departments to the equestrian elite (ibid., pp. 315ff., 324ff.).
84. A constitution of 465 attests the gift of slaves to the imperial court (*CJ* 12.5.4). In the ninth century, the widow Danielis gave five hundred slaves (including a hundred eunuchs) to Basil I (*Theoph. Cont.* 5.74) and then bequeathed all her remaining slaves (three thousand) to Emperor Leo VI (*Theoph. Cont.* 5.77).
85. S. Vryonis, "The Question of the Byzantine Mines."
86. Sodini, "L'artisanat urbain à l'époque paléochrétienne (IVe–VIIe siècles)," pp. 101–104; Jones, *LRE* 2:837–839.
87. *Nov. Just.* 22.8.
88. R. Delmaire, "Les esclaves et *condicionales* fiscaux au bas-empire romain."
89. N. Oikonomides, *Les listes de préséance byzantines des IXe et Xe siècles*, p. 317. On the workers in the imperial workshops, see also Yannopoulos, *La société profane dans l'Empire byzantin*, pp. 227–232 ("Les ouvriers des usines d'État"); he classifies them as "persons whose freedom was limited." *Cf.* H. Bresc, "Le marchand, le marché et le palais dans la Sicile des Xe–XIIe siècles."
90. Al-Muqaddasī, *Descriptio imperri moslemici*, in BGA, 3:147–148, trans. M. Canard, in Vasiliev, 2–2:422–424.
91. Symeon the New Theologian, *The Ethical Discourses*, 2:86–87 (treatise 7). The author contrasts this service to that of strategoi and officers.
92. Delmaire, "Les esclaves et *condicionales* fiscaux au bas-empire romain"; R. Delmaire, *Largesses sacrées et res privata. L'aerarium impérial et son administration du IVe au VIe siècle*, pp. 419ff.
93. Boulvert's *Esclaves et affranchis impériaux sous le Haut-Empire Romain* ends at the time of the Severi. The court organized by Constantine, however, was larger and more varied than that of his predecessors (see R. Guilland, *Recherches sur les institutions byzantines*).
94. Boulvert describes in detail the roles that the emperor's slaves and freedmen filled from the time of Augustus to the third century. He shows not only the importance of slaves and freedmen but also the imperial needs in Rome—both in Italy and in the provinces (see the tables of roles in Boulvert, *Esclaves et affranchis impériaux sous le Haut-Empire Romain*, pp. 201–203, 260–261). Boulvert does not say how these slaves reached the emperor and the court, however.
95. *CJ* 4.42, 12.5.4; Claudius Claudianus, *In Eutropium* 1.152ff.; Agathias 1.16; *Theoph. Cont.* 5.74.
96. See also J. E. Dunlap, *The Office of the Grand Chamberlain in the Late Roman*

Empire; K. Hopkins, "Eunuchs in Politics in the Late Roman Empire"; and Guilland, *Recherches sur les institutions byzantines,* 1:275ff.

 97. By way of example, consider the cases of Narses (Agathias 1.16; Proc., *BP* 1.15.31; Proc., *BG* 3.13; *PLRE* 3:915), Cosmas (Zachariah Mitylenis, 6.2–3; Evag., *HE* 3.22), and Scholasticus (Proc., *BG* 3.40.35; *PLRE* 3:1117.). For all the functions of eunuchs in the courts of the ninth to eleventh centuries, see Oikonomides, *Les listes de préséance byzantines,* pp. 291–301.

 98. *Nov. Leo.* 38.

 99. *Life of Stephen the Younger* 32.36.

100. Zachariah Mitylenis 3.4; 6.3; *PLRE* 3:1244–1245.

101. By imperial policy, that lack of freedom of movement was imposed on the *illustres* as well (Dagron, *Naissance d'une capitale,* pp. 165ff.).

102. P. Magdalino, "The Byzantine Aristocratic *Oikos.*"

103. *Iviron II* 44, 47.

104. The prosopography is detailed in J. Lefort's commentary (*Iviron II,* pp. 152–153, 173–176).

105. See P. Gautier, *Le typikon du sébaste Grégoire Pakourianos.*

106. In the ninth to eleventh centuries, the aristocratic title *kouropalatos* was attributed to military leaders.

107. Lemerle, *Boïlas, test.*

108. *Life of Andrew the Fool,* prol. 2.

109. *Peira* 42.15; Kekaumenos 4 (168).

110. This underestimation is related to the idea of the decline of Roman slavery.

111. P. Lemerle, *The Agrarian History of Byzantium from the Origins to the Twelfth Century,* pp. 65–66.

112. G. Ostrogorsky, "La commune rurale byzantine. Loi agraire—Traité fiscal—Cadastre de Thèbes"; see also G. Ostrogorsky, "Le grand domaine dans l'Empire byzantin"; G. Ostrogorsky, "The Peasant's Preemption Right, an Abortive Reform of the Macedonian Emperors"; and G. Ostrogorsky, *Quelques problèmes d'histoire de la paysannerie byzantine,* pp. 71ff.

113. I. F. Fichman, "Sklaven und Sklavenarbeit im spätrömischen Oxyrynchos (im historischen Längsschnitt)"; I. F. Fichman, "Slaves in Byzantine Oxyrynchos"; J. Gascou, "Les grands domaines, la cité et l'État en Égypte byzantine. Recherches d'histoire agraire, fiscale et administrative"; R. S. Bagnall, *Egypt in Late Antiquity,* chap. 3, "Country Villages."

114. Note on this subject N. Svoronos's work on the *Novellae* of the tenth-century emperors (Svoronos, *Nov. Mac.*).

115. A *typikon* is the charter of a monastery governing its administrative, economic, and ritual life.

116. I have not included the terms *paroikoi* and *douloparoikoi* because these categories are contained within those already mentioned.

117. Patlagean, "'Économie paysanne' et 'féodalité byzantine.'"

118. Y. Rotman, "Formes de la non-liberté dans la campagne byzantine aux VIIe–XIe siècles."

119. Ibid., pp. 507–509.
120. For examples, see Oikonomides, *Fiscalité et exemption fiscale à Byzance,* pp. 133–134.
121. *Iviron II* 44, 47.
122. As in the case of the two slaves who remained with Philaretos; *Life of Philaretos,* pp. 60–62. See also J. W. Nesbitt, "The Life of St. Philaretos (702–792) and Its Significance for Byzantine Agriculture." See the different interpretation of M. Loos, "Quelques remarques sur les communautés rurales et la grande propriété terrienne à Byzance (VIIe–XIe siècles)."
123. Gascou, "Les grands domaines, la cité et l'État en Égypte byzantine."
124. Precisely because of the payment of property rents through fiscal obligations; Patlagean, "'Économie paysanne' et 'féodalité byzantine'"; Gascou, "Les grands domaines, la cité et l'État en Égypte byzantine," pp. 12–23.
125. Bagnall, *Egypt in Late Antiquity,* chap. 3, "Country Villages."
126. Biezunska-Malowist, *L'esclavage dans l'Égypte gréco-romaine,* chap. 3, "Les emplois des esclaves," pp. 150–158, and for agriculture, esp. pp. 74–82; See O. Montevecchi's pioneering "Ricerche di sociologia nei documenti dell'Egitto greco-romano. III.—I contratti di compra-vendita."
127. Dölger, *Der Traktat des Cold. Marc. Gr. 173,* p. 115. See also C. M. Brand, "Two Byzantine Treatises on Taxation," which provides an English translation.
128. *Life of Philaretos,* pp. 60–62.
129. John of Ephesus, *Lives of Thomas and Stephen,* in John of Ephesus, *Eastern Saints,* PO 17:191.
130. Life of Leo Luke of Sicily 1–3; *Life of Elias Spēlaiōtēs* 94ff.
131. *Peira* 6.21.
132. The *paroikoi* are mentioned in the cadastre for the village of Radolibos (*Iviron II* 53) but are absent from Symbatios Pakourianos's will (*Iviron II* 44). Mary Pakouriana mentions them (ibid., 47), but only for purposes of charity.
133. A *Novella* of Romanus I Lecapenus (934) defines these *dunatoi* at length (Svoronos, *Nov. Mac.* 3).
134. N. Svoronos, *Le cadastre de Thèbes.* Consider as well the wife of the strategos of Thebes mentioned in the *Life of Theodora of Thessalonica* (tenth century), who also owned slaves (*Life of Theodora of Thessalonica* 56).
135. *Iviron II* 44, 47, 50.
136. P. Gautier, *La Diataxis de Michel Attaliate.*
137. *Patmos II* 50.
138. *Life of Theophanes the Confessor* 12.20 (early ninth century); *Life of Theodore Studites II* 8 (ninth century; note that, in the version of that Life written by Michael the Monk, the slaves were domestics); *Life of Theodore Studites I* 5; *Life of Elizabeth of Heraclea* 1–4 (ninth to tenth centuries); *Life of Michael Maleinos* 11 (second half of the tenth century); *Theoph. Cont.* 5.74; 77 (tenth century).
139. Lemerle, *Boïlas, test.* pp. 49–53.
140. For distance from the emperor as a founding element in the Byzantine social hierarchy of the tenth to thirteenth centuries, see J. C. Cheynet, *Pouvoir et*

contestations à Byzance (963–1210). The changes in the definition of power can thus be explained by the changes in the social position of the "new" Byzantine aristocracy and in the definition of forms of dependency in the tenth and eleventh centuries.

141. Ibid. The properties of the monasteries were a separate case.

142. *Lavra I* 6; *Iviron I* 2.

143. Ostrogorsky, *Quelques problèmes d'histoire de la paysannerie byzantine*, p. 26. In 810, Nicephorus I taxed the *paroikoi* residing on the lands belonging to the church, the imperial monasteries, and other tax-exempt demesnes (Theoph. A.M. 6302, pp. 486–487). Nicephorus was trying to find sources of revenue. This measure demonstrates that, as far back as the ninth century, the imperial authorities perceived they were losing revenues to the monasteries.

144. *Leges rusticae* 46–47, 71–72; *Life of Philaretos*, pp. 60–62. Philaretos's life is presented as a Byzantine version of the story of Job. But the detail that Philaretos owns slaves is an addition of the Byzantine author, who substitutes "slaves" for *"upēresia pollē sfodra"* ("a very great household," or literally, "a great many servants") (Job 1:3).

145. *Iviron II* 53, which gives the same dimensions for the properties as the *Cadastre of Thebes*. For Radolibos, see J. Lefort, "Le cadastre de Radolibos (1103), les géomètres et leurs mathématiques"; J. Lefort, "Radolibos: Population et paysage."

146. R. Browning, "Slavery in the Byzantine Empire, 600–1200," pp. 46–48.

147. Oikonomides, "Οἱ Βυζαντινοὶ δουλοπάροικοι."

148. See *Lavra I* 33 (of 1060), *Lavra I* 38 (of 1079) and *Iviron II* 32 (of 1059/1074), which make a distinction between the *douloparoikoi* and the *paroikoi*.

149. In general terms, the social and economic center of gravity shifted from the eastern part of the empire to the western part in the tenth to eleventh centuries.

150. Gautier, *Le Typikon du sébaste Grégoire Pakourianos*, p. 99.

151. Ibid. The text mentions *kinēta* and *autokinēta*. These *autokinēta* were likely merely livestock (even though, in classical legal language, slaves were officially designated by the same term).

152. *Patmos II* 50.

153. Ibid.

154. For example, Philaretos, Elizabeth of Heraclea, Michael Maleinos, the widow Danielis, Theophanes the Confessor, Theodore Studites, and the father of Luke the Younger (*Life of Luke the Younger* 1–4).

155. Indicated from the *Novellae* of Justinian to the will of Theodore Studites and the *Novellae* of the "Macedonian" emperors.

156. See esp. the *Life of Theodore of Sykeon* (seventh century) and Psellus's *Life of Auxentios* (eleventh century), which unfold in a village but give no indication of agricultural labor.

157. Lemerle believes Boïlas was a native of Edessa (Lemerle, *Boïlas, test.*, pp. 49–53).

158. Ibid., pp. 23, 26–27.

159. Ibid., *Boïlas, test.*, p. 60; M. Kaplan, *Les hommes et la terre à Byzance du VIe au XIe siècle. Propriété et exploitation du sol*, p. 347.

160. All these possessions had already been divided up.

161. For example, the widow Danielis, Michael Maleinos, Philaretos, and Elizabeth of Heraclea.

162. *Life of Michael Maleinos* 11; *Theoph. Cont.* 5.74, 77. Note that the *Life of Elizabeth of Heraclea* mentions only *paides* and *paidiskai*, whom Elizabeth freed (*Life of Elizabeth of Heraclea* 4); these were probably domestic slaves. Philaretos lost all his slaves *(oiketai)* but two (a *doulos* and a *paidiskē); Life of Philaretos*, pp. 60–62.

163. *Ekloga* 8.1.1; *Proch. Nom.* 34.8; *Epit. Leg.* 38.

164. *Nov. Just.* 1.1; *Ekloga* 8.1.4; *Proch. Nom.* 18.12; *Nov. Leo.* 37.

165. *Ekloga* 8.1.4, explained in *Proch. Nom.* 7.28.

166. *Nov. Just.* 18.11, 22, 78.3–4 (the children were automatically freed; Beauchamp, *Le statut de la femme à Byzance*, p. 281); *Ekloga* 8.1.3.

167. *Nov. Just.* 22; *Proch. Nom.* 5.4.

168. *Nov. Just.* 22.37.

169. Ibid., 1.1; *Proch. Nom.* 18.12.

170. *Nov. Leo.* 37. For the laws concerning the wills of freedmen, see *Epit. Leg.* 31.

171. *Nov. Leo.* 38.

172. Buckland, *The Roman Law of Slavery*, pp. 437ff.

173. A master who served as godfather at the baptism of his female slave could not marry her because she was considered his daughter (*Proch. Nom.* 7.28), nor could a mistress marry her freedman (*Proch. Nom.* 7.20).

174. *Nov. Just.* 123.17; *Ekloga* 8.3. Note that Byzantine laws do not use the word *patrōn* but continue to call the employer "one's master" *(despotēs autou)*.

175. *Nov. Just.* 78.

176. *Ekloga* 14.2.2 adds the *apeleutheros* to the law of the *Codex Justiniani* (*CJ* 4.20.8).

177. *Nov. Leo.* 25.

178. Ferrari, no. 38; Sathas, *Parisinus g. 2509, fol 161–162*; D. Simon and S. Troianos, eds., *Scorialensis R II 12*. Hence the emancipation act graffiti found in Cappadocia (Thierry, "Libelle d'affranchissement des esclaves à Zelve") by themselves attest the free status of the freedmen.

179. Or rather, he incites the child of his mistress to steal it for him (*Spiritually Beneficial Tales of Paul of Monembasia* 2.5).

180. *Life of Athanasia of Aegina* 12.

181. Lemerle, *Boïlas, test.*, p. 27.

182. *P. Cair. Masp.* 1.67089 and 3.67294.

183. *P. Cair. Masp.* 3.67294 (version A in L. Wenger, "Ein christliches Freiheitszeugnis in den ägyptischen Papyri") includes lines 1 to 29, whereas *P. Cair. Masp.* 1.67089 (version B) has the text between lines 3 and 39 and also contains the end of the original.

184. See Wenger, "Ein christliches Freiheitzeugnis."

185. This is not spelled out by the author. But his son, Victor, was the only person who, in declaring her a slave, could take her possessions. The author himself specifies: "May none of my fellow successors . . . my son and heir Victor . . . bother Martha about having the status of a slave" (lines 18–22). In addition, she had already been examined and questioned and had said that "she was not placed *eleuthera*" (lines 27–28). The circumstances are unknown—both who questioned her and why she gave such a response. But, having given it, she needed the author's certification in order to be judged free and so that her possessions would continue to belong to her.

186. And not an emancipation for a possible marriage between the author and the person in question (L. S. B. MacCoull, "A Cinderella Story from Byzantine Egypt: *P. Cair. Masp.* I 67089 and III 67294"). See also Beaucamp, *Le statut de la femme à Byzance*, 2:53 n. 13.

187. Unlike, for example, *P. Stras.* 1.40 (a labor contract, *paramonē*, for a *katadoulos*).

188. See M. Melluso, *La schiavitù nell'età giustinianea* (pp. 225–230), which explains this papyrus in terms of economic dependency.

189. *SB* 3.6097.

190. A deed of sale for slaves from Byzantine Italy (undated) illustrates the opposite case: a master needed a document to testify that he had acquired his slave legally (Ferrari, no. 37); that was also the case in sixth-century Egypt (*P. Stras.* 1404).

191. Ferrari, no. 38.

192. Thierry, "Libelle d'affranchissement des esclaves à Zelve." These graffiti, which occupy the entire arcosolium, are not written as an epitaph and do not mention that the author is dead. In addition, it is not clear that the author was emancipating all his slaves. It is simply noted that he freed two of them: τὸν Δ[. . .], τὸν Νικόλα[ον].

193. With the exception of the Cappadocian emancipation act.

194. Only in the deed from Byzantine Italy (Ferrari, no. 38).

195. Simply because the nature of the property given to the freedman was different in the two cases.

196. *Lavra I* 1; Lemerle, *Boïlas, test.;* Robinson, *Carbone* 10 (59). In Robinson, *Carbone* 11 (61), the slave, Anna, is identified as the author's daughter.

197. Lemerle, *Boïlas, test.*, pp. 26–27.

198. *Lavra I* 1 (composed in 897).

199. *Cf.* for Byzantine Italy, the documents of Saint Elias of Carbone; for Macedonia, *Lavra I* 1; and, for Asia Minor, Boïlas's will.

200. *Nov. Leo.* 37. For the laws concerning freedmen's wills, see *Epit. Leg.* 31.

201. Lemerle, *Boïlas, test.*, p. 26.

202. That is, if they become pagans, Muslims, or heretics (anti-Chalcedonians). These slaves are called *oiketika prosopa*. Boïlas had other slaves whom he bequeathed to his daughters, along with lands and livestock.

203. Lemerle, *Boïlas, test.*, p. 27 (paying them *rogai* and *annonai*).

204. *Iviron II* 44.

205. Ibid., 47.
206. See the procuration of Sister Mary, *Iviron II* 46.
207. Cheynet (*Pouvoir et contestations à Byzance*, chap. 7, "Les formes de dépendance") illustrates how an *oikos* and its dependents functioned.
208. Magdalino, "The Byzantine Aristocratic *Oikos*."
209. As seen in the wills of Gregory Pakourianos, Symbatios Pakourianos, and his widow, Sister Mary.
210. Lemerle, *Boïlas, test.*, pp. 49–53.
211. Note that *apodoulos* was a new term in the Byzantine language; see also *Suidae Lexicon*, 1:358, 3932, s.v. "Ἀριστοφάνης" (the Souda is a compilation dating from between the late tenth and early eleventh century).
212. *Iviron II* 47.
213. Kekaumenos 4 (168).
214. *Peira* 42.17.
215. Nicephorus Bryennios, *Histoire* 2.26.
216. Note, however, that the documents of Saint Elias of Carbone concern the author's daughter (though she is designated as his slave).
217. In contrast, for example, to a four-year labor contract *(paramonē)* (*P. Stras.* 1.40).
218. *Iviron II* 47. She sent this same Stephanos to the quaestor with the procuration she composed after her husband's death (*Iviron II* 46).
219. Gautier, *Le typikon du sébaste Grégoire Pakourianos*, pp. 29, 33, 93.
220. *Theodore Tiron, Miracle of the Dragon* 4.
221. *Spiritually Beneficial Tales of Paul of Monembasia* 2.5.
222. *Life of Luke the Younger* 4–8.
223. Lemerle, *Boïlas, test.*, p. 22.
224. Because the lands of the village of Radolibos in Macedonia were bequeathed by Symbatios Pakourianos's widow to the monastery of Iviron, the couple's wills have been preserved in the archives of the monastery.
225. Gautier, *Le typikon du sébaste Grégoire Pakourianos*, p. 92.
226. *Theoph. Cont.* 5.77. The expression "thema of Longobardia" literally meant the territories under the control of the Lombardians. It was used ambiguously by the Byzantines to refer to the provinces of Puglia and Basilicata but also to other Italian territories (Benevento, Capua, Salerno, Naples, Amalfi, and Gaeta) that recognized the authority of the Byzantine emperor but did not pay taxes to him (V. von Falkenhausen, *La dominazione bizantina nell'Italia meridionale dal IX all'XI secolo*, pp. 31–41). Leo VI's action may therefore show the political-economic importance of the emancipation of such a large number of slaves.
227. Let me cite, by way of example, the transfer of a Chypriot population by Justinian II (Theoph. A.M. 683, p. 365) and the 810 transfer by Nicephorus I (ibid., A.M. 6302, p. 486).
228. *Life of Andrew the Fool* 2–5.
229. *Life of Elias the Younger* 14.

230. *Life of Andrew the Fool* 1; *Life of Elias the Younger* 4.
231. *Life of Matrona of Perge* 44; *Life of Michael Maleinos* 11 (with *legata*); *Life of Elizabeth of Heraclea* 4 (with *legata*); *Life of Nilus of Rossano* 5; *Life of Theophanes the Confessor* 12.20; *Life of Theodore Studites II* 8.
232. Life of Matrona of Perge 44.

4. Evolution of the Concept of Unfreedom

1. [The King James Version is used throughout the chapter.—Trans.]
2. P. Garnsey, *Ideas of Slavery from Aristotle to Augustine.*
3. J. A. Glancy, *Slavery in Early Christianity.*
4. P. Gruszka, "Die Ansichten über das Sklaventum in den Schriften der kappadozischen Kirchenväter."
5. Ibid., p. 109.
6. Gruszka himself introduces that cleavage between slaves and free persons. As I have shown, that position resulted from the view that a single cleavage dominated society.
7. Not having exhaustively verified that vast literature, I rely on the references cited in Garnsey, Glancy, and Gruszka.
8. See Garnsey, *Ideas of Slavery from Aristotle to Augustine,* pp. 173–188 ("II. Paul"); Glancy, *Slavery in Early Christianity,* pp. 57ff., and her analysis of the Gospels (ibid., chap. 4, "The Figure of the Slave in the Sayings of Jesus").
9. See also Ephesians 6:6–8 and 1 Timothy 6:1–2: "Let as many servants as are under the yoke count their own masters worthy of all honour, that the name of God and his doctrine be not blasphemed. And they that have believing masters, let them not despise them, because they are brethren; but rather do them service, because they are faithful and beloved, partakers of the benefit."
10. This tallies with I. Biezunska-Malowist's thesis (*L'esclavage dans l'Égypte gréco-romaine*). Similarly, the writings of Ambrose and Augustine refer to slavery as a doctrinal and philosophical idea but do not develop any concrete precepts.
11. Gruszka provides references to the master-slave relationship that appear in the writings of Gregory of Nazianzus and Basil of Caesarea, explaining the circumstances (Gruszka, "Die Ansichten über das Sklaventum," pp. 112–115).
12. The writings of the Cappadocian fathers speak only of Christian slaves.
13. Gruszka, "Die Ansichten über das Sklaventum," p. 114.
14. Mansi 2:1101. In "L'anathème du concile de Gangres contre ceux qui, sous prétexte de christianisme, incitent les esclaves à quitter leurs maîtres," J. de Churuca explains that the council joined forces against the monastic movement of Eustathians, who were not "anti-slavery agitators" but tended toward an "extreme rigorism." See also P. Brown, *Poverty and Leadership in the Later Roman Empire,* pp. 36–37. The central problem of the third canon was the requirement that the master give his consent before a slave could become a monk. I agree with Churuca's argument that the doctrine on slavery pro-

claimed by the bishops meeting in Gangra reflected the principles already expressed in the Epistles of Paul. For the dating of the Council of Gangra, see A. Laniado, "Note sur la datation conservée en syriaque du concile de Gangres."

15. *Nov. Just.* 5.2, 123.17.

16. Basil, *Letters* 115; Gregory of Nazianzus, *Letters* 79.

17. Ibid. As a matter of fact, he does not say so explicitly but suggests that the owner's consent was needed before ordination.

18. S. Perentidis, "L'ordination de l'esclave à Byzance."

19. The law of asylum promulgated under Justinian is very explicit; it is the bishop or the higoumene who frees the slave by his authority within the church and not by the sacrament (*Nov. Just.* 5.2, 123.17, 123.35).

20. Gruszka, "Die Ansichten über das Sklaventum," pp. 112–113.

21. Gregory of Nazianzus, *Testamentum*, in *Clavis patrum graecorum* 2:189. The will dates from 390–391, when Gregory was patriarch of Constantinople. See M. F. Martroye, "Le testament de saint Grégoire de Nazianze."

22. Note that, among his heirs, he names the church of Nazianzus and his emancipated slave, Gregory, who became a deacon.

23. *Life of Matrona of Perge* 44; *Life of Michel Maleinos* 11; *Life of Elizabeth of Heraclea* 4; *Life of Theophanes the Confessor* 12.20; *Life of Theodore Studites I* 5; *Life of Theodore Studites II* 8. These differ from the emancipation of Andrew the Fool (*Life of Andrew the Fool* 5), which was a result of his mental illness.

24. *Life of Melania the Younger* 9–11, 18; *Life of Symeon the Fool*, pp. 58–59 (pp. 124–125).

25. *Life of Marcellus Acemetes* 30.

26. *Life of Matrona of Perge* 44.

27. *The Life of Melania the Younger* is attributed to Gerontius, the abbot who oversaw the monasteries of Saint Melania in Palestine in the second half of the fifth century (Gorce, ed., *Vie de Sainte Mélanie*, pp. 54–60).

28. Palladius, *Historia Lausiaca* 61.

29. *Life of Melanie the Younger* 10–11.

30. Ferrari, no. 38; Dain, *Paris sup. gr. 1238;* Sathas, *Parisinus gr. 2509 fol. 161–162.* They all come from tenth- and eleventh-century Italy. Acts of emancipation for the same period in the documents of Asia Minor do not invoke that formula. But it is not possible to conclude that this was a regional difference. Note as well that the formula was not part of the *manumissio in ecclesia.*

31. John Chrysostom, *Homilae XXIV in Epistolam ad Ephesios* 22.2 (PG 62:155–161).

32. I am simplifying a great deal here (following Garnsey, *Ideas of Slavery from Aristotle to Augustine*, pp. 191–219).

33. Aristotle, *Politics* 1278b32–38; 1253b20–1256b39 (for a complete discussion of his theory, see Garnsey, *Ideas of Slavery from Aristotle to Augustine*, pp. 11–14, 115–127.

34. A paraphrase of *Dig.* 1.5.4.

35. In contrast to the *Digesta*, which does not necessarily define war as a negative phenomenon.

36. The Greek word *porneia* had two senses: relations in exchange for payment or simply a nonconjugal and nonadulterous relationship.
37. Pitra, *Juris eccl.* 2:625–626.
38. Ibid., *Juris eccl.* 2:344, canon 182. For the dating of the canon, see Grumel, *Reg. pat.*, nos. 407–407a, vol. 1, pts. 2–3:52–53. On the marriages of slaves, see Candidus, frag. 6.
39. *Life of Symeon the Fool*, pp. 95–96 (pp. 161–162).
40. *Life of Theodore of Sykeon* 140, 147.
41. *Life of Mary the Younger* 5. The humane attitude toward slaves had earlier been expressed by Seneca (*Ad Lucilium epistulae morales* 47, pp. 307–309, Gummere trans.): "But this is the kernel of my advice: Treat your inferiors as you would be treated by your betters. And as often as you reflect how much power you have over a slave, remember that your master has just as much power over you. 'But I have no master,' you say. You are still young; perhaps you will have one." In the Roman era, that attitude remained very rare, however; see the master-slave relationship in the Roman era as developed in K. Bradley, *Slaves and Masters in the Roman Empire: A Study in Social Control*.
42. Morphologically, *Adonai* is actually a plural form, literally meaning "my lords," like the Hebrew word *Elohim* (God, *theos*). Nevertheless, both words are used in the Old Testament as singular constructions ("My Lords says, does," and so on).
43. Garnsey, *Ideas of Slavery from Aristotle to Augustine*, pp. 220–235; and Garnsey, "Sons, Slaves, and Christians," esp. p. 108.
44. See Garnsey, "Sons, Slaves, and Christians," as well as the "perpetual slave" state toward God described by Ignatius (Harrill, *The Manumission of Slaves in Early Christianity*, p. 185).
45. According to Roman law, a slave could be the property of more than one person, as was the case in an inheritance or when the slave was in the service of an organization, for example. All the same, these cases were not common, and imperial legislation dealt with the dissolution of such a possession (*CJ* 6.43.3.1; 7.7.1.5).
46. The tetragrammaton was therefore likely rendered as *Adonai* when spoken aloud, as is still the case today.
47. Similarly, the relation between God and believer is equivalent to that between father and son (Garnsey, "Sons, Slaves, and Christians").
48. And after the fourth century (*Nov. Post. Just.*, coll. 1, nov. 7, a *Novella* of Justin II of 572, repeated in *App. Eklo.* 8.2–3).
49. *CJ* 1.13.1–2; *CTh* 4.7.1. See F. Fabbrini, *La manumissio in ecclesia*; F. Fabbrini, "Un nuovo documento relativo alla *manumissio in ecclesia*"; C. Giannelli, "Alcuni formulari relativi all '*manumissio in ecclesia*' tratti da eucologi italo-greci e slavi." In addition, in *The Manumission of Slaves in Early Christianity*, chap. 4, Harrill describes the social custom of a group of people collectively emancipating slaves in temples. That custom, known since antiquity and adopted by churches and synagogues in the first to third centuries, may suggest a more ancient origin for the *manumissio in ecclesia*.

50. *CTh* 4.7.1, which differs from the version in *CJ*, where a document of emancipation must be signed. See Fabbrini, *La manumissio in ecclesia*, pp. 47–80.

51. Fabbrini, *La manumissio in ecclesia*, pp. 132–133.

52. Fabbrini relies on the evidence in *Acta Sancti Alexandri* (*AASS*, May 1, 371ff.); "Et Praefectum urbi quoque Hermem cum uxore et sorore filiis baptizaret, cum mille duecentis quinquaginta servis suis uxoribus quoque et filiis eorum, quos omnes in die Santo Paschae prius fecit fieri ingenuos et ita baptizari" (Fabbrini, "Un nuovo documento relativo all *manumissio in ecclesia,*" p. 217 n. 27).

53. *Nov. Just.* 142; a violation of the ban on castration carried the death penalty.

54. *CTh* 15.8.2; *CJ* 11.41.6–7 (Buckland, *The Roman Law of Slavery*, p. 603). In this case, moral grounds gave the church the power to intervene in the master-slave relationship.

55. *Ekloga* 8.1.4.

56. Ibid., 8.1.1, where *manumissio in ecclesia* appears alongside emancipation in public.

57. *Proch. Nom.* 7.28, unlike *manumissio in ecclesia*, which was a unilateral act by the bishop.

58. Const. Porph., *De cerimon.* 2.49 (p. 695).

59. For example, in all the cases cited above where the master freed his slaves.

60. *Life of Thaddaeus.*

61. *Life of Andrew the Fool* 1.

62. *Spiritually Beneficial Tales of Paul of Monembasia* 9.

63. As in the case of Thaddaeus *(Life of Thaddaeus).*

64. The author indicates, however, that the child in question was not baptized because "the Scythians are not Christians" (ibid.). "Newly purchased" slaves received new names upon entering the *oikos* "even if they are of the same faith," "just as Abraham was renamed by God" (*Life of Makarios of Pelekete* 4).

65. Roman law stipulated that the status of a child came from its mother (*Dig.* 1.5.5.2; *Nov. Post. Just.*, coll. 1, nov. 6; *Proch. Nom.* 34.5–7). If the mother had the status of *eleuthera* during her pregnancy (even if she was reduced to slavery later on), the child received the status of *eugenēs* (*Proch. Nom.* 34.5–7). The children of a slave and his mistress were *eleutheroi* (*CJ* 9.11; *App. Eklo.* 4.4).

66. Beaucamp, *Le statut de la femme à Byzance* (especially on the sexual relationship between a master and a slave, as it existed in the law and in practice, 1:280ff.); J. Evans Grubbs, *Law and Family in Late Antiquity*, on the legislation of Constantine I.

67. Evans Grubbs, *Law and Family in Late Antiquity*, chap. 6: "Sex and Status: Legislation on 'Mixed-Status' Unions."

68. The most important laws to which I refer were: *Nov. Irene*, p. 26 (between 797 and 802); *Nov. Leo.* 100, 101 (between 886 and 912); *Nov. Post. Just.*, coll. 4, nov. 35 (from 1095). See also the story of Philoromus, whose mother was a slave and whose father was free (Palladius, *Historica Lausiaca* 45).

69. *Nov. Post. Just.*, coll. 4, nov. 35.

70. *Ekloga* 8.1.4.
71. *Nov. Post. Just.*, coll. 4, nov. 35.
72. Pitra, *Juris eccl.* 2:346, canon 199.
73. *Life of Basil the Younger*, fol. 28v–29v, 39ff.
74. Ibid., fol. 94.
75. *Peira* 38.3.
76. Ibid.
77. *Nov. Leo.* 101.
78. Ibid., 100.
79. Ibid., 100, 101; *Nov. Irene*, p. 26.
80. *Nov. Post. Just.*, coll. 4, nov. 35; H. Köpstein, "Zur Novelle des Alexios Komnenos zum Sklavenstatus (1095)," pp. 167–168.
81. *Nov. Post. Just.*, coll. 4, nov. 35.
82. This case also reveals a change in the relation between master and freedman, when compared to that in the *Ekloga* and the legislation of Leo VI, which state that the freedman cannot bear witness against his master (*Ekloga* 14.2.2, which adds the freedman to the law of *CJ* 4.20.8; *Nov. Leo.* 25).
83. In the eleventh century, Peter the Chartophylax raised the question of whether the church had to prevent the communion of slaves joined by their masters outside religious marriage. He replied that after Alexius Comnenus's measure, masters had to marry their slaves by religious marriage (RP, *Syntagma* 5:371). Unlike in canon 199 of the *Nomocanon 14 titulorum*, it was now the masters who would be punished.
84. A. Ducloux, *Ad ecclesiam confugere. Naissance du droit d'asile dans les églises (IVe–milieu du Ve. s.)*; J. Gaudemet, *L'Église dans l'Empire romain (IVe–Ve siècles)*, pp. 282–284.
85. Gaudemet, *L'Église dans l'Empire romain*, pp. 249–250; *CTh* 9.45.3 (of 397) for "all those who are bound by obligations toward individuals or toward the state"; *CJ* 1.12.6 (of 466) renders asylum void in certain cases.
86. Mansi 3:12; RP, *Syntagma* 3:248–252. See Ducloux, *Ad ecclesiam confugere*.
87. RP, *Syntagma* 3:507–508.
88. Hefele-Leclercq, *Conciles* 2, pt. 1:126–129, canons 64, 85 in the *Codex canonum Ecclesiae Africanae*, Mansi 3:769, 781.
89. Hefele-Leclercq, *Conciles* 2, pt. 2:779ff. See also Melluso, *La schiavitù nell'età giustinianea*, pp. 257–277 for the West.
90. *Nov. Just.* 5.2, 123.35; and also with a colonus who fled the obligation he had to cultivate the land. Melluso, *La schiavitù nell'età giustinianea*, pp. 201ff.
91. *Nov. Just.* 123.17.
92. Ibid. and 123.35.
93. Ibid., 123.35. For both slave and colonus; for the secular landowner who concealed the colonus of another, the statute of limitations was thirty years (E. Patlagean, *Pauvreté économique et pauvreté sociale à Byzance IVe–VIIe siècles*, pp. 286, 335).
94. Despite the imperial legislation, which is very forthright on this subject, the

Nomocanon attributed to Photios speaks explicitly of the status of *eleutheros* and of *eugenēs* (*Nomocanon I,* chap. 36, in Pitra, *Juris eccl.* 2:480).

95. *Nov. Just.* 123.17.

96. In other words, because his bishop's duties were related not only to affairs internal to the church, his role exceeded the framework of the church's autonomy.

97. *Life of Hypatios* 21; *Life of Theodore of Sykeon* 147. The Hellenistic roots of the practice lay in the asylum offered by temples (P. Debord, "Religion et mentalité des esclaves en Asie Mineure"), which was adopted by the Roman cult of the emperor (G. Freyburger, "Le droit d'asile à Rome"). Hence the statue of the emperor gave protection to the slave against his master's violence (*CJ* 1.25.1; *CTh* 9.44; Bradley, *Slaves and Masters in the Roman Empire,* pp. 124–125). Anne Ducloux's *Ad ecclesiam confugere. Naissance du droit d'asile dans les églises (IVe–milieu du Ve s.)* shows, however, that the right of asylum resurfaced in the fourth century within the atmosphere of Christological struggles and did not perpetuate the Hellenistic custom.

98. *Nov. Just.* 123.35, which adds to *Nov. Just.* 5.2 that the slave who robbed his master would be sent back to him.

99. RP, *Syntagma* 5:48–49 (Grumel, *Reg. pat.,* vol. 1, pts. 2–3, no. 887, p. 376; oddly, it is translated in this edition as "relating to a guilty serf").

100. *"Pasan autou despoteian ekhein kai kuriotēta"* (RP, *Syntagma* 5:48–49).

101. *Nov. Post. Just.,* coll. 3, nov. 11 (between 945 and 959). See Ruth Macrides's commentary, "Justice under Manuel I Komnenos: Four *Novellae* on Court Business and Murder," pp. 190ff. That *Novella* postdated another from the same emperor that rendered asylum void (*Nov. Post. Just.,* coll. 3, nov. 10). Macrides resolves this contradiction and provides commentary (ibid., 192 n. 273).

102. *Life of Symeon the New Theologian* 52–57.

103. For the types of killers finding asylum in the church in the eleventh to thirteenth centuries and the social context of that legislation, see R. Macrides, "Killing, Asylum, and the Law in Byzantium."

104. *Nov. Just.* 7, praef., 7.1, 7.3, 32.1, 120.1.

105. Beginning with Diocletian's reform, the private properties of individuals were overseen by the public tax collector. In the seventh to ninth centuries, the owner also lost his right of *derelictio,* that is, the right to give up his land with its obligations for thirty years, after which the land was declared *klasma,* land of the fisc. As Danuta Gorecki shows, the difference between *possessio* and *dominium* was becoming attenuated (D. Gorecki, "A Farmer Community of the Byzantine Middle Ages: Historiography and Legal Analysis of Sources").

106. *Nov. Just.* 7, praef., 120.1.

107. Consider, for example, the slaves of Gregory of Nazianzus; the father of Theodora of Thessalonica, a *protopresbuteros* surrounded by slaves (*Life of Theodora of Thessalonica* 3–4); the slaves of a deacon in the *Life of Theodore of Sykeon* 94; and Anthimos, a priest and chorepiscopus of the kastron of Eritas

in Cappadocia who also owned slaves (Thierry, *Libelle d'affranchissement des esclaves à Zelve*).

108. Hefele-Leclercq, *Conciles* 2, pt. 2:1080.

109. *ACO* 1–3 ("Collectionis Casinensis sive synodici a rustico diacono compositi," pt. 1, 64), p. 178.

110. One of the freedmen whom Gregory of Nazianzus mentions in his will. In addition, he bequeaths two female slaves to a lady who "shall free them if she wishes"; "otherwise [they] will return to the church" (Gregory of Nazianzus, *Testamentum*).

111. *Life of Matrona of Perge* 44, 47.

112. *Life of Tribunus*, in John of Ephesus, *Eastern Saints*, PO, 18:665–666. See also the references in the documents of the Athos archives cited below.

113. Here I am following Melluso, *La schiavitù nell'età giustinianea*, pp. 219–221.

114. In his will, Theodore Studites says that monasteries must not own slaves or female animals (Theodore Studites, *Testamentum*, in PG 99:1816D; 1817, chap. d). He takes that prohibition from his uncle Plato, the higoumene of Sakkudion (Theodore Studites, *Oratio XI—Laudatio S. Platonis Hegumeni*, in PG 99:824–825, chap. 4.23). See also the editor's emendation of the word *douloi* to *doulai* (ibid., 825 n. 14) and the explanation of J. Pargoire ("Une loi monastique de saint Platon"). See F. J. Leroy, "La réforme Studite," p. 191 and nn. 72–76. Theodore Studites also mentions this subject in a letter to his student Nicholas (*Theodori Studitae Epistulae* 10), in that case only for slaves *(douloi)*, and in his catecheses (*Theodori Studitae Parva Catechesis* 13, p. 48). In both Lives, Theodore Studites frees his slaves (*Life of Theodore Studites I* 5; *Life of Theodore Studites II* 8).

115. Here I am relying solely on the hagiographical narratives.

116. *Lavra I* 27.

117. Ibid., 34.

118. *Xenophon* 1 (of 1089).

119. Patlagean, *Pauvreté économique et pauvreté sociale,* pp. 328–340 ("Le mouvement des hommes").

120. Ibid., p. 333.

121. *Life of Matrona of Perge* 8–10ff., 24; *Spiritually Beneficial Tales of Paul of Monembasia* 13.

122. *Life of Nikon Metanoeite* 12.

123. *Life of Matrona of Perge* 47. She sends the eunuchs to a monastery for men.

124. *Lives of Thomas the Armenian*, in John of Ephesus, *Eastern Saints*, PO 17:290.

125. *Hieronymi sancti Epistulae* 108.20 (J. Labourt trans.) [my translation from the French—Trans.].

126. Ibid.

127. See also ibid., 108.27, in which Jerome relates how Eustochium, daughter of Paula, cares for Paula as an *anchilla.* Palladius recounts the story of Melania the Elder, who follows ascetic saints to serve them in their exile in Palestine while wearing "the blouse of a *paidarios"* (Palladius, *Historia Lausiaca* 46).

128. *Spiritually Beneficial Tales of Paul of Monembasia* 8.
129. Monks and slaves all received new names.
130. In several documents from the Athos archives; MM, *Patmos* 20 (MM, 6:81–90) of 1093; and a will of the higoumene mentioning a dead monk *(to pneumatikon mou paidion)* who had his own *paidia* (ibid., p. 84). See also the case of a murderer who serves the other monks in a monastery: *Life of Symeon the New Theologian* 52–57.
131. *Imperatoris Justiniani Novellae quae vocantur sive constitutiones quae extra codicem*, ed. K. E. Zachariä von Lingenthal, vol. 1, pt. 1, pp. x–xii, quoted in Patlagean, *Pauvreté économique et pauvreté sociale*, p. 335. Von Lingenthal believes the *Novella* is apocryphal. For the relation between that *Novella* and the later legislation of Constantine VII and Manuel I Comnenus, see Macrides, "Justice under Manuel I Komnenos," pp. 191–192 and n. 271.
132. *Imperatoris Justiniani Novellae quae vocantur*, chap. 5. See Melluso, *La schiavitù nell'età giustinianea*, pp. 238–240.
133. *Laudatio S. Theodori a. Chrysipp*, miracle 11, *AASS*, paragraph 22; Sigalas, ed., *Des Chrysippos von Jerusalem Enkomion auf den hl. Johannes den Täufer*, pp. 73–74.
134. *Life of Hypatios* 21. This Life is dated by its editor, Bartelink, to the mid-fifth century (ibid., p. 11). On Beck's dating to the sixth century (*Kirche und theologische Literatur im byzantinischen Reich*, p. 404), see Bartelink, ed., *Vie d'Hypatios*, p. 11 n. 2.
135. *Life of Theodore of Sykeon* 147.
136. Compare the story recounted by Leontius of Neapolis, in which the saint purchases slaves mistreated by their master and frees them (*Life of John of Cyprus* 34).
137. *Life of Theodore of Sykeon* 84, 91, 94, and 140.
138. *Life of Mary the Younger* 5.
139. But Theodore, taken by the soul of Joseph the Hymnographer, was not "home" (*Synax. Const.*, April 3, p. 584).
140. *Synax. Const.*, July 30, p. 855. The oldest manuscript of the *Synaxarion of Constantinople* dates from the mid-tenth century (Patlagean, "L'entrée de la Sainte Face d'Edesse à Constantinople en 944," pp. 38–39 and n. 5).
141. *Nov. Leo.* 9–10, for slaves who become, respectively, a cleric, a monk, and a bishop.
142. The *Life of Joseph the Hymnographer* dates from the late ninth century (*ODB* 2:1074). The date of the entry on that saint in the *Synaxarion of Constantinople* corresponds to that of the *Novella* of Constantine VII on the same subject.
143. *Nov. Post. Just.*, coll. 3, nov. 13. The same emperor tried to render asylum void for murderers (*Nov. Post. Just.*, coll. 3, nov. 10) but then reestablished it (*Nov. Post. Just.*, coll. 3, nov. 11). See Macrides's commentary in "Justice under Manuel I Komnenos," which explains that these were two parts of the same law.
144. *Life of Luke the Younger* 4–8. For the soldiers guarding the roads, see E. Malamut, *Sur la route des saints byzantins*, pp. 273–274.

145. *Life of Luke the Younger* 4–9, and 2, in which Luke's father does not want to be treated like a "fugitive slave."

146. Malamut, *Sur la route des saints byzantins*, pp. 108ff.

147. *Life of Luke the Younger* 10–16.

148. *Life of Nikon Metanoeite* 15. The author indicates that parents must be given all due respect, but God must be respected before them. For his journey, see Malamut, *Sur la route des saints byzantins*, pp. 262–265.

149. Attested, for example, by the *Novella* of Alexis Comnenus (*Nov. Post. Just.*, coll. 4, nov. 35).

150. Lemerle, *Boïlas, test.*; Thierry, *Libelle d'affranchissement des esclaves à Zelve.*

151. *Spiritually Beneficial Tales of Paul of Monembasia* 2.5.

152. *Life of John of Cyprus* 21.

153. *Life of Symeon the Fool*, pp. 85–86 (pp. 151–152).

154. *Life of Hypatios* 21.

155. *Life of Andrew the Fool* 1.

156. Ibid., 2.

157. Ibid., 5.

158. L. Rydén, *The Life of St. Andrew the Fool* 1:41–57; L. Rydén, "The Date of the Life of Andreas Salos"; L. Rydén, "The Life of St. Basil the Younger and the Date of the Life of St. Andreas Salos." In "The Life of St. Andrew the Fool Reconsidered," C. Mango dates the work to the early eighth century. I retain Rydén's dating, which corresponds better to the new image of the slave in the hagiographical literature of the tenth to eleventh centuries. All the same, it is likely that the author used an eighth-century archetype and that the hero's slave status was a late addition.

159. Rydén, "The Life of St. Basil the Younger"; *Life of Basil the Younger*, fol. 6 verso–8 verso.

160. *Life of Basil the Younger*, fol. 28 verso–29 verso and 39ff.

161. *Life of Basil the Younger*, fol. 68–106.

162. This part is not found in the version of the *Acta Sanctorum*. See E. Patlagean, "Byzance et son autre monde. Observations sur quelques récits," pp. 203–204, and Rydén, "The Life of St. Basil the Younger."

163. In any event, emancipation is not mentioned.

164. *Life of Basil the Younger*, fol. 94–94 verso.

165. Ibid., where she is accused of having led a life of fornication because she did not marry the man with whom she lived. The angels accompanying her explain to the demons that her condition of slavery was the reason.

166. *Life of Basil the Younger*, fol. 118ff., 137 verso ff. See also C. Angelidi, Δοῦλοι στήν Κωνσταντινούπολη τόν Ι´ αι´. Ἡ μαρτυρία τοῦ βίου ὁσίου Βασιλείου τοῦ Νέου.

167. And not only with reference to Andrew.

168. A few examples: *Life of Theodore of Sykeon* 84, 92, 94, 140; *Life of Basil the Younger*, fol. 137 verso and ff.; *Life of Athanasia of Aegina* 16.

169. *Life of Andrew the Fool* 21; *Life of Symeon the Fool*, p. 80 (p. 146).

170. *Life of Theodore of Sykeon* 84, 29, 94.

171. *Life of Andrew the Fool* 2; *Life of Basil the Younger*, fol. 137 verso and ff.; that church is identified as the Saint Anastasia Church *en tois Domninou embolois* (Rydén, *The Life of Andrew the Fool*, 2:306 n. 5).

172. *Life of Theodore of Sykeon* 140.

173. Ibid., 147; *Life of Symeon the Fool*, pp. 95–96 (pp. 161–162); *Life of Andrew the Fool* 2; *Life of Basil the Younger*, fol. 137 verso and ff.

174. See also *Lives of Thomas and Stephen*, in John of Ephesus, *Eastern Saints*, PO 17:199–200, and *Life of Theodora of Thessalonica* 25–26. In the latter case, the second master is greed. See Matthew 6:24: "No man can serve *(douleuein)* two masters: for either he will hate the one, and love the other; or else he will hold to the one, and despise the other. Ye cannot serve God and mammon."

175. H. Wallon, *Histoire de l'esclavage dans l'Antiquité*, pp. 261–264; for classical Greek literature, esp. pp. 326–330; for classical Latin literature, pp. 506–513.

176. W. Fitzgerald, *Slavery and the Roman Literary Imagination* (see pp. 28–31 for the example of Horace); I. Weiler, "Inverted *Kalokagathia.*" See also the articles collected in *Representing the Body of the Slave*, ed. T. Wiedemann and J. Gardner. For the slave in Greek tragedy, see V. Citti, "Esclavage et sacré dans le langage tragique."

177. K. McCarthy, *Slaves, Masters, and the Art of Authority in Plautine Comedy*. See also, on Juvenal, M. Garrido-Hory, *Juvénal, esclaves et affranchis à Rome*.

178. Fitzgerald, *Slavery and the Roman Literary Imagination*, pp. 32ff.

179. E. Lévy, "Les esclaves chez Aristophane." See also K. Bradley, "Animalizing the Slave: The Truth of Fiction," which analyzes the story of Lucius's fabulous transformation into an ass in Apuleius's *Metamorphoses* as an example of the representation of the slave in Roman society. Apuleius, however, chose the ass's fictive point of view, inverting the usual perspective of the literature of his age. That perspective of "animalizing the slave" went hand in hand with the violent treatment of slaves in the same era. As a result, according to Bradley, slaves themselves felt inferior (Bradley, *Slaves and Masters in the Roman Empire*; K. Bradley, *Slavery and Society at Rome*, chap. 9, "To Be a Slave").

180. As a counterexample, let me cite the stories of the *paidiskē* Alexandra (Palladius, *Historia Lausiaca* 5); of Moses the Ethiopian (19), a slave who becomes a brigand; and of Sisinnius, "from a servile condition but free in the eyes of the faith" (49). But in all these cases, the servile condition plays no role in the story, and the author does not present these slaves in any relationship with their masters.

181. For the attitude of Byzantine historiography toward another famous slave figure—Spartacus—see J. Irmscher, "Die byzantinische Spartakustradition." Spartacus is considered not a hero but a negative figure. That is exactly the point of view of Psellus, who mentions him in describing the attempted coup d'état against Emperor Constantine IX (*Chronographia*, "Constantine IX," 134).

182. Herodotus, *Histories* 2.134; Plutarch, *Solon* 6, 28 (in Plutarch, *Lives*).

183. *P. Oxy.* 1800, according to C. Ludwig, *Sonderformen byzantinischer Hagiographie und ihr literarisches Vorbild. Untersuchungen zu den Viten des Äsop, des Philaretos, des Symeon Salos und des Andreas Salos*.

184. B. E. Perry, *Aesopica I: A Series of Texts Relating to Aesop or Ascribed to Him or Closely Connected with the Literary Tradition That Bears His Name*, vol. 1; B. E. Perry, "Some Addenda of the Life of Aesop"; B. E. Perry, *Studies in the Text History of the Life and Fables of Aesop;* B. E. Perry, "The Text Tradition of the Greek Life of Aesop"; G. A. Karla, *Vita Aesopi. Überlieferung, Sprache und Edition einer frühbyzantinischen Fassung des Äsopromans.*

185. *P. Oxy.* 1800; Ludwig, *Sonderformen byzantinischer Hagiographie und ihr literarisches Vorbild.*

186. According to Perry, another version of the *Life of Aesop*, derived directly from the second-century archetype, gave rise to new versions in the thirteenth to fourteenth centuries. See also the recension of Karla, *Vita Aesopi. Überlieferung, Sprache und Edition*, pp. 35–45.

187. I. T. A. Papademetriou, *Aesop as an Archetypal Hero*, chap. 1.

188. *Life of Aesop (G)* 9.

189. Ibid., 15.22–25.

190. Philonenko, ed., *Joseph et Aséneth*, pp. 1–15, 99–109; C. Burchard, "The Present State of Research on Joseph and Aseneth"; C. Burchard, *Gesammelte Studien zu Joseph und Aseneth*, pp. 297–310. Both Philonenko and Burchard disagree with the opinion of the first editor, P. Batiffol, that the work was written in the fifth century. Versions in Syriac, Armenian, Slavonic, Latin, and Ethiopian are known, the oldest manuscript dating from the tenth century.

191. The character of Pentephrese is analogous to that of Potiphar in Genesis.

192. *Joseph and Aseneth* 4.

193. Philonenko, ed., *Joseph et Aséneth*, pp. 99–109.

194. *Joseph and Aseneth*, 24.8–9, M. Philonenko translation [my translation from the French—Trans.].

195. E. E. Urbach, "The Laws regarding Slavery," p. 165.

196. I. Mendelsohn, *Slavery in the Ancient Near East*, pp. 51–54. The law among the Imamian Shiites is different, however: the child is born free if one of his parents is free ("'Abd," *Ency. of Islam*, 1:24–26). But note the changes in Jewish law in the Roman era cited in C. Hezser, "The Social Status of Slaves in the Talmud Yerushalmi and in Graeco-Roman Society."

197. Burchard gives an overview of the textual tradition of that narrative, of which fifteen Greek manuscripts dating to between the tenth and seventeenth centuries are known ("The Present State of Research on Joseph and Aseneth," pp. 312–314).

198. *Life of Elias the Younger* 6ff.

199. Ibid., 10–12.

200. *Life of Elias Spēlaiōtēs I* 23; *Life of Elias Spēlaiōtēs II* 14.

201. *Life of Elias Spēlaiōtēs I* 28–30; *Life of Elias Spēlaiōtēs II* 15.

202. *Life of Elias Spēlaiōtēs I* 28–30; *Life of Elias Spēlaiōtēs II* 15.

203. *Life of Mary the Younger* 7.

204. *Life of Fantinos the Younger* 19–20.

205. *Life of Elias the Younger* 9–11.

206. Ibid., 9, 12ff.

207. *Life of Joseph the Hymnographer* 3 (unlike the biblical Joseph, who dreams that his brothers and parents bow down before him [Gen. 37:5–10]).
208. *Life of Joseph the Hymnographer* 6ff.
209. Ibid., 13ff.
210. *Synax. Const.,* April 3, p. 584.
211. This was probably Theodore Tyron (Theodore the Recruit), whose ability to find fugitive slaves is described by Chrysippos of Jerusalem (late fifth century): *Laudatio S. Theodori a. Chrysipp,* miracle 11, *AASS,* paragraph 22; Sigalas, ed., *Des Chrysippos von Jerusalem Enkomion auf den hl. Johannes den Täufer,* pp. 73–74.
212. *Spiritually Beneficial Tales of Paul of Monembasia* 8; Methodius, *In Praise of Nicholas of Myra* 42–43; *Three Miracles of Nicholas of Myra* 8ff; *Life of Nilus of Rossano* 68–70; *Life of Nikon Metanoeite* 20, 23.
213. *Life of Theoctiste of Lesbos* 15. There were also political motives behind that work.
214. H. Delehaye, "La Vie de saint Théoctiste de Lesbos," pp. 196–199.
215. In contrast to Theoctiste, Mary of Egypt leaves the city to lead the life of a desert ascetic.
216. *Life of Theoctiste of Lesbos* 1ff.
217. *Spiritually Beneficial Tales of Paul of Monembasia* 8.
218. *Life of Elias the Younger* 4. This happens to him twice, the first time when he is a child (*Life of Elias the Younger* 6–7). At that time, the Arabs do not succeed in bringing the captives to their territories because the slaves are liberated by Byzantine maritime forces (*Life of Elias the Younger* 8). The second time, Elias is brought to Egypt (*Life of Elias the Younger* 9). It is interesting to note that the author uses the same device to warn of the saint's fate as in the biblical story of Joseph: a dream (Gen. 37:5–10).
219. *Life of Nikon Metanoeite* 20.
220. *Life of John of Cyprus* 21. In this episode, the master obliges his slave to sell him. See also the story Palladius tells about Serapion, who sells himself to convert his purchasers. Once that mission is accomplished, they want to set him free. When he refuses, they give the money to the poor. Serapion sells himself again for the same reason (Palladius, *Histoira Lausiaca* 37).
221. See Glancy, *Slavery in Early Christianity,* chap. 1, "Bodies and Souls: The Rhetoric of Slavery," on the use of the term *sōmation* in the first to second centuries. This book deals with the perception of slaves as bodies (the word *sōma,* or body, is a synonym for "slave"). The author shows that the slave-body association is explicit in ancient authors, and thus in keeping with the representation of the slave as a narrative object.
222. The author of the *Life of Basil the Younger* does not provide any information on Theodora's life outside her master's house.
223. *Life of Andreas the Fool* 1.
224. D. Afinogenov, "The Church Slavonic Life of St. Thaddaios the Martyr of the Second Iconoclasm."
225. Ibid., pp. 329–337.

226. See J. Pargoire, "Saint Thaddée l'Homologète"; C. van der Vorst, "S. Thaddée Studite"; and the two letters from Theodore Studites addressed to Thaddaeus (*Theodori Studitae Epistulae* 126, 183).

227. *Synax. Const.*, December 29, pp. 354–355 (see also *BHG* 2414–2415).

228. Ibid. See Afinogenov's objection ("The Church Slavonic Life of St. Thaddaios the Martyr," p. 322), for a comparison between these two versions.

229. Ibid., pp. 321–322. Pargoire ("Saint Thaddée l'Homologète") and van der Vorst ("S. Thaddée Studite") are unaware of the existence of the Slavonic version. They indicate that the emperor named "Leo" in the Life is Leo V the Armenian (r. 813–820).

230. The *Life of Thaddaeus* is only five pages long.

231. *Spiritually Beneficial Tales of Paul of Monembasia* 8, 9.

232. *Life of Andrew the Fool* 21.

233. Ibid.

234. Ibid., 17.

235. J. C. Cheynet, *Pouvoir et contestations à Byzance (963–1210)*, pp. 287–289.

236. There is reason to wonder whether this implies two different perceptions of how to become a saint: some became saints because they chose to lead a spiritual life dedicated to God; others, increasingly from the ninth century on, were chosen by God from their birth to become saints. In both cases, however, the saint placed his body *en douleia* to God. That is not just an allegorical expression. The *douleia* was sometimes expressed, for example, as asceticism (that is, bodily suffering).

237. *Spiritually Beneficial Tales of Paul of Monembasia* 8. Miracles differ from witchcraft in that they are done for a good cause (ibid., and *Life of Elias the Younger* 43). The most characteristic example is the *Life of Leo of Catania*, which contrasts the saint to the witch Heliodorus.

238. Because the sense of the word "servant" does not include the role that results from a position of submission and that is an obligation assigned by that position, I think it necessary to retain the Greek word *doulos*. Recall that, for a service that is not obligatory in nature, there was another word in Greek during the entire era concerned, namely, *upēresia* (*upēretēs* for "servant").

239. A. Cameron, "Images of Authority: Elites and Icons in Late Sixth-century Byzantium," pp. 33–34.

240. Ibid., p. 12.

241. See also A. Cameron, "The Language of Images: The Rise of Icons and Christian Representation."

242. Note the verse from Matthew (6:24): "No man can serve *(douleuein)* two masters *(kurioi):* for either he will hate the one, and love the other; or else he will hold to the one, and despise the other."

243. Unlike the saints, who were *oi douloi tou theou*.

244. For that reason, I do not translate *douleia* here simply as "service" (as A. Kazhdan and M. McCormick do in "The Social World of the Byzantine Court," pp. 189–195).

245. *Nov. Post. Just.*, coll. 3, nov. 25.

246. For example, on the question of marriage (Evans Grubbs, *Law and Family in Late Antiquity*) or family life (G. Nathan, *The Family in Late Antiquity: The Rise of Christianity and the Endurance of Tradition*).

247. *Dig.* 48.8.4, in cases where the master has his slave castrated; A. Watson, *Roman Slave Law*, pp. 63, 128.

248. In *The Roman Law of Slavery* (p. 37 and n. 5), Buckland shows that the roots of this legislation lie in the Institutes of Gaius.

249. *CJ* 7.17.1.2 (Buckland, *The Roman Law of Slavery*, p. 419); Melluso, *La schiavitù nell'età giustinianea*, pp. 115ff.

250. Suetonius, *Domitianus* 7, in *Vies des douze Césars;* Dio Cassius 57.2.

251. *Dig.* 48.8.6 (for the dating of this law to the era of Nerva, see W. Eck, "Neratius," *RE* sup. 14; 286 and Dio Cassius 48.2); *Dig.* 48.8.4; 1.3; 8.11; *CJ* 4.42.1–2; *Nov. Just.* 142.

252. I shall not expatiate here on the phenomenon of eunuchs in the Roman Empire but will deal with the subject elsewhere.

253. *CJ* 4.42.1–2. Confiscations of castrated slaves can already be discerned in the legislation of Hadrian, *Dig.* 48.8.4. The master who castrates his slave "bona merito fisco meo vindicari debere"; that property also includes the slave. Note that the word *bona* is replaced by *"mancipio . . . confiscando,"* in the law of Constantine (*CJ* 4.42.1).

254. *CJ* 12.5.4. The master has five years to reclaim him—the statute of limitations.

255. J. E. Dunlap, *The Office of the Grand Chamberlain in the Later Roman and Byzantine Empire;* R. Guilland, *Recherches sur les institutions byzantines*, 1:165ff.

256. For the Justinian legislation on this subject, see Melluso, *La schiavitù nell'età giustinianea*, pp. 122–131.

257. Note on this subject the indications in the *Peira* (29, 39); the only information on freedmen (apart from emancipation itself) is rather odd. It involves a person who presents a freedman (*apeleutheros:* it is not clear whether it is his own) to the court who accuses another of having stolen a deposit. The freedman summoned as a witness participated in the theft. The judges do not accept his testimony and deem him unreliable because he could himself be charged. In addition, the *Peira* cites the judges, who exclude that witness as a "lowly and vulgar" person. It is tempting to believe that these observations stem from the fact that he was *apeleutheros*, but that may not have been the reason. In any event, it is possible to say that the status of freedmen still existed as such in the mid-eleventh century.

258. Note that in 343 the church was not supposed to appear too revolutionary or to advance ideas opposed to the law of the empire.

259. That also demonstrates the difference between hagiography and the patristic literature. These were not simply two different types of literature intended for different audiences. The writers were also sometimes from different milieus. See Rydén, *The Life of St. Andrew the Fool*, 1:57–71 ("The Author and His Conceptual Cosmos") and the author's description of himself in the *Life of Basil the Younger* (fol. 35 verso, 44 verso and ff.).

260. Theoph. A. M. 6302 (p. 487).

261. Appian, *The Civil Wars* 4.13. According to that description, *majestas* was not at issue.

262. *Life of Stephen the Younger* 32, 36. This slave does not achieve her aim and, in receiving her punishment, dies (76). The emperor orders her mistress, the pious Anna, to "behave like a good slave of the emperor" *(oiketēs tou basileōs)* and to denounce the saint.

263. The author of the Life declares that during the iconoclastic persecutions, the emperor ordered slaves to denounce their masters (ibid., 64).

264. Bradley, *Slavery and Society at Rome*, pp. 165–173.

265. *Peira* 30.5. Leontius of Neapolis had already designated the master and his slave *sundouloi*. But in the seventh century he was addressing the master, whereas the *Peira* addresses the slave.

266. *Nov. Leo.* 11, 37, 38, 40, 49, 60, 69, 100, and 101. Only two *Novellae* deal with the slave as property (*Nov. Leo.* 29, 66). *Nov. Leo.* 60 prohibits castration, once again granting freedom to a castrated slave (thus repeating the *Novella* of 558: *Nov. Just.* 142). Note the terminological difference between the *Novellae* of Leo VI that speak of the slave as property and those that speak of the slave as individual. The terms used are, in the first case, *andrapodon* and *therapaina*, and, in the second, *doulos* and *oiketēs*.

267. *Nov. Leo.* 100 allows someone who wants to marry a person of slave status to sell himself to the slave's master if the master does not want to sell his slave. The *Novella* affirms that the suitor will not remain a slave after the master's death. If the suitor does not want to sell himself and does not have the means to buy the slave in order to marry her, the *Novella* establishes another legal means: the suitor will work for wages in the master's home until he accumulates the value agreed upon between them. It is clear that the innovation introduced by the *Ekloga* in 741 (*Ekloga* 8.2) opened new legal options. Note that, unlike the *Ekloga*, the *Novella* of Leo VI determined a fixed wage of two *nomismata* per year of work. Another *Novella* from the same emperor also makes provisions for the case of a quasi-marital union between two slaves when one is emancipated (*Nov. Leo.* 101, which does not use the term *gamos* here). This case is treated in the same way as in the previous *Novella*.

268. *Nov. Post. Just.*, coll. 4, nov. 35.

269. According to Roman law, free persons sentenced to death lost their free status and thus found themselves slaves of the state, even when they were awaiting or currently on trial. That situation deprived them of all the rights they had when free: their marriages were annulled, and their property reverted to the fisc. It was for that reason that Roman citizens preferred to commit suicide rather than be charged with a capital crime. Suicide, which demonstrated that they possessed themselves, left them of free status, and their property went to their heirs. See J. Burdon, "Slavery as Punishment in Roman Criminal Law," which describes the different types of "penal slaves" and shows the development of the Roman penal system in this regard.

270. In this case, however, even though the convict had the status of a slave, his enslavement did not last because he was executed.

271. Buckland, *The Roman Law of Slavery,* pp. 404ff.; Melluso, *La schiavitù nell'età giustinianea,* pp. 52–59.
272. *Nov. Just.* 22.8.
273. Nevertheless, in "Prisons et crimes dans l'Empire romain," J. U. Krause shows that there was no limit on how long someone could be held awaiting trial.
274. Patlagean, "Byzance et le blason pénal du corps," pp. 406–408.
275. Ibid., pp. 408–413.
276. See P. Garnsey, *Social Status and Legal Privilege in the Roman Empire,* chaps. 4–6, who discerns what he calls "the dual-penalty system."
277. Patlagean, "Byzance et le blason pénal du corps," p. 413. Hence "hagiography illuminates and perfectly confirms a general tendency of Byzantine civilization, clearly stated in the sixth century and perceptible earlier, which was to respond to a criminal offense not by doing away with the guilty party but by an alternative whereby those who could do so paid with their wealth, to the benefit of the victim and usually of the state, while those who could not do so had a part of their body cut off, the only solution, moreover, for the most serious violations and for political disqualifications" (pp. 421–422). Similarly, Burdon ("Slavery as Punishment in Roman Criminal Law," pp. 80–83) indicates that mutilations were sometimes inflicted on the condemned, citing Eusebius, "De Martyribus Palaestinae," 328, 329 (PG 20:1484), though in that case the punishment was castration (officially prohibited).
278. *Dig.* 1.5.4; *Inst. Just.* 1.3; Melluso, *La schiavitù nell'età giustinianea,* pp. 28–29.
279. R. Taubenschlag, *The Law of Greco-Roman Egypt in the Light of the Papyri 332 B.C.–640 A.D.,* p. 56 n. 33; J. Ramin and P. Veyne, "Droit romain et société: Les hommes libres qui passent pour esclaves et l'esclavage volontaire"; A. Lintott, "La servitude pour dettes à Rome." As for the scope of the practice, see Glancy, *Slavery in Early Christianity,* pp. 80–85, who gives an overview of the historical debate.
280. Buckland, *The Roman Law of Slavery,* pp. 427ff.; Melluso, *La schiavitù nell'età giustinianea,* pp. 111ff.
281. Buckland, *The Roman Law of Slavery,* pp. 427–433 ("Fraudulent Sale of Freeman"). There are no extant mentions prior to the third-century jurists cited in the *Digesta* (*Dig.* 1.5.5.1, 4.4.9.4, 40.14.2).
282. *CTh* 4.8.6.
283. Contrary to M. Morabito's belief (*Les réalités de l'esclavage d'après le Digeste,* p. 72).
284. *Life of John of Cyprus* 21; Palladius, *Historia Lausiaca* 37.
285. *CTh* 4.8.6 (Buckland, *The Roman Law of Slavery,* pp. 420–422); M. Kaser, *Das römische Privatrecht,* 1:60. For the definition of that power qua right, see Y. Thomas, "*Vitae necisque potestas.* Le père, la cité, la mort," which defines *ius vitae necisque* as "the power to kill, which entails that of letting live" (p. 510). Note as well the next sentence: "The right to death is in that way an abstract definition of power" (p. 500). See also the different viewpoint of R. Westbrook, "Vitae Necisque Potestas."
286. *CJ* 4.43.1.

287. Buckland, *The Roman Law of Slavery,* pp. 420–422; Kaser, *Das römische Privatrecht,* 2:131, 142, 205. See the explanatory analysis with bibliography in Melluso, *La schiavitù nell'età giustinianea,* pp. 33ff.

288. Buckland, *The Roman Law of Slavery,* p. 421 n. 1 (according to *Fragmenta Vaticana* 34, quoted by Buckland); see also *CJ* 4.43.2; and Melluso, *La schiavitù nell'età giustinianea,* pp. 37ff., who cites the *Novella* of Constantine on the subject, *CTh* 5.10.1 of 329.

289. Basil, "Homilia II. in Psalmum XIV," 4, in PG 29:277. For Egypt, see Biezunska-Malowist, *L'esclavage dans l'Égypte gréco-romaine,* pp. 19ff.; and I. F. Fichman, "Economic Aspects of Individual Dependency in Roman and Late Egypt." The Phrygians sold their children as slaves: P. Veyne, "Vie de Trimalcion," p. 16n. 6 (who cites Philostratus, *Vita Appoll.* 8.7.12); Taubenschlag, *The Law of Greco-Roman Egypt,* pp. 56 nn. 34–36, 104–105 n. 30; M. Lemosse, "L'enfant sans famille en droit romain"; Glancy, *Slavery in Early Christianity,* p. 71.

290. *Nov. Val.* 33 (32 in the Haenel edition), following Buckland, *The Roman Law of Slavery,* p. 421. On all issues relating to children sold in the Roman era, see J. Boswell, *The Kindness of Strangers,* pp. 67–75 and 163–166.

291. *Nov. Just.* 18.11. Probably with the intent of strengthening the family by preventing a family from finding half its members enslaved and half free.

292. *Nov. Just.* 123.17.

293. *CTh* 11.2.1–2 (Buckland, *The Roman Law of Slavery,* p. 420 n. 14). See P. Nessana II, 56, in which a father hires out his son *en paramonē*.

294. Patlagean, *Pauvreté économique et pauvreté sociale à Byzance,* p. 154; *Nov. Just.* 14; Theoph. A. M. 5855 (p. 51); Glancy, *Slavery in Early Christianity,* pp. 54–55.

295. *Nov. Just.* 134.7. The practice is attested by *P. Lond.* 6 (1915) of about 330 (following Fichman, "Economic Aspects of Individual Dependency in Roman and Late Egypt," pp. 163–164).

296. Buckland, *The Roman Law of Slavery,* p. 402; *Nov. Just.* 153. For the practice, see Taubenschlag, *The Law of Greco-Roman Egypt,* p. 55 n. 30; and Glancy, *Slavery in Early Christianity,* pp. 74–76, who cites the second- and third-century church fathers' opposition to the abandonment of children. See also the information of Anna Comnena on the education of orphans who "must be raised as free beings and not as slaves" (*Alexiad* 7.3).

297. *Nov. Just.* 22.12, 32.1.

298. Most references are from the eastern provinces.

299. Nonetheless, that word sometimes continued to be used in a legal context, as in Boïlas's will (Lemerle, *Boïlas, test.,* p. 27), which says of his freedmen, "for I want them to remain *eugeneis* and free."

300. *Nov. Leo.* 59, which affirms that the act of selling oneself was still being practiced.

301. *Nov. Leo.* 100.

302. B. Lewis, *Race and Slavery in the Middle East: An Historical Enquiry,* pp. 5–7; M. Gordon, *Slavery in the Arab World,* p. 24; Guemara, "La libération et le

rachat des captifs. Une lecture musulmane," pp. 334–335 n. 7. Lewis points out that this was a legal development and that the act of selling oneself because of debt, and the punishment of reducing a Muslim to slavery were, like the act of selling one's children, prohibited by the first caliphs (though he does not specify which ones).

303. *Nov. Post. Just.*, coll. 4, nov. 35. For the children abandoned in medieval western Europe, see Boswell, *The Kindness of Strangers.*
304. Köpstein, "Zur Novelle des Alexios Komnenos zum Sklavenstatus (1095)," p. 164.

Appendix A: Terminology

1. *Nov. Just.* 22.12; *Ekloga* 17.42.
2. I follow the criteria established by the legal definition of slavery. Freedmen are infrequently mentioned in saints' Lives and never by their specific terms, *apeleutheroi* and *apodouloi.*
3. Nevertheless, the difference between this term and the others, and its application to slaves, are important with respect to the provenance of slaves. In the same way, I deliberately excluded the words *desmios* and *desmeuō (δέσμιος, δεσμεύω)*, literally "in chains" and "to chain up," respectively. They are primarily used in historiographical works to refer to chained and generally enslaved prisoners.
4. H. Köpstein, "Zum Bedeutungswandel von ΣΚΛΑΒΟΣ/SCLAVUS"; H. Köpstein, "Zum Fortleben des Wortes δοῦλος und anderer Bezeichnungen für den Sklaven im Mittel- und Neugriechischen." See also H. Ditten, *Ethnische Verschiebungen zwischen der Balkanhalbinsel und Kleinasien vom Ende des 6. bis zur zweiten Hälfte des 9. Jahrhunderts,* pp. 260ff.
5. See also P. Lemerle, ed., *Les plus anciens recueils des miracles de S. Démétrius,* 1:173 n. 14.
6. H. Kahane and R. Kahane, "Notes on the Linguistic History of 'Sclavus.'"
7. Ibid., p. 353.
8. Const. Porph., *De admin.* 32.
9. This might have consequences for the word *sklavos* as well.

Appendix C: Prices

1. E. Ashtor, *Histoire des prix et des salaires dans l'Orient médiéval;* C. Morrison, "Monnaie et prix à Byzance du Ve au VIIe siècle"; J. C. Cheynet, E. Malamut, and C. Morrison, "Prix et salaires à Byzance (Ve–XVe siècles)"; Y. Ragib, "Les marchés aux esclaves en terre d'Islam."

Bibliography

1. Legislative Sources

General

Regesten des Kaiserurkunden des oströmischen Reiches von 565–1453. Edited by Franz Dölger and Peter Wirth. 5 vols. Munich-Berlin: Oldenbourg, 1924–1962.

Legal Sources

Appendix Eclogae. Edited by Dieter Simon and Spyros Troianos. In *Font. min.* 3, pp. 34–125. Frankfurt: Klostermann, "ForByzRecht 4," 1979.

Basilicorum libri LX. Edited by H. J. Scheltema, D. Holwerda, and N. Van der Wal. 8 vols. text, 9 vols. scholia. Groningen: Wolters, 1953–1988; edited by Carl Wilhelm Ernst Heimbach. 5 vols. Leipzig: Barth, 1833–1850.

Codex Theodosianus. Edited by Theodor Mommsen and Paul Martin Meyer. Berlin: Weidmannos, 1962.

Corpus Juris Civilis (Institutiones Justiniani, Digesta, Codex Justinianus, Novellae Justiniani). Edited by Paul Krueger, Theodor Mommsen, and Rudolf Schoell. 3 vols. in 5 parts. Berlin: Weidmannos, 1954–1959; R. W. Lee, *The Elements of Roman Law, with a Translation of the Institutes of Justinian.* 2nd ed. London: Sweet & Maxwell, 1949.

Ecloga. Das Gesetzbuch Leons III. und Konstantinos' V. Edited by Ludwig Burgmann. Frankfurt: Lowenklau-Gesellschaft, "ForByzRecht 10," 1983.

Ecloga privata aucta. In Zepos, *JGR* 6:4–47.

Epanagoge. In Zepos, *JGR* 2:230–368.

Das Eparchenbuch Leons des Weisen. Edited by Johannes Koder. Vienna: Verlag des Österreichischen Akademie der Wissenschaften, "CFHB 33," 1991.

Epitome Legum: In Zepos, *JGR* 4:265–285; Jürgen Maruhn, ed., "Der Titel 50 der Epitome," in *Font. min.* 3, pp. 194–210. Frankfurt: Kostermann, "ForByzRecht 4," 1979; Jürgen Maruhn, "Eine zyprisch Fassung eherechtlicher Titel der Epitom." In *Font. min.* 4, pp. 218–255. Frankfurt: Klostermann, "ForByzRecht 7," 1981.

Gaius, *Institutiones.* Edited by Emil Seckel and Bernhard Kuebler. London: Duckworth, 1988 (1st ed. 1939).

Imperatoris Justiniani Novellae quae vocantur sive constitutiones quae extra codicem. Edited by Karl Eduard Zachariä von Lingenthal. Leipzig: Teubner, 1881.

Leges militares (version A). Edited by Walter Ashburner. In Zepos, *JGR* 2:75–79.

Leges militares (version B). Edited by E. Korzenszky. In Zepos, *JGR* 2:80–89.

Leges navales; Lex rhodia. Edited by Walter Ashburner. In Zepos, *JGR* 2:91–103.

Leges rusticae; Nomos georgikos. Edited by Walter Ashburner. In Zepos, *JGR* 2:67–71; E. E. Lipshits, I. P. Medvedev, and E. K. Piotrovskaia, eds. *Vizantiiskii zemledelcheskii zakon.* Leningrad: Leningradskoe otd-nie "Nauka," 1984.

Legum Iustiniani imperatoris vocabularium. Edited by Gian Gualberto Archi and Anna Maria Bartoletti-Colombo. "*Pars Latine.*" 10 vols. plus indexes. Milan: Cisalpino-Goliardica, 1975–1979; "*Pars Graeca.*" 6 vols. plus indexes. Milan: Cisalpino-Goliardica, 1984–1989.

Liber legum novellarum divi Valentiniana Augusti. In *Leges Novellae ad Theodosianum pertinentes,* ed. Paul Martin Meyer. Berlin: Weidmannos, 1962, 2:69–154.

Novellae et Aureae Bullae imperatorum post Justinanum. In Zepos, *JGR* 1 (col. 1 for the years 566–866; col. 2 for 886–910; col. 3 for 911–1057; col. 4 for 1057–1204).

Die Novellen der Kaiserin Eirene. Edited by Ludwig Burgmann. In *Font. min. 4,* pp. 1–33. Frankfurt: Klostermann, "ForByzRecht 7," 1981.

Les Novelles de Léon le Sage. Edited by Pierre Noailles and Alphonse Dain. Paris: Les Belles Lettres, "Nouvelle coll. de textes et documents," 1944.

Les Novelles des empereurs macédoniens. Concernant la terre et les Stratitotes. Edited by Nicolas Svoronos and G. Gounaridis (posthumous edition). Athens: Centre de recherches byzantines, 1994.

Peira, in Zepos, *JGR* 4:9–260.

Prochiros Nomos. In Zepos, *JGR* 2:107–228 and 395–410.

Zepos, Ioannes, and Panagiotes Zepos, eds. *Jus Graecoromanum.* 8 vols. Athens: Georgion Phexis & uiou, 1931.

Ecclesiastical Sources

Acta Conciliorum Oecumenicorum. Edited by Eduard Schwartz, Johannes Straub, and Rudolf Schieffer. 4 vols. in 27 parts. Berlin: De Gruyter, 1922–1974.

Acta Conciliorum Oecumenicorum, series secunda. Edited by Rudolf Schieffer. 4 vols. in 5 parts. Berlin: De Gruyter, 1984–1995.

Joannou, Périclès-Pierre. *Les canons des conciles oecuméniques.* Grottaferrata: Pontificia Commissio ad redigendum Codicem Iuris Canonici Orientalis, 1962.

———. *Les canons des synodes particuliers.* Grottaferrata: Pontificia Commissio ad redigendum Codicem Iuris Canonici Orientalis, 1962.

Mansi, Giovanni Domenico. *Sacrorum Conciliorum nova et amplissima collectio.* 53

vols. in 58 parts. Paris: Welter, 1901–1927; repr. Graz: Akademische Druck-U. Verlagsanstalt, 1960–1962.

Pitra, Jean-Baptist. *Juris ecclesiastici Graecorum historia et monumenta.* 2 vols. Rome, 1864, 1868.

Les Regestes des Actes du Patriarcat de Constantinople. Edited by Venance Grumel, Vitalien Laurent, and Jean Darrouzès. 2 vols. in 8 parts. Paris: Institut français d'études byzantines, 1932–1979.

Rhalles, Giorgios Alexandrou, and Michael Potles, eds. Σύνταγμα τῶν θείων καὶ τῶν ἱερῶν κανονῶν. 6 vols. Athens: Gregore, 1852–1859; repr. 1966.

Hebrew-Aramaic Sources

Assaf, Simha. *The Responsa of the Geonim in the Manuscripts of the Genizah* (in Hebrew). Jerusalem: Makor, 1928.

Jerusalem Talmud. In *Havruta Lalomed, Responsa Project.* Ramat-Gan: Bar-Ilan University, 2001.

Talmud of Babylonia. Edited by Jacob Neusner. 36 vols. Atlanta: Scholars Press, 1994–.

2. Nonlegislative Documentary Sources for the Byzantine Empire

Papyrological Collections

Casson, Lionel, and Ernest Leopold Hettich, eds. *Excavations at Nessana.* Vol. 2. Princeton, N.J.: Princeton University Press, 1950.

Greek Papyri in the British Museum. Vol. 6: *The Jewish Troubles in Alexandria and the Athanasian Controversy Illustrated by Texts from Greek Papyri in the British Museum.* Edited by H. Idir Bell and W. E. Crum. London, 1924.

Kölner Papyri. Vol. 3. Edited by Bärbel Kramer and Robert Hübner. Opladen: Westdeutscher Verlag, 1980.

Kraemer, Caspar John, ed. *Excavations at Nessana.* Vol. 3. Princeton, N.J.: Princeton University Press, 1958.

Maspero, Jean, ed. *Papyrus grecs d'époque byzantine. Catalogue général des antiquités égyptiennes du musée du Caire.* 3 vols. Cairo: Institut français d'archéologie orientale, 1910–1916.

The Oxyrhynchus Papyri. London: Egypt Exploration Society, 1889–1988.

Papiri greci e latini. Rome: Società italiana per la ricerca dei papiri greci e latini in Egitto, 1920–.

Preisigke, Friedrich, ed. *Griechische Papyrus der kaiserlichen Universitäts—und Landesbibliothek zu Strassburg.* Leipzig: Hinrichs, 1912–1920.

Sammelbuch griechischer Urkunden aus Ägytpen. Edited by Friedrich Preisigke, Friedrich Bilabel, Emil Kiessling, and Hans-Albert Rupprecht. Wiesbaden: Harrassowitz, 1915–.

Collections of Archival Documents from the Empire

Archives de l'Athos. Edited by G. Millet, P. Lemerle, and J. Lefort. Paris: Lethielleux, 1937–.

Ἔγγραφα Πάτμου. 2 vols. Edited by E. Branousē and M. Nostazopoulou-Pelekidē. Athens: Ekdoseis Ethnikou Hidrymatos Ereunōn, 1980.

Guillou, André, ed. *Corpus des Actes Grecs d'Italie du sud et de Sicile: Recherches d'histoire et de géographie.* 5 vols. Vatican City: Biblioteca apostolica vaticana, 1967–1980.

Miklosich, Franz, and Joseph Müller, eds. *Acta et diplomata graeca medii aevi sacra et profana.* 6 vols. Vienna: Gerold, 1860–1890.

Pacta Veneta 4: I trattai con Bisanzio 992–1198. Edited by Marco Pozza and Giorgio Ravegnani. Venice: Il cardo, 1993.

Robinson, Gertrude, ed. *History and Cartulary of the Greek Monastery of St. Elias and St. Anastasius of Carbone.* 3 vols. Rome: Pont. Institutum Orientalium Studiorum, "OrChr 44, 63, 62," 1928–1930.

Sathas, Constantinus N., ed. Μεσαιωνικῆς Βιβλιοθήκης. 4 vols. Athens, Venice, and Paris, 1872–1894; repr. Hildesheim: G. Olms Verlag, 1972.

Tafel, Gottlieb Lukas Friedrich, and Georg Martin Thomas, eds. *Urkunden zur Ältern Handels- und Staatsgeschichte der Republik Venedig.* 3 vols. Amsterdam: Hakkert, 1964.

Economic Treatises, Treatises on Taxation, and Cadastres

Dölger, Franz. *Der Traktat des Cold. Marc. Gr. 173.* In F. Dölger, *Beiträge zur Geschichte der byzantinischen Finanzverwaltung, besonders des 10. und 11. Jahrhunderts.* Leipzig: Teubner, "Byzantinisches Archiv 9," 1927; repr. Hildesheim: G. Olms, 1964, pp. 3–9, 113–156.

Karayannopulos, Johannes, ed. *Le traité Zavorda.* In J. Karayannopulos, "Fragmente aus den Vademecum: Eines byzantinischen Finanzbeamtem." In *Polychronion: Festschrift Franz Dölger zum 75. Geburztstag,* edited by Peter Wirth, pp. 318–334. Heidelberg: Winter, 1966.

Oikonomides, Nicolas, ed. *Le traité de Philothée (899).* In part 2 of N. Oikonomides, *Les listes de préséance byzantines des IXe et Xe s.* Paris: CNRS, "Le monde byzantine 4," 1972.

Schilbach, Erich, ed. *Le traité fiscal du Paris. sup. gr. 676 (fol. 89–92 verso).* *Byzantinische metrologische Quellen.* In *Géométries du fisc byzantin,* ed. J. Lefort, R. Bondoux, J. C. Cheynet, J. P. Grélois, V. Kravari, and J. M. Martin, pp. 60–77. Paris: Lethielleux, "Réalités byzantines 4," 1991.

Svoronos, Nicolas, ed. *Le cadastre de Thèbes.* In "Recherches sur le cadastre byzantin et la fiscalité aux XIe–XIIe siècles: Le cadastre de Thèbes (planches I à VIII)," ed. N. Svoronos. *BCH* 83 (1959): 1–166.

Other Documents

Dain, Alphonse, ed. *Parisinus suppl. gr. 1238, fol. 20*. In A. Dain, "Une formule d'affranchissement d'esclave." *REB* 22 (1964): 238–240.

Fabbrini, Fabrizio, ed. *Crypt.Γ. β., IV, fol. 120–120 verso*. In Fabrizio Fabbrini, "Un nuovo documento relativo alla manumissio in ecclesia." *Rendiconti della Classe di Scienze morali, storiche e filogiche*, ser. 8, 16/5–6 (1961): 214–215.

Ferrari, G., ed. "Fomulari notarili inediti dell'età bizantina, cod. Vat. gr. 86." *Bulletino dell'Istituto Storico Italiano* 31 (1910): 41–128.

Gautier, Paul, ed. *La Diataxis de Michel Attaliate*. *REB* 39 (1981): 5–143.

———. *Le typikon du sébaste Grégoire Pakourianos*. *REB* 42 (1984): 5–145.

Giannelli, C., ed. *Vat. gr. 1833, fol. 52*. In C. Giannelli, "Alcuni formulari relativi alla 'manumissio in ecclesia' tratti da ecologi italo-greci e slave," pp. 137–138. *Rivista di cultura classica e medioevale* 1/2 (1959): 127–147.

Lemerle, Paul, ed. *Le testament d'Eustathios Boïlas (avril 1059)*. In P. Lemerle, *Cinq études sur le XIe siècle byzantin*, pp. 15–63. Paris: CNRS, "Le monde byzantin 6," 1977.

Oikonomides, Nicolas, ed. *Patmiacus 171 (fol. 516)*. In N. Oikonomides, "Quelques boutiques de Constantinople au Xe siècle; Prix, loyers, imposition." *DOP* 26 (1972): 345–356.

Pertusi, Agostini, ed. *La Crisobolla del 992*. In A. Pertusi, "Venezia e Bisanzio nel secolo XI," pp. 155–160 of *La Venezia del Mille*. Florence: Sansoni, "Storia della civiltà veneziana 10," 1965.

Sathas, Constantinus N., ed. *Parisinus gr. 2509, fol. 161–162*. In C. Sathas, *MB* 6:617–618.

Simon, Dieter, and Spyros Troianos, eds. *Scorialensis R II 12*. In "Dreizehn Geschäftsformulare," 13:294–295, *Font. min.*, pp. 262–295. Frankfurt: Klostermann, "ForByzRecht 3," 1977.

Thierry, Nicole, ed. "Libelle d'affranchissement des esclaves à Zelve (Xe s.)." In N. Thierry, "Enseignments historiques de l'archéologie cappadocienne," *TM* 8 (1981): 500–519; repr. in Nicole Thierry, *Haut Moyen Âge en Cappadoce*. Vol. 2, chap. 18, pp. 329–333. Paris: Geuthner, 1994.

3. Nonlegislative Documentary Sources Outside the Byzantine Empire

Assaf, Simha. "Ancient Acts of the Genizah of Palestine, Egypt, and North Africa" (in Hebrew). *Tarbiz* 9/1 (1937): 11–34, 196–218.

Mann, Jacob. *The Jews in Egypt and in Palestine under the Fatimid Caliphs: A Contribution to Their Political and Communal History, Based Chiefly on Genizah Material hitherto Unpublished*. 2 vols. Oxford: Oxford University Press, 1900–1922; repr. Oxford, 1969.

———. *Texts and Studies in Jewish History and Literature*. 2 vols. Cincinnati: Hebrew Union College Press, 1931 (Vol. 1); Philadelphia, 1935 (Vol. 2).

270   **Bibliography**

4. Hagiographical Sources

Hagiographical narratives are cited with the corresponding reference to Halkin, *BHG,* followed by the editor's name. Unless page numbers are indicated, all references are to the chapters or paragraphs noted and numbered in the edition cited.

Acta Sanctorum. 71 vols. Paris: Société des bollandistes, 1863–1940.

Bibliotheca hagiographica latina antiquae et mediae aetatis. 3 vols. Brussels: "SubsHag 6A–B and 12," 1889–1901.

Halkin, François. *Bibliotheca hagiographica graeca 3e éd.* 3 vols. in 1 part. Brussels: "SubsHag 8A," 1957; *Auctarium Bibliothecae hagiographicae graeca.* Brussels: "SubsHag 47," 1969; *Novum auctarium Bibliothecae hagiographicae gracae.* Brussels: "SubsHag 65," 1984.

In Praise of Theodore Tyron: Laudatio S. Theodori a. Chrysipp (BHG 1765c), *AASS* (Nov. 4): 55–72; Anthonios Sigalas, *Des Chrysippos von Jerusalem Enkomion auf den hl. Johannes den Täufer.* Berlin: Teubner, "Byzantinisches Archiv 7," 1921; Anthonios Sigalas, *Des Chrysippos von Jerusalem Enkomion auf den hl. Johannes den Täufer. Untersuchungen und Ergänzungen zu den Schriften des Chrysippos,* pp. 91–93. Athens: Verlag der Byzantinisch-neugreichischen Jahrbücher, "Texte und Forschungen zur byzantinisch-neugreichischen Philologie 20," 1937.

John of Ephesus. *Eastern Saints.* Edited and translated by Ernest Walter Brooks. PO 17:1–304; 18:311–697; 19:152–273.

Life of Andrew the Fool (BHG 115z–117): Lennart Rydén, ed. *Life of St. Andrew the Fool.* 2 vols. Uppsala: Acta Universitatis Upsaliensis, "Studia Byzantina Upsaliensis 4/1–2," 1995.

Life of Athanasia of Aegina (BHG 180): "Vie de sainte Athanasie d'Égine." In François Halkin, *Six inédits d'hagiologie byzantine,* pp. 179–195. Brussels: "SubsHag 74," 1987.

Life of Auxentios (BHG 203): Elizabeth E. Fischer, Βίος καὶ πολιτεία τοῦ ὁσίου πατρὸς ἡμῶν Αὐξεντίου τοῦ ἐν τῷ Βουνῷ. Stuttgart: Teubner, 1994.

Life of Basil the Younger (BHG 263): "Vita S. Basilii Iunioris, dans Parisinus gr. 1547." *AASS* (March 3): 20–32.

Life of Basil the Younger (BHG 263–264): "Vie de Basile le Jeune dans Moscou gr. 249," fol. 2–66; S. G. Viliskij, ed. Odessa: Zapiski Imperatorskogo novorossijskogo universita, 1911, pp. 286–326; fol. 351–378; S. G. Viliskij, ed. Odessa: Zapiski Imperatorskogo novorossijskogo universita, 1911, pp. 326–346; fol. 66–351; A. N. Veselovskij, ed. St. Petersburg: "Sbornik Otdelenija ruskogo jazyka i slovesnosti Imperatorskoj akademii nauk 46, 53." 1891–1892, part 6, supp. 3–174.

Life of Blaise of Amorion (BHG 278): "Vita Blasii Amoriensis." *AASS* (Nov. 4): 657–659.

Life of Elias Spēlaiōtēs I (BHG 581): "Vita S. Eliae Spelaeotae." *AASS* (Sept. 3): 343–888.

Life of Elias Spēlaiōtēs II: Vicenzo Saletta, trans., "Vita di S. Elia Speleota secondo il manoscritto Cryptense B. b; XVII." *Studi meridionali* 3/4 (1970): 445–453; 4/2–3 (1971): 272–315; 5/1 (1972): 61–96.

Life of Elias the Younger (BHG 580): Giuseppe Rossi Taibbi, "Vita di Sant'Elia il Giovane." Palermo: Istituto Siciliano di Studi Bizantini e Neoellenici, 1962.

Life of Elizabeth of Heraclea (BHG 2121): François Halkin, "Sainte Élisabeth d'Héraclée, abbesse à Constantinople," *AB* 91 (1973): 251–264; "Zur Vita des Äbtissein Elisabeth von Konstantinopel," *AB* 92 (1974): 287–288.

Life of Fantinos the Younger (BHG 1509b): Enrica Follieri, *La vita di San Fantino il Giovane.* Brussels: "SubsHag 77," 1993.

Life of George of Amastris (BHG 668): "Zhitie S. Georgia amastriskago." In V. G. Vasil'evskij, *Trudy.* Vol. 3. Petrograd, 1915, pp. 1–71.

Life of Gregory the Decapolite (BHG 711): Francis Dvornik, *La vie de Saint Grégoire le Décapolite et les Slaves macédoniens au IXe siècle.* Paris: Champion, 1926.

Life of Hypatios (BHG 760): G. J. M. Bartelink, *Vie d'Hypatios.* Paris: Éd. du Cerf, "SC 177," 1971.

Life of John of Cyprus (BHG 886): Leontius of Neapolis, "Vie de Jean de Chypre." In *Vie de Syméon le Fou et Vie de Jean de Chypre,* ed. André-Jean Festugière and Lennart Rydén. Paris: Geuthner, 1974.

Life of Joseph the Hymnographer (by Theophanes the Monk) (BHG 944): "Vita Ioseph hymnigraphi a. Theophane monastère." In Athanasios Papadopoulos-Keameus, *Monumenta graeca et latina ad historiam Photii patriarchae pertinentia.* Vol. 2, pp. 1–14. St. Petersburg, 1901.

Life of Lazarus of Mount Galesios (BHG 979): "Vita S. Lazari auctore Gregorio monacho." *AASS* (Nov. 3): 508–606.

Life of Leo Luke of Sicily (BHL 4842): "La Vita di S. Leone vescovo di Catani." *AASS* (March 1): 97–102.

Life of Leo of Catania (BHG 981): A. Acconcia Longo, "La vita di S. Leone vescova di Catania e gli incantesimi del mago Eliodoro." *RSBN* 26 (1989): 80–98.

Life of Leo of Catania (vita metrica) (BHG 981c): D. Raffin, "La Vita metrica anonima su Leone de Catania." *BollBadGr* 16 (1962): 33–48.

Life of Luke the Younger (BHG 994): Carolyn L. Connor and W. Robert Connor, *The Life and Miracles of Saint Luke of Steiris.* Brookline, Mass.: Hellenic College Press, 1994.

Life of Makarios of Peleketes (BHG 1003): I. Van den Gheyn, "Acta S. Macarii hegumeni monasterii Pelecetes." *AB* 16 (1897): 142–163.

Life of Marcel Acemetes (BHG 1027z): Gilbert Dagron, "La vie ancienne de saint Marcel l'Acémète." *AB* 86 (1968): 271–321.

Life of Mary of Egypt (BHG 1042): "Vita Mariae Aegyptiae," PG 87:3697–3726.

Life of Mary the Younger (BHG 1164): "Vita S. Mariae Iunioris," *AASS* (Nov. 4); 692–705.

Life of Matrona of Perge (BHG 1221): "Vita prima S. Matronae," *AASS* (Nov. 3): 790–813.

Life of Melania the Younger (BHG 1241): Denys Gorce, *Vie de Sainte Mélanie.* Paris: Éd. du Cerf, "SC 90," 1962.

Life of Melania the Younger (Latin Version) (BHL 5885): Charles de Smedt, "Vita Sanctae Melaniae junioris," *AB* 8 (1889): 19–63.

Life of Melania the Younger by Metaphrastes (BHG 1242): Symeon Metaphrastes, "Vita et conversatio Sanctae Melanae Romanae," PG 116:753–794.

Life of Michael Maleinos (BHG 1292): Louis Petit, "Vie et office de S. Michel Maleïnos." Paris: "Bibliothèque hagiographique orientale 4," 1903, pp. 7–26.

Life of Nahum: "Zhitie Nauma." In B. N. Floria, A. A. Tarilov, and S. A. Ivanon, *Krillo-metodiesvskoj tradicii posle Kirala i Mefodija.* St. Petersburg: Aletejja, 2000, pp. 286–288.

Life of Nicetas of Medicium (BHG 1341): "Vita S. Nicetae Confessoris." *AASS* (April 1): xxii–xxxiii.

Life of Nicholas of Sion (BHG 1347): Ihor Ševcenko and Nancy Petterson Ševcenko, *The Life of St. Nicholas of Sion.* Brookline, Mass.: Hellenic College Press, 1984.

Life of Nikon Metanoeite (BHG 1366, 1367): Denis F. Sullivan, *The Life of St. Nikon.* Brookline, Mass.: Hellenic College Press, 1987.

Life of Nilus of Rossano (BHG 1370): P. Germano Giovanelli, Βίος καὶ πολιτεία τοῦ ὁσίου πατρὸς ἡμῶν Νείλου τοῦ Νεοῦ. Badia di Grottaferrata, 1972; Antonis Fyrigos, corr., "La vita di S. Nilo da Rossano edita da Giovanni Matteo Carophyllis," *RSBN* 24 (1987): 119–239.

Life of Philaretos (BHG 1511z): Lennart Rydén, *The Life of St. Philaretos the Merciful Written by His Grandson Niketas.* Uppsala: Acta Universitatis Upsaliensis, "Studia Byzantina Upsaliensis 8," 2002.

Life of Stephen the Younger (BHG 1666): Marie-France Auzépy, *La vie d'Étienne le Jeune par Étienne le Diacre.* Aldershot, Hampshire: Variorum, 1997.

Life of Symeon the Fool (BHG 1677): Leontius of Neapolis, "Vie de Syméon le Fou." In André-Jean Festugière and Lennart Rydén, eds., *Vie de Syméon le Fou et Vie de Jean de Chypre.* Paris: Geuthner, 1974.

Life of Symeon the New Theologian (BHG 1692): I. Hausherr and G. Horn, *La Vie de Syméon de Nicetas Stethatos.* Rome: Pontifical Institute for Oriental Studies, "OrChr 12 (45)," 1928.

Life of Thaddaeus: D. Afinogenov, "The Church Slavonic Life of St. Thaddaios the Martyr of the Second Iconoclasm," *AB* 119/2 (2001): 313–338.

Life of Theoctiste of Lesbos (BHG 1723–1724): "Vita S. Theoctistae," *AASS* (Nov. 4): 224–233.

Life of Theodora of Thessalonica (BHG 1737, 1739): Symeon A. Paschalides, Ὁ βίος τῆς ὁσιομυροβλύτιδος Θεοδώρας τῆς ἐν Θεσσαλονίκῃ. Διήγηνσῃ περὶ τῆς μεταθέσεως τοῦ τιμίου λειψάνου τῆς ὁσίας Θεοδώρας. Thessalonica: Kentro Hagiologikōn Meletōn, 1991.

Life of Theodore of Sykeon (BHG 1748): André-Jean Festugière, *Vie de Théodore de Sykéon.* 2 vols. Brussels, "SubsHag 48," 1970; D. Baker, corr., *SChH* 13 (1976): 83–96; J. O. Rosenquist, corr. *Eranos* 78 (1980): 163–174.

Life of Theodore Studites I (BHG 1754): "Vita et conversatio S. Theodori abbatis monasterii Studii a Michele monacho Studia," PG 99:234–327.

Life of Theodore Studites II (BHG 1755): Vasilij Vasil'evic Latyšev, "Vita S. Theodori

Studitae in codice Mosquensi musei Rumianzoviani no. 520." *VizVrem (BX)* 21 (1914): 255–304; PG 99:113–233.

Life of Theophanes the Confessor (BHG 1787z): Vasilij Vasil'evic Latyšev, *Methodii Patriarchae Constantinopolis, Vita S. Theophanis Confessoris.* Moscow: Memoirs of the Academy of Russia, 8th ser., 13/4 (1918).

Methodius. *In Praise of Nicholas of Myra (BHG* 1352*):* "Methodii Encomium." In Gustav Anrich, *Hagios Nicolaos der Heilige Nikolaos in der griechischen Kirche,* pp. 151–182. Berlin: Teubner, 1931.

Miracles of Artemios (BHG 173): Virgil S. Crisafulli and John W. Nesbitt, *The Miracles of St. Artemios.* Leiden: Brill, 1997; Paul Lemerle, ed. *Les plus anciens receuils des miracles de S. Démétrius.* 2 vols. Paris: CNRS, 1979–1981.

Spiritually Beneficial Tales of Paul of Monembasia (narratives numbered 1–14 correspond to *BHG* 1449; 1449e; 1449f; 1449m; 1075d; 1449g; 1449nb; 1449b; 1449e; 1449h; 873n; 1449a; 1449k; 1175): John Wortley, *Les récits édifiants de Paul, évêque de Monembasie, et d'autres auteurs.* Paris: CNRS, 1987.

Synaxarium Ecclesia Constantinopolitanae: Propylaeum ad Acta Santorum Novembris. Edited by Hippolyte Delehaye. Brussels, 1902.

Theodore Tyron, Miracle of the Dragon (BHG 1766): *AASS* (Nov. 4): 46–48.

Three Miracles of Nicholas of Myra (BHG 1355): "Thaumata tria." In Gustav Anrich, *Hagios Nikolaos der Heilige Nikolaos in der griechischen Kirche,* pp. 183–197. Berlin: Teubner, 1913.

5. Other Greek Sources of a Hagiographical or Imaginative Nature

Digenis Akritis: Elizabeth Jeffreys, *Digenis Akritis: The Grottaferrata and Escorial Versions.* Cambridge, U.K.: Cambridge University Press, "Cambridge Medieval Classic 7," 1998.

Joseph and Aseneth (Greek Version): Marc Philonenko, ed. *Joseph et Aséneth.* Leiden: Brill, "Studia post-biblica 13," 1968 (for the Syriac, Armenian, and Slavonic versions, see C. Burchard, *Gesammelte Studien zu Joseph und Aseneth).*

Life of Aesop (G): "Vita Aesopi vulgaris (cod. G. Morgan nr. 397)." In Ben Edwin Perry, *Aesopica I,* pp. 35–80. Urbana: University of Illinois Press, 1952.

Life of Aesop (W): "Vita Aesopi Westermaniana (cod. W)." In Ben Edwin Perry, *Aesopica I,* pp. 81–110. Urbana: University of Illinois Press, 1952.

6. Nonhagiographical Literary Sources (Historiographical, Epistolary, Geographical, Theological)

Spellings of authors' names have been anglicized.

Greek Works

Agathias Myrinaei. *Historiarum Livri Quinque.* Edited by Rudolf Keydell. 2 vols. Berlin: De Gruyter, "CFHB 2–2A," 1967.

Appian. *Les guerres civiles à Rome.* Edited by P. Torrens. 4 vols. Paris: Les Belles Lettres, 1993–2000.

Aristophanes. *Ploutos.* In Aristophanes, *Oeuvres,* ed. Victor Coulon. Vol. 5. Paris: Les Belles Lettres, "G. Budé, série grecque," 1972.

Aristotle. *Politique.* Edited by Jean Aubonnet. 5 vols. Paris: Les Belles Lettres, "G. Budé, série grecque," 1968–1989.

Basil. *Lettres.* Edited by Yves Courtonne. 3 vols. Paris: Les Belles Lettres, "G. Budé série grecque," 1957–1966.

Candidus. *Fragmenta.* In Roger C. Blockley, *The Fragmentary Classicising Historians of the Later Roman Empire,* pp. 464–471 (notes, pp. 472–473). 2 vols. Liverpool: Cairns, 1981–1983.

Clavis patrum graecorum. Edited by Maurice Geehard. 7 vols. and supp. Turnhout: Brepols, "CChr," 1983–1998.

Comnena, Anna. *Aléxiade.* Edited by Bernard Leib. 4 vols. Paris: Les Belles Lettres, "G. Budé, série byzantine," 1937–1976.

Constantine Porphyrogenitus. *De administrando imperio.* Edited by Gyula Moravcsik, translated by Romilly Heald Jenkins. Washington, D.C.: Dumbarton Oaks, "CFHB 1," 1967.

———. *De cerimoniis aulae byzantinae.* Edited by Joannes Jacobus Reiskii. In Constantine Porphyrogenitus, *Opera omnia,* Vol. 2.

———. *Opera omnia.* 3 vols. CSHB, 1829–1840.

Cosmas Indicopleustes. *Topographie chrétienne.* Edited by Wanda Wolska-Conus. 2 vols. Paris: Éd. du Cerf, "SC 141, 159," 1968–1970.

Dio Cassius. *Histoire romaine.* Edited by Marie-Laure Freuburger-Galland, translated by Jean-Michel Roddaz, François Hinard, and Pierre Cordier. 3 vols. Paris: Les Belles Lettres, "G. Budé, série grecque," 1991–2002.

Eunapius. *Fragmenta.* In Roger C. Blockley, *The Fragmentary Classicising Historians of the Later Roman Empire,* pp. 6–123 (notes pp. 129–150). Liverpool: Cairns, 1981–1983.

Evagrius. *Historia ecclesaistica.* Edited by J. Bides and L. Parmentier. London: Metheun, 1898.

The Greek New Testament. Edited by K. Aland, M. Black, C. M. Martini, B. M. Metzger, and A. Wikgrem. Stuttgart: United Bible Societies, 1968 (1st ed. 1966).

Gregory of Nazianzus. *Lettres.* Edited by Paul Gallay. 2 vols. Paris: Les Belles Lettres, "G. Budé, série grecque," 1964–1967.

———. *Testamentum.* In PG 37:389–394.

Herodotus. *Histoires.* Edited by Philippe-Ernst Legrand. 9 vols. Paris: Les Belles Lettres, "G. Budé, série grecque," 1968–1970 (1st ed. 1932–1954).

John Chrysostom. *Homiliae XXIV in Epistolam ad Ephesios.* PG 62:9–176.

Kaminiates, Ioannes. *De expugnatione Thessalonicae.* Edited by Gertrud Böhlig. Berlin: De Gruyter, 1973.

Kekaumenos. *Raccomandazioni e consigli di un galantuomo* (Στρατηγικόν). Edited by Maria Dora Spadaro. Alexandria: Edizioni dell'Orso, 1998.

Leōn Choirosphaktēs. Correspondence edited and translated by Georgios T. Kolias. In Georgios T. Kolias, *Léon Choerosphactès, magistre, proconsul et patrice.* Athens: Verlag der Byzantinisch-neugriechischen Jahrbücher, 1939.

Leonis Diaconi Historiae. Edited by Charles Benoît Hase. CSHB, 1828.

Leonis Imperatoris Tactica sive de re militari liber. Edited by J. Lamius. PG 107:669–1119.

Malalas Ioannes. *Chronographia.* Edited by Ioannes Thurn. Berlin: De Gruyter, "CFHB 5," 2000. [Pagination to the L. Dindorf edition (CSHB, 1831), provided by Thurn, is given in parentheses.]

Malchus. *Fragmenta.* In Roger C. Blockley, *The Fragmentary Classicising Historians of the Later Roman Empire,* pp. 402–455 (notes 456–462). Liverpool: Cairns, 1981–1983; Lia Raffaella Cresci, ed., *Malco di Filadelfia Frammenti.* Naples: Bibliopolis, "Byzantina et Neo-Hellenica Neapolitana 9," 1982.

Menander Protector. *Fragmenta.* In Roger C. Blockley, *The History of Menander the Guardsman: Introductory Essay, Text, Translation, and Historiographical Notes.* Liverpool: Cairns, 1985.

Nicephorus Bryennios. *Histoire.* Edited by Paul Gautier. Brussels: Éd. de Byzantion, "CFHB 9," 1975.

Nicephoros, Patriarch of Constantinople. *Short History.* Edited by Cyril Mango. Washington, D.C.: Dumbarton Oaks, "CFHB 13," 1990.

Nicetae Choniatae Historiae. Edited by Jean Louis van Dieten. New York: De Gruyter, "CFHB 11/1," 1975.

Olympiodorus. *Fragmenta.* In Roger C. Blockley, *The Fragmentary Classicising Historians of the Later Roman Empire,* pp. 162–209 (notes pp. 211–220). Liverpool: Cairns, 1981–1983.

Palladius. *Historia Lausica.* Edited by G. J. M. Bartelink. Milan: A. Monadori, Fondazione Lorenzo Valla, "Vita dei santi 2," 1974.

Πάτρια Κωνσταντινουπόλεως. Edited by T. Preger. In *Scriptores originum constantinopolitanarum.* Vol. 2. Leipzig: Teubner, 1907.

Pausanias. *Oeuvres.* Edited by Michel Casevitz, translated by Jean Pouilloux. 3 vols. Paris: Les Belles Lettres, "G. Budé, série grecque," 1992–2000.

Plutarch. *Vies.* Edited and translated by R. Flacelière, E. Chambry, M. Juneau, and E. Simon. Paris: Les Belles Lettres, 1964–1983.

Priscus. *Fragmenta.* In Roger C. Blockley, *The Fragmentary Classicising Historians of the Late Roman Empire,* pp. 227–377 (notes pp. 379–400). Liverpool: Cairns, 1981–1983.

Procopius Caesariensis. *Opera omnia.* Edited by Jacob Haury. 2 vols. Leipzig: Teubner, 1962–1963 (Vol. 1: *De bello persico;* Vol. 2: *De bello gothico).*

Psellus, Michael. *Chronographie.* Edited by Émil Renauld. 2 vols. Paris: Les Belles Lettres, "G. Budé, série byzantine," 1967.

Scylitzes, Ioannes. *Synopsis historiarum.* Edited by Ioannes Thurn. Berlin: De Gruyter, "CFHB 5," 1973.

Seneca. *Ad Lucilium epistulae morales.* Translated by Richard M. Gummere. 3 vols. Cambridge, Mass.: Harvard University Press, 1917–1925; *Lettres à Lucilius.*

Edited by François Préchac, translated by Henri Noblot. 5 vols. Paris: Les Belles Lettres, "G. Budé, série latine," 1945–1964.

Septuaginta. Id est Testamentum graece iuxta LXX interpretes. Edited by Albert Rahlfs. Stuttgart: Württembergische Bibelanstalt, 1979 (1st ed. 1935).

Suidae Lexicon. Edited by Ada Adler. 5 vols. Leipzig: Teubner, 1928–1938.

Sylloge Tacticorum quae olim "inedita Leonis Tactica" dicebatur. Edited by Alphonse Dain. Paris: Les Belles Lettres, 1938.

Symeon the New Theologian. *Traités théologiques et éthiques.* Edited by Jean Darrouzès. 2 vols. Paris: Éd. du Cerf, "SC 122, 129," 1966–1967; *On the Mystical Life: The Ethical Discourses.* Translated by Alexander Golitzin. 2 vols. Crestwood, N.Y.: St. Vladimir's Seminary Press, 1995–1997.

Theodori Studitae Epistulae. Edited by Georgios Fatouros. 2 vols. Berlin: De Gruyter, "CFHB 31/1–2," 1991.

Theodori Studitae Parva Catechesis. Edited by Emmanuel Auvray. Paris: Lecoffre, 1891.

Theodore Studites. *Oratio XI.—Laudartio S. Platonis Hegumeni.* PG 99:803–850.
———. *Testamentum.* PG 99:1813–1823.

Theophanes Confessor. *Chronographia.* Edited by Carl de Boor. 2 vols. Leipzig: Teubner, 1883–1885; repr. Hildesheim: G. Olms, 1963 [All references are to the universal locators (A. M.) indicated by Theophanes, followed by the pagination of the de Boor edition]; Cyril Mango and Roger Scott, *The Chronicle of Theophanes Confessor.*

Theophanes Continuatus. Edited by Immanuel Bekker. CSHB, 1838; corrected by Kazimierz Kumaniecki, *Byzantion* 7 (1932): 235–237.

Zosimus. *Histoire nouvelle.* Edited by François Paschoud. 6 vols. Paris: Les Belles Lettres, "G. Budé, série grecque," 1971–1989.

Latin Works

Agobardi Lugdunensis Opera omnia. Edited by Lieven van Acker. Turnhout: Brepols, "CChr Continuatio Mediavalis 52," 1981.

Ambrose. *De officiis.* Edited by Maurice Testard. 2 vols. Paris: Les Belles Lettres, "G. Budé, série latine," 1984–1992.

Ammian Marcellinus. *Histoire.* Edited by Guy Sabbah. 6 vols. Paris: Les Belles Lettres, "G. Budé, série latine," 1968–1999.

Claudius Claudianus. *In Eutropium.* Edited by Pierre Fargues. Paris: Hachette, 1933.

Excerpta ex Historiis Arabum, De Expeditionibus syriacis Nicephor Phocae et Ioannis Tzimiscis. Edited by Charles Benoît Hase. CSHB, 1828, appendix to *Leonis Diaconi Historiae.*

Hieronymi Sancti Epistulae. Edited and translated by J. Labrout. 5 vols. Paris: Les Belles Lettres, "G. Budé, série latine," 1949–1955.

Liudprandi Cremonensis Opera omnia. Edited by Paolo Chiesa. Turnhout: Brepols,

"CChr Continuatio Mediavalis 156," 1998 ("Antapodosis," pp. 1–150; "Relatio de Legatione Constantinopolitana," pp. 187–218).

Res Gestae Divi Augusti. Edited by Victor Ehrenberg and Arnold Hugh Martin Jones, reprinted by P. A. Brunt and J. M. Moore. London: Oxford University Press, 1978.

Suetonius. *Vies des douze Césars.* Edited by Henri Ailloud. 3 vols. Paris: Les Belles Lettres, "G. Budé, série latine," 1964–1967.

Tacitus. *Annales.* Edited by Pierre Wuilleumier. 4 vols. Paris: Les Belles Lettres, "G. Budé, série latine," 1969–1976.

Arabic Works

Abū al-Faraj al-Isbahānī. *Kitāb al-Aghānī.* 9 vols. Cairo: Wizārāt al-Thaqāafah wa-al-Irshād al-Qawmī, 1963–1964.

Alf Layla wa-Layla. Edited by Maximilian Habicht and Heinrich Fleischer. 13 vols. Cairo: Dār al-Kutub al-Misriyya, 1998 (1st ed. Breslau, 1825–1843); *The Thousand and One Nights: From the Earliest Known Sources.* Edited by Muhsin Mahdi. 2 parts. Leiden: Brill, 1984.

Al-Balādhurī. *Kitāb Futūh al-Buldān.* Edited by Michael Jan de Goeje. Leiden: Brill: 1968 (1st. ed. 1866); new edition by Fuat Sezgin. Frankfurt: Institut für Geschichte der Arabisch-Islamischen Wissenschaften an der Johann Wolfgang Goethe-Universität, "Islamic Geography 42," 1992; *The Origins of the Islamic State, Kitāb Futūh al-Buldān.* Translated by Khuri Philp Hitti. Vol. 1. New York: Columbia University Press, 1916.

Ibn Fadlān. *Voyage chez les Bulgares de la Volga.* Translated by Marius Canard. Paris: SPAG (Papyrus), 1988.

Ibn Hawqal. *Kitāb Sūrat al-ard.* In Ibn Hawqal, *Opus geographicum,* BGA 3; *Configuration de la terre.* Translated by Johannes Hendrik Kramers and Gaston Wiet. 2 vols. Beirut: Dār Maktabat al-Hayāh, 1964.

Ibn Khordādhbih. *Kitāb al-Masālik wa'l-mamālik.* BGA 6.

Ibn Rusta. *Kitāb al-A'laq al-nafīsa.* BGA 7.

The Koran. Translated by N. J. Dawood. New York: Penguin, 1999; *Le Coran.* Translated by Sheikh Si Boubakeur Hamza. 2 vols. Paris: Maisonneuve et Larose, 1972; *Le Coran.* Translated by Denise Masson. Paris: Gallimard, "Bibliothèque de la Pléiade 190," 1967.

Al-Mas'ūdī. *Kitāb al-Tanbīh wa'l-ishrāf,* BGA 8; new edition by Fuat Sezgin. Frankfurt: Institut für Geschichte der Arabisch-Islamischen Wissenschaften an der Johann Wolfgang Goethe-Universität, "Islamic Geography 41," 1992; *Le livre de l'avertissement et de la révision.* Translated by B. Carra de Vaux. Paris: Imprimerie nationale, 1896.

———. *Murūj al-dhahab wa-ma'adin al-jawhar: Les prairies d'or* (books 1–7). Translated by C. Barbier de Meynard and Pavet de Courteille, corrected by Charles Pellat. 4 vols. Paris: Société asiatique, 1962–1989 (1st ed. 1861–1917);

The Meadows of Gold: The Abbasids (book 8). Translated by Paul Lunde and Caroline Stone. London: Kegan Paul, 1989.

Al-Muqaddasī. *Aḥsan al-taqāsīm fī ma'rifat al-aqālīm: La meilleure répartition pour la connaissance des provinces.* Translated by André Miquel. Damascus: Institut français de Damas, 1963; *The Best Divisions for the Knowledge of the Regions.* Translated by Basil Anthony Collins. Reading, U.K.: Garent, Centre for Muslim Contribution to Civilization, 1994.

———. *Description de l'Occident musulman aux IVe–Xe siècles: Extrait du "Kitāb Aḥsan al-takāsīm fī ma'rifat al-aqālīm."* Edited and translated by Charles Pellat. Algiers: Carbonel, 1950.

Al-Tabarī. *Ta'rīkh al-rusul wa'l-mulūk.* Edited by Michael Jan de Goeje. Leiden: Brill, 1879–1901.

Yaḥyā Ibn Sa'īd al-Antāq (Abu'l-Farāj). PO 18, 23. In *Histoire de Yahya-ibn-Sa'īd d'Antioche: Continuateur de Sa'īd-ibn-Bitriq,* ed. and trans. Ignace Kratchkovsky and Alexander Alexandrovich Vasiliev, 5:701–833; 3:349–520; PO 47, ed. and trans. Ignace Kratchkovsky, François Micheau, and Gérard Troupeau. 4:373–559.

Hebrew Work

Ibn Daud, Abraham. *The Book of Tradition (Sefer Ha-Qabbalah).* Edited and translated by Gerson D. Cohen. Philadelphia: Jewish Publication Society of America, 1967.

Syriac Works

Michael the Syrian. *Chronique.* Edited and translated by Jean-Baptiste Chabot. 4 vols. Paris: Culture et civilisation, 1963 (1st ed. 1899).

Zachariah Mitylenis. *Zachariah of Mitylene, the Syriac Chronicle Known as that of Zachariah Mitylene,* trans. Frederick John Hamilton and Ernest Walter Brooks. London: Metheun, 1899.

Armenian Work

The Armenian History Attributed to Sebeos. Edited and translated by Robert Tomson, commentary by James Howard-Johnston. 2 vols. Liverpool: Liverpool University Press, 1999.

Russian Work

The Laurentian Chronicle: The Russian Primary Chronicle; Laurentian Text. Translated by Samuel Hazzard Cross and Olgerd P. Shobowitz-Wetzor. Cambridge, Mass.: Mediaeval Academy of America, 1953.

General Studies

Unless otherwise indicated, all references are to the pagination of the most recent edition cited.

Beck, Hans Georg. *Kirche und theologische Literatur im byzantinischen Reich.* Munich: Beck, "Handbuch der Altertumswissenschaft," 1959.

Berkowitz, Luci, Karl A. Squitier, and William A. Johnson. *Thesaurus linguae graecae: Canon of Greek Authors and Works.* 3rd ed. Oxford: Oxford University Press, 1990.

Bruce, William C., ed. *An Historical Atlas of Islam.* Leiden: Brill, 1981.

Buchwald, Wolfgang, Armin Hohlweg, and Otto Prinz, eds. *Dictionnaire des auteurs grecs et latins de l'Antiquité et du Moyen Âge,* trans. Jean-Denis Berger and Jacques Billen. Turnhout: Brepols, 1991.

Chantraine, Pierre. *Dictionnaire étymologique de la langue grecque: Histoire des mots.* 2 vols. Paris: Klincksieck, 1968–1980.

Du Cange, Charles du Fresne. *Glossarium mediae et infimae latinitatis.* 10 vols. Niort: Fabre, 1883–1887.

Hefele, Karl-Joseph, and Henri Leclercq. *Histoire des conciles.* 11 vols. in 21 parts. Paris: Librairie Letouzey et Ané, 1907–1952.

Hunger, Herbert. *Die hochsprachliche profane Literatur des Byzantiner.* 2 vols. Munich: Beck, 1978.

Jones, Arnold Hugh Martin, John Robert Martindale, and J. Morris. *The Prosopography of the Later Roman Empire.* 3 vols. Cambridge, U.K.: Cambridge University Press, 1992.

Karayannopulos, Johannes, and Günter Weiss. *Quellenkunde zur Geschichte von Byzanz (324–1453).* 2 vols. Wiesbaden: Harrassowitz, "Schriften zur Geistesgeschichte des östlichen Europa 14," 1982.

Kaser, Max. *Das römische Privatrecht.* 2 vols. Munich: Beck, "Handbuch der Altertumswissenschaft," 1971–1975.

Lampe, Geoffrey William Hugo. *A Patristic Greek Lexicon.* Oxford: Clarendon Press, 1968.

Liddell, H. G., and R. Scott. *A Greek-English Lexicon,* revised by H. S. Jones and R. Mackenzie. Oxford: Clarendon Press, 1968.

Sophocles, Evangelinus Apostolides. *Greek Lexicon of the Roman and Byzantine Periods (from b.c. 146 to a.d. 1100).* 2 vols. Cambridge, Mass.: Harvard University Press, 1914.

Talbert, Richard J. A., ed. *Barrington Atlas of the Greek and Roman World.* Princeton, N.J.: Princeton University Press, 2000.

Van der Wal, Nicolaas. *Manuale Novellarum Iustianiai: Aperçu systématique du contenu des Novelles de Justinien.* Groningen: Wolters-Swets & Zeitlinger, 1964.

Van der Wal, Nicolaas, and Jan H. A. Lokin. *Historiae Iuris graeco-romani delineatio: Les sources du droit byzantin de 300 à 1453.* Groningen: Forsten, 1985.

Winkelmanns, F., R. J. Lilie, C. Ludwig, T. Pratsch, I. Rochow, W. Brandes, J. R. Martindale, and B. Zielme, eds. *Prosopographie der mittlebyzantinschen Zeit.* Berlin: De Gruyter, 1999–.

Critical Studies

Afinogenov, Dimitri. "The Church Slavonic Life of St. Thaddaios the Martyr of the Second Iconoclasm." *AB* 119/2 (2001): 313–338.

Ahrweiler, Hélène. *Byzance et la mer. La marine de guerre, la politique et les institutions maritimes de Byzance aux VIIe–XVe siècles.* Paris: PUF, 1966.

———. "Les relations entre les Byzantins et les Russes au IXe siècle." *Bulletin d'information et de coordination de l'Association internationale des études byzantines* 5 (1971): 44–70; repr. as chap. 7 of Hélène Ahrweiler, *Byzance: Les pays et les territoires.* London: Variorum, 1976.

Amirante, Luigi. *Prigionia di guerra. Riscatto e postliminium.* Naples: Jovene, 1969–1970.

Andreau, Jean. *Banque et affaires dans le monde romain, IVe siècle av. J.-C.–IIIe siècle apr. J.-C.* Paris: Éd. du Seuil, 1999.

———. "Originalité de l'historiographie finleyenne, et remarques sur les classes sociales. In *Table ronde tenue à Rome autour de M. I. Finley sur "Ancient Slavery and Modern Ideology." Opus* 1 (1982): 181–185.

———. "Vingt ans après *L'économie antique* de M. I. Finley. Présentation du dossier de *L'économie antique." Annales HSS* 50 (1995): 947–960.

Angelidi, Christine. "Δοῦλοι στήν Κωνσταντινούπολη τόν Ι′αι′. Ἡ μαρτυρία τοῦ βίου ὁσίου Βασιλείου τοῦ Νέου." *Symmeikta* 6 (1985): 33–51.

Antoniadis-Bibicou, Hélène. *Recherches sur les douanes à Byzance: L'octava,' le 'kommerkion' et les commerciaires.* Paris: Colin, "Cahiers des Annales 20," 1963.

Ashburner, Walter. "The Byzantine Mutiny Act." *JHS* 46 (1926): 80–109.

———. "A Byzantine Treatise on Taxation." *JHS* 35/1 (1915): 76–84.

———. "The Farmer's Law." *JHS* 30 (1910): 85–108; *JHS* 32 (1912): 68–95.

Ashtor, Eliyahu. "Aperçus sur les Radhanites." *Revue suisse d'histoire* 27 (1977): 245–275; repr. as chap. 2 in Eliyahu Ashtor, *Studies on the Levantine Trade in the Middle Ages.* London: Variorum, 1978.

———. "Gli Ebrei nel commercio mediterraneo nell'alto medioevo (sec. X–XI)." In *Gli Ebrei nell'alto medioevo* 1:401–487.

———. *Histoire des prix et des salaires dans l'Orient médiéval.* Paris: SEVPEN, "Monnaie, prix, conjoncture 8," 1969.

———. *Studies in the Levantine Trade in the Middle Ages.* London: Variorum, 1978.

Assaf, Simha. "Slaves and Slave Trade among the Jews in the Middle Ages" (in Hebrew). *Zion* 4 (1939–1940): 91–125.

———. *Texts and Studies in Jewish History* (in Hebrew). Jerusalem: Mosad ha-Rav Kuk, 1946.

Bagnall, Roger S. *Egypt in Late Antiquity.* Princeton, N.J.: Princeton University Press, 1993.

Barthélemy, Dominique. "Qu'est-ce que le servage en France au XIe siècle?" *RH* 287/2 (1992): 233–284.

Bashab, E. *Sheviya and Pedut: Captivity and Ransom in Mediterranean Jewish Society* (in Hebrew). Jerusalem, 1980.

Beaucamp, Joëlle. *Le statut de la femme à Byzance (IVe–VIIe siècles).* 2 vols. Paris: De Boccard, "TM Monographies," 1990, 1992.

Bendall, S. "Slaves or Soldiers?" *Nomismatika Chronika* 8 (1989): 41–43.

Beševliev, Veselin. *Die protobulgarischen Inschriften.* Berlin: Akademie-Verlag, "BBA 23," 1963.

Biezunska-Malowist, Izabela. *L'esclavage dans l'Égypte gréco-romaine. Seconde partie: Période romaine.* Translated by J. Wolf. Breslau: Polska Akademia Nauk, "Archiwum filologiczne 35," 1974.

Bloch, Marc. *La société féodale.* Paris: Albin Michel, 1989 (1st ed. 1939).

———. "Comment et pourquoi finit l'esclavage antique." *Annales ESC* 2/2 (1947); repr. in Marc Bloch, *Mélanges historiques* 1:261–285. Paris: EPHE, 1963.

———. "Liberté et servitude personnelles au Moyen Âge, particulièrement en France: Contribution à une étude des classes." *Anuario de Historia del Derecho español* (1933): 5–101; repr. in Marc Bloch, *Mélanges historiques* 1:210–258. Paris: EPHE, 1963.

———. *Mélanges historiques.* New ed. Paris: EPHE, 1963.

Blockley, Roger C. *The Fragmentary Classicising Historians of the Later Roman Empire: Eunapius, Olympiodorus, Priscus, and Malchus.* 2 vols. Liverpool: Cairns, 1981–1983.

Bonnassie, Pierre. "Survie et extinction du régime esclavagiste dans l'Occident du haut Moyen Âge." *CahCM* 28 (1985): 307–343.

Boswell, John. *The Kindness of Strangers: The Abandonment of Children in Western Europe from Late Antiquity to the Renaissance.* New York: Pantheon, 1988.

Botte, Roger, ed. *L'ombre portée de l'esclavage: Avatars contemporains de l'oppression sociale.* Issue of *Journal des africanistes* 70/1–2 (2000).

Boulvert, Gérard. *Esclaves et affranchis impériaux sous le Haut-Empire Romain: Rôle politique et administratif.* Naples: Jovene, "Biblioteca di Labeo 4," 1970 (1st ed. Aix-en-Provence, 1964).

Boyer, Régis. *L'Islande médiévale.* Paris: Les Belles Lettres, "Guide Belles Lettres des civilisations," 2002 (1st ed. 2001).

Bradley, Keith. "Animalizing the Slave: The Truth of Fiction." *JRS* 90 (2000): 110–125.

———. *Slavery and Society at Rome.* Cambridge: Cambridge University Press, 1994.

———. *Slaves and Masters in the Roman Empire: A Study in Social Control.* Brussels: Latomus, "Latomus 185," 1984.

Brand, Charles M. "Two Byzantine Treaties on Taxation." *Traditio* 25 (1969): 35–60.

Braund, David. "Privacy under the Principate and the Ideology of Imperial Eradication." In *War and Society in the Roman World,* ed. John Rich and Graham Shipley, pp. 195–212. London: Routledge, 1993.

Bresc. Henri. "Le marchand, le marché et le palais dans la Sicile des Xe–XIIe siècles." In *Mercati et mercanti nell'alto medioevo,* pp. 285–321.

Bresc, Henri, ed. *Figures de l'esclave au Moyen Âge et dans le monde moderne.* Paris: L'Harmattan, 1996.

Brown, Peter. *Poverty and Leadership in the Later Roman Empire.* Hanover, N.H.: University Press of New England, "Menahem Stern Jerusalem Lectures," 2002.

Browning, Robert. *Byzantium and Bulgaria: A Comparative Study across the Early Medieval Frontier.* London: Temple Smith, 1975.

———. "Slavery in the Byzantine Empire, 600–1200" (in Russian). *VizVrem* 14 (1958): 38–55.

Buckland, William Warwick. *The Roman Law of Slavery.* Cambridge, U.K.: Cambridge University Press, 1970 (1st ed. 1908).

Burchard, Christoph. *Gesammelte Studien zu Joseph und Aseneth.* Leiden: Brill, "Studia Veteris Testamenti Pseudepigrapha 13," 1996.

———. "The Present State of Research on Joseph and Aseneth." In *New Perspectives on Ancient Judaism, II: Religion, Literature, and Society in Ancient Israel, Formative Christianity and Judaism, Ancient Israel and Christianity,* ed. J. Neusner, P. Borgen, and E. S, Freichs, pp. 31–52. Lanham, Md.: University Press of America, 1987; repr. in Christoph Burchard, *Gesammelte Studien zu Joseph und Aseneth,* pp. 297–320. Leiden: Brill, 1996.

Burdon, J. "Slavery as Punishment in Roman Criminal Law." In *Slavery and Other Forms of Unfree Labour,* ed. Leonie J. Archer, pp. 68–85. London: Routledge, 1988.

Cahen, Claude. "Y a-t-il eu des Radhanites?" *Revue des études juives,* 14th ser., 3 (1964): 499–505.

Cameron, Averil. *Changing Cultures in Early Byzantium.* Aldershot, Hampshire: Variorum, 1996.

———. *Continuity and Change in Sixth-century Byzantium.* London: Variorum, 1981.

———. "Cyprus at the Time of the Arab Conquests." *Cyprus Historical Review* 1 (1992); repr. as chap. 6 of Averil Cameron, *Changing Cultures in Early Byzantium.* Aldershot, Hampshire: Variorum, 1996.

———. "Images of Authority: Elites and Icons in Late Sixth-century Byzantium." *P & P* 84 (August 1979); repr. as chap. 18 of Averil Cameron, *Continuity and Change in Sixth-century Byzantium.* London: Variorum, 1981.

———. "The Language of Images: The Rise of Icons and Christian Representation." In *The Church and the Arts,* ed. Diana Wood. Oxford, U.K.: Blackwell, "Studies in Church History 28," 1992; repr. as chap. 12 of Ameril Cameron, *Changing Cultures in Early Byzantium.* Aldershot, Hampshire: Variorum, 1996.

————. *The Later Roman Empire, A.D. 284–430.* Cambridge, Mass.: Harvard University Press, 1993.

————. "The Mandylion and Byzantine Iconoclasm." In *The Holy Face and the Paradox of Representation,* ed. Herbert L. Kessler and Gerhard Wolf, pp. 33–54. Bologna: Nuova Alfa, "Villa Spelman Colloquia 6," 1998.

————. *The Mediterranean World in Late Antiquity. A.D. 395–600.* London: Routledge, "Routledge History of the Ancient World," 1993.

Campagnolo-Pothitou, Maria. "Les échanges de prisonniers entre Byzance et l'Islam aux IXe et Xe siècles." *Journal of Oriental and African Studies* 7 (1995): 1–55.

Canard, Marius. *Byzance et les musulmans du Proche-Orient.* London: Variorum, 1973.

————. "Deux épisodes des relations diplomatiques arabo-byzantines au Xe siècle." *Bulletin d'études orientales de l'Institut français de Damas* 13 (1949–1950): 51–69; repr. as chap. 12 of Marius Canard, *Byzance et les musulmans du Proche-Orient.* London: Variorum, 1973.

————. *Histoire de la dynastie des Hamdanides de Jazîra et de Syrie.* Paris: PUF, "Publications de la faculté des lettres d'Alger 21," 1953.

————. "La prise d'Héraclée et les relations entre Hârûn al-Rashîd et l'empereur Nicéphore Ier." *Byzantion* 32 (1962); repr. as chap. 18 of Marius Canard, *Byzance et les musulmans du Proche-Orient.* London: Variorum, 1973.

————. "Quelques 'à-côtés' de l'histoire des relations entre Byzance et les Arabes." In *Studi orientalistici in onore di Giorgio Levi Della Vida,* pp. 98–119. Rome: Istituto per l'Oriente, 1956; repr. as chap. 15 of Marius Canard, *Byzance et les musulmans du Proche-Orient.* London: Variorum, 1973.

Cankova-Petkova, Genoveva. "Contribution au sujet de la conversion des Bulgares au christianisme." *Byzantino-Bulgarica* 4 (1973): 21–40.

Carrié, Jean-Michel. "Le 'Colonat du Bas-Empire': Un mythe historiographique." *Opus* 1 (1982): 351–370.

————. "'Colonato del Basso Impero': La resistenza del mito." In *Terre, proprietari e contadini dell'Impero romano. Dall'affitto agrario al colonato tardo-antico: Atti dell'Incontro internazionale di studio, Capri, 16–18 octobre 1995,* ed. Elio Lo Cascio, pp. 75–150. Rome: Nuova Italia Scientifica, 1997.

————. "Esclavage antique et idéologie moderne dans *Ancient Slavery and Modern Ideology.*" In *Table ronde tenue à Rome autour de M. I. Finley sur "Ancient Slavery and Modern Ideology.*" *Opus* 1 (1982): 161–170.

————. "Un roman des origines: Les généalogies du 'Colonat du Bas-Empire.'" *Opus* 2/1 (1983): 205–251.

Cheikh-Moussa, A. "Figures de l'esclave chanteuse à l'époque abbasside." In *Figures de l'esclave au Moyen Âge et dans le monde moderne,* ed. H. Bresc, pp. 31–76. Paris: L'Harmattan, 1996.

Cheynet, Jean-Claude. *Pouvoir et contestations à Byzance (963–1210).* Paris: Publications de la Sorbonne, "Série Byzantina Sorbonensia 9," 1990.

Cheynet, Jean-Claude, Élisabeth Malamut, and Cécile Morrison. "Prix et salaires à Byzance (Xe–XVe siècles)." In *Hommes et richesses dans l'Empire byzantin II. VIIIe–VXe siècles*, ed. V. Kravari, J. Lefort, C. Morrison, pp. 339–374. Paris: Lethielleux, "Réalités byzantines 3," 1991.

Christides, Vassilios. *The Conquest of Crete by the Arabs (ca. 824): A Turning Point in the Struggle between Byzantium and Islam*. Athens: Akadēmia Athēnōn, 1984.

————. "Raid and Trade in the Eastern Mediterranean: A Treatise by Muhammad bn. 'Umar, the Faqih from Occupied Moslem Crete, and the Rhodian Sea Law, Two Parallel Texts." *Graeco-Arabica* 5 (1993): 63–102.

Chrysos, Evangelos. "Some Aspects of Roman-Persian Legal Relations." *Klēronomia* 8 (1976): 1–60.

Cipollone, Giulio, ed. *La liberazione dei 'captivi' tra christianità e islam. Oltre la crociata e il Ghiad: Tolleranza e servizio e servizio umanitario. Atti del Congresso interdisciplinare di studi storici (Roma, 16–19 settembre 1998) organizzato per l'VIII centenario dell'approvazione della regolo dei Trinitari da parte del Papa Innocenzo III il 17 dicembre 1998/15 safar, 595 H.* Vatican City: Archivio segreto vaticano, "Collectanea archivi vaticani 46," 2000.

Citti, Vittorio. "Esclavage et sacré dans le langage tragique." In *Religion et anthropologie de l'esclavage et des formes de dépendance: Actes du XXe colloque du GIREA, Besançon 46, novembre 1993*, ed. Jacques Annequin and Marguerite Garrido-Hory, pp. 91–99. Paris: Les Belles Lettres, "Annales littéraires de l'université de Besançon 534, Centre de recherches d'histoire ancienne 133," 1994.

Cohen, Gerson D. "The Story of the Four Captives." *Proceedings of the American Academy for Jewish Research* 29 (1960–1961): 55–131.

Condominas, Georges, ed. *Formes extrêmes de dépendance, contribution à l'étude de l'esclavage en Asie du Sud-Est* (J. Klein, H. Stern, E. T. Magnnon, A. Gurreiro, P. Beaujard, M. A. Martin, K. Sok, L. F. F. R. Tomaz, B. Milcent, J. P. Dimenichiani, B. D. Ramiaramana, B. Brac de la Perrière, and A. Doré). Paris: EHESS, "Civilisations de société," 1998.

Crone, Patricia. *Slaves on Horses: The Evolution of the Islamic Polity*. Cambridge, U.K.: Cambridge University Press, 1980.

Cursi, Maria Floriana. *La struttura del 'Postliminium' nella republica e nel principato*. Naples: Jovene, "Pubblicazioni dell'Istituto di diritto romano e dei diritti dell'Oriente mediterraneo 73," 1996.

Da Costa-Loubillet, G. "Saints de Constantinople aux VIIIe, IXe et Xe siècles." *Byzantion* 24 (1954–1956): 179–263 and 453–511; 25–27 (1957): 783–852.

————. "Saints de Grèce aux VIIIe, IXe et Xe siècles." *Byzantion* 31 (1961): 309–369.

————. "Saints de Sicile et Italie méridionale." *Byzantion* 29–30 (1959–1960): 89–173.

Dagron, Gilbert. *Naissance d'une capitale: Constantinople et ses institutions de 300 à 451*. Paris: PUF, "Bibliothèque byzantine, Études 7," 1974.

Debord, Pierre. "Religion et mentalité des esclaves en Asie Mineure." In *Religion et anthropologie de l'esclavage et des formes de dépendance: Actes du XXe colloque du GIREA Besançon 46, novembre 1993,* ed. Jacques Annequin and Margurite Garrido-Hory, pp. 137–145. Paris: Les Belles Lettres, "Annales littéraires de l'université de Besançon 534, Centre de recherches d'histoire ancienne 133," 1994.

De Churuca, J. "L'anathème du concile de Gangres contre ceux qui, sous prétexte de christianisme, incitent les esclaves à quitter leurs maîtres." *Revue historique de droit français et étranger* 60 (1982): 261–278.

Delehaye, Hippolyte. "La Vie de sainte Théoctiste de Lesbos." *Byzantion* 1 (1924): 191–200.

Delmaire, Roland. "Les esclaves et *condicionales* fiscaux au bas-empire romain." *Topoi orient-occident* 9/1 (1999): 179–189.

———. *Largesses sacrées et res privata: L'aerarium impérial et son administration du IVe au VIe siècle.* Rome: EFR, "Coll. de l'EFR 21," 1989.

De Souza, Philip. *Piracy in the Graeco-Roman World.* Cambridge, U.K.: Cambridge University Press, 1999.

Ditten, Hans. *Ethnische Verschiebungen zwischen der Balkanhalbinsel und Kleinasien vom Ende des 6. bis zur zweiten Hälfte des 9. Jahrhunderts.* Berlin: Akademie-Verlag, "BBA 59," 1993.

Dockès, Pierre. *La libération médiévale.* Paris: Flammarion, "Nouvelle bibliothèque scientifique," 1979.

Dozy, R. *Recherches sur l'histoire et la littérature d'Espagne.* Paris: Brill, 1881.

Duby, Georges. *Guerriers et paysans, VIIIe–XIIe siècles, premier essor de l'économie européenne.* Paris: Gallimard, "Bibliothèque des histoires," 1973.

———. *La société aux XIe et XIIe siècles dans la région mâconnaise.* Paris: EHESS, "Bibliothèque générale de l'EHESS," 1988 (1st ed. 1953).

Ducloux, Anne. *Ad ecclesiam confugere: Naissance du droit d'asile dans les églises (IVe–milieu du Ve s.).* Paris: De Boccard, "De l'archéologie à l'histoire," 1994.

Ducrey, Pierre. *Guerre et guerriers dans la Grèce antique.* Paris: Payot, 1985.

Dunlap, James Eugene. *The Office of the Grand Chamberlain in the Later Roman and Byzantine Empire.* London: Macmillan, "University of Michigan Studies Humanistic Series 14/2," 1924.

Espéronnier, M. "Les échanges commerciaux entre le monde musulman et les pays slaves d'après les sources musulmanes médiévales." *CahCM* 23/1 (1980): 17–27.

———. "Villes et commerce: La Khazarie et la Bulgarie de la Volga, d'après les textes arabes et persans des IXe et Xe siècles." In *Les centres proto-urbains russes entre Scandinavie, Byzance et Orient,* ed. M. Kazanski, A. Nercessian, and C. Zuckerman, pp. 409–424. Paris: Buchet-Chastel, "Réalités byzantines 7," 2000.

Evans Grubbs, Judith. *Law and Family in Late Antiquity: The Emperor Constantine's Marriage Legislation.* Oxford: Oxford University Press/Clarendon Press, 1995.

Fabbrini, Fabrizio. *La manumissio in ecclesia.* Milan: Giuffrè, "Pubblicazioni dell'Istituto di diritto romano e dei diritti dell'Oriente mediterraneo 40," 1965.

———. "Un nuovo documento relativo alla manumissio in ecclesia." *Rendiconti della Classe di Scienze morali, storiche e filogiche* ser. 8, 16/5–6 (1961): 211–222.

Falkenhausen, Vera von. *La dominazione bizantini nell'Italia meridonale dal IX all'XI secolo*. Bari: Ecumenica Editrice, 1978.

Ferluga, Jadran. "Der byzantinische Handel auf der Balkanhalbinsel vom VII. bis zum Anfang des XIII. Jahrhunderts." In *Papers Presented at the 5th International Congress of South-East European Research Studies Held in Belgrad, 11th–16th September, 1984*, pp. 31–52. Skopje: Institute of National History, 1988; repr. in Jadran Ferluga, *Untersuchungen zur byzantinischen Provinzverwaltung. VI.–XIII. Jahrhundert*, pp. 159–174. Amsterdam: Hakkert, 1992.

——. "Les îles dalmates dans l'Empire byzantin." *ByzF* 6 (1927); repr. in Jadran Ferluga, *Byzantium and the Balkans: Studies on the Byzantine Administration and the Southern Slavs from the Seventh to the Twelfth Centuries*, pp. 97–130. Amsterdam: Hakkert: 1976.

——. "Mercati e mercanti fra mar Nero e Adriatico: Il commercio nei Balcani dal VII all'XI secolo." In *Mercati et mercanti nell'alto medioevo*, pp. 443–498.

——. "Navigation et commerce dans l'Adriatique aux VIIe et VIIIe siècles." *ByzF* 12 (1987): 39–51; repr. in Jadran Ferluga, *Untersuchungen zur Byzantinischen Provinzverwaltung. VI.–XIII. Jahrhundert*, pp. 449–461. Amsterdam: Hakkert, 1992.

——. *Untersuchungen zur byzantinischen Provinzverwaltung. VI.–XIII. Jahrhundert*. Amsterdam: Hakkert, 1992.

Festugière, André-Jean. *Les moines d'Orient*. 3 vols. in 4 parts. Paris: Éd. du Cerf, 1961–1963.

Fichman, I. F. "Economic Aspects of Individual Dependency in Roman and Late Egypt" (in Russian). *Vestnik Drevneï Istorii* (1981/1): 77–99; translated into French by J. Gaudey in *Esclavage et dépendance dans l'historiographie soviétique récente*, ed. M. M. Mactoux and E. Geny, pp. 157–184. Paris: Les Belles Lettres, "Annales littéraires de l'université de Besançon 577, Centre de recherches d'histoire ancienne 149," 1995.

——. "Sklaven und Sklavenarbeit im spätrömischen Oxyrhynchos (im historischen Längsschnitt)." *Jahrbuch für Wirtschaftgeschichte* (1973/2): 149–208.

——. "Slaves in Byzantine Oxyrhynchos." In *Akten des XIII international Papyrologenkongress* (Munich: Beck, 1974), pp. 117–124 (pp. 57–60).

Finley, Moses Immanuel. *Ancient Slavery and Modern Ideology*. New York: Viking, 1980.

——. *Economy and Society in Ancient Greece*. New York: Viking, 1982.

Fitzgerald, William. *Slavery and the Roman Literary Imagination*. Cambridge, U.K.: Cambridge University Press, "Roman Literature and Its Contexts," 2000.

Fournet, Jean-Luc. *Hellénisme dans l'Égypte du VIe siècle: La bibliothèque et l'oeuvre de Dioscore d'Aphrodité*. 2 vols. Cairo: Institut français d'archéologie orientale, 1999.

Freyburger, Gérard. "Le droit d'asile à Rome." *Les études classiques* 60/2 (1992): 139–151.

Friedman, Yvonne. *Encounter between Enemies: Captivity and Ransom in the Latin Kingdom of Jerusalem*. Leiden: Brill, "Cultures, Beliefs, and Traditions. Medieval and Early Modern Peoples 10," 2002.

———. "The 'Great Precept' of Ransom: The Jewish Perspective." In *La liberazione dei 'captivi' tra Cristianità e Islam,* ed. G. Cipollone, pp. 161–172. Vatican City: Archivio segreto vaticano, "Collectanea archivi vaticani 46," 2000.

Garnsey, Peter. *Ideas of Slavery from Aristotle to Augustine.* Cambridge, U.K.: Cambridge University Press, 1996.

———. *Social Status and Legal Privilege in the Roman Empire.* Oxford: Clarendon, 1970.

———. "Sons, Slaves, and Christians." In *The Roman Family in Italy: Status, Sentiment, Space,* ed. Beryl Rawson and Paul Weaver, pp. 101–122. Canberra: Clarendon Press, 1997.

Garnsey, Peter, and Richard P. Saller. *The Roman Empire: Economy, Society, and Culture.* Berkeley: University of California Press, 1987.

Garrido-Hory, M. *Juvénal. Esclaves et affranchis à Rome.* Besançon: Presses universitaires franc-comtoises, "Série des index thématiques des références à l'esclavage et à la dépendance 6," 1998.

Gascou, Jean. "Les grands domaines, la cité et l'état en Égypte byzantine: Recherches d'histoire agraire, fiscale et administrative" *TM* 9 (1985): 1–96.

Gaudemet, Jean. *L'Église dans l'Empire romain (IVe–Ve siècles).* Paris: Sirey, 1958.

———. "Ordre public et charité chrétienne: La loi du 27 juillet 398." *Studi tardoantichi* 1 (1986): 245–264; repr. in J. Gaudemet, *Droit et société aux derniers siècles de l'empire romain,* pp. 197–216. Naples: Jovene, 1992.

Giannelli, Ciro. "Alcuni formulari relativi alla 'manumissio in ecclesia' tratti da eucologi italo-greci e slavi." *Rivisti di cultura classica e medioevale* 1/2 (1959): 127–147.

Gibb, Hamilton A. R. "Arab-Byzantine Relations under the Umayyad Caliphate." *DOP* 12 (1958): 221–233.

———. "The Fiscal Rescript of 'Umar II." *Arabica* 2/1 (1955): 1–16.

Gieysztor, Aleksander. "Les juifs et leurs activités économiques en Europe orientale." In *Gli Ebrei nell'alto medioevo* 1:489–528.

———. "Les marchés et les marchandises entre le Danube et la Volga aux VIIIe–XIe siècles." In *Mercati et mercanti nell'alto medioevo,* pp. 499–522.

Gil, Moshe. "The Radhanite Merchants and the Land of Radhan." *Journal of the Economic and Social History of the Orient* 17/3 (1974): 299–328.

Glancy, Jennifer A. *Slavery in Early Christianity.* Oxford: Oxford University Press, 2002.

Goitein, Shelomo Dov. *A Mediterranean Society: The Jewish Communities of the Arab World as Portrayed in the Documents of the Cairo Genizah.* 6 vols. Berkeley: University of California Press, 1967–1993.

———. "Autographs of Yehuda Halevi" (in Hebrew). *Tarbiz* 25 (1955–1956): 393–416.

Golden, Peter B. "Khazaria and Judaism." *Archivum Eurasiae Medii Aevi* 3 (1983): 127–156.

Gordon, Murray. *Slavery in the Arab World.* New York: New Amsterdam, 1989.

Gorecki, Danuta. "A Farmer Community of the Byzantine Middle Ages: Historiography and Legal Analysis of Sources." *BS/EB* 9/2 (1982): 169–198.

———. "The Slavic Theory in Russian Pre-revolutionary Historiography of the Byzantine Farmer Community." *Byzantion* 56 (1986): 77–107.

Greatrex, Geoffrey. *Rome and Persia at War, 502–532.* Leeds: Cairns, 1998.

Gruszka, Peter. "Die Ansichten über das Sklaventum in den Schriften der kappadozischen Kirchenväter." *Antiquitas* 10 (1983): 106–118.

Guemara, Raoudha. "La libération et le rachat des captifs: Une lecture musulmane." In G. Cipollone, ed., *La liberazione dei 'captivi' tra Cristianità e Islam,* pp. 333–344. Vatican City: Archivio segreto vaticano, "Collectanea archivi vaticani 46," 2000.

Guilland, Rodolphe Joseph. *Recherches sur les institutions byzantines.* 2 vols. Amsterdam: Hakkert, "BBA 35," 1967.

Hadjinicolaou-Marava, Anna. *Recherches sur la vie des esclaves dans le monde byzantin.* Athens: Institut français d'Athènes, 1950.

Harrill, James Albert. *The Manumission of Slaves in Early Christianity.* Tübingen: Mohr-Sieback, "Hermeneutische Untersuchungen zür Theologie," 1995.

Harvey, Alan. *Economic Expansion in the Byzantine Empire 900–1200.* Cambridge, U.K.: Cambridge University Press, 1989.

Heers, Jacques. *Esclaves et domestiques au Moyen Âge dans le monde méditerranéen.* Paris: Fayard, 1981.

Hendy, Michael F. *Studies in the Byzantine Monetary Economy, c. 300–1450.* Cambridge, U.K.: Cambridge University Press, 1985.

Hezser, Catherine. "The Social Status of Slaves in the Talmud Yerushalmi and in Graeco-Roman Society." In *The Talmud Yerushalmi and Graeco-Roman Culture,* Vol. 3, ed. Peter Scräf. Tübingen: Mohr-Siebeck, 2002.

Hopkins, Keith. "Eunuchs in Politics in the Late Roman Empire." *Proceedings of the Cambridge Philological Society* 189 (1963): 62–80; repr. as chap. 3 in Keith Hopkins, *Conquerors and Slaves.* Cambridge, U.K.: Cambridge University Press, 1978.

———. *Conquerors and Slaves.* Cambridge, U.K.: Cambridge University Press, 1978.

Horden, Peregrine, and Nicholas Purcell. *The Corrupting Sea: A Study of Mediterranean History.* Oxford: Blackwell, 2000.

Irmscher, Johannes. "Die byzantinische Spartakustradition." *Antiquitas* 10 (1983): 55–61.

Isaac, Benjamin. "Bandits in Judaea and Arabia." *Harvard Studies in Classical Philology* 88 (1984): 171–203; repr. in Benjamin Isaac, *The Near East under Roman Rule.* Leiden: Brill, "Nemosyne Bibliotheca Classica Batava Supplementum," 1993.

Ivakin, G. "Kiev aux VIIIe–Xe siècles." In *Les centres proto-urbains russes entre Scandinavie, Byzance et Orient,* ed. M. Kazanski, A. Nercessian, and C. Zuckerman, pp. 225–239. Paris: Buchet-Chastel, "Réalités byzantines 7," 2000.

Jacoby, David. "The Byzantine Outsider in Trade (c. 900–c. 1350)." In *Strangers to Themselves: The Byzantine Outsider. Papers from the Thirty-second Symposium of*

Byzantine Studies, University of Sussex, Brighton, March 1998, ed. Dion C.
Smythe. Aldershot, Hampshire: Ashgate/Variorum, 2000, pp. 129–147.

———. "Une classe fiscale à Byzance et en Romanie latine: Les inconnus du fisc,
éleuthères ou étrangers." In *Actes du XIVe Congrès international des études
byzantines. Bucarest, 1971.* Vol. 2. Bucharest: Editura Academiei Republicii
Socialiste Românîa, 1975, pp. 139–152; repr. as chap. 7 in David Jacoby,
Recherches sur la Méditerranée orientale du XIIe au XVe siècle. London: Variorum,
1979.

———. "What Do We Learn about Byzantine Asia Minor from the Documents of
the Cairo Genizah?" In *Byzantine Asia Minor (Sixth–Twelfth Cent.),* ed. Steilos
Lampakis, pp. 83–95. Athens: Instituto Byzantinōn Eruōn, Speros Basil Vryonis
Center for the Study of Hellenism, 1998.

Jenkins, Romilly James Heald. "Cyprus between Byzantium and Islam, A.D. 688–
965." In *Studies Presented to David Moore Robinson,* Washington University, St.
Louis, 1953, pp. 1006–1014; repr. as chap. 22 in Romilly James Heald Jenkins,
Studies on Byzantine History of the Ninth and Tenth Centuries. London: Variorum,
1970.

Jones, Arnold Hugh Martin. *The Later Roman Empire 284–602.* 3 vols. Oxford:
Blackwell, 1964.

Kahane, Henri, and Renée Kahane. "Notes on the Linguistic History of 'Sclavus.'"
In *Studi in onore di Ettore Lo Gatto e Giovanni Maver,* pp. 345–360. Rome:
Sansoni, 1962.

Kaplan, Michel. *Les hommes et la terre à Byzance du VIe au XIe siècle: Propriété et exploitation du sol.* Paris: Publications de la Sorbonne, "Série Byzantina
Sorbonensia 10," 1992.

Karla, Grammatiki A. *Vita Aesopi. Überlieferung. Sprache und Edition einer
frühbyzantinischen Fassung des Äsopromans.* Wiesbaden: Dr. Ludwig Reichert
Verlag, "Serta Graeca 13," 2001.

Kazanski, M., A. Nercessian, and C. Zuckerman, eds. *Les centres proto-urbains russes
entre Scandinavie, Byzance et Orient.* Paris: Buchet-Chastel, "Réalités byzantines
7," 2000.

Kazhdan, Alexander. *Authors and Texts in Byzantium.* Aldershot, Hampshire: Variorum, 1993.

———. "The Corporations and Government Workshops of Constantinople in the
Ninth and Tenth Centuries" (in Russian). *VizVrem* 6 (1953): 132–155.

———. "The Concepts of Freedom *(eleutheria)* and Slavery *(douleia)* in Byzantium." In *La notion de liberté au Moyen Âge: Islam, Byzance, Penn-Paris-
Dumbarton Oaks Colloquia, 4 Sessions des 12–15 octobre 1982,* ed. George Makdisi,
Dominique Sourdel, and Janine Sourdel-Thomine. Paris: Les Belles Lettres,
1985.

———. "Hagiographical Notes." *Byzantion* 53 (1983): 538–558; 54 (1984): 176–
192; *BZ* 78 (1985): 49–55; *Byzantion* 56 (1986): 148–170; *Erytheia* 9/2 (1988):
197–209, repr. as chaps. 3–7 in Alexander Kazhdan, *Authors and Texts in Byzantium.* Aldershot, Hampshire: Variorum, 1993.

————. "Slaves and *Misthioi* in Byzantium, Ninth to Eleventh Centuries" (in Russian). *Uchenye zapiski Tul'skij gosudarstvenyj pedagogicheskij institua* 2 (1951): 63–88.

————. "Some Questions Addressed to the Scholars Who Believe in the Authenticity of Kaminiates' 'Capture of Thessalonica.'" *BZ* 71 (1978): 301–314; repr. as chap. 12 in Alexander Kazhdan, *Authors and Texts in Byzantium.* Aldershot, Hampshire: Variorum, 1993.

Kazhdan, Alexander, and Michael McCormick. "The Social World of the Byzantine Court." In *Byzantine Court Culture from 829 to 1204,* ed. Henri Maguire, pp. 167–215. Washington, D.C.: Dumbarton Oaks, 1997.

Kennedy, Hugh. "Byzantine-Arab Diplomacy in the Near East from the Islamic Conquests to the Mid-eleventh Century." In *Byzantine Diplomacy: Papers from the Twenty-fourth Spring Symposium of Byzantine Studies,* ed. J. Shepard and S. Franklin, pp. 133–143. Aldershot, Hampshire: Variorum/Ashgate, 1992.

Khadduri, Majid. *War and Peace in the Law of Islam.* New York: AMS Press, 1979 (1st ed. 1955).

Khalilieh, Hassan S. *Islamic Maritime Law: An Introduction.* Brill: Leiden, 1998.

Khouri, R. "Ἀνεπίσημες ἀνταλλαγές, ἐξαγορές καί ἀπελευθερώσεις Βυζαντινῶν καί Ἀράβων αἰχμαλώτων." *Graeco-Arabica* 4 (1991): 109–113.

Klingshirn, William. "Charity and Power: Caesurius of Arles and the Ransoming of Captives in Sub-Roman Gaul." *JRS* 75 (1985): 183–203.

Koder, Johannes. "Delikt und Strafe im Eparchenbuch: Aspekte des mittelalterlichen Korporationswesens in Konstantinopel." *JÖB* 41 (1991): 113–131.

————. "Maritime Trade and the Food Supply for Constantinople in the Middle Ages." In *Travel in the Byzantine World,* ed. R. Macrides, pp. 109–124. Aldershot, Hampshire: Ashgate/Variorum, 2002.

Kolendo, Jerzy. "Les Romains prisonniers de guerre des Barbares au Ier et au IIe siècle." *Index. Quaderni camerti di studi romantistici. International Survey of Roman Law* 15 (1987): 227–234.

Kolias, Taxiarchis G. "Kriegsgefangene, Sklavenhandel und die Privilegien der Soldaten: Die Aussage der Novelle von Ioannes Tzimisikes." *BS* 56 (1995): 129–136.

Kolias-Dermitzaki, Athina. "Some Remarks on the Fate of Prisoners of War in Byzantium (Ninth–Tenth Centuries)." In G. Cipollone, ed., *La liberazione dei 'captivi' tra Cristianità e Islam,* pp. 583–620. Vatican City: Archivio segreto vaticano, "Collectanea archivi vaticani 46," 2000.

Köpstein, Helga. "Die byzantinische Sklaverei in der Historiographie der letzten 125 Jahre." *Klio* 43–45 (1965): 560–576.

————. "Einige Aspekte des byzantinischen und bulgarischen Sklavenhandels im X. Jahrhundert: Zur Novelle des Joannes Tzimiskes über Sklavenhandelszoll." In *Actes du premier congrès international d'études balkaniques et sud-est européennes,* 3:237–247. Sofia: Académie bulgare des sciences, 1966.

———. "Paroiken in frühen Byzanz: Zu problemen von Terminus und Status." *Buzantiaka* 12 (1992): 181–214.

———. "Sklaven in der 'Peira.'" In *Font. min. 9*, pp. 1–33. Frankfurt: Klostermann, "ForByzRecht 19," 1994.

———. "Sklaverei in Byzanz." *Das Altertum* 27 (1981): 94–101.

———. "Zum Bedeutungswandel von ΣΚΛΑΒΟΣ /SCLAVUS." *ByzF* 7 (1979): 67–88.

———. "Zum Fortleben des Wortes doulos und anderer Bezeichnungen für den Sklaven im Mittel- und Neugriechischen." In *Untersuchunghen Ausgewahlter Altgriechischer Sozialer Typenbegriffe und Ihr Fortleben in Antike und Mittlealter,* ed. Elisabeth Charlotte Welskopf, pp. 319–353. Berlin: Akademie-Verlag, 1981.

———. "Zur Novelle des Alexios Komnenos zum Sklavenstatus (1095)." *Actes du XVe Congrès international d'études byzantines.* Vol. 4, pp. 60–172. Athens : Association internationale des études byzantines, 1976.

———. *Zur Sklaverei im Ausgehenden Byzanz: Philologisch-historische Untersuchung.* Berlin: Akademie-Verlag, "BBA 34," 1966.

———. "Zur Sklaverei in byzanzinischer Zeit." *Acta antiqua scientiarum hungaricae* 15 (1967): 359–368.

Krause, Jens-Uwe. "Prisons et crimes dans l'Empire romain." In *Carcer. Prison et privation de liberté dans l'Antiquité classique. Actes du colloque de Strasbourg (5 et 6 décembre 1997),* ed. C. Bertrand-Dagenbach, A. Chauvot, M. Matter, and J. M. Salamito, pp. 117–128. Paris: De Boccard, 1999.

Kravari, Vassiliki, Jacque Lefort, and Cécile Morrison, eds. *Hommes et richesses dans l'Empire byzantin II. VIIIe–XVe siècles.* Paris: Lethielleux, "Réalités byzantines 3," 1991.

Laniado, Avshalom. "Note sur la datation conservée en syriaque du concile de Gangre." *OrChrP* 61 (1995): 195–199.

Lee, R. W. Lee. *The Elements of Roman Law, with a Translation of the Institutes of Justinian.* 2nd ed. London: Sweet & Maxwell, 1949.

Lefort, Jacques. "Le cadastre de Radolibos (1103), les géomètres et leurs mathématiques." *TM* 8 (1981): 269–313.

———. "Radolibos: Population et paysage." *TM* 9 (1985): 195–234.

Lemerle, Paul. *The Agrarian History of Byzantium from the Origins to the Twelfth Century.* Translated by G. MacNiocaill. Galway: Galway University Press, 1979.

———. *Cinq études sur le XIe siècle byzantin.* Paris: CNRS, "Le monde byzantin 6," 1977.

Lemosse, M. "L'enfant sans famille en droit romain." *Recueil de la Société Jean-Bodin* 35 (1975): 257–270.

Leroy, François Joseph. "La réforme Studite." *OrChrAn* 153 (1958): 181–214.

Letsios, Dimitres. "Die Kriegsgefangenschaft nach Auffassung der Byzantiner." *BS* 53 (1992): 213–227.

———. "Sea Trade as Illustrated in the 'Rhodian Sea Law' with Special Reference to the Reception of Its Norms in the Arabic Ecloga." *Graeco-Arabica* 6 (1995): 209–225.

Lévy, E. "Captivus redemptus." *Classical Philology* 38/3 (1943): 159–176.

———. "Les esclaves chez Aristophane." In *Actes du colloque 1972 sur l'esclavage,* pp. 29–46. Paris: Les Belles Lettres, "Annales littéraires de l'université de Besançon 163, Centre de recherches d'histoire ancienne 11," 1974.

Lewis, Bernard. *Race and Color in Islam.* New York: Harper & Row, 1971.

———. *Race and Slavery in the Middle East: An Historical Enquiry.* New York: Oxford University Press, 1990.

Lieu, Samuel. "Captives, Refugees, and Exiles: A Study of Cross-Frontier Civilian Movements and Contacts between Rome and Persia from Valerian to Jovian." In *The Defence of the Roman and Byzantine East,* ed. P. Freeman and D. Kennedy, 2:475–505. Oxford: BAR, "BAR International Series 297," 1986.

Lintott, Andrew. "La servitude pour dettes à Rome." In *Carcer: Prison et privation de liberté dans l'Antiquité classique,* ed. C. Bertrand-Dagenbach et al., pp. 19–25. Paris: De Boccard, 1999.

Loos, Milan. "Quelques remarques sur les communautés rurales et la grande propriété terrienne à Byzance (VIIe–XIe s.)." *BS* 39 (1978): 3–18.

Ludwig, Claudia. *Sonderformen byzantinischer Hagiographie und ihr literarisches Vorbild: Untersuchungen zu den Viten des Äsop, des Philaretos, des Symeon Salos und des Andreas Salos.* Frankfurt: Lang, "BBS 3," 1997.

MacCoull, Leslie S. B. "A Cinderella Story from Byzantine Egypt: *P. Cair. Masp.* I 67089 and III 67294." *Byzantion* 62 (1992): 380–388.

MacMullen, Ramsay. *Changes in the Roman Empire: Essays in the Ordinary.* Princeton, N.J.: Princeton University Press, 1999.

———. "Late Roman Slavery." *Historia* 36/3 (1987): 359–382; repr. as chap. 23 in Ramsay MacMullen, *Changes in the Roman Empire: Essays in the Ordinary.* Princeton, N.J.: Princeton University Press, 1999.

Macrides, Ruth. "Justice under Manuel I Komnenos: Four Novels on Court Business and Murder." In *Font. min.* 6, pp. 99–204. Frankfurt: Klostermann, "ForByzRecht 11," 1984.

———. "Killing, Asylum, and the Law in Byzantium." *Speculum* 63/3 (1988): 509–538.

———, ed. *Travel in the Byzantine World: Papers from the Thirty-fourth Spring Symposium of Byzantine Studies,* Birmingham, April 2000. Aldershot, Hampshire: Ashgate/Variorum, 2002.

Maffi, Alberto. *Ricerche sur postliminium.* Milan: Giuffrè, 1992.

Magdalino, Paul. "The Byzantine Aristocratic *Oikos.*" In *The Byzantine Aristocracy IX–XIII Centuries,* ed. M. Angold, pp. 92–111. Oxford: BAR, "BAR International Series 221," 1984; repr. as chap. 3 of Paul Magdalino, *Tradition and Transformations in Medieval Byzantium.* Aldershot, Hampshire: Variorum, 1991.

———. *Tradition and Transformations in Medieval Byzantium.* Aldershot, Hampshire: Variorum, 1991.

Malamut, Élisabeth. *Les îles de l'Empire byzantin, VIIIe–XIIe siècles.* 2 vols. Paris: Publications de la Sorbonne, "Byzantina Sorbonensia 8," 1988.

———. *Sur la route des saints byzantins.* Paris: CNRS, "CNRS histoire," 1993.

Mango, Cyril. "The Life of St. Andrew the Fool Reconsidered." *RSBS* 2 (1982): 297–313.

Mango, Cyril, and Roger Scott, trans. *The Chronicle of Theophanes Confessor: Byzantine and Near Eastern History* A.D. *284–813.* Oxford: Clarendon Press, 1997.

Martroye, M. François. "Le testament de saint Grégoire de Nazianze." *Mémoires de la Société nationale des antiquaires* 76 (1924): 219–263.

Marx, Karl. *Das Kapital: A Critique of Political Economy.* Edited by Friedrich Engels, condensed by Serge L. Levitsky. Washington, D.C.: Regnery Gateway, 1996.

Marx, Karl (with Friedrich Engels). *The German Ideology: Including Theses on Feuerbach and Introduction to the Critique of Political Economy.* Amherst, N.Y.: Prometheus, 1998.

McCarthy, Kathleen. *Slaves, Masters, and the Art of Authority in Plautine Comedy.* Princeton, N.J.: Princeton University Press, 2000.

McCormick, Michael. "Byzantium on the Move: Imagining a Communications History." In *Travel in the Byzantine World*, ed. R. Macrides, pp. 3–29. Aldershot, Hampshire: Ashgate/Variorum, 2002.

———. "New Light in the 'Dark Ages': How the Slave Trade Fuelled the Carolingian Economy." *P&P* 177 (November 2002): 17–54.

———. *Origins of the European Economy: Communications and Commerce,* A.D. *300– 900.* Cambridge, U.K.: Cambridge University Press, 2001.

———. "Voyageurs, monnaies et esclaves." In *Les échanges au Moyen Âge, dossiers d'archéologie* 256 (September 2000): 44–47.

Melluso, Marco. *La schiavitù nell'età giustinianea: Disciplina giuridica e rilevanza sociale.* Besançon: Presses universitaires franc-comtoises, "Série Esclavage et dépendance," 2000.

Mendelsohn, Isaac. *Slavery in the Ancient Near East: A Comparative Study of Slavery in Babylonia, Assyria, Syria, and Palestine from the Middle of the Third Millennium to the End of the First Millennium.* Oxford: Oxford University Press, 1949.

Mentxaka, Rosa. "Sobre la existencia de un *ius pignoris* del redentor sobre el cautivo redimido en el derecho romano clasico." *Revue internationale des droits de l'Antiquité,* ser. 3, 32 (1985): 273–337.

Mez, Adam. *The Renaissance of Islam.* Translated by S. K. Bakhsh and D. S. Margoliouth. Patna: Jubilee Printing and Publishing, 1937.

Montevecchi, Orsolina. "Ricerche di sociologia nei documenti dell'Egitto greco-romano. III. I contratti di compra-vendita." *Aegyptus* 19 (1939): 11–53.

Morabito, Marcel. *Les réalités de l'esclavage d'après le Digeste.* Paris: Les Belles Lettres, "Annales littéraires de l'université de Besançon 254, Centre de recherches d'histoire ancienne 39," 1981.

Morrison, Cécile. "Monnaie et prix à Byzance du Ve au VIIe siècle." In *Hommes et richesses dans l'Empire byzantin I*, ed. P. Zech, pp. 239–260. Paris: Lethielleux, "Réalités Byzantines 3," 1989.

Nathan, Geoffrey. *The Family in Late Antiquity: The Rise of Christianity and the Endurance of Tradition.* London: Routledge, 2000.

Nesbitt, John W. "A Geographical and Chronological Guide to Greek Saint Lives." *OrChrP* 35 (1969): 443–489.

———. "The Life of St. Philaretos (702–792) and Its Significance for Byzantine Agriculture." *GOrThR* 14/2 (1969): 150–158.

Noonan, Thomas Schaub. "Byzantium and the Khazars: A Special Relationship?" In *Byzantine Diplomacy: Papers from the Twenty-fourth Spring Symposium of Byzantine Studies*, ed. J. Shepard and S. Franklin, pp. 109–132. Aldershot, Hampshire: Variorum/Ashgate, 1992.

———. "The Impact of the Islamic Trade upon Urbanization in the Rus' Lands: The Tenth and the Early Eleventh Centuries." In *Les centres proto-urbains russes entre Scandinavie, Byzance et Orient,* ed. M. Kazanski, A. Nercessian, and C. Zuckerman, pp. 379–393. Paris: Buchet-Chastel, "Réalités byzantines 7," 2000.

———. "The Khazar-Byzantine World of the Crimea in the Early Middle Ages: The Religious Dimension." *Archivum Eurasiae Medii Aevi* 10 (1998–1999): 207–230.

———. "Khazaria as an Intermediary between Islam and Eastern Europe in the Second Half of the Ninth Century: The Numismatic Perspective." *Archivum Eurasiae Medii Aevi* 5 (1985): 175–200.

———. "Les Khazars et le commerce oriental." In *Les échanges au Moyen Âge, dossiers d'archéologie* 256 (September 2000): 82–85.

———. "Volga Bulgharia's Tenth-century Trade with Samanid Central Asia." *Archivum Eurasiae Medii Aevi* 11 (2000–2001): 140–218.

———. "What Does Historical Numismatics Suggest about the History of Khazaria in the Ninth Century?" *Archivum Eurasiae Medii Aevi* 3 (1983): 265–281.

Nosov, E. "Rjurikovo, Gorodišče et Novgorod." In *Les centres proto-urbains russes entre Scandinavie, Byzance et Orient,* ed. M. Kazanski, A. Nercessian, and C. Zuckerman, pp. 143–172. Paris: Buchet-Chastel, "Réalités byzantines 7," 2000.

Oikonomides, Nicolas. *Byzantium from the Ninth Century to the Fourth Crusade.* Aldershot, Hampshire: Variorum, 1992.

———. "Οἱ Βυζαντινοὶ δουλοπάροικοι." *Symmeikta* 5 (1983): 295–302; repr. as chap. 9 of Nicolas Oikonomides, *Byzantium from the Ninth Century to the Fourth Crusade.* Aldershot, Hampshire: Variorum, 1992.

———. "Le dédoublement de saint Théodore et les villes d'Euchaïta et d'Echaneia." *AB* 104 (1986): 327–335.

———. *Fiscalité et exemption fiscale à Byzance (IXe–XIe s.).* Athens: Institut de recherches byzantines, Fondation nationale de la recherche scientifique, 1996.

———. "Le kommerkion d'Abydos, Thessalonique et le commerce bulgare au IXe siècle." In *Hommes et richesses dans l'Empire byzantin II. VIIIe–XVe siècles,* ed. V. Kravari, J. Lefort, and C. Morrison, pp. 241–248. Paris: Lethielleux, "Réalités byzantines 3," 1991.

———. *Les listes de préséances byzantines des IXe et Xe siècles.* Paris: CNRS, "Le monde byzantin 4," 1972.

———. "Le marchand byzantin des provinces (IXe–XIe s.)." In *Mercati e mercanti nell'alto medioevo*, pp. 633–665.

———. "Quelques boutiques de Constantinople au Xe siècle: Prix, loyers, imposition." *DOP* 26 (1972); repr. as chap. 8 of Nicolas Oikonomides, *Byzantium from the Ninth Century to the Fourth Crusade*. Aldershot, Hampshire: Variorum, 1992.

———. "Silk Trade and Production in Byzantium from the Sixth to the Ninth Century: The Seals of Kommerkiarioi." *DOP* 40 (1986): 33–53.

Ostrogorsky, Georg. "La commune rurale byzantine: Loi agraire—Traité fiscal—Cadastre de Thèbes." *Byzantion* 32 (1962): 139–166.

———. "Le grand domaine dans l'Empire byzantin." *Recueils de la Société Jean Bodin* 4 (1949): 38ff.

———. *The History of the Byzantine State*. Translated by Joan Hussey. New Brunswick, N.J.: Rutgers University Press, 1969 (1st ed. Munich, 1940).

———. *Die ländliche Steuergemeinde des byzantinischen Reiches im X. Jahrhundert*. Amsterdam: Hakkert, 1969 (1st ed. Stuttgart, 1927).

———. "The Peasant's Preemption Right: An Abortive Reform of the Macedonian Emperors." *JRS* 37 (1947): 117–126.

———. *Quelques problèmes d'histoire de la paysannerie byzantine*. Translated by H. Grégoire. Brussels: Éd. de Byzantion, "Corpus Bruxellense Historiae Byzantinae," 1956.

Papademetriou, Ioannes-Theophanes A. *Aesop as an Archetypal Hero*. Athens: International Center for Humanistic Research, "Studies and Researches 39," 1997.

Pargoire, J. "Saint Thaddée l'Homologète." *EO* 9 (1906): 37–41.

———. "Une loi monastique de saint Platon." *BZ* 8 (1899): 98–101.

Patlagean, Évelyne. "Byzance et le blason pénal du corps." In *Du châtiment dans la cité. Supplices corporels et peine de mort dans le monde antique. Table ronde organisée par l'EFR avec le concours du Centre national de la recherche scientifique (Rome 9–11 novembre 1982)*, pp. 405–426. Rome: EFR, "Coll. de l'EFR 79," 1984.

———. "Byzance et les marchés du grand commerce vers 830–vers 1030: Entre Pirenne et Polanyi." In *Mercati e mercanti nell'alto medioevo*, pp. 587–629.

———. "Byzance et son autre monde: Observations sur quelques récits." In *Faire croire. Modalités de la diffusion et de la réception des messages religieux du XIIe au XVe siècle. Table ronde (Rome, 22–23 juin 1979)*, pp. 201–221. Rome: EFR, "Coll. de l'EFR 51," 1981.

———. "'Économie paysanne' et 'féodalité byzantine.'" *Annales ESC* 30/6 (1975): 1371–1396; repr. as chap. 3 of Évelyne Patlagean, *Structures sociales, famille, chrétienté à Byzance*. London: Variorum, 1981.

———. "L'entrée de la Sainte Face d'Édesse à Constantinople en 944." In *La religion civique à l'époque médiévale et moderne (Chrétienté et Islam)*. Rome: EFR, "Coll. de l'EFR 213," 1995, pp. 21–35; repr. in Évelyne Patlagean, *Figures du pouvoir à Byzance (IXe–XIIe siècles)*, pp. 37–52. Spoleto: Centro italiano di studi sull'alto Medioevo, "Collectanea 13," 2001.

———. *Figures du pouvoir à Byzance (IXe–XIIe siècles)*. Spoleto: Centro italiano di studi sull'alto Medioevo, "Collectanea 13," 2001.

————. "Nommer les Russes en grec, 1081–1294." In *Le origini e lo sviluppo della cristianità slavo-bizantina*, ed. S. W. Swierkosz-Lenart, pp. 123–141. Rome: Istituto storico italiano per il Medio Evo, "Nuovi studi storici 17," 1992.

————. *Pauvreté économique et pauvreté sociale à Byzance, IVe–XIIe siècles.* Paris: Mouton, "Civilisations et sociétés 48," 1976.

————. *Structures sociales, famille, chrétienté à Byzance.* London: Variorum, 1981.

————. "Variations impériales sur le thème romain." In *Roma fra oriente e occidente. SettStu* 49 (Spoleto: Centro italiano di studi sull'alto Medioevo, 2002): 1–47.

Patoura, Sophia. Οἱ αἰχμάλωτοι ὡς παράγοντες ἐπικοινωνίας καὶ πληροφόρησης (4ος–10ος αἰ.). Athens: Kentro Vyzantinōn Ereunōn, 1994.

Patterson, Orlando. *Slavery and Social Death: A Comparative Study.* London: Harvard University Press, 1982.

Perentidis, Stavros. "L'ordination de l'esclave à Byzance." *Revue historique de droit français et étranger* 59 (1981): 231–248.

Perry, Ben Edwin. *Aesopica I. A Series of Texts Relating to Aesop or Ascribed to Him or Closely Connected with the Literary Tradition That Bears His Name.* Vol. 1. Urbana: University of Illinois Press, 1952.

————. "Some Addenda of the Life of Aesop." *BZ* 59 (1966): 285–304.

————. *Studies in the Text History of the Life and Fables of Aesop.* Haverford, Pa.: American Philological Association, "Philological Monographs 7," 1936.

————. "The Text Tradition of the Greek Life of Aesop." *Transactions and Proceedings of the American Philological Association* 64 (1933): 198–244.

Pertusi, Agostino. "Venezia e Bisanzio nel secolo XI." In *La Venezia del Mille*, pp. 117–160. Florence: Sansoni, "Storia della civiltà veneziana 10," 1965.

Pipes, Daniel. *Slave Soldiers and Islam: The Genesis of a Military System.* New Haven, Conn.: Yale University Press, 1981.

Poly, Jean-Pierre, and Éric Bournazel. *La mutation féodale, Xe–XIIe siècles.* Paris: PUF, "Nouvelle Clio 16," 1980.

Popovic, Alexandre. *La révolte des esclaves en Iraq aux IIIe–Xe siècles.* Paris: Geuthner, "Bibliothèque d'études islamiques 6," 1976.

Poppe, Andrzej. "The Political Background to the Baptism of Rus': Byzantine-Russian Relations between 986–989." *DOP* 30 (1976): 197–244.

Preisigike, Friedrich. "Ein Sklavenkauf des 6. Jahrhunderts. P. gr. Str. Inv. Nr. 1404." *Archiv für Papyrusforschung* 3 (1906): 415–424.

Puškina, T. "Les trouvailles monétaires de Gnezdovo: Un marqueur des relations commerciales." In *Les centres proto-urbains russes entre Scandinavie, Byzance et Orient*, ed. M. Kazanski, A. Nercessian, and C. Zuckerman, pp. 213–224. Paris: Buchet-Chastel, "Réalités byzantines 7," 2000.

Ragib, Yusuf. "Les esclaves publics aux premiers siècles de l'Islam." In *Figures de l'esclave au Moyen Âge et dans le monde moderne*, ed. H. Bresc, pp. 7–30. Paris: L'Harmattan, 1996.

————. "Les marchés aux esclaves en terre d'Islam." In *Mercati et mercanti nell'alto medioevo*, pp. 721–766.

Ralph-Johannes, Lilie. *Handel und Politik: Zwischen dem byzantinischen Reich und den italienischen Kommunen Venedig. Pisa und Genua in der Epoche der Komnenen und der Angeloi (1081–1204).* Amsterdam: Hakkert, 1984.

Ramin, J., and P. Veyne. "Droit romain et société: Les hommes libres qui passent pour esclaves et l'esclavage volontaire." *Historia* 30 (1981); repr. in Paul Veyne, *La société romaine,* pp. 247–280. Paris: Éd. du Seuil, "Points. Histoire," 1990.

Reinach, M. T. "Un contrat de mariage du temps de Basile le Bulgaroctone." In *Mélanges offerts à M. Gustave Schlumberger à l'occasion du quatre-vingtième anniversaire de sa naissance (17 octobre 1924),* 1:118–132. Paris: Geuthner, 1924.

Rostovtzeff, Michael Ivanovich. *The Social and Economic History of the Roman Empire.* Oxford: Clarendon Press, 1926.

Rotman, Youval. "Formes de non-liberté dans la campagne byzantine aux VIIe–XIe siècles." In *Mélanges de l'EFR, Moyen Âge* 112/2 (2000): 499–510.

Rougé, Jean. *Recherches sur l'organisation du commerce maritime en Méditerranée sous l'Empire romain.* Paris: SEVPEN, 1966.

Rydén, Lennart. "The Date of the Life of Andreas Salos." *DOP* 32 (1978): 127–155.

———. *The Life of St. Andrew the Fool.* 2 vols. Uppsala: Acta Universitatis Upsaliensis, "Studia Byzantina Upsaliensis 4/1–2," 1995.

———. "The Life of St. Basil the Younger and the Date of the Life of St. Andreas Salos." In *Okeanos: Essays Presented to Ihor Sevcenko on His Sixtieth Birthday by His Colleagues and Students,* ed. Cyril Mango and Omeljan Pritsak, pp. 568–577. Cambridge, Mass.: Harvard University Press, "Harvard Ukranian Studies 7," 1984.

Ste. Croix, Geoffrey Ernest Maurice de. *The Class Struggle in the Ancient Greek World from the Archaic Age to the Arab Conquests.* London: Duckworth, 1981.

Sanna, Maria Virginia. *Nuove ricerche in tema di postliminium e redemptio ab hostibus.* Cagliari: Éd. AV, "Biblioteca di studi e ricerche di diritto romano e di storia del diritto," 2001.

Saradi-Mendelovici, Hélène. *Le notariat byzantin du IXe au XVe siècle.* Athens: National University of Athens, Sophie N. Saripolou Library, 1992.

Schilbach, Erich. *Byzantinische Metrologie.* Munich: Beck, 1970.

Sedyh, V. "Timerevo—Un centre proto-urbain sur la grande voie de la Volga." In *Les centres proto-urbains russes entre Scandinavie, Byzance et Orient,* ed. M. Kazanski, A. Nercessian, and C. Zuckerman, pp. 173–197. Paris: Buchet-Chastel, "Réalités byzantines 7," 2000.

Shahid, Irfan. *Byzantium and the Arabs in the Sixth Century.* 2 vols. in 3 parts. Washington, D.C.: Dumbarton Oaks, 1995–2002.

———. "Byzantium and Kinda." *BZ* 53 (1960): 57–78; repr. as chaps. 4–5 of Irfan Shahid, *Byzantium and the Semitic Orient before the Rise of Islam.* London: Variorum, 1988.

Shapira, D. "Two Names of the First Khazar Jewish Beg." *Archivum Eurasiae Medii Aevi* 10 (1998–1999): 231–241.

Shaw, Brent D. "Bandits in the Roman Empire." *P&P* 105 (November 1984): 3–52.

Shepard, Jonathan. "Constantinople—Gateway to the North: The Russians." In

Constantinople and Its Hinterland: Twenty-seventh Spring Symposium on Byzantine Studies Papers, ed. Cyril Mango and Gilbert Dagron, pp. 243–260. Aldershot, Hampshire: Variorum, 1995.

Shepard, Jonathan, and Simon Franklin, eds. *Byzantine Diplomacy: Papers from the Twenty-fourth Spring Symposium of Byzantine Studies,* Cambridge, March 1990. Aldershot, Hampshire: Variorum/Ashgate, 1992.

Simeonova, Liliana. "In the Depths of Tenth-century Byzantine Ceremonial: The Treatment of Arab Prisoners-of-War at Imperial Banquets." *BMGS* 22 (1998): 75–104.

Sjuzjumov, M. J. "Occupations and Commerce in Constantinople in the Early Tenth Century" (in Russian). *VizVrem* 4 (1951): 11–41.

Sodini, Jean-Pierre. "L'artisanat urbain à l'époque paléochrétienne (IVe–VIIe s.)." *Ktèma* 4 (1979): 71–119.

Sorlin, Irène. "Les traités de Byzance avec la Russie au Xe siècle." *Cahiers du monde russe et soviétique* 2/3–4 (1961): 313–360, 447–475.

————. "Voies commerciales, villes et peuplement de la Rôsia au Xe siècle d'après le *De administrando imperio* de Constantin Porphryogénète." In *Les centres proto-urbains russes entre Scandinavie, Byzance et Orient,* ed. M. Kazanski, A. Nercessian, and C. Zuckerman, pp. 337–356. Paris: Buchet-Chastel, "Réalités byzantines 7," 2000.

Stratos, Andreas Nikolaou. *Byzantium in the Seventh Century.* Translated by M. Ogilvie-Grant. 5 vols. Amsterdam: Hakkert, 1968–1980 (1st ed. Athens, 1965–1977).

Talbot, Alice-Mary, ed. *Holy Women of Byzantium: Ten Saints' Lives in English Translation.* Translated by N. Constas, J. Featherstone, C. Mango, M. Kouli, A. C. Hero, V. Karras, L. F. Sherry, A. M. Talbot, A. E. Laiou, P. Halsall. Washington, D.C.: Dumbarton Oaks, "Byzantine Saints' Lives in Translation," 1996.

Taubenschlag, Rafal. *The Law of Greco-Roman Egypt in the Light of the Papyri 332 B.C.–640 A.D.* Warsaw: Polish Philological Society-Herald Square Press, "Eus supplementa 19/2," 1944.

Testart, Alain. "L'esclavage comme institution." *L'homme. Revue française d'anthropologie* 145 (January–March 1998): 31–70.

Thomas, Yan. "*Vitae necisque potestas:* Le père, la cité, la mort." In *Du châtiment dans la cité. Supplices corporels et peine de mort dans le monde antique. Table ronde organisée par l'EFR avec le concours du Centre national de la recherche scientifique (Rome 9–11 novembre 1982),* pp. 499–548. Rome: EFR, "Coll. de l'EFR 79," 1984.

Tibi, Ahmad. "Byzantine-Fatimid Relations in the Reign of Al-Mu'izz Li-Din Allah (r. 953–957 A.D.) as Reflected in Primary Arabic Sources." *Graeco-Arabica* 4 (1991): 91–107.

Toubert, Pierre. *Les structures du Latium médiéval: Le Latium méridional et la Sabine du IXe à la fin du XIIe siècle.* 2 vols. Rome: EFR, "Bibliothèque des écoles françaises d'Athènes et de Rome," 1973.

Toynbee, Arnold Joseph. *Constantine Porphyrogenitus and His World.* Oxford: Oxford University Press, 1973.

Treadgold, Warren T. "The Bulgars' Treaty with the Byzantines in 816." *RSBS* 4 (1984): 213–220.

Urbach, Efraim Elimelech. "The Laws Regarding Slavery" (in Hebrew). *The Annual of Jewish Studies;* repr. in Efraim Elimelech Urbach, *The World of the Sages, Collected Studies,* pp. 178–227. Jerusalem: Y. L. Magnes, 1964.

Van der Vorst, C. "S. Thaddée Studite." *AB* 31 (1912): 157–160.

Vasiliev, Alexander Alexandrovich. *Byzance et les Arabes.* 2 vols. in 3 parts. Brussels: Institut de philologie et d'histoire orientales, "Corpus Bruxellense Historiae Byzantinae," 1935–1968.

———. *History of the Byzantine Empire 324–1453.* 2 vols. Madison: University of Wisconsin Press, 1954 (1st English ed. 1928).

Verlinden, Charles. *L'esclavage dans l'Europe médiévale.* 2 vols. Vol. 1, *Péninsule ibérique-France.* Brugge: De Tempel, Ghent Rijksuniversiteit Faculteit der Letteren en Wijsbegeerte. Vol. 2, *Italie—Colonies italiennes du Levant—Levant Latin—Empire byzatnin.* Ghent: Rijksuniverseiteit, 1977.

———. "Guerre et traite comme sources de l'esclavage dans l'empire byzantin aux IXe et Xe siècles." *Graeco-Arabica* 5 (1993): 207–227.

———. "La traite des esclaves: Un grand commerce international au Xe siècle." In *Mélanges Edmond-René Labande: Études de civilisation médiévale (IXe–XIIe siècles),* pp. 721–730. Poitiers: Centre d'études supérieures de civilisation médiévale, 1975.

———. "Les Radaniya: Intermédiaires commerciaux entre les mondes germano-slave et gréco-arabe." *Graeco-Arabica* 6 (1995): 111–124.

Vernant, Jean-Pierre. "La lutte des classes." *Eirene: Studia Graeca et Latina* 4 (1965): 5–19; repr. in Jean-Pierre Vernant and Pierre Vidal-Naquet, *Travail et esclavage en Grèce ancienne,* pp. 59–78. Brussels: Complexe, "Historiques 14," 1988.

Vernant, Jean-Pierre, and Pierre Vidal-Naquet. *Travail et esclavage en Grèce ancienne.* Brussels: Complexe, "Historiques 14," 1988.

Verri, Pietro. *Le leggi penali militari dell'impero bizantino nell'alto medioevo.* Rome: Tip. della Scuola Ufficiali Carabinieri, "Rassegna della giustizia militare sup. 1–2," 1978.

Veyne, Paul. *La société romaine.* Paris: Éd. du Seuil, "Points. Histoire," 1990.

———. "Vie de Trimalcion." *Annales ESC* 16/2 (1961); repr. in Paul Veyne, *La société romaine,* pp. 13–57. Paris: Éd. du Seuil, "Points. Histoire," 1990.

Vidal-Naquet, Pierre. "Les esclaves grecs étaient-ils une classe?" *Raison présente* 6 (1968), in *Ordres et classes. Colloque d'histoire sociale, Saint-Cloud, 24–25 mai 1967,* ed. D. Roche, pp. 29–36. Paris: Mouton, "Congrès et colloques 12," 1973; repr. in Jean-Paul Vernant and Pierre Vidal-Naquet, *Travail et esclavage en Grèce ancienne,* pp. 81–93. Brussels: Complexe, "Historiques 14," 1988.

———. "Réflexion sur l'historiographie grecque de l'esclavage." *Actes du Colloque 1971 sur l'esclavage.* Paris: Les Belles Lettres, "Annales littéraires de l'université de Besançon 140, Centre de recherches d'histoire ancienne 6," 1972, pp. 25–44; repr. in Jean-Paul Vernant and Pierre Vidal-Naquet, *Travail et esclavage en Grèce ancienne*, pp. 95–122. Brussels: Complexe, "Historiques 14," 1988.

Vryonis, Speros. "The Question of the Byzantine Mines." *Speculum* 37 (1962): 1–17.

Wallon, Henri Alexandre. *Histoire de l'esclavage dans l'Antiquité*. Paris: Laffont, 1988 (1st ed. 1847).

Watson, Alan. *Roman Slave Law*. Baltimore, Md.: Johns Hopkins University Press, 1987.

Weiler, I. "Inverted Kalokagathia." In *Representing the Body of the Slave*, ed. T. Wiedemann and J. Gardner, pp. 11–28. London: Frank Cass Publishers, 2002.

Wenger, Leopold. "Ein christliches Freiheitszeugnis in den ägytpischen Papyri." In *Festgabe Albert Ehrhard*, ed. A. M. Koeniger, pp. 451–478. Bonn: Schroeder, 1922.

Westbrook, Raymond. "Vitae Necisque Potestas." *Historia Zeitschrift für alte Geschichte* 48/2 (1999): 203–223.

Whittaker, C. R. "Labour Supply in the Later Roman Empire." In *Table ronde tenue à Rome autour de M. I. Finley sur "Ancient Slavery and Modern Ideology."* Opus 1 (1982): 171–179.

Wiedemann, Thomas, and Jane Gardner, eds. *Representing the Body of the Slave*. London: Frank Cass Publishers, 2002.

Yannopoulos, Panayotis A. *La société profane dans l'Empire byzantin des VIIe, VIIIe et IXe siècles*. Louvain: Université de Louvain, "Recueil de travaux d'histoire et de philologie," 1975.

Zuckerman, Constantin. "On the Date of the Khazars' Conversion to Judaism and the Chronology of the Kings of the Rus Oleg and Igor." *REB* 53 (1995): 237–270.

———. "Short Notes: Two Notes on the Early History of the Thema of Cherson." *BMGS* 21 (1997): 210–222.

———. "Le voyage d'Olga et la première ambassade espagnole à Constantinople." *TM* 13 (2000): 647–672.

Index